RE-IMAGINING POLICING IN CANADA

Edited by Dennis Cooley

The nature of policing is undergoing a radical transformation. In Canada, as in other nations in the Western world, many of the policing services that were provided by public forces in the past are being gradually handed over to private security agencies. Complex networks of policing that include a mix of public and private security providers are emerging, and this development has serious implications for how Canadians inter-act with one another. For instance, if residents of a gated community or members of a downtown business association pay for their own policing services rather than rely on the public police, whose law is being en-forced?

With this collection, Dennis Cooley has brought together some of the top minds in criminology and policing to examine how policing is changing across the country. The essays describe the character and constitution of security in Canada and explore the implications of these changes in terms of larger questions about power, social control, justice, and law. Wide-ranging and topical, *Re-imagining Policing in Canada* will prove essential reading for policy makers and scholars alike.

DENNIS COOLEY is the deputy minister of justice for the Government of Yukon.

Re-imagining Policing in Canada

Edited by Dennis Cooley

UNIVERSITY OF TORONTO PRESS
Toronto Buffalo London

© University of Toronto Press Incorporated 2005
Toronto Buffalo London
Printed in Canada

ISBN 0-8020-3681-3 (cloth)
ISBN 0-8020-8503-2 (paper)

Printed on acid-free paper

Library and Archives Canada Cataloguing in Publication

Re-imagining policing in Canada / edited by Dennis Cooley.

ISBN 0-8020-3681-3 (bound).   ISBN 0-8020-8503-2 (pbk.)

1. Police – Canada.   I. Cooley, Dennis, 1964–

HV8157.R44 2005   363.2'0971   C2004-905143-1

University of Toronto Press acknowledges the financial assistance to
its publishing program of the Canada Council for the Arts and the
Ontario Arts Council.

University of Toronto Press acknowledges the financial support for
its publishing activities of the Government of Canada through the
Book Publishing Industry Development Program (BPIDP).

Contents

RE-IMAGINING POLICING IN CANADA

Introduction: Re-imagining Policing in Canada

DENNIS COOLEY

Policing is often thought to be a core responsibility of the state. In liberal democratic societies, to arrest, detain, search, and otherwise restrict an individual's liberty represents a formidable expression of power. Public police forces are authorized to restrict an individual's liberty, but they do so within the constraints of the 'rule of law,' which means that they must operate in a fair and unbiased manner and in accordance with elaborate protocols that have been developed to hold public police forces accountable for their actions.[1]

Throughout the Western world, the demand for security has altered the urban landscape. In Canada, we have seen a rise in the number of 'gated communities'[2] – residential communities built behind security fences – and in the United States, gated communities have metastasized into private cities.[3] 'Mass private property'[4] turns what would otherwise be considered public space, ordinarily policed by public police, into private property governed by private security. Business associations are hiring security companies to patrol public streets in downtown shopping districts. Private security companies regularly patrol low-income housing complexes in cities across Canada. A new network of control and governance allows private corporations to fortify their territories and produce their own private order maintenance systems.

The emergence of fortified communities suggests that a gap exists between expectations of security and the services that the public police can provide. Such communities call into question some fundamental assumptions of our society: if residents of a gated community or members of a downtown business association pay for their own policing services rather than relying on the public police, whose law is being enforced? If some businesses and communities pay for their own service, should they be subject to the same level of taxation as those who rely on the public police? Are principles of democratic accountability eroded as more and more policing is undertaken by private security organizations? The transformation in how policing services are delivered will have serious implications for how Canadians interact with one another in their communities.

This volume explores the consequences that the privatization of security has had and will have on policing in Canada. The perception that there is an increasing need for security, the response of the public and private sectors to this demand for security, and the impact of such transformations on the delivery of policing activities have created tensions for law and public policy. If policing is less and less a public responsibility, what are the implications for issues of fundamental justice? It is customarily thought that police organizations are answerable to the law, that they aspire to impartiality, and that they work within a culture of independence. From a market perspective, private security agencies are answerable to their employer, they are not working with similar imperatives of independence and impartiality, and they are not independent. But what happens when there is a clash of interests between those who are in charge of securing public and private space and those who live and work in those spaces? Are the current legal theories supporting a public-private distinction meaningful? What do these theories obscure? Can we develop different conceptual tools that better reflect the evolution of policing? This volume tests current assumptions about policing in our society and moves us to a more nuanced and layered understanding of the evolution of policing in Canada.

The chapters in this volume were originally prepared for the Law Commission of Canada as background research for its project on public and private policing. The Law Commission of Canada is an independent federal law reform agency that advises Parliament on how to improve and modernize Canada's laws. The commission seeks to engage Canadians in the renewal of the law to ensure that it is relevant, responsive, equally accessible to all, and just. The commission is interested in exploring how law has responded to Canadians' changing expectations for security. The way in which our values may have been transformed by the intermingling of public and private actors in the field of security is an ideal focus for a study of changing social relationships.

The commission's project on security arose out of an examination of the intersection of law and communities. The commission was interested in examining how the law solidifies some and undermines or erases other notions of community: why is it that the law recognizes, supports, and nurtures some communities and not others? An investigation of the needs of different types of communities for order and security and of how the evolving relationship between private security and public police responds to these needs offers a way of examining how law can be used to help build and sustain vibrant communities. The coexistence of (and, at times, competition between) publicly funded institutions and private firms is not unique to the security field. However, the public-private divide in the world of security presents particular challenges: will the private sector provide security in a way that is compatible with our values of equality and human dignity in a democratic society? Is the current division of labour between public police and private security the best way to provide policing? These questions are asked at a time when we are increasingly concerned about security. The chapters in this volume provided an analytical and empirical framework for the commission's discussion paper *In Search of Security: The Roles of Public Police and Private Agencies* and subsequent work.[5]

Transformations in Policing

The chapters in this volume describe the changing character and constitution of security in Canada and explore the implications of these changes in terms of larger questions about power, social control, justice, and law. A foundation of sociological thought in the twentieth century was that democratic states, through their monopoly over the means of coercion, were responsible for the provision of security. According to Max Weber's classic formulation, the state is the only institution in society that can claim to legitimately use force in its dealings with other members of society. In liberal-democratic societies, this has traditionally been achieved through the creation of state-controlled police forces. The Royal Canadian Mounted Police has jurisdiction over federal policing, as well as policing in some provinces and municipalities. There are also a number of other public police forces such as the Ontario Provincial Police, La Sûreté du Québec, and the Royal Newfoundland Constabulary. Many municipalities and Aboriginal communities across the country have their own police forces.

Manning,[6] among others, argues that the idea of 'the state as the holder of the monopoly of the legitimate use of force' no longer corresponds to the empirical reality. Given that private police forces outnumber public police forces in many countries, the state no longer holds a monopoly on the use of legitimate force. Moreover, 'the armed (and continually arming) American population' likely possesses far more conventional firepower than do public police forces. Finally, the state's monopoly of policing powers has also been ceded in large measure to the 'in-house' security providers of multinational corporations and to private security providers.

The line between what is and what is not an official police function is also becoming increasingly blurred. This is not a new development, nor is it one that is restricted to Canada.[7] Rigakos (in this volume) and others[8] have shown that private and public security institutions have coexisted for the past several hundred years. What is new, however, is the degree to which the state's monopoly on policing has been eroded.

A common contention of all the chapters in this volume is that there has been a 'decoupling of ... security from the state.'[9] Although the state is still a significant player in the delivery and regulation of policing, it is no longer the only institutional actor involved in offering guarantees of security to citizens. There are now a range of private policing organizations that include, for example, private security firms, insurance companies, forensic accountants, and private in-house corporate security. These private agencies have moved beyond simply protecting private property to a broader array of policing activities. They are actively engaged in order maintenance, as well as in the investigation and prevention of crime in public spaces. Policing powers are increasingly dispersed across a network of public and private agencies.

Like other state functions, over the past two decades policing has been reconfigured and rationalized in the light of neoliberal characteristics of governance. Police services are focusing on core policing functions and individuals, and businesses are increasingly purchasing security on the free market. A new governing rationality is emerging that reflects what Nikolas Rose has described as the 'death of the social.'[10] The triumph of neoliberalism over welfarist policies signals a new relationship between individuals and the institutions of governance. The emerging governance relationships do not represent a retrenchment of governing capacity (i.e., 'less' government) so much as a reconfiguration of governance relationships. As Rose argues, governance is likely to be achieved not through

politically directed, nationally territorialized, bureaucratically staffed and programmatically rationalised projects of a centrally concentrated State, but through activating the self-governing properties of the subjects of government themselves in a whole variety of locales and localities – enterprises, associations, neighbourhoods, interest groups and, of course, communities.[11]

As Garland[12] argues, what is emerging is governance not through society but through the regulated and accountable choices of autonomous agents – citizens, consumers, parents, employees. Citizenship and governance are expressed in terms of individual freedom, personal responsibility, and self-fulfilment. State agencies redefine their mission in terms of a targeted consumer population whom they will service rather than for the public good.[13]

The chapters in this volume underscore the shortcomings of analyses that presuppose a public-private divide. Hermer and his colleagues contend that attempts to categorize policing agencies into 'public' versus 'private' forms is inevitably misleading, and Rigakos argues that this distinction tends to conceal more than it reveals. A wide variety of agents are now engaged in a diversity of security activities in Canada, and these can seldom be assigned exclusively to either the public or the private sphere. The chapters in this volume re-imagine policing by moving beyond the binary public-private distinction.

Policing in Canada

As of 2002, there were approximately 320 public police services in Canada employing 58,414 police officers. Since policing in Canada is a shared responsibility of the federal and provincial governments, policing is provided by a mix of federal, provincial, and municipal services. Most notably, there is the Royal Canadian Mounted Police (RCMP). The RCMP is a national police force that provides federal, national, and international police services, as well as contract policing services for certain provinces and municipalities across Canada. The RCMP enforces federal statutes throughout Canada and is also involved in combating organized crime, the illegal drug trade, and customs and immigration violations. The RCMP provides technical support to the entire law-enforcement community in Canada. This support includes forensic laboratory, identification, computerized police information, intelligence, and training services. Thus, the RCMP plays a pivotal role in shaping the delivery of policing services in Canada.

The Canadian constitution provides that the 'administration of justice' – which includes providing policing services – is a provincial responsibility. Provinces can provide policing services directly, or they can contract with the RCMP to provide the services. Ontario and Quebec[14] are the only two provinces that provide full provincial policing.

Most provincial legislation requires cities and towns to provide their own policing services. There are three ways that municipalities can provide policing services: they can form their own police service; they can share policing services with another municipality; or they can enter into an agreement for contract policing with a provincial police service or with the RCMP. Municipal police services vary greatly in size: some (such as the Toronto Police Service and the Montreal Urban Community Police Department) employ several thousand officers, others fewer than twenty.

It is possible that, in the future, public police will have to compete directly with private security for municipal policing contracts. For example, the *Police Services Act* of Ontario was amended to allow municipal councils the option to 'adopt a different method of providing police services.' Some private security executives have argued that this amendment allows private security companies to bid directly on municipal policing services.[15]

Public policing services in Canada have felt the squeeze of tightening budgets in recent years. The amount of resources spent on policing in Canada has remained relatively constant since the 1990s[16] and, as Figure I.1 indicates, although the rate of police officers per 100,000 population has increased over the past three years, the general trend since 1972 has been for the rate to decline. At the same time, police have been asked to provide more services. Crime has become more sophisticated, and this increases the demand placed on public police. For example, police services require highly skilled personnel to respond to international and domestic organized crime, computer-related crime, and, most recently, threats of terrorism.

As a result of additional demands and limited resources, many police organizations have rationalized their services. It has been argued that this has created an 'expectation gap' – a gap between what citizens expect of their police service and the services that they actually receive. The growth of private security can be seen as a response to this 'expectation gap.'[17]

For the last three decades, private policing organizations (including 'in-house' and private contract security) have grown while the actual number of police officers in Canada has steadily declined relative to the population. Reliable data on the growth of private security in Canada do not exist.[18] However, it is generally agreed that sometime in the late

FIGURE I.1: Police officers per 100,000 population, Canada, 1962–2002

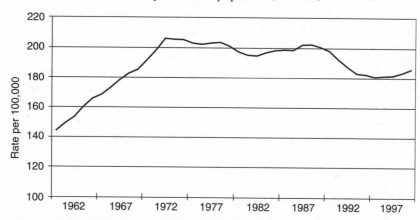

Source: Canadian Centre for Justice Statistics, *Police Resources in Canada*, 2002 Cat. No. 85-225-XIE (Ottawa: Statistics Canada, 2002)

1960s or early 1970s the number of individuals employed in the private security sector appears to have overtaken the number of public police officers. Statistics Canada reports that in 1996 there were 59,090 police officers in Canada, compared to 82,010 private security officers and private investigators.[19] According to these data, roughly two-thirds of security providers in Canada are employed in the private sector. This figure underestimates the actual number of private security employees because it only includes private security officers and investigators and does not include forensic accountants, insurance investigators, private 'in-house' security officers, and others engaged in security work.

In 1997, Statistics Canada conducted a survey of private investigation and security services companies in Canada.[20] Based on a random sample, the survey estimated that the private investigation and security services industry generated more than $2 billion in revenue that year and comprised some 2,746 establishments. Since the survey included only investigation and security services companies, this figure likely underestimates the total revenue generated by private security activities in Canada. The amount of revenue would be higher if the survey included, for example, forensic accountants, security consultants, and internally provided corporate and institutional security services.

It is difficult to compare security arrangements in different countries because of the lack of reliable data. In general, however, most Western nations have seen a growth in private security over the past thirty years. Compared to European countries, Canada, the United States, South Africa, and Australia all have more private security officers than public police officers. In European countries, public police tend to outnumber private security.[21]

We have limited awareness of the scope of private security activities. The rent-a-cop teenager who patrols a shopping centre is the visible tip of the security iceberg. Alongside street patrols and security guards in shopping centres, for example, there exists a very different side of the industry. The 'high-end' security industry is a mix of 'in-house' or 'for hire' forensic accountants, investigators, consultants, loss prevention specialists, and computer programmers who engage in security work for, among others, banks, credit bureaus, insurance companies, retail outlets, stock exchanges, and other private corporations, as well as for government organizations. These highly skilled, well-resourced, and technologically sophisticated security professionals operate, for the most part, beyond the view of most Canadians; yet they wield considerable power and authority.[22]

The events of 11 September 2001 changed the security landscape in Canada and abroad. Following the terrorist attacks on New York city and Washington, the Canadian government responded by increasing public police budgets and introducing 'anti-terrorist' legislation. In October 2001, the federal government announced a $280-million 'anti-terrorism plan' that included additional funding for the RCMP and the Ministry of the Solicitor General. In its December 2001 budget, the federal government presented a five-year $7.7 billion security initiative that included an allocation of $1.6 billion to strengthen intelligence and policing.

Immediately following the terrorist attacks, many questioned whether governments have relinquished too much of their responsibility for security to the private sector and, in response, the federal and provincial governments developed task forces to better coordinate police and security services. What is interesting is that these task forces were almost exclusively composed of public policing officials. Speaking of the United States, Manning[23] notes five trends in U.S. policing following 11 September: an increased visible federal presence in security work; the use of new, largely untested modes of surveillance; the development of a homeland security bureaucracy; a rhetorical focus on 'terrorism' by federal agencies; and, finally, complementing these four trends, the ongoing militarization of local policing that had already been occurring in the United States. At the same time, however, there has also been an increase in demand for private security services as businesses reassess their security plans in light of the 'new reality.' Indeed, many of the new technologies that governments are implementing in airports and at border crossings and other sensitive installations are manufactured, installed, and operated by private security firms. The net effect of 11 September may be a growth in both public police and private security services and the development of denser and more complex networks of relationships between the two.

Networked Policing

Beyond the sheer growth in the number of private security personnel and the contribution of the industry to the economy, there has been a qualitative change in the type of services that the private security industry provides. Policing in Canada, and throughout the world, is in the process of changing from a system in which public police forces provided almost all of our policing services to one in which policing services are provided by a range of public and private agencies. The idea of 'privatization' is a useful concept with which to begin thinking about changes in the nature of policing, but it is also limiting. It is becoming increasingly apparent that the issue is not simply redrawing the line between what is and what is not a public or private policing responsibility, as if they were two distinct and separate entities. It is progressively more difficult to differentiate between public and private: the line between public police and private security has blurred. In addition, policing in general (both public and private) has increasingly been viewed as a commodity.

Complex *networks* of policing that reflect a mix of public and private security providers are emerging. Johnston and Shearing refer to the complex of policing institutions as *nodal* and *networked governance*.[24] They argue that in an era of *networked governance* the key question is not the dividing line between public and private policing. Rather, the key issue – both theoretically and from a policy perspective – is the coordination of networks of state and non-state actors. Thus, in many urban areas, we are witnessing not simply two-tiered policing but *multilevel* policing: the public police contract out patrol services to private security firms; in some instances, private security firms help fund public police investigations; private police resolve complaints that were once within the exclusive domain of the public police; public police and private security firms cooperate in investigations; and private organizations hire public police to provide security for private functions. According to Stenning,

> it is now almost impossible to identify any function or responsibility of the public police which is not, somewhere and under some circumstances, assumed and performed by private police in democratic societies. Policing policy-makers are nowadays resigned to the fact that any effective policing is likely to require some combination, collaboration or 'networking' between public and private providers, and that the lines between the responsibilities of these various providers are likely to be difficult, if not impossible, to clearly demarcate.[25]

To use Bayley and Shearing's phrase, policing has become 'multi-lateralized.'[26]

It is not simply the case that private security is moving in to fill a void left by the public police. Nor can it be said that public and private police agencies exist in a wholly antagonistic relationship. Casting the issue in terms of 'public police versus private police' misses the point that networks of policing are more often than not *complementary* and mutually supportive.[27] The chapter by Hermer and colleagues in this volume offers ample evidence to show that there is 'a significant degree of diffusion of functions' between state and non-state policing agencies. Huey, Ericson, and Haggerty provide numerous examples where the goals, activities, and mentalities of public police and private security intersect in a complementary fashion. Indeed, the chapter by Murphy and Clarke shows that in Edmonton the relationship between the Edmonton Police Service and private security agencies has been formalized. The convergence of public and private policing is further enhanced by the back-and-forth movement of both high-ranking and front-line personnel between public and private policing agencies.[28]

Re-imagining Policing in Canada

The chapters in this volume explore different aspects of networked policing. Hermer and colleagues acknowledge that shifts in the ideological, institutional, and practical character of policing have taken place over the past four decades and argue that legal reforms are necessary. Indeed, if policing is to reflect core democratic values, the authors argue, it must be fair, equitable, and just, in addition to being inclusive of all members of the community in both its processes and its benefits.

Law plays a critical role in structuring policing arrangements. The federal government is the sole authority on matters of criminal law and procedure, while the responsibility for regulating non-state policing agencies, as well as various activities of property owners and businesses that are relevant to policing, lies with the provinces. But at a more general level, the conception of policing embodied in both provincial and federal statutes is limited. The activities of *law enforcement* and *crime prevention* are treated almost exclusively as outputs produced by *police forces* and *police services.* This 'atomized' view of policing creates considerable uncertainty about the powers and responsibilities of state versus non-state policing authorities.

Hermer and his colleagues maintain that because the agencies engaged in policing are not isolated from one another in their operations or in their impacts, reform must address networks of policing as coherent wholes. The parameters of the debate over law reform must be extended to address how the multiplicity of state and non-state resources that are presently engaged in policing can be harnessed to provide the most effective and acceptable policing for communities (whether at the local, regional, national, or international level). They suggest *policing* boards as a radical but realistic reform option. A policing board would have broad legal and 'market' authority to hold accountable all agencies that are involved in the process of policing – including both the state police and non-state bodies. Moreover, the board would be given authority to inquire into the conduct of *any* policing agency – including but not limited to the state police – and thereby hold that agency publicly accountable for its policing practices and apply disciplinary measures when appropriate.

The three chapters on policing urban centres in Canada provide a social context for many of the ideas that are presented by Hermer and colleagues. For example, Hermer and colleagues claim that one of the characteristics of policing in the twenty-first century is the development of community policing programs where public involvement is solicited to assist the police in making decisions about the efficient and effective deployment of resources. In his chapter, Mopas examines the process by which communities are 'mapped out' and how this mapping process is implicated in the dispersion of power. Mopas examines the creation of distinct communities in Vancouver's Downtown Eastside. As he notes, the creation of distinct communities has political implications as merchants, property owners, residents, and others who use the space struggle to define the community in their image. Mopas illustrates how 'community policing' is a reflection of how the community is defined. In the Downtown Eastside, through the use of different policing strategies, a number of subareas or neighbourhoods have been able to separate themselves and remain distinct from the larger community.

Huey, Ericson, and Haggerty's chapter also examines urban Vancouver to describe the fusion between amusement and consumption that is increasingly present in urban design and to explore the impact of this trend on approaches to order and security. Urban entertainment destinations are now commonplace in Canada. They are high-consumption areas that utilize forms of entertainment as a means of retailing goods and services. Attempts to create such sites of consumption and pleasure may be compromised by the pre-existence of various forms of 'urban blight' that are commonly associated with the inner city. Business improvement associations in many Canadian cities have turned to private security firms to respond to any number of 'quality of life' issues that plague retailers and consumers (such as panhandling, graffiti, 'squeegee kids,' and street youth).

Huey, Ericson, and Haggerty examine the impact and implications of these programs in the context of the Gastown and Granville Mall neighbourhoods of Vancouver. Their research focuses on three programs that utilize private security services: the Downtown Vancouver Business Improvement Association's 'Downtown Ambassadors' and 'Loss Prevention Officers' programs, and the Gastown Business Improvement Society's 'Security Patrol' program. They examine the working aspects of these programs, explore their impact on the neighbourhood, and look at levels of cooperation with police. They explore the adoption of 'broken windows' as a philosophy by these programs, and how this philosophy is translated into policing practices on the street. The findings lead to a critique of both the 'broken windows' thesis and of current conceptions of consumer culture.

Huey and colleagues suggest that these areas are characterized by 'retail-oriented policing.' Retail-oriented policing is 'about creating and preserving images that are desired by consumers from within specific targeted "lifestyles."' They contend that these new policing practices are both leading to, and exacerbating, divisions within neighbourhoods. Policing oriented towards commercial interests and aimed at preserving the commercialized 'identity' of spaces 'involves the use of various levels of coercion to ensure that the wholeness of this new "identity" is preserved.' This image of wholeness is achieved only through exclusion of those parts that do not 'belong.' The 'broken windows' philosophy supports this process, through its prioritization of commercial interests over those of other community interests.

Murphy and Clarke's work explores the flip side of the coin – the impact of the growth of the private sphere on the public sector. Their research shows just how different the outcomes of public service rationalization can be. While both Halifax and Edmonton have faced roughly similar fiscal and ideological pressures, the impact on the organization of policing services in each city has differed. In Halifax, there has been a return to a traditional, reactive crime-fighting style, whereas Edmonton has responded to the fiscal crunch by instituting proactive, community-style policing. These points of divergence offer an opportunity to examine a variety of organizational and operational policing practices and different models of public and private policing governance, and to explore policing policy issues and directions.

Murphy and Clarke's findings give empirical substance to claims that trends in policing are linked to broader transformations in the economy and shifts in mentalities of governance. Indeed, changes in the relationship between public police and private security in both locales can be traced to governmental initiatives shaped by fiscal and political pressures. The increasing cost of public policing coupled with a shift to neoliberal attitudes of government and governance have limited the expansive growth characteristic of the liberal, welfare-state model. Nevertheless, their case studies suggest the need to examine how responses to global trends are shaped by local forces. In Nova Scotia, provincial governments have a history of not intervening in municipal affairs, and private security has been able to grow in Nova Scotia with minimal government regulation. Limited government intervention has meant that there has been little effort to rationalize or integrate public and private policing: policing and security are in effect self-regulated, loosely networked, largely beyond public scrutiny, and guided primarily by market forces and values. On the other hand, policing and security in Alberta were drawn into a larger, self-conscious restructuring process carried out by the government of Alberta. As a result, private security was integrated in a diverse policing network with the Edmonton public police as the central hub of its operations. Murphy and Clarke's study affirms the pluralization of policing thesis, but – most importantly – concludes that the pluralization of policing is attenuated by local political cultures and historical factors.

Rigakos confronts a fundamental question of the four preceding chapters: is it possible to re-imagine *the activities of policing* within a

..ceptual framework that moves beyond the public-private distinction? Rather than accepting the existing structure of police organizations and activities, Rigakos organizes policing practices in terms of their relation to the more basic substratum of human activities. Beginning from the assumption that 'policing' is not limited to the work done by public police officers, Rigakos develops a typology of order and security arrangements based on a general classification of policing activities. He identifies five types of policing activity: (1) polemic; (2) sentry-dataveillant; (3) investigative; (4) patrol; and (5) civic-sumptuary. These categories overcome some of the problems associated with continuing to employ the public-private dichotomy and provide a refreshingly different perspective on the constitution of order and security. More importantly, they allow us to move beyond questions associated with the sectoral designation of a given officer in order to appreciate both the fluidity in the types of activities engaged in by each and how these may vary in location. Furthermore, this categorization of policing activities can be applied in empirical contexts in order to better understand the day-to-day constitution of order and security. As such, the work represents a promising theoretical contribution to the literature on policing and security.

Finally, as former chair (from 1991 to 1995) of the Metropolitan Toronto Police Services Board, the civilian agency responsible for the governance of Canada's largest municipal police service, Susan Eng looks at policing as a 'public good.' Policing is often characterized as a social contract between citizens and the state: individuals give up certain liberties, and the state guarantees that policing will be equitable and impartial. Different governing bodies are responsible for ensuring that policing policies and practices properly meet public needs and expectations. For Eng, there exists a *democratic gap* between the mandate and the practice of these agencies. Not everyone is equal before the law; some segments of society are overpoliced and do not have a real voice in shaping police policies. The discrepancy between the 'law on the books' and the 'law in practice' creates a democracy gap.

The increasingly prevalent role played by private security exacerbates this gap. Private policing caters to the interests of private property owners and businesses. Those who are policed are dealt with according to overriding commercial interests. There is no social contract between those working in private security and those being policed.

Like Hermer and colleagues, Eng opts for policing boards as a mechanism to provide effective, democratic, and community-driven oversight of public and private policing agencies. A new legislative framework could be developed to ensure that policing boards reflect core democratic values in policing. Such a framework could build upon and improve the current system of oversight for the public police. A governance body with an overall mandate to translate community safety and security needs into policing policies, standards, and practices (for both the public police and private security) would better ensure civilian oversight and accountability in public policing and address accountability concerns with private security. For Eng, the establishment of an effective governance model, one that encompasses both public and private security, would allow the state to fulfil its role in the social contract as the guarantor that the provision of services reflects democratic values. The challenge is to ensure that services are provided to all segments of society, not just to those who can afford them.

Issues for Law Reform

Does the public-private distinction make sense anymore? The chapters in this volume call into question the conventional wisdom that public police respond to violations of the public law such as the Criminal Code, whereas private police patrol private property. As Stenning[29] argues, a great deal of our law links the geography that is policed to the policing function. The courts often assume that *public* property is policed by *public* police because there is a *public* interest. On the other hand, *private* police are responsible for policing *private* property. Stenning argues that it is increasingly difficult to defend the geographic generalization for two reasons. First, the public police are not confined to the policing of public spaces. Second, with the growth of 'mass private property' such as malls, leisure complexes, and sports facilities, private property can no longer be thought of as private space. These public spaces are being policed by private police. As Hermer and colleagues argue in their contribution to this volume, these are communal spaces. Changes in property relations, therefore, require a reconsideration of the regulation of policing.

The courts, through the doctrine of state agency, have retained the legal fiction that state and private interests can be disentangled.[30] The Charter of Rights and Freedoms does not apply to interactions between two private individuals. Through the doctrine of state agency, however, the Charter does apply when an individual exercises authority derived from the state. For example, anyone – whether a peace officer, a security guard, or a private citizen – who effects an arrest is deemed to be acting as an agent of the state and therefore is bound to respect the Charter.[31] However, the Charter does not apply to detentions of a private citizen by another private citizen. So as long as a private security officer detains but does not arrest an individual, the Charter does not apply. As the networks of public and private policing become more and more dense, the question of when a private security agent is acting as an agent of the state and therefore subject to the Charter will become more and more difficult to answer.

The current regulatory environment may not adequately reflect the reality of the emerging networks of public and private policing in Canada. Should legislation attempt to shore up the distinction between public police and private security? For example, policy makers could attempt to bolster the doctrine of state agency so that regulations set out what actions private security agencies and personnel can and cannot perform. Or should Canada's policy be geared towards effective regulation of the new networks of policing that have developed? Should we develop policing policies that encompass the activities of both the public sector and the private sector, policies that can manage the relationship between these two service providers?

The goal of law reform should be to provide a regulatory framework that promotes democratic policing values. As Susan Eng reminds us, accountability is a critical issue. The effectiveness of accountability measures for the public police is a contentious issue. Some argue that public police officers are unfairly treated by an inefficient oversight system. Others claim that existing oversight mechanisms are weak and lack broad-based community representation. Some argue that private security officers are much less accountable for their actions than are public police because legislation does not establish independent oversight mechanisms that can be used to hold private security officers accountable.

Perhaps the question is not only whether private and public policing bodies are accountable, but to whom. Existing methods of accountability may not reflect the reality that policing is no longer solely provided by the public police. Perhaps it is not simply that private security ought to be brought under the mechanisms of accountability that currently exist for the public police. Rather, it may be that law reform efforts should be directed towards the development of innovative oversight mechanisms that reflect the new reality of networks of public and private policing in Canada. If we accept the assumption that policing includes activities undertaken by both the public police and private security agencies, then should we not look to broader forms of regulation that encompass the policing sector as a whole? The type of policing boards proposed by Eng and by Hermer and colleagues is one promising avenue for law reform.

The chapters in this volume make it clear that it is no longer feasible to think about issues such as accountability, oversight, and democratic policing solely in terms of the public police. The challenge is to think creatively about how to refashion governance relationships to reflect emerging networks of policing.

Notes

1 Eng and Hermer and colleagues (in this volume) question the degree to which these protocols are effective, leaving this democratic oversight open to debate.

2 Edward James Blakely and Mary Gail Snyder, *Fortress America: Gated Communities in the United States* (Washington, D.C.: Brookings Institution Press, 1997).

3 Evan McKenzie, *Privatopia: Homeowner Associations and the Rise of Residential Private Government* (New Haven, Conn.: Yale University Press, 1994).

4 Clifford D. Shearing and Philip C. Stenning, 'Private Security: Implications for Social Control' (1983) 30:5 Social Problems 493.

5 Law Commission of Canada, *In Search of Security: The Roles of Public Police and Private Agencies* (Ottawa: Law Commission of Canada, 2002). In addition, the commission sponsored In Search of Security: An International Conference on Policing and Security in Montreal in February 2003. Information about the conference is available on the commission's website: www.lcc.gc.ca.

6 Peter K. Manning, 'Policing New Social Spaces,' in J.W.E. Sheptycki, ed., *Issues in Transnational Policing* (London: Routledge, 2000) 175.

7 Jaap De Waard, 'The Private Security Industry in International Perspective' (1999) 7:2 European Journal on Criminal Policy and Research 143; Vera Institute of Justice, *The Public Accountability of Private Police: Lessons from New York, Johannesburg, and Mexico City* (New York: Vera Institute of Justice, August 2000).

8 For example, see David Bayley and Clifford Shearing, 'The New Structure of Policing: Description, Conceptualization and Research Agenda' (Washington, D.C.: National Institute of Justice, 2001); Stephen Spitzer and Andrew T. Scull, 'Social Control in Historical Perspective: From Private to Public Responses to Crime,' in David F. Greenberg, ed., *Correction and Punish-ment* (Beverly Hills: Sage Publications, 1977); C. Shearing and P. Stenning, 'Modern Private Security: Its Growth and Implications,' in Michael Tonry

and Norval Morris, eds, *Crime and Justice: An Annual Review of the Research*, vol. 3 (Chicago: University of Chicago Press, 1981).

9 N. Walker, 'Decoupling Police and State,' in E. Bort and R. Keat, eds, *The Boundaries of Understanding: Essays in Honour of Malcolm Anderson* (Edinburgh: International Social Science Institute, 1999) 75.

10 Nikolas Rose, 'The Death of the Social? Re-figuring the Territory of the Government' (1996) 25:3 Economy and Society 327.

11 Ibid., 352.

12 David Garland, *The Culture of Control; Crime and Social Order in Contemporary Society* (Chicago: University of Chicago Press, 2001).

13 See also M. Foucault, 'On Governmentality' (Autumn 1979) 6 Ideology and Consciousness 5; C. Gordon, *Power/Knowledge: Selected Interviews and Other Writings, 1972–1977 / Michel Foucault* (Brighton: Harvester Press, 1980).

14 While technically a provincial police force, the Royal Newfoundland Constabulary provides policing services to the three largest cities in Newfoundland (St John's, Corner Brook, and Labrador City). The RCMP provides contract policing for other Newfoundland municipalities.

15 Law Commission of Canada, *supra* note 5 at 22. See also G.S. Rigakos, *The New Parapolice: Risk Markets and Commodified Social Control* (Toronto: University of Toronto Press, 2002) 115.

16 Canadian Centre for Justice Statistics. *Police Resources in Canada*, 2002 Cat. No. 85-225-XIE (Ottawa: Statistics Canada, 2002).

17 Law Commission of Canada, *supra* note 5 at 24–5.

18 Sanders provides some useful data on the size and scope of the private security industry in Canada. See Trevor Sanders, 'Rise of the Rent-A-Cop: Private Security in Canada, 1991–2001,' paper presented at In Search of Security: An International Conference on Policing and Security, Montreal, February 2003.

19 Karen Swol, 'Private Security and Public Policing in Canada,' *Juristat* 18:3 (Ottawa: Statistics Canada, Canadian Centre for Justice Statistics, 1998, catalogue no. 85-002-XPE98013) at 1.

20 Statistics Canada, *Annual Survey of Investigation and Security Service* (1997).

21 De Waard, *supra* note 7.

22 For a review of different aspects of the high-end public and private security industry, see Stephen Schneider, *Combating Money Laundering in Canada: Exploring the Role of Private Sector Financial Investigative Agencies*, report prepared for the Law Commission of Canada, September 2003; James W. Williams and Margaret E. Beare, 'Private Agencies and Public Dilemmas: Contemplating Reform in the Forensic Accounting and Corporate Inves-

tigation Industry,' report prepared for the Law Commission of Canada, September 2003; Sheptycki, *supra* note 6.

23 Peter Manning, 'Three Modes of Security,' paper prepared for In Search of Security: An International Conference on Policing and Security, Montreal, February 2003.

24 Les Johnston and Clifford Shearing, *Governing Security: Explorations in Policing and Justice* (London: Routledge, 2003) 18.

25 Philip Stenning, 'Powers and Accountability of Private Police' (2000) 8 European Journal of Criminal Policy and Research at 328.

26 Bayley and Shearing, *supra* note 8.

27 Stenning, *supra* note 25.

28 Les Johnston, 'Transnational Private Policing: The Impact of Global Commercial Security,' in J.W.E. Sheptycki, ed., *Issues in Transnational Policing* (London: Routledge, 2000) 31.

29 Stenning, *supra* note 25.

30 For a comprehensive review of the law relating to police and private security, see N.J. Groot, *Canadian Law and Private Investigations* (Toronto: Irwin Law, 2001).

31 *In R. v. Lerke* [1986], 24 C.C.C. (3d) 129, Alta. C.A., it was held that the power to arrest is derived from the sovereign and is therefore the exercise of a state function. Because an arrest is a state function, the Charter applies regardless of whether the person making the arrest is a peace officer or a private citizen.

1 Policing in Canada in the Twenty-first Century: Directions for Law Reform

JOE HERMER, MICHAEL KEMPA, CLIFFORD SHEARING,
PHILIP STENNING, AND JENNIFER WOOD

The radical innovation of our time is the turn by the state to markets, public as well as private, to deliver public goods. Post-industrial states continue to finance public goods, but they have stepped back from directly delivering these goods to their citizens. Some are quite deliberately stimulating the creation of public markets, where providers of public goods compete directly for public money. The post-industrial state is increasingly a partner and contractor, working jointly with other institutions – private as well as public – to set the terms on which others deliver public goods. The state contracts out the work that it expects can be done more efficiently by others, whether that work is maintaining military bases, providing policing, delivering development assistance, supplying military training, managing prisons, running schools, providing security at airports, or delivering health care. The hope and the promise is that through the logic of markets, competition will increase efficiency. This change in the way the state works – through markets rather than as a manager and operator – is the most significant change since the development of the rational, efficient, bureaucratic state a century ago.

> Janice Gross Stein, *The Cult of Efficiency* (the 2001 Massey Lectures),
> (Toronto: Anansi, 2001), 66

The world will be policed collectively, or it will not be policed at all.

> Hendrik Hertzberg, 'Tuesday and After,' *The New Yorker*,
> 24 September 2001, 28

Introduction

During the last four decades of the twentieth century some very significant changes occurred in policing in Canada and other democratic countries. These changes involved not only a restructuring of the institutions through which policing is undertaken but also the development of new techniques for actually accomplishing policing goals. In this chapter, we review what is known about these changes, their social implications, and their relevance for a reconsideration of the role of law in achieving more effective, realistic, just, equitable, and democratic policing in Canada.

We should make clear at the outset of our discussion what we mean when we use the term 'policing.' Until relatively recently, as we shall discuss in more detail below, 'policing' was a term typically used to describe the work done by public police officers and services ('the police'). Thus, there was an implicit assumption that you could discover what 'policing' was all about by just looking at what 'the police' were doing. There are still many people (in fact, probably still the majority) who understand and use the term 'policing' in this sense. In light of the significant changes that we will be reviewing in this paper, however, we shall be using the term 'policing' in a different, rather broader sense. This is because, as we shall illustrate in what follows, not only are the kinds of activities that 'the police' have traditionally been involved in now undertaken by many other people and institutions, but also many other people and institutions have been finding new and different ways to achieve similar objectives to those of the police (i.e., new forms, strategies, and methods of policing), as well as deploying policing for other, different objectives.

For these reasons, which we shall discuss in more detail in this chapter, we believe that it is no longer useful to think of 'policing' as just what 'the police' do. Instead, we shall be using the term 'policing' throughout this paper to mean *any activity that is expressly designed and intended to establish and maintain (or enforce) a defined order within a community.* While policing is most commonly performed by organizations or groups formally organized for the purpose, whether under state or non-state auspices (such as police services, private security companies, etc.), it is often performed by individuals who may have policing responsibilities included in more general job responsibilities (e.g., a receptionist, ticket collector, or sales clerk), or by citizens as an aspect of their general civic or communal responsibilities (e.g., Neighbourhood Watch, Block Parents, etc.). Indeed, as we shall discuss in more detail below, such 'responsibilization' of the citizenry to assume policing tasks is becoming increasingly common with the growing prominence of 'neoliberal' conceptions of governance.

Of course, our use of the term 'policing' in this way needs some further elaboration. In particular, we need to clarify what we mean by 'a defined order' and what we mean by a 'community.'

A 'defined order' is a set of explicit or implicit norms designed to regulate behaviours (conduct), relationships, or expression, and to provide for the establishment of institutions and procedures. Order may be formally defined (e.g., through laws enacted by a legislature), or more informally defined (e.g., by customs and traditions passed on from one generation to another). Commonly, however, the order that is actually policed in practice varies somewhat from the order that is formally prescribed. Thus, for instance, the formal law may prohibit the driving of a vehicle on the highway in excess of 80 kilometres per hour, but police may in practice enforce the law only against drivers who drive at more than 90 or 100 kilometres per hour. Social scientists have offered many explanations for such 'gaps' between the 'law on the books' and the 'law in action,' but these need not concern us here. The existence of such gaps, however, indicates that ascertaining the 'order' which is actually the basis for policing in any given context poses an empirical question which cannot be answered by simply consulting the formal law, and that in most circumstances the role of the law in policing is mediated both by social norms generally and by the particular cultures of the organizations charged with policing.

Orders are typically defined with a view to achieving particular objectives, and policing is the means through which such objectives are sought to be achieved. One objective that is most commonly identified with formal laws (and hence as an objective of policing) is the achievement of security and safety for members of the community being policed. Indeed, providing assurances of security is regarded as such a powerful justification for policing that it is often claimed to be its objective even when this is questionable. In an interview, for instance, the Minister of Foreign Affairs of the Taliban government in Afghanistan claimed that that government's repressive laws and policing against women and girls were required to restore 'security and order' to the country, which had experienced war and disorder for two decades.[1] Many observers, however, argue that these laws and policing were really more about imposing a religious ideology of male domination, involving gross violations of human rights, than about guaranteeing anyone's 'security.' What this example illustrates is that claims about the objectives of order and policing are often open to legitimate contestation, and cannot necessarily be accepted at face value.

While security and safety are the objectives most commonly claimed for policing by state authorities, they are certainly not the only discernible objectives of policing, and this is becoming increasingly the case as the definitions of order and policing are undertaken by an ever-wider variety of state and non-state authorities. Even in the case of policing by state authorities, objectives that have either little, or at best tenuous, connection to security and safety, or that are actually incompatible with those objectives, can be identified. Thus, in many countries, policing is undertaken with the explicit or implicit objective of suppressing political dissent or particular minority groups (e.g., apartheid policing in South Africa prior to the 1990s). Even the pursuit of 'justice' as an objective of order and policing may sometimes be seen as incompatible, or tenuously compatible, with objectives of security and safety.[2]

Some scholars have characterized non-state policing broadly as 'policing for profit.'[3] While we believe that this represents an exaggerated, and often inaccurate, stereotyping of non-state policing, it is no doubt an accurate description of the principal objective of much non-state policing, and it illustrates that the objectives of order and policing are largely determined by the particular interests of the state or non-state authorities who define order and sponsor the policing of it.[4]

It will be obvious that these policing objectives are neither mutually exclusive nor necessarily easily reconcilable; for instance, a measure to enhance security may not be perceived as just or supportive of fundamental human rights, and a measure to achieve justice may be perceived as threatening to security. Furthermore, policing undertaken to further private interests often will not satisfactorily reflect broader public interests and may even be in conflict with them. It will be obvious, too, that these concepts are inevitably quite political, in the sense that what may be perceived as 'security' or 'justice' by one person may be experienced as insecurity or injustice by another, depending on their relative positions or status in a community. Thus, for instance, a policing operation designed to 'clean up' the streets of a downtown shopping area may be perceived by home-owners or business entrepreneurs in the area as improving the security or safety of the area, but may be perceived and experienced as oppressive, threatening, and unjust by the principal 'targets' of the operation, such as homeless people, unemployed youth, people begging, and so on, who feel that they, too, should be recognized as having a right to frequent the area because it is supposed to be a 'public' place. We consider such situations in more detail later in this chapter. For present purposes, however, it is sufficient to note that order and policing most commonly reflect some attempt to achieve a balance between such competing interests in a community.

Because policing, as we understand it, is essentially about establishing and maintaining order, it will be obvious that the role of law (and law reform) with respect to policing is both direct and indirect. On the one hand, the law plays a key role in defining the 'order' that forms the basis for policing. As we shall illustrate, although most people think first of the criminal law when thinking about the legal order with which policing is concerned, the criminal law is in fact only one area of the law (and in some circumstances by no means the most influential one) through which the order that is maintained through policing is defined and policing itself is shaped. One of the challenges for law reformers in this area, therefore, is to identify what kinds of law reform might best contribute to the kind of legal environment for policing that best reflects core values. In this chapter, we endeavour to identify at least the range of different kinds of law and law reform that this challenge brings into play.

Much more directly, of course, the law can shape policing through the enactment or judicial recognition of rules and procedures, and of institutions, through which policing is carried out, governed, and held accountable. In this chapter, we argue that law reformers need to pay attention to both these ways in which the law can shape and influence policing.

Just as we have defined 'policing' broadly for the purposes of our analysis, so we also adopt a broad definition of 'community.' In this chapter, we take 'community' to mean a collectivity, whether it be defined in terms of a specific geographic area, by a sense of shared identity – on the basis, for instance, of gender, nationhood, race, ethnicity, or sexual orientation – or by a shared sense of goals organized through economic, political, or cultural activity. While a 'community' often reflects all three of these attributes (e.g., the 'gay community' in some cities), it is important to note that some of the most active communities are ones that are 'imagined,'[5] in the sense that they are not based in a particular physical space or territory (e.g., the 'virtual communities' of cyberspace). Communities, of course, do not just happen – they are shaped, influenced, facilitated, and constrained by a host of factors, including the law. And, as we shall illustrate in this chapter, the nature of communities, in turn, has an influence on how they are policed, and by whom. Consequently, law reformers who are interested in policing need also to pay attention to the ways in which the law shapes communities that are the sites of policing.

In addressing the role of law in policing in Canada, we start from the assumption that, in a democracy such as ours, a principal objective of lawmakers should be to establish a legal environment for policing that is supportive of essential democratic values – fair, equitable, and just policing that is as inclusive as possible and in which fundamental human rights of everyone are recognized, upheld, and protected. As we shall illustrate, all of these notions (fairness, equity, justice, inclusiveness, and respect for human rights) are also 'political' in the sense that what is accepted as 'fair,' 'equitable,' 'just,' and so on, within a given society or community is, in a true democracy, typically determined through some process of political negotiation and compromise that requires a balancing of competing interests. 'Policing,' then, is inevitably and by definition 'political' in this sense. Accordingly, in this chapter we do not attempt to come up with any prescriptions for what policing should be done, by whom it should be done, or how; rather, we attempt to identify the kinds of legal reform strategies most likely to produce a legal environment that is most conducive to the development of a democratic politics of policing – that is to say, political processes most likely to produce and promote policing that reflects the core ideals (such as fairness, equity, justice, inclusiveness, protection of human rights, etc.) most valued in a democracy.

To accomplish this objective, our chapter begins with a brief description of the current legal environment within which policing is currently undertaken in Canada, highlighting the various ways in which the law currently shapes, influences, facilitates, and inhibits different ways of conceiving of, and doing, policing. We then consider the important changes that have occurred during the last forty years or so, not only in who does policing, but in what policing seeks to accomplish and how it is done. We pay particular attention to some significant social, economic, and political shifts that have, directly or indirectly, led to these important changes in policing. We provide illustrations of the ways in which the law has 'lagged behind' these changes so that it no longer adequately reflects and responds to the realities either of policing itself or of the contexts in which it occurs. We also note that one of the most important effects of this legal anachronism is that the current legal framework now supports and facilitates policing that does not always optimally reflect or promote those core democratic ideals we claim to value so highly.

We then consider the ways in which policing creates and shapes 'spaces' within communities, ways that in turn influence the way people live and the opportunities available to them. We consider the nature of these spaces, and in particular address the issue of whether they are usefully thought about nowadays in terms of a conventional 'public-private' dichotomy, rather than in terms of their 'communal' character, and some implications of this for the policing of such spaces. We pay particular attention to the ways in which policing 'sorts' populations into those who do and do not have access to such communal spaces and regulates such access; and we consider what kinds of legal reform might generate a legal environment supportive of policing that would better reflect the democratic ideals of equity and inclusiveness. We also recognize that not all of the 'spaces' that require policing in Canada are nowadays purely geographical spaces (e.g., cyberspace) or confined within our national boundaries.

While the primary focus of our discussion is on developments here in Canada, we recognize that the kinds of developments in policing we are witnessing are not only not unique to Canada, but are nowadays responding to, and being influenced by, significant developments beyond our borders (e.g., globalization, market restructuring, and geopolitical shifts). In addition to identifying some of these, and their implications for policing in Canada, we also describe some innovative ideas and experimental approaches to policing (and to reforming the legal environment in which it is undertaken) in other jurisdictions, from which we may be able to draw some valuable lessons for policy and legal reform in Canada.

We conclude with a summary of the principal arguments developed in the chapter, and outline what we consider to be the most important implications of our analysis for future law reform with respect to policing in this country. We make some specific recommendations as to what should be given priority in this respect.

In recent years, it has become common to differentiate between 'public' and 'private' policing – indeed, some of us, in our earlier writings, have contributed to this dichotomous view of policing. As we explain in this chapter, however, recent developments have rendered this analytical dichotomy of increasingly doubtful utility for understanding policing at the beginning of the new millennium. Accordingly, we have opted to discuss policing primarily in terms of 'state' and 'non-state' policing, although this approach, too, is by no means free from difficulties. By 'state' policing, we mean policing that is in some significant way undertaken under the auspices of public, governmental authorities, whether these be at a local, regional, national, or international level (e.g., Interpol). And we use the term 'non-state policing' as a residual category to comprehend policing (again within whatever space, whether defined geopolitically or otherwise) that is not undertaken under such public, governmental auspices. While we recognize that these are not entirely 'watertight' categories, and that the character of some policing will still be ambiguous in these terms, we nevertheless believe that, especially when considering the role of law with respect to policing, these terms have some advantages over the more conventional labels of 'public' and 'private' policing.

The Current Legal Environment

The legal environment within which policing occurs in Canada is complex and consequently not easy to summarize briefly. We start, however, by describing the more direct ways in which policing is regulated through the law, and then consider the broader range of laws that indirectly shape and influence policing.

Constitutionally, the responsibility for legislation most directly related to policing is divided between the federal Parliament and provincial legislatures. Paragraph 91(27) of the *Constitution Act* vests the Parliament of Canada with the exclusive authority to enact criminal law and procedure, and it is under this head of legislative authority that most of the legal powers for criminal law enforcement (a vital tool for much policing) are enacted. Such legislation sets out not only the criminal law enforcement powers of state police officers (mostly referred to as 'peace officers' in the legislation) but also those of non-state individuals (including ordinary citizens) who may be engaged in policing activities. While federal legislation makes clear distinctions between the criminal law enforcement powers of peace officers, owners of property, and ordinary citizens,[6] however, it does not explicitly recognize the existence of specific non-state policing institutions or personnel such as contract and in-house security guards or investigators. Rather, these latter agents have the same criminal law enforcement powers as ordinary citizens and as the property owners for whom they work (and whose legal agents they are).

Paragraph 92(14) of the *Constitution Act*, on the other hand, vests provincial legislatures with exclusive authority to legislate with respect to the 'administration of justice' within their respective provinces, and it is pursuant to this head of legislative authority that most state police services in Canada are established and regulated.[7] In addition, paragraph 92(13) vests provincial legislatures with exclusive authority to legislate in relation to 'property and civil rights' in their respective provinces, and paragraph 92(16) vests similar authority with respect to 'all matters of a merely local or private nature in the province.' It is under these heads of legislative authority that provinces regulate various non-state policing institutions such as contract security agencies and their personnel, as well as various activities of property owners and businesses that are relevant to policing (e.g., the rights of employers to exercise control over their employees, of landlords and property owners with respect to their tenants and invitees, of educational institutions with respect to their students, etc.). Paragraph 92(15) allows provincial legislators to legislate with respect to the enforcement of provincial laws, thus providing another important source of legal powers for those doing policing (e.g., under trespass statutes,[8] highway traffic legislation etc.).

The apparently sharp distinction between the legal status and authority of state and non-state police, however, is complicated by a number of factors. One of these is the common practice whereby non-state police personnel are granted 'special constable' status for specific, limited purposes (e.g., to enforce municipal parking by-laws or provincial trespass legislation on private property). Such appointments give non-state police the status, authority, and powers of state 'peace officers' when engaged in those functions with respect to the private property that they police. Among other implications, this means that such non-state police are partly legally accountable to (and subject to control and governance by) state authorities, as well as to their private employers, for those of their functions to which their special constable appointments relate.[9]

A similar blurring of legal status and accountability arises when state police officers provide services directly under contract to private employers during their off-duty hours (often referred to as 'special pay duty' when officially sanctioned, and as 'moonlighting' when not so sanctioned).[10] Private employers of state police officers for such purposes are most typically corporations (such as the SkyDome Corporation in Toronto, which hires municipal police officers to maintain order at major league baseball games), but they may also be private citizens (e.g., who hire an off-duty state police officer to protect wedding gifts and ensure order at a wedding reception).

Finally, there are police personnel who are employed by organizations that are 'quasi-public' but also have some 'private' characteristics. University police or security personnel hired by Crown corporations (such as hydro providers, transit authorities, and public housing authorities) are good examples of such legally 'hybrid' police personnel. Although they are employed by organizations that have many 'public' characteristics and can be considered state organizations, their role (and often their legal status and authority) is in many ways more similar to that of non-state security personnel employed by private corporations, and is frequently further complicated by the fact that they also hold limited special constable appointments.

In sum, it can be observed that there is no straightforward legal dichotomy between state and non-state police. Rather, there exists in law a continuum of police legal status and authority, with clearly state police at one end and equally clearly non-state police at the other, and a whole range of 'quasi-state' and 'hybrid' police in between.

Of equal and growing importance to the legal environment for policing since its adoption in 1982, has been the Canadian Charter of Rights and Freedoms. This document, which is entrenched in the *Constitution Act*, sets out minimum constitutional standards (enumerated rights and freedoms of citizens) to which all legislation and governmental activities must conform.[11] The Charter has particularly significant implications (usually entailing constraints of various kinds) for the policing activities of state authorities, since policing so often involves restraints on liberty and invasions of privacy (and hence encroachments on rights and freedoms). Because the standards set out in the Charter apply only to *governmental* activities, however, the constraints it imposes on policing activities rarely if ever apply to the policing activities of non-state authorities, unless such non-state authorities can be considered to be acting in some way as agents of the state.[12] Thus, the legal environment generally provides much greater latitude for coercive and intrusive policing activities of non-state authorities than for those of state authorities.[13] As might be expected, the application of the Charter to those police in the middle of the public-private spectrum just discussed is often a matter of some uncertainty and an evolving case law.

In many, if not most, cases in which order and policing must be scrutinized for conformity with the Charter, values and interests must be balanced in arriving at a conclusion. The recent judgment in *R. v. Banks*,[14] involving a challenge to the constitutionality of a provision of Ontario's *Safe Streets Act*, provides a good illustration of this. The provision in question prohibits anyone, while on a roadway, from soliciting a person who is in or on a stopped, standing, or parked vehicle (the accused were 'squeegee kids'). Justice Babe held that, despite the fact that this provision of the act violated the accused's freedom of expression guaranteed by section 2(b) of the Charter, such violation was 'a reasonable limit prescribed by law' that 'can be demonstrably justified in a free and democratic society' under section 1 of the Charter, in order to protect the rights of citizens generally to use the streets and roadways without harassment, molestation, or fear.[15] The case illustrates how section 1 of the Charter has, in practice, given the courts, rather than legislatures, the ultimate authority to determine what is or is not 'demonstrably justified' order and policing in our Canadian democracy, at least when Charter rights and freedoms are at issue.[16] Anticipating the courts' resolutions of such issues thus poses a special challenge for law reformers in this area.

A notable feature of the current laws with respect to policing in Canada is that they rarely refer to 'policing' as such. Rather, policing tends to be alluded to by reference to police 'forces' or 'services.' For example, section 31 of the Ontario *Police Services Act*[17] provides that a municipal or regional 'Police Services Board' is 'responsible for the provision of police services and for law enforcement and crime prevention in the municipality.' The section then goes on to specify the principal things that such a board should be doing to fulfil this responsibility, all of which relate to the governance and supervision of the municipal 'police force.'[18] The word 'policing' does not appear anywhere in this statute.[19] Thus, the statute presents a view of policing as a function essentially associated with the role and work of state police institutions and personnel ('peace officers'). At the level of discourse, therefore, the law shapes discussion of, and arrangements for, policing in significant ways. Thus, in Ontario, as in most other jurisdictions, there are no officially recognized institutions that have responsibility for 'policing' as such (as opposed to 'police services').

The British Columbia *Police Act*[20] is a bit of an exception in this respect. Section 2 of the act provides that the minister[21] 'shall ensure that an adequate and effective level of policing is maintained throughout the Province.' Subsequent provisions of this legislation, however, make it clear that, as in the Ontario statute, 'policing' is conceived in the British Columbia statute as a function to be achieved through the establishment and work of state police forces. Thus, section 15 of the act states that municipalities of a certain size

> shall provide, in accordance with this Act and the regulations,
> (a) policing in the municipality with a police force of sufficient numbers
>   (i) to adequately enforce municipal bylaws, the criminal law and the laws of the Province, and
>   (ii) to maintain law and order in the municipality, and

(b) adequate accommodation and materiel for
   (i)   the operations of and use by the police force required under
         paragraph (a), and
   (ii) the detention of persons required to be held in custody.

When enacted in 1988, the act also provided for the British Columbia
Police Commission, a provincial oversight body.[22] Its functions, however,
as delineated in section 42 of the act, are related to the oversight of
provincial and municipal police forces and constables, police boards
(local governing authorities for state police forces), and 'police operations and procedures,' rather than of policing more generally. Despite
the use of the word 'policing' in the statute, therefore, it is clear that this
law embodies a conception of policing that focuses on the role and work
of state police institutions. As in other provinces, non-state providers of
policing services, to the extent that they are regulated at all, are regulated under separate legislation that typically refers to 'private security'
rather than private policing.[23] The law thus does not encourage a holis-
tic approach to 'policing,' and tends to convey a conception of policing
as essentially about *law enforcement* and *crime prevention*.
   One of the practical implications of this atomized view of policing in
the law is that uncertainty arises as to where the responsibilities of the
state's policing authorities end and those of non-state policing authorities begin. This uncertainty has been greatly aggravated during the last
forty years or so with the emergence, especially but by no means exclusively in urban areas, of various new forms of property ownership, and in
particular of what Shearing and Stenning have termed 'mass private
property' – property that is privately owned but that is in fact publicly
used (in the sense that members of the general public are routinely
invited, even encouraged, to frequent it).[24] Although conventional
wisdom suggests that, because it is legally 'private' property (i.e., it is
privately owned), the responsibility for policing it does not belong primarily to state policing authorities, the public character of the use of
such property (i.e., from the point of view of its use it resembles a 'public
place' more than simply private space) raises doubts about this. Moreover, the 'spillover' effects frequently associated with such places (i.e.,
the additional policing problems they may generate in neighbouring
public places) sometimes raise questions as to whether the responsibility
for the policing of such spillover effects should be borne by the state's
policing authorities or by the mass private property owners.[25] Courts and

inquiries have also had to wrestle with the question of the appropriateness of the application of non-state law enforcement powers, such as those under trespass laws, on such 'publicly used private property.'[26] Only relatively recently have the courts begun to recognize that these developments in the nature of property call for a more nuanced approach to the legal distinction between private citizens on the one hand and 'the public' on the other, one which takes into account that not all privately owned property is alike and that the character of some property (as 'public' or 'private,' in terms of the access to it of different 'publics') can be quite ambiguous.[27]

The traditional deference to the rights of property owners in the law[28] has enormous implications for policing. On the one hand, the right of private property owners to privacy has translated into substantial restraints on the right of state officials such as police officers to enter such property, or place it under surveillance, without either the consent of the owner or occupier(s) of the property or a judicial warrant (which typically requires proof of reasonable and probable grounds to believe that criminal conduct is taking place on the property – an 'articulable cause'). On the other hand, and more importantly for policing, the law recognizes the right of the owner or occupier of property, either personally or through an agent (e.g., an employed non-state security guard) to control activity, behaviour, and movement on the property and to 'defend' the property from unauthorized access, predation, or damage, and in some circumstances to employ physical force and/or pervasive and continuous random surveillance in doing so. All of these activities (control of access and movement, use and threat of physical force, surveillance, etc.) are essentially policing activities. Unlike their deployment by state police, however, which is significantly constrained by the requirements of the Charter and the need for 'articulable cause,' their deployment by property owners and their agents within the confines of their property is (sometimes with the exception of physical force or the threat of it)[29] relatively unconstrained by the law.[30] These legal rights of property owners thus provide an essential foundation and legitimation for non-state policing.

At the heart of this legal regime is the critical legal proposition that the extent of the right to privacy (and the right to police it and to protect oneself against invasions of it) is precisely commensurate with the legal ownership or occupancy of real and personal property. Nowhere has this legal proposition been more emblematically stated than in the famous dictum in *Semayne's Case*[31] that 'the house of everyone is to him as his castle and fortress, as well for his defence against injury and violence, as for his repose.' In the subsequent leading case of *Entick v. Carrington*, the English courts confirmed that this right to privacy will normally prevail even over the interests of the sovereign:

> Our law holds the property of every man so sacred, that no man can set his foot upon his neighbour's close without his leave; if he does he is a trespasser though he does no damage at all; if he will tread upon his neighbour's grounds he must justify it by law.[32]

These ancient general legal principles have been affirmed by Canada's highest court in recent cases.[33]

Another essential feature of the current legal environment for policing is the deference accorded in the law to freedom of commerce, and the associated freedom of contract that, although thought to have been somewhat eroded during the 1970s and 1980s, is now said to be gaining new ascendancy.[34] As Karl Marx and others long ago emphasized, these two freedoms, and their recognition and legitimation through the law, are essential foundations of a capitalist market economy.[35] Their implications for policing are profound, for they allow for the commodification of security, safety, and policing through contractual arrangements in which the contracting parties are treated as equals and free.[36] Thus, for instance, submission to policing procedures can be made a condition (through the terms of a contract) of access to services, property, or other facilities. While freedom of contract is certainly not absolute in our law – for instance, antidiscrimination laws generally prohibit discrimination against members of racial, ethnic and other identifiable groups in contracts for the provision of services to the public[37] – our laws of contract, whether in relation to the provision of services or to employment, generally allow great freedom for 'private' negotiation of security and policing arrangements (e.g., that customers or employees consent to searches of their person or belongings as a condition of entry to retail premises). The fact that contracting parties often do not actually have equal bargaining power (e.g., an individual contracting with a bank for access to credit facilities) means that powerful institutions are often able to effectively impose such arrangements on their customers as a condition of access to the services they control. The law typically supports such arrangements. Although customers are notionally 'free' not to enter into such contracts, the reality is often that declining to do so would make life extremely difficult if not intolerable (e.g., international travel would be much more difficult if one were not willing to buy airline tickets or submit to searches before boarding aircraft[38] – yet the law treats such transactions as contracts freely entered into by equal contracting parties). In some instances, legislatures have stepped in to regulate the terms that may and may not be included in such contracts (residential tenancy legislation provides a good example of this). But never, to our knowledge, has there been any explicit, systematic, public consideration of the extent to which policing, security, and safety arrangements should or should not, in light of some broader public interest, be allowed to be the subject of private contractual agreements.[39]

By contrast, the courts have tended to urge strict observance of the rights and freedoms of citizens in places traditionally regarded as 'public'[40] – for instance, in applying the provisions of the Charter of Rights and Freedoms to the regulation and policing of such places[41] – although they have sometimes authorized limitations on such rights for some people in the interests of upholding conflicting rights and interests of the majority.[42] The courts have shown considerable reluctance, however, to apply such standards to places of 'mass private property' and other quasi-public places.[43]

The close association between the authority for policing and the nature of the property in relation to which it is undertaken means inevitably that policing itself is indirectly, but very influentially, shaped by laws that govern the character of property and the uses to which it may be put (i.e., planning and zoning laws, such as those permitting and governing 'gated communities' and forms of 'mass private property'). Typically, such laws are enacted very locally (i.e., through municipal by-laws) within the framework of relevant general provincial statutes setting out broad principles and institutions through which local decisions may be appealed, and so on. Equally importantly, such laws typically allow for substantial negotiation and political input into their administration, allowing for the possibility that security and safety arrangements (including the allocation of responsibility for them between state and non-state police) can be explicitly negotiated as part of the process for zoning approval for areas of mass private property such as malls and shopping centres.[44]

Finally, it is most important to remember that a great deal of policing is achieved without the input of police personnel (state or non-state), through the deployment of technology and the vigilance of ordinary citizens and employees. Thus, for instance, surveillance cameras (both real and 'dummy') are commonly deployed in the expectation that they will achieve effective policing merely by the deterrent effects of their visible presence, regardless of whether anyone is actually monitoring them. Ordinary employees such as receptionists, ticket collectors, and sales clerks have policing functions (such as access control, surveillance, and compliance monitoring) built into their job descriptions. While some of these policing activities are directly regulated through law,[45] many are not. Nevertheless, both state and non-state policing are regulated (or at least influenced, facilitated, or constrained) by a host of laws (such as licensing laws; privacy, data, and consumer protection laws; workplace health and safety laws), as well as by specific policing legislation and the common law of property, contract, and tort.

In sum, the current legal environment within which policing is undertaken in Canada is multifaceted and quite complex. It frequently reflects concepts (such as what is 'public' and what is 'private') and associated ideas about the appropriate roles of the state and non-state authorities in securing order and enforcing laws, and in governing and holding accountable those who do policing, the appropriateness of which is increasingly being called into question as the modern realities of both property relations and use, and of policing itself, evolve. It is to these evolving realities of policing and property relations that our discussion therefore now turns.

Trends and Directions in Policing

In this section we describe the forms of policing that have developed within the context of the legal framework we outlined above, along with broader social, political, and economic trends that have an impact on policing.[46] In doing so we focus on Canadian developments and some global developments that connect with and raise concerns for the Canadian case.

Nodal Governance

We are witnessing a fundamental shift in the ways in which governance is being conceived, institutionalized, and delivered. This is having profound implications for the entire enterprise of crime control, and for policing more specifically.[47]

Within the welfare liberal mode of governance that has dominated the Western political landscape for much of this century, states took responsibility for planning and administering a wide range of governmental services,[48] including policing.[49] State governments, and their police forces, were hierarchically organized, and governance was centralized.[50] As state governments grew larger and larger so too did their police services. These highly 'professionalized' services 'owned' policing.[51] With the expansion of state police services, the role and importance of non-state forms of policing relatively declined.[52]

The erosion of welfare liberal approaches to governance in many democratic nations (as well as the restructuring of many authoritarian regimes) that has occurred in recent years has taken place in the context of the changing technological, economic, and political landscape associated with 'globalization.'[53] As part of these shifts, many state functions have been devolved to non-state agencies, both sub- and supranationally. This has occurred both with and without state support.[54]

Neoliberal political rationality has been central to these developments.[55] It has promoted governing arrangements that operate through and for *communities*. This has shifted the focus of governance away from 'the social' realm that was so central to welfarism. With this shift in focus has come an increased reliance on local knowledge and an emphasis on the value of more direct forms of citizen participation in carrying out the business of governance. A central mechanism used to effect these values has been 'the market': the commodification of governmental services permits local entities to participate in governance and to shape the ways in which it is carried out through the exercise of purchasing power.

Concurrently with an increasing reliance upon the market as the primary medium of information (i.e., 'local preferences and needs') and service distribution, a range of non-state agencies has reassumed a more focal role in governance. These agencies include for-profit as well as not-for-profit institutions such as volunteer associations. The reemergence of many forms of *non-state* agencies in the process of governance highlights the fact that state government, while it has played and continues to play an important role in directing the contemporary reinvention of governance, does not dominate all aspects of this process.

That being said, considerable restructuring of state agencies has been taking place as governments themselves increasingly recognize their position as one agency within a broader governmental *network* wherein service planning, provision, and control are spread across a greater number of state and non-state institutional players, or *nodes*.[56] Increasingly, states are focusing their attention on the 'steering' rather than the 'rowing'[57] of governance.[58]

The nodes that take part in nodal governance relate to one another in a wide variety of ways, which are characterized by differing degrees of official and tacit coordination. In some cases, network activities and outcomes are determined by a very small number of dominant nodes. The influence of such dominant nodes can be accepted and resisted by other nodes to varying degrees. In other networked arrangements, there is no conscious coordination of nodal activity – yet even in such instances of 'benign neglect,' the activity of individual nodes cannot help but impact upon the activity of the others, shaping the character of the overall network of governance that emerges. A key academic and policy challenge is to uncover the implications of these different permutations of nodal governance for different segments of the population.

Agencies, Mentalities, and Technologies for Policing

With the emergence of nodal governance, a range of non-state institutions has reassumed a prominent role in the process of policing. In many cases, these agencies deploy techniques and forms of power (i.e., 'technologies') that reflect and reinforce different understandings (i.e., 'mentalities') of what policing is intended to accomplish, and how.

PAID NON-STATE POLICING

The latter half of the twentieth century saw a substantial global expansion in paid non-state policing, frequently referred to generically as the 'private security industry.'[59] This expansion was extensive in both wealthier nations and nations in transition to full democracy. In Canada and the United States, for example, the ratio of non-state policing agents to state agents is estimated at 2 or 3 to 1. While this represents a veritable explosion in private security manpower in North America over the past four decades, the rate and scope of expansion of the industry has been less dramatic yet substantial and steady throughout the balance of the Western democratic nations of Europe, particularly in the cases of the Netherlands, the United Kingdom, and Germany.[60] In some parts of the democratizing world – for example, South Africa, where the ratio is estimated to be between 5 and 7 to 1 – paid non-state policing is becoming increasingly pervasive as citizens explore alternative means of attaining security in the context of an overwhelmed state.[61]

As we have detailed in the previous section, the sources of authority of paid non-state policing personnel differ substantially from those of the state police. The former derive their authority largely through exercising the rights of property ownership of their employers, while the latter are first and foremost charged with the administration of criminal law and a general right to use coercive force (which also yields substantial symbolic authority).[62] Criminal law by definition concerns itself primarily with sanctioning past wrongs, whereas the role of representing the powers and interests of property ownership both enables and necessitates a set of policing mentalities and practices that are future-oriented: the activities of paid non-state policing are predominantly oriented towards risk reduction and harm/loss minimization.[63] As such, paid non-state policing agencies most often focus upon eliminating the conditions that permit loss to occur, through such techniques as forcibly excluding and/or removing undesirable persons who disrupt profitable order, and engaging surveillance and environmental design techniques that either discourage undesirable conduct or permit it to be caught before it causes serious harm or disruption.[64]

There are a growing number of distinct local auspices under which such services of paid non-state policing agencies are contracted. At the local level, single businesses may hire a company to watch over their premises and the common spaces associated with them. A more recent practice involves the pooling together of resources by businesses and/or residential communities to purchase the services of paid non-state policing.[65] Both forms of sponsorship arrangements were observed in Mopas's study (also published in this book) of Vancouver's Downtown Eastside (DTES). These forms of 'private' policing often spill over into surrounding 'public' spaces such as streets and courtyards. Finally, governments also hire non-state policing agencies to protect state assets and the common spaces associated with them.[66] Here, explicitly 'public' interests are being served through 'private' resources purchased as commodities within governmental markets.

Non-state policing is increasingly in evidence at national and international levels.[67] For example, non-state policing agencies with central offices in 'established' democracies – most notably concentrated in the United States – have established far-flung networks of 'branch' offices abroad. These networks present difficult accountability dilemmas to states, especially since companies engaged in these practices often do so specifically to avoid regulatory restrictions.[68]

A further trend in transnational non-state policing is for states to deploy hired mercenaries in 'peacekeeping' functions. These security forces have, thus far, been used primarily to train state forces. Apparently, there exists a 'professional code' that bars support for actions undertaken on behalf of either governments or liberation movements that are not recognized as 'legitimate' by the international community.[69] Though there appears to be limited growth within this sector, there is some evidence to support the concern that the companies involved in this work may be breaching international law.[70]

Beyond conventional forms of paid non-state policing, there has also been an increase in recent years in what might be called the 'secondary' paid non-state policing sector. Included in this category are paid agencies that are involved in policing but do not regard this as their primary focus. Examples are the 'community service representatives' or 'city ambassadors' found in many cities of the United States and Western Europe. These agents are often hired by local levels of government, and their primary role is to act as 'public concierges' and 'information agents' for people (often tourists) passing through public spaces; secondarily, they serve a surveillance and information-relay function to both conventional non-state as well as state policing personnel.[71]

Both primary and secondary paid non-state policing agencies have been assuming a greater role in policing forms of 'supranational' spaces 'above' and 'beyond' national territories.[72] For instance, as a consequence of the technological and legal difficulties in policing the Internet through traditional mechanisms of state-oriented centralized surveillance and control, non-state initiatives now dominate the policing of cyberspace.[73] A key approach has been the setting up of 'intranets,' which amount to 'contractual communities' of Internet users who agree to adhere to standards that are enforced by their Internet Service Provider (ISP). Such ISPs act as technological gatekeepers, screening out information and guarding against user conduct that is deemed offensive to that community of Internet users.

VOLUNTEER NON-STATE POLICING: RESPONSIBILIZED AND
AUTONOMOUS CITIZENSHIP

As we noted above in our review of the current legal environment, the law has traditionally recognized a role for ordinary citizens in the policing of their communities, and still does so. Accordingly, paralleling the recent 'rebirth' of the paid non-state policing sector, and frequently with state encouragement and support (but sometimes in spite of state opposition to it), there has been a great increase in 'voluntary' or 'civil' involvement in policing. Unpaid non-state policing has taken a variety of forms, which Johnston has categorized into two types.[74] The first is wholly autonomous from the state and sometimes – but by no means always – violent in its form. This is what is often disparaged as 'vigilantism.' The second category is understood as 'responsible' civil policing because it is carried out under an umbrella of state regulation.

A major challenge that governments have begun to acknowledge is the need to find ways of limiting forms of such policing that use force illegally. The concern here – as in policing generally – is with establishing effective forms of regulation given that policing takes place to a large extent out of the public view.[75]

'Responsibilized' policing is consistent with the broader neoliberal emphasis on promoting citizen contributions to the provision of governmental services. The most obvious example of this form of policing is the mobilization of citizens by state police agencies as part of community policing programs.[76] Peter Grabosky outlines this relationship as follows:

> community-based policing entails the decentralisation of command, nurturance of and co-operation with citizen crime prevention efforts, a proactive service orientation, and accountability to local communities. In turn, this entails close consultation with local communities, to enable local citizens to define what their crime problems are and to suggest what remedial approaches might be most appropriate.[77]

This promotion of active citizen involvement in policing contrasts with the passive role of citizens emphasized within the 'professional' police era that is associated with the waning politics of 'welfarism.'[78]

The Internet is another sphere where there is a high degree of what can be considered highly 'responsibilized' non-state policing activity. Specifically, Internet users are encouraged by a variety of agencies – including the makers of computer technology, ISPs, businesses that engage in computer commerce, and governments themselves – to deploy protective hardware and software to prevent intrusions into their private communications and saved files, as well as to screen out forms of Internet content that violate their own standards of tolerance.[79]

Autonomous non-state policing is less often analysed and written about in scholarly accounts because of the difficulties of conducting research on this mode of policing. Nevertheless, the existing research indicates that violent autonomous policing is most likely to be found in relatively underprivileged areas that, for such reasons as lack of public resources, are often not effectively serviced by state police.[80] Violent autonomous policing might in such cases be thought of as 'private' policing undertaken 'by' and – at least in theory – 'on behalf of' less well-to-do segments of the population. Researchers have linked the rise of such vigilante activity to high levels of dissatisfaction with the public police and increasing desperation in the face of escalating crime and declining personal safety among the urban and rural poor.[81]

Not all forms of autonomous non-state policing involve violent activity. Examples drawn from states that are presently in transition to democracy, and from Mopas's study of Vancouver's DTES, point to approaches that combine high levels of autonomy (and occasionally forms of minimalist state regulation) with conflict resolution and program building for a safe future. One example is in response to sectarian gang confrontations in Northern Ireland. Here, high-profile volunteer community members mediate between sectarian groups through keeping in constant mobile telephone contact with counterparts on the other side of the conflict.[82]

Further, in some of South Africa's poorest black townships, a growing number of networks of Community Peace Committees convene community gatherings for the purposes of mediating disputes and preventing future breaches of the peace.[83] Solutions to disputes are not dependent upon mobilizing state police agencies but encompass a wide range of personal restitution arrangements and community-building activities. In the context of Vancouver's DTES, Mopas observed an analogous community safety group composed of a range of residents, businesses, and other community members that breaks with traditional approaches to community policing that place the public police in the dominant role of network 'coordinator.' To the extent that such pacific 'autonomous' policing forms have produced tangible improvements in the absolute and perceived levels of safety and quality of life for members of some of South Africa's most marginalized communities,[84] Canadian initiatives of the above form merit further research to determine whether and to what extent they produce benefits above and beyond standard approaches to community policing.

RELATED TRANSFORMATIONS IN STATE POLICING

Associated with the re-emergence of non-state policing is a range of transformations in state policing services. These shifts have also occurred at local, national, and supra/interstate levels.

At the local level, state police agencies have been persuaded by governments to deploy business logics of efficient management to considerably streamline their organizations.[85] A major component of this strategy has been wide-scale adoption of the competitive business principle of 'subsidiarity' – the belief that tasks and decision making ought to be devolved to the lowest possible level within the organization. In many parts of the world, including Canada, this has translated into a major effort to decentralize state policing functions.[86]

Structurally, in many state police services, subsidiarity has resulted in the devolution of decision-making authority to local districts. Such is the case in Ontario where, beginning in 1993, the Ontario Provincial Police undertook a massive process of organizational review and restructuring.[87] Operationally, subsidiarity has been associated with the development of community policing programs where, as we have noted, public involvement is in part solicited to assist the police in making decisions about the efficient and effective deployment of resources.

Other public police-focused approaches to 'community policing' that are premised upon an intolerance of disorder are also spreading widely. Perhaps the best-known example is the 'Zero Tolerance' approach deployed in New York City since the mid-1990s – an approach that has been modified and implemented in many places throughout North America. Within such programs, 'quality of life' offences are aggressively policed in public spaces because it is believed that cracking down on minor offences will increase security in such spaces in the long run by removing risky elements.[88]

Mopas observed a similar yet distinct policing approach in Vancouver's DTES: the public police were known to be pursuing a 'containment' policy through territorially differential enforcement of antidrug, loitering, and public order legislation to keep drug sales and users 'safely' away from the principal commercial and tourist area of Gastown. This approach is viewed by the Vancouver Police Department as a viable means of minimizing the apparent threat posed by drug users to residents of, and visitors to, the city until such time as drug treatment services are made available in the community.[89]

Within such 'disorder-intolerant' policing programs, we see the marriage of 'private' or 'market' logics of future-oriented risk management and harm reduction with the established state capacities and technologies of coercion and law enforcement.[90] What is common to all such modes of disorder-intolerant policing, is that they deploy coercion not to affect the 'rationality' of actors or alter their behaviour but simply to displace or remove the riskiest and most problematic individuals from the mainstream. As we will later develop in more detail in our discussion of the policing of communal spaces, this process of instrumental removal is often undertaken within a highly emotively charged normative discourse that depicts the targets of instrumental coercion as 'morally corrupt' individuals who have proven themselves undeserving of full community membership and thereby deserving of harsh state sanction.[91]

Related to the introduction of non-state mentalities to state police institutions, local police services in a growing number of jurisdictions within Canada and abroad have come to sell some of their services both to business owners and to the public more generally. A key example is the charging of fees for responding to instances of false sounding of home security systems and for providing traffic direction for special sales events on retail property. At other times, state police enter into 'sponsorship' arrangements with non-state bodies.[92] Sponsorship can take many forms, ranging from direct financial contributions to state police coffers to the provision of office space, clerical support, and/or equipment in support of particular state policing initiatives.[93]

Concurrent with the decentralization and marketization of local-level public policing, federal policing has been marked by increasing centralization and militarization.[94] This has been associated with an increasing centralization of 'high policing' functions – policing that involves combating what are perceived as explicit threats to the political, social, and economic order of the nation-state.[95] In uncertain and hotly contested 'globalizing' times, there is a real concern that the state police may be assuming an inappropriate role in quelling legitimate resistance to corporate-dominated global futures, a role that has sometimes been suspected to be at the direct behest of governments. A Canadian illustration of such a concern is the role of the RCMP in quelling student protest at the Asia-Pacific Economic Co-operation (APEC) summit in Vancouver in 1997, and at the Free Trade Agreement of the Americas (FTAA) summit in Quebec City in April 2001. In both instances, the federal police force played a key role in policing what was essentially political/economic protest that ran counter to the economic policy of state governments. The policing of the 1997 APEC meeting has recently been the subject of a review and interim report of an RCMP Public Complaints Commission tribunal, which concluded not only that the RCMP had used excessive force and violated protesters' Charter rights, but also that in two instances RCMP officers had been the object of improper 'interference' by federal government officials.[96] Similar complaints have subsequently been filed by the Canadian Civil Liberties Association against the RCMP and Quebec police with respect to the policing of the 2001 FTAA summit in Quebec City. Concerns have been expressed that the militarization of public order (and especially federal) policing in Canada – thought to be accompanied by increasing politicization – may foreshadow a more general trend towards reliance upon coercion by state police.[97]

There have also been substantial developments at the international and supranational levels of public policing. On the one hand, we have seen a massive expansion of formal and informal cooperation between state policing agencies. Such cooperation is perhaps most fully developed in the context of the European Union, where increased interaction between public police agencies is necessitated and is undertaken within the framework of the Schengen Agreement.[98] This declaration of cooperation abolishes border checks between member states, increasing the free movement of persons. To meet the associated security challenges, the Schengen Agreement includes a range of provisions. Most notable among these are requiring that police services provide other member states with assistance by request; permitting cross-border observation of persons 'presumed to have taken part in a criminal offence where extradition may apply' (though prior permission from the host must be obtained); and creating the authority to pursue a suspect interjurisdictionally (i.e., the right of 'hot pursuit').

Within this legal framework, existing agencies such as Interpol that liaise between various international policing agencies have assumed an increasingly prominent role in coordinating information flows and joint initiatives between national police forces. Additionally, we have seen the creation of wholly new suprastate policing agencies that are funded and supported by public resources and staffed by public bureaucrats but that transcend the boundaries and jurisdiction of individual states. Again, such agencies are especially well developed in the European Union, a notable example being the Trevi Initiative, a high-level ministerial group composed of senior police officers from the E.U. member states and the seven 'Friends of Trevi' who attend its meetings as observers: Austria, Canada, Morocco, Norway, Sweden, Switzerland, and the United States.[99]

Such agencies – which operate outside of the traditional 'public' sphere and are not accountable through conventional police governance authorities – raise a number of important concerns. Brodeur points out that such agencies create the condition of 'plausible deniability' on the part of state agencies that permit or undertake excessive or otherwise inappropriate policing activity inside and outside their borders.[100] Second, the question arises as to what nation ought to have jurisdiction in a given instance: the nation in which an arrest occurs; the nation in which a crime occurs; or the nation of birth of the offender or victim? The principal threat here is that the mechanisms for deciding questions of jurisdiction will be inconsistent, so that offenders will be subjected to varying legal standards in similar instances of criminal activity.[101]

Networks of Policing

In recent years, policing scholarship has shifted from an *institutional* focus on state police agencies to a greater emphasis on the *processes* through which individuals and agencies act – whether directly or through others – to undertake policing.[102] While scholars have begun to examine the ways in which the many nodes involved in networked arrangements for policing relate to one another,[103] less progress has been made in this domain than in identifying the agencies involved.[104] As we noted earlier, there has been a tendency in both the academic literature and legal policy to address and attempt to regulate the operation of policing agencies in isolation from one another, or from the perspective of one over the other, rather than as networks with interrelated practices and outcomes.

Most often, the role of state police is privileged in these analyses: it is often tacitly assumed that state police dominate or direct all other nodes that are involved in policing networks. Conversely, it is too often implied that paid non-state policing agencies and 'autonomous' forms of volunteer non-state policing operate with a greater degree of disconnection from state police than is often actually the case.

Beyond 'domination' and 'independence,' there exists a whole range of ways in which nodes – both sponsors and providers – relate to one another within networks. As we have already noted, agencies that sponsor policing initiatives sometimes band together to pool resources: this is the case in both commercial Business Improvement Districts and within residential communities.[105] We have also highlighted the fact that states have played an active role in the development of networked forms of policing. One of the most important forms of such support is direct funding: it has been well documented, for instance, that the state is one of the largest employers of both private security guards and private investigators.[106] Additionally, the state has on occasion provided local communities with monies to contract for policing services. Equally important is the creation of a legislative environment that requires non-state policing initiatives on private/semi-public property (a practice that has been documented in Spain).[107] Insurance companies also prompt property and business owners to hire non-state policing services to avoid liability on losses due to theft and property damage.[108]

Beyond the relationships that exist between sponsors and providers, providers interact among themselves in a wide variety of ways. Both formal (i.e., codified) and informal interaction take place, at the level of information sharing, resource sharing, and suspect/offender transfers.

Informal arrangements with respect to information sharing involve such measures as keeping open radio channels between state and non-state security bodies and maintaining informal contacts between agencies.[109] More formally, the state police may exercise their legal authority to obtain information that pertains to ongoing criminal investigations from paid non-state policing agencies.

Ericson and Haggerty have documented the ways in which information tends to flow outward from state police to other agencies.[110] According to their analysis, state police have become knowledge/information brokers in a broader network of intelligence-driven policing. Other studies have since supported earlier analyses, suggesting that non-state policing agencies also funnel a good deal of information to state police.[111] Mopas's study in Vancouver's DTES supports the notion that the flow of information occurs in both directions.

A significant amount of 'suspect/offender transfer' back and forth between state and non-state policing agencies has been documented in the literature. On the one hand, paid non-state policing agencies may turn suspects/offenders over to state police when situations become either too complicated or too serious (as when serious violence has occurred or is threatened) for the non-state body to be willing to handle them on its own.[112] This line has been blurred in recent years, where paid non-state policing agencies have been granted special police powers (e.g., through 'special constable' appointments in Canada, or 'deputization' in the United States).[113]

Similarly, in some countries state police have been known to transfer responsibility to 'deal' with suspected offenders to non-state policing bodies, or have apparently hired non-state policing personnel to undertake questionable investigative activities.[114] In some countries, this may go so far as to involve the transfer of suspects to violent 'vigilante' bodies,[115] although such practices happily have never been documented in Canada. One motive for such transfers is that a lower standard of proof is required to justify taking action in the non-state realm.[116] Where a known community 'troublemaker' objects to demands made by non-state policing personnel reflecting the standards of the property owner and is subsequently ejected and/or banned from the property, he or she may be turned over to the public police for violating trespass law when re-entering that space rather than on the basis of an adequately supported suspicion of criminal activity.[117] In Vancouver's DTES, as Mopas relates, there are informal arrangements to exchange information between state and non-state policing bodies and the residents' and merchants' agencies they represent regarding community 'troublemakers,' so that such individuals can be more completely monitored and controlled by state and non-state policing agencies.

The extent of these modes of interaction highlight that there is a significant degree of diffusion of functions – and of the mentalities and technologies that underpin them – between state and non-state policing agencies. Not only is it very difficult to encounter what was once thought of as 'an essential state police function' that is not in many cases also performed by non-state policing agencies (with or without state approval and/or tolerance), but also the sharp demarcation often drawn between the preventive mentality of non-state policing and the past-oriented 'justice' orientation of state police is increasingly dissolving. The evidence to date indicates that innovations in ways of thinking about – and approaching – the problems of policing have frequently originated in the non-state sector, and have subsequently been diffused to the state police.[118] The effect has been that, to a far more significant degree than in the past, state police have adopted a future-oriented set of mentalities and objectives that nevertheless are often carried out through the familiar technologies of coercion and law enforcement and the symbolic authority that derives from these capacities. Conversely, though to a lesser extent, non-state policing agencies have in some instances begun to concern themselves with carrying out a past-oriented 'justice' function, mimicking, in so far as the law permits, the coercive capacity and symbolic authority of state police to the extent that they have discovered this to be a saleable service that the public demands.[119]

The 'commodification' of policing, combined with a growth in forms of 'new communal space' – as discussed below – has resulted in the 'enclavization' of wealthier segments of the population. Residential gated communities and enclosed shopping and entertainment complexes are emblematic of this shift towards 'fortification,' a process that reflects an understanding of security as homogeneity. Critics of these developments point out that the residents or occupants of such enclaves can become effectively cut off from much in the way of diverse cultural or social exchange with the broader society. Life on the inside is in many cases relatively sterile and can be experienced as non-stimulating, while life on the outside is increasingly perceived and reacted to as dangerous and stressful.[120] The 'denizens' [121] of these spaces are confined to their own homes and secure work and leisure spaces, free to administrate 'over a life to which essentially nothing happens.'[122] Unaware of much of what happens outside of their fortified fragments, in many cases the wealthy become fearful of normal social exchange, a withdrawal that is further encouraged by the 'talk of crime' that predominates in transitional and established democratic states alike.[123]

Hence, the fortification or enclavization process serves to sort populations along economic, racial, and other lines, to the extent that 'non-denizens' are 'contained' in the spaces that surround them. One need only look at the 'conduit' spaces, such as streets, sidewalks, and parks, to see evidence of this containment process. Different forms of 'conduit policing' have emerged in response to the twin processes of enclavization and containment, to which we turn in the next section. To preview our discussion of these interrelated policing approaches, we will here highlight that the concentration of non-state policing in privileged non-state spaces coupled with disorder-intolerant state policing initiatives in the conduit spaces that surround them produces a 'democratic gap'[124] between the rich and the poor in what most would consider ought to be a 'public good,' a general right of citizenship: access to effective policing, protection, and personal security.[125]

Policing 'Communal' Space

In carrying out an analysis of the relationship between democratic values and modern policing, it is important to recognize that the established distinction between 'public space' and 'private space' that has often guided such an analysis is artificial and reified. This reification is particularly problematic at the present moment, when the operational reality of policing, in its institutional and strategic forms, is outstripping our capacity to describe and make sense of its operations. In this section, we move beyond this simple public-private dichotomy by evoking the concept of 'communal' space.[126] In drawing out the problematics of the public-private distinction, we describe the characteristics of communal space and, using the case of how homeless people are governed, engage key questions about how policing programs can be carried out that contribute to the constitution of forms of communal space that reflect democratic qualities of tolerance, diversity, and pluralism.

The Social Construction of Space

The concept of 'space' signifies a range of meanings in late-modern society, many of which challenge the Cartesian idea of space as having measurable dimensions within which material objects can exist. We often speak, for example, of psychological space, cyberspace, transnational space, and natural space. Like the word 'community,' which we have defined with some care in relation to policing, space exists as much on the plane of the imagination as it does in a physical way.

With this quality of space in mind, it is important to note that space is both a target and a resource of policing programs. The sponsors and rationalities of the police view space as a territory that is to be ordered in a manner that is consistent with their jurisdiction. However, this order does not simply take space as an object itself; policing programs reconfigure and *produce* the space of the public imagination. Thus, policing blitzes against drunk driving, for example, are not just operations that carry out surveillance, inspection, testing, evidence gathering, suspension, and arrest but are also activities that generate a much broader, highly moralized sphere that is closely linked to notions of risk, responsibility, and citizenship.[127]

The traditional way of exploring how spaces such as streets and highways are policed is to talk in terms of 'public' space, which is implicitly set in opposition to 'private' space – attributes determined by the 'public' or 'private' status of who owns the space. We want to suggest that this distinction between public and private is no longer a sustainable framework with which to understand the auspices and rationalities of policing. It is not just that the boundaries between 'private' and 'public' police are blurred and often difficult to decipher, or that the very nature of policing auspices, devolved through sovereign authority and mediated through administrative law, provide opportunities for a variety of non-state police agents to exercise powers often associated with the order-keeping dimensions of governments. An even more central reason why this distinction does not hold is that space is primarily constituted by social interaction, and often this interaction has little connection to the actual legal status of the space as privately or publicly owned.[128] In other words, just as the fluid and complex dynamics of social interaction constantly undermine distinctions between 'public' and 'private,' so do the spaces constituted by this interaction – spaces such as park benches, street corners, subway carriages, and roadways.

The term 'public' is traditionally used to denote freedom of access and flow, constrained only by prohibitions on conduct as spelled out primarily in criminal law but also in local by-laws. In contrast, 'private' spaces in law are spaces wherein property owners are at liberty to determine how, under what conditions, and by whom such spaces will be shared. There is a 'right of access' that is associated with public space, a space where one can 'form new alliances, gain new insights about the potentials and possibilities of what it means to be human.'[129] For urban theorists such as Lefebvre, spaces such as sidewalks provide people with the ability to exercise a 'right to the city,' a right to mobility that is central to the exercise of the democratic rights of citizenship.[130] A central feature of this 'right to the city' is the opportunity to have unplanned encounters with strangers from different walks of life. In arguing for the 'uses of disorder,' Richard Sennett argues that attempts to sanitize public spaces can have disturbing consequences for the way people relate to one another, and that the vast, lonely 'jungle' of the city can provide a challenging social matrix characterized by diversity and complex experience.[131]

The Concept of 'Communal Space'

In order to acknowledge the constructed and complex character of space, we wish to abandon the category of 'public space.' We suggest that in discussing how spaces such as sidewalks, street corners, or commercial complexes should be governed, we need to move away from the idea of 'public' space (set in opposition to 'private' space), and instead employ the notion of 'communal' space. By *communal space* we signify space where there is a certain collective expectation of common access and use and that people in this space do not depend on exercising a right to private property.

A tentative typology of communal spaces includes the following:

- roadways and sidewalks
- city parks and park paths and laneways
- state and provincial parks, conservation areas, and nature preserves and reserves
- public transportation such as buses and streetcars
- subway cars, platforms, and station areas
- shopping malls and other spaces of 'mass private property'[132] involving public entertainment/exhibition such as sports stadiums and industrial complexes
- places of worship
- outdoor markets

An extensive review of this typology would be a worthwhile project but is not necessary for our purposes. Instead we note a number of preliminary features about this typology of 'communal space' that will allow us to take forward our task of outlining the relationship between democratic values and policing practices.

First, these communal spaces are only loosely connected to what one might term the public institutions of formal government. Thus, we note the irony that most 'public buildings' are not communal. For example, one cannot walk off the streets and through the premises of the government offices in Queen's Park, Toronto, without proper accreditation; the purpose of such space is constituted by qualities that we associate with the requirements of privacy (an orderly workplace in which public servants can do their work without undue interruption). Similarly, public universities, hospitals, parks, and housing areas are governed as forms of private property, often in highly detailed ways, utilizing non-state policing services and devolved state powers in legislation such as trespass to property legislation. Of course, circumstances that are considered to be an emergency sometimes require these spaces to become accessible in a more communal way in terms of serving the public interest. Thus, for instance, when public health officials in the City of Toronto declared a 'heat emergency,' the foyers of many government buildings were set up to enable homeless people to have some air-conditioned place to rest and take fluids, conduct that would normally have led to their eviction by the security staff.[133]

Ironically, some of the spaces that we often think of as intended to be particularly communal and permissive, namely provincial and national parks, are in fact governed by highly detailed and intrusive regulatory programs that often mimic the commercial concerns of non-state policing regimes. [134]

Conversely, space that we often think of as 'private,' such as commercial property where shopping malls or entertainment complexes are located, are places of significant communal interaction. These are spaces that have historically been associated with ideas of the 'public,' hosting major sports and entertainment events that generate collective excitement, national pride, and feelings of transgression and counter-culture. In a culture where self-identity and consumerism are closely linked, such commercial spaces provide opportunities for participation in 'the world of commodities.'

Secondly, the primary quality of communal space is that it is space that is typically characterized by transience: it allows people to flow. To think in terms of how people move through spaces such as sidewalks, entertainment complexes, and roadways is to recognize that communal spaces are designed and policed as transient places; they make up spaces of transience that are designed to facilitate and withstand flow.[135] This quality of transience is recognized by Augé in his conceptualization of the 'non-places of supermodernity,' such as airports, shopping malls, highways, and places involving micro interactions such as encounters with cash machines.[136] In an effort to reconstruct the anthropological notion of 'place,' Augé argues that 'non-places' are spaces not of self-identity but of transience and anonymity, not of shared solidarity, but of strangeness and instruction. In communal space, people are moving anonymously as part of a 'lonely crowd,' moving by foot power or in privately owned vehicles and public transit vehicles such as buses, street-cars, and subway cars. Each of these various types of transient flow provides opportunities for social encounters – the experience of passing by on a sidewalk, sitting on a park bench with neighbours, travelling across the city on a streetcar or underground in a subway or a mall complex.

If one of the primary qualities of many forms of communal space is transience, this is not to say that those who are in communal space should be viewed narrowly as commuters or pedestrians who simply flow past each other in an asocial way. On the contrary, the transience of communal space is highly social, providing various nodes where face-to-face interaction condenses, often among people who do not know one another. In his work *Relations in Public*, Goffman argued that the passing-by experience of people in communal spaces provides opportunities for 'eye communion,' interaction that involves reciprocating 'conversational gifts' and gestures that together form a 'little ceremony.'[137] To explore these social situations, Goffman developed the notion of the 'encoun-ter' for a 'type of social arrangement that occurs when persons are in one another's immediate physical presence.' Encounters are a form of 'focused interaction' where individuals share a secular sacrament of 'eye communion,' a shared sense that the self is always dependent on the involvement of the other.[138]

Even in the case of the apparent isolation of commuters sealed in their own vehicles, the experience of commuting on roadways remains highly interactional and encounter-driven. Cars are inherently social spaces made up by a peculiar mix of visibility and seclusion. The modern vehicle is a sphere of spectacle, consumption, and communication: people talk on their cell phones or to passengers, listen to music, or eat food that is often catered to them by drive-through fast-food merchants.

This expectation and experience of seclusion and privacy collides, in a variety of ways, with the car's participation in a form of space that, unlike a personal dwelling, is rendered visible, inspectable, and contingent on schemes of licensing, insurance, and public law. Squeegee workers exploit the ambiguity of the public character of vehicle space by positioning themselves at the node of the traffic intersection, impinging on the momentarily parked space of the car and the driver. The disruption into the shell of the vehicle, and the expectation for privacy and exclusion that this shell creates, would seem to suggest why so much societal reaction to 'squeegee kids' is greatly out of proportion to any real danger that they actually pose to the commuting public.

'Mass Private Property'

A dominant type of communal space these days, especially in urban areas, is what Shearing and Stenning have termed 'mass private property.'[139] This comprises spaces that, while owned by individual citizens or by corporations, grant particular forms of common access and flow. Examples of such spaces include shopping malls, commercial and some industrial complexes, and recreational theme parks. Within these communal spaces, freedom of access and use is more tightly circumscribed than in what are traditionally thought of as 'public' spaces such as parks, roadways, and other thoroughfares. As we have already detailed, property owners, with the backing of state and non-state authorities and subject to some legal constraints, are entitled to determine who may have access to these spaces and who may be excluded from them.

Freedom of access and flow are thus more curtailed than in traditional 'public' spaces, particularly the 'corridors' or 'conduits,' where criminal and other public law is (in theory at least) the only restraint on freedom.[140] As we have outlined above, access to criminal law, as a strategy, is less relevant to the policing of mass private property than it is in the 'corridors.' There are two main reasons for this, the most obvious being that property owners do not have access to the same legitimate coercive powers of the state and its institutions such as the police. Equally important is the fact that the policing strategies and objectives put into place within these spaces are necessarily aligned with the broader interests of the property owner. These interests are often, but not always, to make a profit and to minimize loss.[141] As such, the particular order that is promoted within these spaces – and the forms of policing associated with it – are constructed to the end of profit maximization and loss minimization. A wider range of conduct (often beyond that proscribed in law) is therefore seen as threatening to the order and security of such spaces. Such conduct can include loitering, begging, and various other forms of importuning conduct (e.g., distributing political or religious materials, busking, etc.).

In addition to the strategy of access control, as enabled in provincial trespass legislation, policing within mass private property can be highly unspecific and embedded in a range of seemingly non-police functions.[142] In particular, policing can take the form of strategies for opportunity reduction and target hardening (such as requiring employees to carry passes or key cards in order to restrict access to certain parts of the building) or physical design strategies (such as installing mirrors that are positioned for people to see around corners). Closed-circuit television and electronic article surveillance have also become popular as techniques for discouraging both employee theft and customer theft in particular. Employees, such as retail salespeople or bank tellers, also serve a policing function, as they are both trained and required to minimize risk and shrinkage through particular forms of surveillance and intelligence gathering. As Garland has expressed it, this approach to policing, which seeks to 'embed'[143] it everywhere, seeks to 'modify the everyday routines of social and economic life by limiting the supply of opportunities, shifting risks, redistributing costs, and creating disincentives. It aims to embed controls in the fabric of normal interaction, rather than suspend them above it in the form of a sovereign command.'[144]

The Eaton Centre, a large urban shopping centre in downtown Toronto, exemplifies a form of mass private property where this form of 'embedded' policing is to be found. Within this space, a particular form of transience is privileged – the 'transient consumer,' a transient whose purpose is to contribute to the profit maximization of the complex. While the space is designed to provide physical comfort to the user (e.g., through cleanliness, air-quality control, etc.), a certain 'flow' of users is promoted not only through access control but also through subtle physical and environmental design features. For example, in order to encourage users to peruse a maximum amount of stores in the complex, long and relatively narrow corridors are accompanied by a conspicuously low number of escalators. Hence, while comfortable and inviting as a place for consumption, the space is designed to prevent, or at least minimize, chances for loitering or, more generally, sedentary flow. While in this space, citizens are encouraged to comply with the particular behavioural standards embodied in a mobile space of consumerism and consumption.

Those who are excluded from mass private property are thus 'contained' within the spaces that surround it – namely, what we have referred to earlier as 'conduits.' This containment effect creates, according to Shearing, a 'conduit policing problem' in the other forms of communal spaces surrounding mass private property enclaves.[145] This problem has been responded to in different ways under different auspices. The non-state patrolling of 'public' space can be seen in the Business Improvement District (BID).[146] BIDs have proliferated over the last twenty years as a more general response to a perceived decline of downtown neighbourhoods as a result of a growth in mass private property (particularly shopping malls) in the suburbs. This suburbanization process has resulted in a decline in the urban core tax base, prompting businesses to band together to sponsor service delivery with regard to maintenance, landscaping, and rubbish collection.[147] BIDs have also attempted to colonize the conduits that connect their 'fortified' spaces by engaging the institutions of non-state policing in the patrolling function. In some instances, businesses have constructed conduit systems that are physically separate from – rising above or below – their 'disorderly' surroundings. These 'sanitized corridors' that connect the enclaves can be seen in 'underground cities' as well as enclosed and raised 'skywalks' that connect shopping outlets and public transit systems. Such slivers of fortified non-state space that connect fortified enclaves appear to be most developed in modern Asian cities.[148] Nevertheless, they have emerged and are spreading in North America.[149]

Another form of conduit policing can be seen in disorder-based initiatives undertaken by public policing organizations. The most extreme example of this is the aforementioned 'Zero Tolerance' approach developed in New York City by former commissioner William Bratton. This program, which had its beginnings in the New York Transit System, was implemented in the mid-1990s. Its objective was to crack down on 'quality of life' offences, such as panhandling, jaywalking, graffiti, 'boom boxes,' and so on. This focus on 'disorderly' conduct was inspired by the theory of 'broken windows,' first articulated by Wilson and Kelling.[150] The premise of 'broken windows' is that, if various forms of physical and social disorder are tolerated at the community level, citizens will become fearful, community 'decay' will ensue, and an air of careless neglect will develop in which more serious forms of crime will flourish. Therefore, if governments and communities focus their efforts on enforcing 'civic morality,'[151] informal social control will be strengthened, standards of morality will be maintained, and crime will be reduced.

The appeal of the 'broken windows' theory is both emotive and instrumental in nature.[152] It is emotive because it harks back to a nostalgic construction of 'community' and 'neighbourhood' as homogeneous environments where clear standards of morality are known and respected.[153] At the same time, it deploys an instrumental logic, suggesting that there is a causal link between relatively minor manifestations of physical and social disorder and serious crime. This logic suggests that 'disorderly' behaviour is a risk to the security of the 'average citizen.' What is also appealing about the disorder-based approach, from the vantage point of policy makers, is that the state police are not required to reinvent or reform themselves. Rather, they are simply being asked to deploy their defining capacities (the exercise of coercion and the enforcement of the law) in a 'targeted' manner. As seen in Mopas's study, this disorder-based approach was manifested in Vancouver's DTES, where coercion is deployed to keep a 'risky' segment of the population – intravenous drug users – 'out of the way.' In these cases, there is little concern with altering the behaviour of the groups being targeted. Instead, a seemingly market-based risk-reduction approach is being coupled with the established state capacities of coercion and law enforcement. Disorder-intolerant policing deploys coercion not to affect the rationality of actors or to alter their behaviour but simply to displace them, or 'contain' them elsewhere. In Ontario, disorder-intolerant policing has been targeted primarily at particular groups of transient street populations, such as those who engage in begging and squeegee work.

Before turning to these examples, we would like to highlight that it is within this dual context of non-state policing directed by wealthier property owners and exclusionary state policing conducted on behalf of the mainstream that developments in both violent and pacific autonomous non-state policing among the poor can occur. The case of South Africa demonstrates these links. Displacement of insecurity into conduit spaces by non-state policing is apparent in this context. Impoverished non-white residential and (informal) 'commercial' areas have experienced an exponential increase in violence and insecurity since the fall of the apartheid regime.[154] In turn, disorder-intolerant forms of state policing deployed in residual public (i.e., 'conduit') spaces have contributed to a deepening alienation between the police and the principal targets of this intolerance – the poor, non-whites, and other marginalized groups. Associated with this has been the rise of both the violent and the non-violent forms of autonomous non-state policing described above, principally among the most disadvantaged areas of South Africa,[155] and indeed, we would suggest, elsewhere in the world.

At the same time, the examples of the policing of marginalized, street-based populations alert us to many of the normative concerns of recent developments in enclavization and conduit policing. We explore these through a more detailed consideration of one example – the policing of homelessness.

Policing Transience: The Case of the Homeless in Communal Space

In Canada, the United States, and Britain, the presence of homeless people, of those who are visibly indigent in communal spaces, has emerged as one of the most significant issues for policing. Homeless populations present particular challenges for democratic policing: they are an extremely vulnerable, marginalized group who rely on communal space for survival. Those who live on the street, however, are often the target of laws and police operations that are carried out in the name of 'safety' and 'security.' Indeed, the emphasis on low-level disorder, associated with the 'broken windows' approach, has inspired a network of prohibitions and restrictions that can be seen as a direct attempt to banish homeless people from many communal spaces.

In an influential essay, Waldron discussed the connection between homelessness and freedom in the context of the first principles of property law.[156] Waldron noted the widespread legal prohibitions against the most basic activities that a homeless person must carry out, such as the freedom to lie on a bench or the freedom to urinate. Because of these prohibitions, homeless people are 'placeless' in a way that makes them unfree to carry out even the most basic living functions. Economically forced to live in the communal spaces of streets and parks, homeless people are punished by laws that create an extraordinary lack of freedom. For Waldron, the issue of homelessness, like other violations of human rights, raises fundamental questions about 'the most basic principles of liberty.'[157]

Homeless people represent a different form of transience from those who have stable housing, in that their transience is one that is not carried out in relation to a sphere of privacy; homeless people attempt to 'take up' a place as part of a strategy of survival where a person has to be intransient in order to sleep, eat, sit, urinate, and so on, and occupy and maintain a body that has nowhere to go. Homeless people are inherently subversive in communal space because their permanent transience is fundamentally different from the temporary transience of most others, who are moving through communal space towards a particular destination.

Policing of homeless people is accomplished almost as much through streetscape design as through more familiar labour-intensive policing strategies. Much of the recent designing of communal space, for instance, has focused on 'target hardening' whereby the permanent transience of the homeless is 'designed out.' A good example of this is the use of 'vagrant bars' on benches in communal space, particularly bus shelters, which make it impossible for someone to lie down on the bench or, in fact, in the most recent design of seating in bus shelters, even to sit for very long.[158] This systematic exclusion of the sort of conduct homeless people engage in is emblematic of how the policing of transience in communal space is linked to socio-economic status – simply put, people who do not have money in their pockets to spend, or do not have a home or job to commute from and to, are being excluded from using communal space.

The exclusionary character of communal space is of course not limited to informal modes of control. The law has come to play a central role in the discriminatory character of the policing of communal space. In Canada, there has been a movement in the last decade to resuscitate and enact a range of loitering and anti-panhandling legislation that falls under the type of law that Waldron would include as an attack on the freedom of the visibly indigent – those who are poor and homeless in communal space. In the last decade, this movement has seen the enactment of a range of municipal by-laws in Canadian cities such as London, Vancouver, Halifax, and Oshawa that prohibit begging, one of the central subsistence activities of homeless people. Enacted in 1999, Ontario's *Safe Streets Act*[159] is the most comprehensive and only provincial law that provides explicitly for the policing of a wide range of begging behaviour, including the conduct of 'squeegee kids.'

Unlike most municipal by-laws, which tend to prohibit alms-giving in the most general way (only occasionally using time and place restrictions), the *Safe Streets Act* is both extraordinarily detailed *and* vague and sweeping.[160] The two main antibegging sections of the act prohibit soliciting in 'an aggressive manner' (subsection 2(2)) and solicitation of a 'captive audience' (subsection 3(2)). Subsection 3(2), under the heading, 'Solicitation of captive audience prohibited' provides that:

'No Person Shall,
  a. solicit a person who is using, waiting to use, or departing from an automated teller machine;

b. solicit a person who is using or waiting to use a pay telephone or a public toilet facility;

c. solicit a person who is waiting at a taxi stand or a public transit stop;

d. solicit a person who is in or on a public transit vehicle;

e. solicit a person who is in the process of getting in, out of, on or off a vehicle or who is in a parking lot; or

f. while on a roadway, solicit a person who is in or on a stopped, standing or parked vehicle.

The capricious character[161] of this section is evident when one considers how 'soliciting' is defined for the purposes of the act:

'solicit' means to request, in person, the immediate provision of money or another thing of value, regardless of whether consideration is offered or provided in return, using the spoken, written or printed word, a gesture or other means. (section 1)

This definition, which includes the making of a request by *any means*, leaves open the question of whether a visibly indigent person – a homeless person who looks to be in a destitute, desperate state that evokes need and want – could be considered to be soliciting *simply by being present* in the wide array of spaces circumscribed by this section. By their very nature, homeless people have no choice but to 'hang around' in public space, attempting to negotiate places in which to exist. While supporters of the Act argue that the spatial specificity of the offence sections do not create a blanket restriction on begging in public space, the reality is that the combined nature of these prohibitions has the effect of broadly covering many of the spaces that homeless people occupy, particularly in the case of sidewalks. This is evident if one thinks of the architecture of public streets: in many stretches of busy urban sidewalks, it would be difficult for a homeless person not to be situated in close proximity to phone booths, parking lots, taxi or transportation stops, or automated banking machines, all of which are ubiquitous features of urban streetscapes. And since the act does not prescribe these places in exact terms, the decision of when someone who is begging is in the vicinity of these places is left to the discretion of the police officer.

Thus, while the act details sets of circumstances in which begging is prohibited, a closer look at the text reveals that the detailing in no way defines those circumstances with precision. Rather, the detailing actually constructs a regime that is vague – leaving ample room for discretionary and capricious enforcement – and potentially extremely sweeping in its reach.

More than any other aspect of the act, this section represents the reintroduction of repealed vagrancy laws that have a history of policing the social status of people.[162] And at the core of the policing of status offences is that people are targeted on the grounds that they are suspicious. As Douglas has pointed out in relation to vagrancy law, policing on the grounds of suspicion is a recipe for discrimination:

> The persons arrested on 'suspicion' are not the sons of bankers, industrialists, lawyers, or other professional people. They, like the people accused of vagrancy, come from other strata of society, or from minority groups who are not sufficiently vocal to protect themselves, and who do not have the prestige to prevent an easy laying-on of hands by the police.[163]

In the summer of 2000, a coalition of lawyers and social service providers in downtown Toronto encouraged those charged under the *Safe Streets Act* to come forward and be part of a challenge to the legislation. That fall, lawyers representing thirteen people charged under the act were bound together for trial, with their lawyers presenting a defence that the act was, in a number of ways, unconstitutional. Most significantly, defence lawyers argued that the *Safe Streets Act* (1) constituted an invasion by the province of the federal Parliament's exclusive legislative jurisdiction over criminal law; (2) infringed upon the right to freedom of expression guaranteed by section 2(b) of the Charter of Rights and Freedoms; and (3) infringed upon the right to life, liberty, and security of the person guaranteed by section 7 of the Charter by denying economic rights necessary for survival.

Justice Babe of the Ontario Court of Justice found all of the defendants guilty as charged, and convicted them. He rejected the first and third of the arguments against the provision in question, but accepted the argument that the provision infringed upon the defendants' freedom of expression. However, he found the infringement to be justified under section 1 of the Charter (which allows for such 'reasonable limits' on Charter rights as can be 'demonstrably justified in a free and democratic society'). He found the limitation on freedom of expression to be reasonable because the act was intended to protect public 'safety.' He found no other violations of the constitution. The case is currently on appeal.

In relation to this case, it is important to note that only those sections of the act under which the thirteen individuals had been charged were under judicial scrutiny. Thus, the constitutionality of one of the most contentious provisions of the act, all but one of the offences under soliciting a 'captive audience,' has not yet been challenged on constitutional grounds. Little is known about how this offence section is being used to police visibly indigent people, both informally and as part of the 2,400 charges that have so far been laid under the act as a whole. Nor is there anything known about how many people have been fined or incarcerated under the *Safe Streets Act*.[164]

The *Safe Streets Act* evokes a number of very significant issues for how 'safety' and 'security' are constituted and policed in our current sociopolitical climate. In the context of our discussion about the relationship between democratic values and the policing of communal space, the act can be viewed primarily as a legal instrument that governs the transience of communal space – of sidewalks, roadways, and curbs. In particular, the offences that target squeegee workers, and the 'captive audience' section, act to exclude people who take up subsistence activities that involve 'soliciting' in communal space, conduct that can be regarded as conflicting with the temporary transience of those who are travelling to work, home, or consumer-oriented destinations. Indeed, as we have noted, the definition of 'soliciting' is sufficiently broad that it could conceivably capture the mere presence of needy and visibly indigent people who, by simply being in particular places in communal space, are viewed as requesting donations.[165] While more research needs to be conducted on how 'the letter' of the *Safe Streets Act* is translated into policing practice, the act is sufficiently broadly framed to allow for exclusionary policing practices that aggravate the 'democracy gap' between the rich and the poor.

Another species of law that has played a major role in governing the transient character of communal spaces is provincial trespass legislation. As we have developed above, although these acts vary across the provinces, they generally provide a powerful tool in authorizing a property owner not just to prohibit or permit access but to create specific conditions for the use of the property. Thus, state and non-state police personnel can enforce prohibitions against such activities as 'loitering' in communal spaces such as public housing property or shopping malls – spaces that are privately owned but where there is an expectation of public thoroughfare and access. The arrest powers provided to non-state policing personnel by trespass legislation are routinely invoked to remove people from such premises. Furthermore, as Mopas's study of the Downtown Eastside of Vancouver indicates, there is growing evidence to suggest that trespass legislation is playing an increasing role in governing communal spaces such as sidewalks, despite the fact that non-state policing personnel typically do not have jurisdiction within such spaces.[166]

In conclusion, we draw attention to two general points that can be made about the transnational character of how policing auspices and programs privilege forms of temporary, consumer-oriented transience in communal space and act to exclude the permanent transience required by people who must live there. First, because of the legal ambiguity of communal space – both in how it appears visually and in terms of property ownership – the policing of transience tends to involve a complex of both state and non-state agents. Many communal spaces appear to be an extension of publicly owned sidewalks and streets but are in fact parcels of privately owned property that are regulated with the use of non-state antitrespass agents. This trend is becoming even more pronounced as commercial property owners intentionally create spaces that appear to mimic an open, cosmopolitan 'public' atmosphere through the use of sidewalk cafés, shopping promenades, and so on. Increasingly, city governments are entering into agreements with the private sector to provide 'public' amenities such as washrooms, bus stops, postering drums, and so on. This colonization of communal space by profit-making interests creates an extremely complex spatial environment, where the functions and responsibilities of state and non-state agents are becoming very difficult to disentangle.

Closely related to this observation is the second feature: that communal spaces are being homogenized through a transnational 'city centre improvement' movement that focuses on profit maximization and the social control of those who are not viewed as active consumers. This homogenization has involved the use of standardized street furniture, storefront design, lighting, closed-circuit camera surveillance, non-state intelligence communications (through, for example, store security radio links and state/non-state information sharing protocols), and the pedestrianization of street and roadway segments in city centre cores. These practices, as we have discussed above, have been given widespread legitimacy by theories of 'disorder-intolerant' policing, making the presence of homeless people even more visible and incongruent with forms of temporary transience. This transnational trend has generated perhaps one of the most visible manifestations of globalization – that streetscapes in different cities such as London, Edinburgh, Copenhagen, New York, or Toronto are starting to look remarkably alike.

Conclusions

In this paper we have sought to document the significant changes in policing that have been occurring, and are continuing to evolve, with an emphasis upon those trends that are most pertinent to Canada. We have considered the implications of these developments for the evolving role of law in providing the legal context and parameters within which policing is undertaken. We have shown that the erstwhile dominant position of the state and its policing institutions in the provision of policing has significantly declined (or been eroded) as a result of the increasing contributions of non-state actors and institutions in the policing of communities. Partnerships in which the state plays the leading role are increasingly being replaced by networks of policing institutions in which, depending on the context and objectives, the state may or may not play a significant role. During the last four or five decades, the distribution of responsibility for policing has been significantly transformed. As well, because of innovations and different conceptions of policing that have influenced both state and non-state providers of policing services, the means, strategies, and technologies through which policing is accomplished have also become a great deal more diverse.

We have reviewed a variety of the social, political, economic, and ideological developments, at local, regional, national, and international levels, that have shaped the direction of these changes in policing in Canada. These include important changes in the nature and uses of property, leading to new types of spaces that cannot be easily understood within the conventional ascriptive framework of 'public' and 'private' places within which, until recently, the law has evolved. Most recently, these include the emergence of 'cyberspace' and the unique policing challenges to which it gives rise. More generally, the law's traditional dichotomy between the 'public' and the 'private' (whether applied to the ownership of property, the rights of citizens in different places, or the limits of authority and jurisdiction for policing) has been increasingly challenged and found wanting as a result of the developments we have described. Furthermore, the tendency to dichotomize 'public' and 'private' policing obscures the fact that 'private' policing has quite as many effects on various 'publics,' both within and outside its domain (i.e., on those whom it includes and those whom it excludes), as 'public' policing has on private citizens. We have suggested that in providing a suitable legal environment for the policing of many of the spaces in our communities, the law should focus on whether they have a communal character, rather than on whether they have conventionally been treated as 'public' or 'private.'

We have reviewed the current legal environment within which policing is undertaken in Canada and noted both its complexity and the fact that it has significantly lagged behind the current realities of policing, of the nature of policing problems, and of the contexts in which policing must now be undertaken. Specifically, the law's attempt to draw a relatively clear demarcation between 'public' policing and 'private' policing constitutes an entirely inadequate response to the complex and fluid networks of policing institutions and the variety of policing contexts and practices that have been evolving in recent decades, and that will continue to evolve. Similarly, the law has failed to respond adequately to changing patterns of property relations and uses and to the social and political implications of modern policing arrangements for these emerging spaces. The result, as we have shown, is that all too often the law recognizes and supports policing arrangements that do not reflect or promote core democratic values such as fairness, equity, inclusiveness, transparency, justice, and the protection of fundamental human rights and civil liberties, and that often benefit a few at the expense of many.

We have considered the ways in which these state and non-state policing agencies tend to relate to one another in carrying out the policing function. Of vital importance here is the observation that while participating nodes in the networks of policing do tend to perform distinct sets of functions using distinct technologies that correspond with distinct mentalities for how they conceptualize and so approach the task of policing, a significant – and apparently increasing – degree of functional overlap and diffusion of mentalities is evident across both state and non-state policing agencies. In many instances, 'private' (non-state) agencies promote preventive order in spaces that are ostensibly 'public,' through the mechanism of powers that accrue to private property ownership. Similarly, in many cases the public police promote preventive order that reflects a market-like risk-minimization rationality in spaces that are more fully 'public,' through the mechanism of their right to deploy coercive force and all of the symbolic power that this also conveys. Such forms of practical and conceptual overlap illustrate the inadequacy of the public-private dichotomy in conceptualizing, and so attempting to regulate, contemporary developments in policing.

We have also examined the outcomes associated with dominant modes of networked policing. One of the key points raised here is that the agencies participating in networks of policing have interrelated (which is not always the same as overlapping or equivalent) functions *and* effects. The rise of paid non-state policing, responsibilized and autonomous forms of volunteer policing, and disorder-intolerant brands of public policing are interrelated phenomena – shifts in one realm prompt further shifts and developments in another, although their respective impacts tend to be concentrated among more and less well-to-do segments of the population. Regulation that seeks to foster particular democratic policing approaches and outcomes must therefore approach policing networks as coherent wholes: regulation that addresses each node in isolation will be inadequate to the task at hand. Table 1.1, below, presents a typological map of these contemporary policing arrangements and the principal ethical concerns they raise.

We have also highlighted how important it is to understand the social processes through which spaces are constructed as 'communal' (be they popularly thought of as 'public' or 'private'), and the different forms of transience that characterize the participation of different segments of the community in these communal spaces. We have pointed out that the policing of such spaces invariably involves some balancing of the respective interests of these different groups with respect to their access to such spaces, and that over-broad laws threaten the fundamental human rights of disadvantaged members of society such as the homeless, the poor, and 'squeegee kids' (categories that, of course, are not mutually exclusive). The outcome all too often results in a 'democratic gap' between the more and less affluent – a gap that cannot be considered compatible with our core democratic values.[167]

Looking to the Future: Directions for Law Reform

We have argued that reforming the law with respect to policing will require more than adaptations to criminal law and other penal statutes and amendments to explicit policing legislation (whether it relates to state or non-state policing). Numerous other areas of the law – the law of contract, tort, labour relations, licensing, urban planning, and zoning, to name but a few – shape the contexts in which policing occurs, and the way (and by whom) policing is accomplished, in important ways. A comprehensive approach to redesigning the legal environment within which policing occurs therefore requires systematic attention to all these different elements in that environment. For a federal state such as Canada, this poses an enormous challenge, since no one level

TABLE 1.1
A typology of policing networks

Linked agencies	Forms of association	Impacts and concerns
• state/state networks • supranational	• Information sharing. • Resource sharing.	• Much of this activity entails legal ambiguity, taking place in the grey area of 'international jurisdiction': lowest standard of democratic protections may be deployed.
• state/non-state (junior partnership) networks • standard community policing • paid private security firms	• Information sharing, from state to non-state agencies and vice versa. • Some community direction of policing activity. A greater degree of direction in the instance of private agencies hired by private citizens.	• Limited community representation on the bodies directing the police. • Accountability only to those with ability to purchase paid private security: resultant democratic 'gap' in distribution of safety and security.
• state/non-state (equal partnership) networks • 'radical' community policing • paid private security firms	• A greater degree of public control of public policing activity – direction of the public police by independent state/non-state bodies. • Information sharing from state to non-state agencies and vice versa.	• A concern that non-representative community interests will mobilize public police resources against marginalized and non-vocal segments of the broader community. • Democratic gap, with the wealthy able to purchase security.

TABLE 1.1
A typology of policing networks (concluded)

Linked agencies	Forms of association	Impacts and concerns
• state/non-state (illegal partnership) networks • vigilantes • paid private security firms	• State handing over suspects to non-state policing bodies. • Tacit state tolerance of vigilante activity. • Paid private security firms handing over suspects to the public police in more extreme cases of disorder or criminal activity.	• Questionable public policing practice of pursuit of lower standard of proof in private realm where there is insufficient evidence to formally prosecute through the state justice system. • Reluctance on the part of non-state policing agencies and their directors to hand suspects/offenders over to public police in all but the most extreme instances of offending (due to profit imperative). This may undermine the public image of primacy of law/respect for the state and its institutions.
• non-state/non-state autonomous networks • vigilantes • pacific community volunteers	• There is sometimes collaboration between civil community-building agencies and violent vigilante groups: informal information and resource sharing.	• Obvious violations of due process and democratic human rights. • Pacific forms of community peace building have the potential to empower poor persons through giving them ownership over their security issues: extending the benefits of local democratic control that are made available to the wealthy through the market.

of government has constitutional authority or responsibility for all these different areas of the law.

It is particularly important, we believe, to try to move the debate over policing reform beyond its current parameters, which tend to polarize discussion of both state and non-state policing institutions and practices. Thus, for instance, in our view the question is not whether policing is most appropriately undertaken by the state or under non-state auspices – a conversation that almost always ends in controversy about the un- doubted failings of both – but, rather, how the multiplicity of state and non-state resources for policing can be harnessed to provide the most effective and acceptable policing for communities (whether at the local, regional, national, or international level). Implicit in this idea of 'effec- tive and acceptable policing' must be the requirement not only that policing recognizes and meets the community's needs for order, security, safety, and justice, but also, and equally importantly, that it recognizes and conforms to the core democratic values we have discussed – fairness, equity,[168] respect for fundamental human rights, inclusiveness, access to justice, and accountability.

Implicit in the approach we are recommending is the need to come to terms with the changing political, economic, and social realities of Canada and other Western nations, and in particular the changing relationships between, and respective roles of, the state and civil society, and the implications of these changes for how and by whom policing will be done in the twenty-first century. Thus, for instance, if discussions of non- state policing institutions continue to be conducted within a framework of increasingly outdated assumptions about the role of the state, it is unlikely that the very real potential of such institutions to contribute to effective policing of our communities will be recognized or realized.

In our paper we have sought to show that such institutions are now, and will inevitably be in the future, deeply involved in policing at all levels, from the most local to the international arena. The choice for law reformers is between recognizing these realities and attempting to re- form the law to take the greatest advantage of them in the broader public interest and in accordance with democratic values, or ignoring them and risking losing the initiative entirely in shaping public policy with respect to policing. As the quotation from Gross Stein with which we began our paper makes clear, even when the provision of a public good such as policing becomes the subject of a market-place, the state can still play a crucial role in determining and enforcing minimum requirements for the operation of such a market. In the case of policing, however, that role cannot be fulfilled effectively on the basis of outdated understandings of the provision of policing as a monopoly of the state, or by considering only the negative or problematic features, and not the productive potential, of non-state provision.

A most important part of our argument emphasizes the inevitably political nature of policing policy, and of policing itself. This reality has all too often not been candidly acknowledged or addressed by legislators or courts, which have sought, rather, to 'insulate' policing from politics. Because of the political nature of policing and the complexity of the challenge for redesigning the legal environment within which it occurs, it would make no sense for us to try to present in this paper a detailed blueprint for legal reform with respect to policing in Canada. Instead, what we recommend as a vital first step towards this end are legal reforms that will establish and support new institutions for the governance of policing (as opposed just to the governance of police) and the development of policing policy. Through such reforms and institutions, a more appropriate politics of policing will become possible – by which we mean a politics of policing that will be as inclusive as possible, and that will be more likely to generate policing policy and practices which reflect and promote the kinds of core democratic values outlined in this paper. Of course, it must be recognized that, to be adequate and effective, even this suggested first step in policing-related law reform would require a great deal of cooperation between lawmakers and policy makers at different levels of government in Canada.

In this connection, we would draw the reader's attention to some recent recommendations and experiments, in Canada and elsewhere, that we believe provide potentially valuable guidance in pursuing such an ambitious agenda of law reform with respect to policing. Of interest are a set of proposals for holding non-state policing to account recently made by a prominent chief constable in the United Kingdom.[169] This program would place the state police at the centre of a regulatory network for monitoring all local agencies (state and non-state) that are active in the process of policing.

More radical, and in our view more realistic and appropriate, in this respect are the recent recommendations of the Independent Commission on Policing in Northern Ireland (ICPNI) chaired by Chris Patten. The Patten Report's most innovative components are recommendations for the creation of new institutions and political processes to address what has so far been a particularly divisive politics of policing in that jurisdiction.

Two principal mechanisms were recommended by the independent commission to regulate the range of state and non-state agencies involved in policing in Northern Ireland. Foremost among these were the commission's calls for the establishment of a *Policing* (as opposed to *Police*) Board. This board would be constituted to be representative of the 'communities' it serves. Further, as its name would suggest, the Policing Board, as envisaged by the ICPNI, would have very broad legal and what can be called 'market' authority to hold accountable all agencies involved in policing – including both state police and non-state bodies.

With regard to legal powers, the board would be given broad authority to inquire into the operational conduct of *any* policing agency – including but not limited to the state police – empowering it to hold that agency publicly accountable for its policing practices and to apply disciplinary or remedial measures as and when appropriate.

With regard to 'market' authority, the board would be charged with administering a *policing* (as opposed to *police*) budget that would enable it to support a range of state and non-state agencies that can make a positive contribution to policing while conforming to democratic standards and values. While the state police might continue to command the greater part of this budget, they would not own it outright. Thus, the state police and other state and non-state providers of policing services under collective 'community' auspices would have to justify support from this budget by demonstrating their capacity and commitment to provide effective and acceptable policing to the community. Inappropriate or unacceptable policing activity could be responded to not only through traditional legal sanctions and responses, but also through termination or suspension of budgetary support. Thus the legal authority of the Policing Board would be reinforced through its legislated capacity to engage a public (and publicly accountable) market for policing.

Such ideas, although not very familiar to Canadians, are not entirely new here,[170] and have been at least hinted at, if not yet fully elaborated, in some recent official policy documents on policing and policing governance policy.[171]

The two most important elements of such proposals, from the point of view of this paper, are (i) that institutions for the governance of policing and the development and implementation of policing policy must recognize and provide a voice for all those in a community, whether state or non-state actors (and, of course, including the state police service), who can potentially contribute to the effective policing of the community, and (ii) that a policing budget (rather than just a budget for a state police service) should be established, for support from which all potential contributors to effective policing can compete on equal terms.

We believe that such institutions of governance could be designed to reflect and promote those core democratic values to which we have referred and, in turn, would be most likely to generate policing policies and practices that would similarly reflect and promote such values.

Such institutions would be suited to the governance of policing and the development of policing policy in geographic communities within Canada, however defined. Even more challenging, however, will be the task of designing institutions of this kind for the governance of policing on the international level and of 'virtual' communities in cyberspace. Both of these domains, because they extend far beyond Canada's borders, while at the same time having very significant implications for Canada, will, of course, require a degree of international cooperation that extends far beyond the remit of law reform institutions in Canada. Nevertheless, the law in Canada will need to be reformed so as to provide a legal environment for policing within which these challenges can be addressed.

As we have emphasized many times in this paper, law reform respecting policing will need to be informed by an understanding of recent developments in the nature of property relations and the constitution of 'communal' spaces. With respect to these communal spaces especially (whether they be on public or private property), the challenge for law reform will be to strike an appropriate balance between the interests of different groups of users of such spaces. Such a balance would (i) take account of users' different economic and social circumstances and needs; (ii) respect and protect the fundamental human rights of all of them; (iii) be as equitable and inclusive as possible; (iv) recognize that not all citizens have equal access to political power or communicative opportunities; (v) be open to public accountability, scrutiny, and critique; and (vi) provide effective mechanisms through which grievances can be heard and fairly adjudicated and abuses be redressed and/or corrected. As Von Hirsch and Shearing have recently written,

> It may well be that current trends concerning ownership and organization of common spaces are difficult or impossible to reverse. This, however, does not mean that we must be quiescent while the freedoms we value are eroded. The task facing us is that of rethinking our regulatory framework in ways that recognize these new styles of ownership and management, while at

the same time preserving important values and liberties. What is required, in particular, is the development of a normative framework that will give adequate recognition to rights of free access in the newly-emerging common spaces and in the spaces still in possession of public authorities.[172]

We conclude our paper with the hope that the material we have presented herein will inform and stimulate further discussions of the law reform challenges presented by the developments in policing here and elsewhere that we have documented. While we most certainly recognize the magnitude of these challenges, we are equally confident that the conceptual tools required to address them are beginning to be within our grasp, and that resources are available, both in Canada and elsewhere, that will help us to develop and apply them.

Notes

1 CNN, documentary on the Taliban, aired 26 August 2001.
2 Many Chileans, for instance, have opposed the current pursuit of justice against that country's former dictator, General Augusto Pinochet, on the ground that it threatens security and political stability in the country.
3 S. Spitzer and A. Scull, 'Privatization and Capitalist Development: The Case of the Private Police' (1977) 25 Social Problems 18; N. South, *Policing for Profit: The Private Security Sector* (London: Sage Publications, 1988).
4 Wood and Shearing, for instance, have argued that the principal objectives of policing in a university environment are the establishment and maintenance of an environment conducive to learning, teaching and research, equity, and human rights, entailing equal access for students, faculty, and other members of the university 'community,' freedom from sexual harassment, and so on. Jennifer Wood and Clifford Shearing, 'Securing Safety on Campus: A Case Study' (1998) 40:1 Canadian Journal of Criminology 81.
5 B. Anderson, *Imagined Communities: Reflections on the Origins and Spread of Nationalism* (London: Verso, 1983).
6 Sections 494 and 495 of the Criminal Code, dealing with powers of arrest without warrant of citizens, property owners, and peace officers.
7 There are, however, some federally established state policing agencies, of which the Royal Canadian Mounted Police is the most well known. The constitutional authority of the federal Parliament to establish such agencies has been recognized by the Supreme Court of Canada as 'necessarily incidental' to its authority to enact criminal law and procedure, as well as pursuant to its residual authority to legislate for 'peace, order and good

government' (the so-called POGG power) throughout Canada. See, for example, *The Queen and Archer v. White*, [1956] S.C.R. 154; *Attorney General of Quebec and Keable v. Attorney General of Canada et al.* [1979] 1 S.C.R. 218 at 242. Paragraph 92(8), vesting provincial legislatures with exclusive jurisdiction to legislate with respect to 'municipal institutions in the province' is also relevant for the establishment of municipal and regional police services and police governing authorities.

8 George Rigakos and D. Greener, 'Bubbles of Governance: Private Policing and the Law in Canada' (2000) 15:1 Canadian Journal of Law and Society 145.

9 The mechanisms and institutions through which special constables are held publicly accountable, however, are different in most jurisdictions from those through which regularly appointed public police officers are held publicly accountable. For instance, the Special Investigations Unit, under section 113 of Ontario's *Police Services Act*, has jurisdiction to investigate actions of police officers that have resulted in deaths or serious injuries but does not have jurisdiction with respect to special constables appointed under the act. For further detail on this issue, see British Columbia Police Commission, *Special Provincial Constables: A Plan for Accountability* (Vancouver, B.C.: Police Commission, 1991); K. Taylor, 'The Role of Special Provincial, Special Municipal and Auxiliary Constables in British Columbia' (1994), research paper prepared for the Commission of Inquiry into Policing in British Columbia (available from the B.C. Ministry of the Attorney General); British Columbia, Commission of Inquiry into Policing in British Columbia (Mr Justice Wallace T. Oppal, Commissioner), *Closing the Gap: Policing and the Community – The Report, Volume 2* (Vancouver: Author, 1994), F-32–F-46; Manitoba Law Reform Commission, *Report on Special Constables*, Report No. 96 (Winnipeg: Manitoba Law Reform Commission, 1996).

10 Philip Stenning, 'Off-duty Conduct,' Discussion Paper 7 (Ottawa: RCMP External Review Committee, 1991); and A. Reiss, *Private Employment of Public Police* (Washington, D.C.: U.S. Government Printing Office, 1988).

11 The Charter, s. 32. Section 1, however, allows for limited exceptions to this requirement when such exceptions can be 'demonstrably justified in a free and democratic society.'

12 *R. v. Lerke*, [1986] 49 C.R. (3rd) 324, in which the Alberta Court of Appeal held that a citizen, when exercising the powers of a citizen to arrest under the Criminal Code, was to be considered as acting as an agent of the state.

13 In the United States, where the Bill of Rights imposes similar constraints on governmental activities, the courts have demonstrated a substantial willingness to impose those constraints on private policing activities by holding

that in certain circumstances private authorities can be considered to be in effect exercising 'governmental' functions. For a detailed account and analysis of this trend, see D. Sklansky, 'The Private Police' (1999) 46 U.C.L.A. Law Review 1165. So far, Canadian courts have displayed little inclination to follow this judicial trend: see *R. v. Shafie*, [1989] 47 C.C.C. (3rd) 27 (Ont. C.A.); *R. v. Fitch*, [1995] 93 C.C.C. (3rd) 185 (B.C.C.A.); and the Supreme Court of Canada's decision in *R. v. M. (M.R.)*, [1999] 129 C.C.C. (3rd) 361; as well as Justice L'Heureux-Dubé's comments on this subject in *Committee for Commonwealth v. Canada*, [1991] 77 D.L.R. (4th) 385, at 423–5. For a Canadian case in which it was held that a non-state security person, in executing a citizen's arrest pursuant to the Criminal Code, was to be considered as acting as an agent of the state, see *R. v. Lerke, supra* note 12. See also Rigakos and Greener, *supra* note 8; and Philip Stenning, 'Powers and Accountability of Private Police' (2000) 8:3 European Journal on Criminal Policy and Research 325.

14 2001. O.J. No. 3219.

15 Justice Babe rejected, as unsupported by evidence, the defendants' claim that this provision was being enforced discriminately by police. The case thus involved a judgment about the constitutionality of the order being policed, rather than about the policing itself.

16 Legislatures do, of course, have the option of having the 'last word' on such issues by invoking the so-called notwithstanding clause (*Constitution Act*, s. 33), in order to exempt legislative provisions from the application of the Charter. Understandably, given the heavy political price likely to be exacted for doing so, legislators are extremely reluctant to resort to this option (a constraint fully intended by the framers of the *Constitution Act*).

17 R.S.O. (1990) c. P.15.

18 Section 5 of the act does provide for the possibility that 'police services' may be provided through a 'different method,' if approved by the Ontario Civilian Commission on Police Services (a provincial oversight body), thus apparently allowing for the possibility that a municipality could contract for such services from a non-state provider. So far, however, despite some discussions of such a possibility in one Ontario municipality, no such arrangement has yet been proposed or approved in the province.

19 Interestingly, section 2 of the Ontario *Police Act* (the predecessor of the *Police Services Act*) provided that 'Every city and town is responsible for the *policing* of and maintenance of law and order in the municipality *and* for providing and maintaining an adequate police force in accordance with the *police needs* of the municipality': see *Police Act*, R.S.O. [1980] c. 381, s. 2 (emphasis added).

20 R.S.B.C. [1996] c. 367.
21 Responsibility for police services in the province has recently been transferred from the portfolio of the attorney general to the revived portfolio of the solicitor general in British Columbia.
22 The B.C. Police Commission was abolished and replaced by a 'Director of Police Services' and a 'Police Complaint Commissioner' by amendments to the *Police Act* passed in 1997 (see *Police Amendment Act,* S.B.C. 1997, c. 37, s. 36).
23 Ontario's *Private Investigators and Security Guards Act,* R.S.O. [1990] c. P. 25, of which there is a counterpart in every province.
24 Clifford Shearing and Philip Stenning, 'Modern Private Security: Its Growth and Implications,' in M. Tonry and N. Morris, eds, *Crime and Justice: An Annual Review of Research,* vol. 3 (Chicago: Chicago University Press, 1981) 193–245; and T. Jones and T. Newburn, *Private Security and Public Policing* (Oxford: Clarendon Press, 1998) at 46–51 and 104–14.
25 For a recent example of such discussions, see 'Fantino Wants More Policing near Woodbine,' *Globe and Mail* (20 April 2001) A23. See also W. Walsh and E. Donovan, 'Private Security and Community Policing: Evaluation and Comment' (1989) 17:3 Journal of Criminal Justice 187.
26 *Harrison v. Carswell,* (1976) 25 C.C.C. (2nd) 186 S.C.C.; Raj Anand (Chair), Ontario Task Force on the Law Concerning Trespass to Publicly-Used Property as It Affects Youth and Minorities, *Report* (Toronto: Ministry of the Attorney General of Ontario, 1987); and Rigakos and Greener, *supra* note 8.
27 *University of British Columbia v. Berg,* [1993] 2 S.C.R. 354, in which the majority of the Supreme Court of Canada proposed a 'relational approach' in distinguishing between different 'publics' with respect to security arrangements for a particular facility (in this case, denial of a key to a university building).
28 Interestingly, property rights are not included among the rights and freedoms enumerated in the Canadian Charter of Rights and Freedoms.
29 See most recently, *R. v. Asante-Mensah,* [2001] O.J. No. 3819, in which the Ontario Court of Appeal held that a private citizen is entitled to use reasonable force in making an arrest pursuant to his or her powers under trespass legislation.
30 Although the law places fewer constraints on the use of such powers by non-state police than is the case for state police, the law does provide substantial mechanisms through which non-state police may be held accountable for their exercise. See Stenning, *supra* note 13 at 336–45.
31 *Semayne's Case* [1604] 5 Co. Rep. 91a, 77 E.R. 194.
32 *Entick v. Carrington* (1765) 19 St. Tr. 1029, at 1029.

33 *Eccles v. Bourque*, [1975]. 2 S.C.R. 739, at 743; *Canada (Director of Investigation and Research, Combines Investigation Branch) v. Southam Inc.*, [1984] 2 S.C.R. 145, at 157; and more recently *R. v. Feeney*, [1997] 2 S.C.R. 13.
34 F. Buckley, ed., *The Fall and Rise of Freedom of Contract* (Durham, N.C.: Duke University Press, 1999).
35 H. Collins, *Marxism and Law* (Oxford: Oxford University Press, 1984) ch. 4. See also M. Cain and A. Hunt, eds, *Marx and Engels on Law* (London and New York: Academic Press, 1979) ch. 3.
36 This includes collective agreements under labour legislation, which not uncommonly include provisions concerning safety, security, and policing in the workplace. See, for example, Philip Stenning and Clifford Shearing, *Search and Seizure Powers of Private Security Personnel* (Ottawa: Minister of Supply and Services Canada, 1979).
37 The Ontario Human Rights Code, R.S.0. 1990, c. H.19.
38 As is well known, following the terrorist attacks in the United States on 11 September 2001, there has been renewed discussion about the respective roles of state and non-state policing authorities in securing airports and aircraft.
39 Of course, the division of responsibility for policing between state and non-state providers has been the subject of discussion in a number of academic, policy, and judicial contexts (e.g., the Oppal Inquiry in British Columbia, *supra* note 9; the Anand Task Force report, *supra* note 26; and *Harrison v. Carswell*, *supra* note 26). However, many of these examinations have been quite limited in scope, and rarely have the broad principles underlying such distribution of responsibility been fully, adequately, or systematically set out and publicly discussed.
40 In *Committee for Commonwealth v. Canada*, *supra* note 13, the Supreme Court of Canada held that even some places 'owned by government' (in this case an airport) are more appropriately treated as 'public' places, in which citizens' Charter rights should be strictly protected and upheld, rather than as privately owned places whose owners have legally recognized freedom to limit the rights of those who frequent them. The court acknowledged that in Canada the courts have not yet been willing, as the courts in the United States have, to treat privately owned 'mass private property' analogously to the way they treat such government-owned 'public' places.
41 *Peterborough (City) v. Ramsden*, [1993] 2 S.C.R. 1084; *R. v. Greenbaum*, [1993] 1 S.C.R. 674; *R. v. Sharma*, [1993] 1 S.C.R. 650 (both Supreme Court of Canada decisions).
42 In the case of *R. v. Banks*, *supra* note 14 at 12–13. See also *supra* note 15 at 55–6.

43 *Russo v. Ontario Jockey Club*, (1988) 62 O.R. (2nd) 731 (Ont. H.C.); *R. v. Shafie*, (1989) 47 C.C.C. (3rd) 27 (Ont. C.A.); and *R. v. M (M.R.)*, (1999) 129 C.C.C. (3rd) 361 (S.C.C.).

44 For instance, when the downtown Toronto Eaton Centre was approved in the 1970s, a condition of the approval was that a general public right of access to the subway station through certain of the centre's privately owned passageways be maintained; *R. v. Layton*, (1988) 38 C.C.C. (3rd) 550 (Ont. Prov. Ct); and *Cadillac Fairview Corp. Ltd. v. R.W.D.S.U.*, (1990) 71 O.R. (2nd) 206 (Ont. C.A.).

45 For instance, in response to a complaint under the recently enacted *Personal Information Protection and Electronic Documents Act, 2000*, s. C., c. 5, the federal privacy commissioner has recently issued two rulings making it illegal to mount surveillance cameras that (even if on private property) include surveillance of the public street, online: http://www.privcom.gc.ca/media/nr-c/nt_010620_e.asp?V=Print and http://www.privcom.gc.ca/media/nrc/02_05_b_011004_e.asp?V=Print.

46 The analysis presented throughout this section connecting developments in policing with broader social, political, and economic trends characteristic of 'late modernity' has been informed in large part by David Garland's macroscopic genealogy of the contemporary culture and practice of 'crime control.' See David Garland, *The Culture of Control: Crime and Social Order in Contemporary Society* (Chicago: University of Chicago Press, 2001).

47 P. O'Malley and D. Palmer, 'Post-Keynesian Policing' (1996) 25:2 Economy and Society 137; P. O'Malley, 'Policing, Politics, Post-Modernity' (1997) 6:3 Social and Legal Studies 363; Ian Loader, 'Plural Policing and Democratic Governance' (2000) 9:3 Social and Legal Studies 323; L. Johnston, *Policing Britain: Risk, Security and Governance* (Harlow: Longman, 2000); L. Johnston, *The Rebirth of Private Policing* (London: Routledge, 1992); C. Shearing, 'Reinventing Policing: Policing as Governance,' in F. Sack, M. Vob, D. Frehsee, A. Funk, and H. Reinke, eds, *Privatisierung Staatlicher Kontrolle: Befunde, Konzepte, Tendenzen* (Baden-Baden: Nomos Verladsgellschaft, 1995); A. Crawford, *The Local Governance of Crime: Appeals to Community and Partnerships* (Oxford: Clarendon, 1997); M. Kempa, R. Carrier, J. Wood, and C. Shearing, 'Reflections on the Evolving Concept of "Private Policing"' (1999) 7:2 European Journal on Criminal Policy and Research 197.

48 J.R. Gusfield, 'Constructing Ownership of Social Problems: Fun and Profit in the Welfare State' (1989) 36:5 Social Problems 431; P. Miller and N. Rose, 'Political Power beyond the State: Problematics of Government' (1992) 43:2 British Journal of Sociology 173; N. Rose, 'The Death of the Social? Refiguring the Territory of Government' (1996) 25:3 Economy and Society 327;

D. Held, A. McGrew, D. Goldblatt, and J. Perraton, *Global Transformations: Politics, Economics, and Culture* (Cambridge: Polity Press, 1999); A. Giddens, *The Third Way: The Renewal of Social Democracy* (Cambridge: Polity Press, 1998); J. Gray, *Endgames: Questions in Late Modern Political Thought* (Cambridge: Polity Press, 1997); U. Beck, *World Risk Society* (Cambridge: Polity Press, 1999); M. Foucault, 'Governmentality,' in G. Burchell, C. Gordon, and P. Miller, eds, *The Foucault Effect: Studies in Governmentality* (Chicago: University of Chicago Press, 1991) 87.

49 See, especially, R. Reiner, *The Politics of the Police*, 3rd ed. (Oxford and New York: Oxford University Press, 2000); O'Malley and Palmer, *supra* note 47; Johnston 2000 and 1992, *supra* note 47.

50 Beck; Gray; and Foucault, all *supra* note 48.

51 Reiner, *supra* note 49.

52 Spitzer and Scull, *supra* note 3; Jones and Newburn, *supra* note 24; T. Jones and T. Newburn 'The Transformation of Policing? Understanding Current Trends in Policing Systems' (2002) 25 British Journal of Criminology 129; Shearing and Stenning, *supra* note 24; Johnston 2000 and 1992, *supra* note 47; Kempa et al., *supra* note 47.

53 Held et al., *supra* note 48; S. Strange, *The Retreat of the State: The Diffusion of Power in the World Economy* (Cambridge: Cambridge University Press, 1996); R. Falk, *Predatory Globalisation: A Critique* (Cambridge: Polity Press, 1999); K. Ohmae, *The End of the Nation State: The Rise of Regional Economies* (London: HarperCollins, 1996).

54 O'Malley and Palmer; O'Malley; and Johnston 2000 all *supra* note 47; R. Batley, 'Public-Private Relationships and Performance in Service Provision' (1996) 33:4, 5 Urban Studies 723; H. Werlin, 'The Slum Upgrading Myth' 36:9 Urban Studies 1523.

55 Rose, *supra* note 48; O'Malley and Palmer, and O'Malley, *supra* note 47; Giddens, *supra* note 48.

56 M. Castells, *The Rise of the Network Society: The Information Age. Economy, Society and Culture*, vol. 1 (Cambridge, Mass., and Oxford: Blackwell, 1996); C. Shearing, 'A Nodal Conception of Governance: Thoughts on a Policing Commission' (2001) 11 Policing and Society 3–4, Special Issue on Policing in Northern Ireland, 259; C. Shearing, '"A New Beginning" for Policing' (2000) 27:3 Social and Legal Studies 386.

57 Many popular texts addressing contemporary political reform make use of this 'steering versus rowing' metaphor. See, for example, D. Osborne and T. Gaebler, *Reinventing Government: How the Entrepreneurial Spirit Is Transforming the Public Sector* (New York: Plume, 1993); W. Eggers and J. O'Leary, *Revolu-*

tion at the Roots: Making Our Government Smaller, Better, and Closer to Home (New York: The Free Press, 1995).

58 See, for example, J. Braithwaite, 'The New Regulatory State and the Transformation of Criminology' (2000) 40 British Journal of Criminology 222; P.N. Grabosky, 'Using Non-governmental Resources to Foster Regulatory Compliance' (1995) 8:4 Governance: An International Journal of Policy and Administration 527; P.N. Grabosky, 'Beyond the Regulatory State' (1994) 27 The Australian and New Zealand Journal of Criminology 192; G. Smith and D. Wolfish, *Who's Afraid of the State? Canada in a World of Multiple Centres of Power* (Toronto: University of Toronto Press, 2001).

59 D. Sklansky, *supra* note 13; Johnston, *supra* note 47; J. De Waard, 'The Private Security Industry in International Perspective' (1999) 7:2 European Journal on Criminal Policy and Research 143.

60 G. Campbell and B. Reingold, 'Private Security and Public Policing in Canada,' *Juristat* 14:10 (Ottawa: Statistics Canada, Canadian Centre for Justice Statistics, 1994); Shearing and Stenning, *supra* note 24; Rigakos and Greener, *supra* note 8. Swol reports a 126 per cent increase in persons employed in the guarding industry over the period 1971–91, from 51,220 to 115,570 personnel, coupled with a 71 per cent increase in the private investigations field, from 3,460 to 5,925 personnel. By way of contrast, persons employed in public police services increased by 41 per cent over this same period, from 41,148 to 56,774 personnel. Because of the deployment of more restrictive measurement criteria in the 1996 census, the total number of paid private security personnel is listed in these later measures as 82,010, compared with 59,090 public police officers. See K. Swol, 'Private Security and Public Policing in Canada,' *Juristat* 18:3 (Ottawa: Statistics Canada, Canadian Centre for Justice Statistics, 1998).

61 J. Irish, *Policing for Profit: The Future of South Africa's Private Security Industry*, Institute for Security Studies Monograph Series No. 39 (Halfway House, South Africa: Institute for Security Studies, 1999); M. Schönteich, 'Fighting Crime with Private Muscle: The Private Sector and Crime Prevention' (2000) 8:5 African Security Review, online: http://www.iss.co.za/Pubs/ASR/8No5/Contents.html; De Waard, *supra* note 59; Johnston, *supra* note 47. We should here highlight that the policing of more marginalized segments of the population is dominated by the forms of 'fully autonomous' (in most cases 'vigilante') policing that we turn to describe next.

62 Stenning, *supra* note 13; Michael Mopas and Philip Stenning, 'Tools of the Trade: The Symbolic Power of Private Security – An Exploratory Study' (2001) 11:2 Policing and Society 67–97.

63 Johnston, *supra* note 47; Jones and Newburn, *supra* note 24.
64 Ibid.; Clifford Shearing, 'The Unrecognised Origins of the New Policing: Linkages between Private and Public Policing,' in M. Felson and R.V. Clarke, eds, *Business and Crime Prevention* (Monsey, N.Y.: Criminal Justice Press, 1997) 219–30.
65 J. Murphy, 'The Private Sector and Security: A Bit on BIDs' (1997) 9 Security Journal 11–13; L. Noaks, 'Private Cops on the Block: A Review of the Role of Private Security in Residential Communities' (2000) 10 Policing and Society 143.
66 Jones and Newburn, *supra* note 24; C. Parenti, *Lockdown America: Police and Prisons in the Age of Crisis* (London and New York: Verso, 1999).
67 Johnston, *supra* note 47; L. Johnston, 'Transnational Private Policing: The Impact of Global Commercial Security,' in J. Sheptycki, ed., *Issues in Transnational Policing* (London and New York: Routledge, 2001) 21; J. Sheptycki, 'Transnational Policing and the Makings of a Modern State' (1995) 35:4 British Journal of Criminology 613; J. Sheptycki, 'Editorial' (forthcoming) Policing and Society (Special Issue on Cross-Border Police Co-Operation).
68 Johnston, *supra* note 67.
69 J.C. Zarate, 'The Emergence of a New Dog of War: Private International Security Companies, International Law and the New World Disorder' (1998) 34 Stanford Journal of International Law 75.
70 D. Shearer, 'Dial an Army' (1997) 8:9 The World Today 203; D. Shearer, 'Portrait of a Private Army' (1998) 112:73 Foreign Policy; P. Alexander, 'South Africa's Veterans Recruit Army of Outlaws,' *Electronic Telegraph* 681 (April 1997), online: www.telegraph.co.uk; J. Harker, 'Mercenaries: Private Power, Public Insecurity?' *New Routes* (1998), online: www.life-peace.org; W. Reno, 'Privatising War in Sierra Leone' (1997) 96 Current History 227.
71 D. Nogalla and F. Sack., '"Private" Reconfigurations of Police and Policing; The Case of Germany,' paper presented for the GERN-Seminar, 'Police et Sécurité: Contrôle Social et L'Interaction Public – Privé,' Hamburg, Germany, 1998; R. Hesseling, 'Functional Surveillance in the Netherlands: Exemplary Projects' (1995) 6:2 Security Journal 1–25; J. Greene, T. Seamon, and P. Levy, 'Merging Public and Private Security for Collective Benefit: Philadelphia's Center City District' (1995) 14:2 American Journal of Police 3–20.
72 Johnston, *supra* note 67; Johnston, *supra* note 47.
73 D. Wall, 'Policing the Virtual Community: The Internet, Cyberspace, and Cyber-crime,' in P. Francis, P. Davies, and V. Jupp, eds, *Policing Futures: The Police, Law Enforcement and the Twenty-first Century* (London: Macmillan; New York: St Martin's Press, 1997) 208; D. Wall, 'Policing the Internet: Maintain-

ing Order and Law on the Cyberbeat,' in Y. Akdeniz, C. Walker, and D. Wall, eds, *The Internet, Law and Society* (Harlow: Longman, 2001); A. Kozinski, 'Finding Justice in the Internet Dimension' (1997) 20 Seattle University Law Review 619; E. Wise, 'Criminal Law: Sex, Crime and Cyberspace' (1996) 43 The Wayne Law Review 101; I. Kerr, 'Personal Relationships in the Year 2000: Me and My ISP' (31 August 2001) Report to the Law Commission of Canada.

74 Johnston, *supra* note 47; L. Johnston, 'Private Policing in Context' (1999) 7:2 European Journal on Criminal Policy and Research 175.

75 This is not only because much policing is 'low visibility' physically; in some instances, it appears, the public is not anxious to know how policing is done, even when reasonable inquiry or vigilance could establish this. In the case of politicians who are notionally 'responsible' for policing, this desire not to be informed about policing methods has been referred to as reflecting a principle of 'plausible deniability.' See E. Mann and J. Lee, *RCMP vs The People* (Don Mills, Ont.: General Publishing, 1979).

76 O'Malley and Palmer, *supra* note 47.

77 P.N. Grabosky, 'Law Enforcement and the Citizen: Non-Governmental Participants in Crime Prevention and Control' (1992) 2 Policing and Society 249 at 254.

78 O'Malley and Palmer, *supra* note 47; P. Kratcoski and D. Dukes, eds, *Issues in Community Policing* (Cincinnati: Anderson Publishing, 1995).

79 *Supra* note 73, all.

80 P. Hillyard, 'Policing Divided Societies: Trends and Prospects in Northern Ireland and Britain,' in Francis et al., *supra* note 73, 163–85; P. Hillyard, 'Paramilitary Policing and Popular Justice in Northern Ireland,' in M. Findlay and U. Zvekic, eds, *Alternative Policing Styles: Cross-Cultural Perspectives* (Deventer and Boston: Kluwer Law and Taxation Publishers, 1993), 139–56; D. Aitkenhead, 'Rough Justice' *Daily Mail and Guardian* (Johannesburg, South Africa, 29 May 2000); B. Baker, 'Taking the Law into Their Own Hands: Fighting Crime in South Africa,' paper presented at the 29th Joint Sessions of Workshops, ECPR, Grenoble, 6–11 April 2001; D. Nina and S. Russell, 'Policing "By Any Means Necessary": Reflections on Privatisation, Human Rights and Police Issues – Considerations for Australia and South Africa' (1977) 3:2 Australian Journal of Human Rights, online: http://www.austlii.edu.au/au/journals/AJHR/#52.

81 Ibid.; T. Caldeira, 'Building up Walls: The New Pattern of Segregation in Sao Paulo' (1996) 48:1 International Social Science Journal 55–65; T. Caldeira, *City of Walls: Crime, Segregation, and Citizenship in Sao Paulo* (Berkeley: University of California Press, 2000); M. Huggins, 'Urban Violence and

Police Privatization in Brazil: Blended Invisibility' (2000) 27:2 Social Justice 113–34; E. Leeds, 'Cocaine and Parallel Polities in the Brazilian Urban Periphery: Constraints on Local-Level Democratisation' (1996) 31:3 Latin American Research Review 47–83.

82 J. Dee, 'Unsung Hero Was Heart and Soul of Peace Process' *Irish Times* (17 June 2001).

83 Clifford Shearing, 'Transforming Security: A South African Experiment,' in J. Braithwaite and H. Strang, eds, *Restorative Justice and Civil Society* (Cambridge: Cambridge University Press, 2001) 19; Braithwaite, *supra* note 58; D. Roche, 'Restorative Justice and the New Regulatory State in South African Townships' (2002) 42 British Journal of Criminology 514; P. O'Malley, *The Promise of Risk: From Actuarial Justice to a Politics of Security* (forthcoming: author's draft, cited with permission).

84 The Community Peace Programme, as part of the School of Government, University of Western Cape, has been coordinating such community dispute resolution forums in Zwelethemba, the program's principal pilot area, since 1997. To assess the efficacy of this program, a random sample of members of the Zwelethemba community were surveyed by researchers at the School of Government on several occasions. Over the space of the first two years of the project, the percentage of people who felt that disputes were being handled in more appropriate ways within the community over the previous six-month period increased from 19.7 per cent to 49 per cent, while those who felt the situation had stayed the same or become worse decreased from 80.3 per cent to 35 per cent.

85 For a critique of such approaches within state policing agencies, see, for example, P. Manning, 'A Dramaturgical Perspective,' in B. Forst and P. Manning, *Privatization of Policing: Two Views* (Washington, D.C.: Georgetown University Press, 1999) 51.

86 Ontario Provincial Police, *Organisational Review: A Process and Model for Change* (Toronto: Queen's Printer, 1995); J. Wood, 'Reinventing Governance: A Study of Transformations in the Ontario Provincial Police,' PhD. diss., University of Toronto, 1999; P. McKenna, *Foundations of Policing in Canada* (Scarborough, Ont.: Prentice Hall Canada Career and Technology, 1998).

87 Ontario Provincial Police, *supra* note 86; Wood, *supra* note 86.

88 W. Bratton, 'Crime Is Down in New York: Blame the Police,' in N. Dennis, ed., *Zero Tolerance: Policing in a Free Society* (London: Institute of Economic Affairs, Health and Welfare Unit, 1997) 29; C. Pollard, 'Zero Tolerance: Short-Term Fix, Long-Term Liability?' in Dennis, ed., ibid., 43.

89 F. Bula, 'Downtown Eastside: A Fix at Last?' *Vancouver Sun* (19 November

2001) B1 and B2, describing the current 'four pillars' approach being developed to respond to problems of drug abuse in the DTES. Perhaps not surprisingly, plans to locate treatment facilities within the Chinatown district have met with considerable resistance from business people in that neighbourhood.

90 Johnston, *supra* note 47.

91 A. Crawford, 'Community Safety and the Quest for Security: Holding Back the Dynamics of Social Exclusion' (1998) 19:3–4 Policy Studies 237; Johnston, *supra* note 47; B. Fischer, 'Community Policing: A Study of Local Policing, Order and Control,' PhD diss., University of Toronto, 1998; B. Fischer, 'Community Policing – Some Observations and Reflections on Its Social, Legal and Democratic Implications,' in S. Einstein and M. Amir, eds, *Policing, Security and Democracy: Special Aspects of 'Democratic Policing'* (Huntsville, Tex.: Office of International Criminal Justice, 2001) 35.

92 Grabosky, *supra* note 77; P. Grabosky, 'Private Sponsorship of Public Policing' (forthcoming: author's draft, cited with permission).

93 The Alberta Energy Company provided the RCMP with financial contributions, computers, software, and technical support to assist in the service's massive undercover investigation of anti-industrial activist Weibo Ludwig: see C. Blatchford, 'AEC Gave RCMP Computers and Software: Deployed to Track "Persons of Interest"' *National Post* (23 February 2000) A1 and A11.

94 Johnston, *supra* note 47; D. Bayley and C. Shearing, *The New Structure of Policing: Description, Conceptualization and Research Agenda* (Washington, D.C.: U.S. Department of Justice, National Institute of Justice, 2001).

95 J.P. Brodeur, 'High Policing and Low Policing: Remarks about the Policing of Political Activities' (1983) 30:5 Social Problems 507. Hillyard, *supra* note 80; Johnston, *supra* note 47; Parenti, *supra* note 66; Bayley and Shearing, *supra* note 94.

96 Commission for Public Complaints against the RCMP (T. Hughes, Q.C., Commissioner), *Commission Interim Report* (31 July 2001) File No. PC 6910–199801. See also W. Pue, ed., *Pepper in Our Eyes: The APEC Affair* (Vancouver: University of British Columbia Press, 2000); Richard Ericson and A. Doyle, 'Globalization and the Policing of Protest: The Case of APEC 1997' (1999) 50:4 The British Journal of Sociology 589; and Philip Stenning, 'Red Serge, Grey Suits, Blue Skies and a Dark Cloud: Some Thoughts on the Hughes Report on the Policing of the 1997 APEC Conference' *Canadian Literary Review* (March 2002).

97 Bayley and Shearing, *supra* note 94.

98 A. Swart, 'Police and Security in the Schengen Agreement and the Schengen Convention,' in H. Meijers et al., eds, *Schengen: Internationalisation of*

Central Chapters of the Law of Aliens, Refugees, Privacy, Security and Police (Utrecht: Kluwer Law and Taxation Publishers, 1991); C. Joubert and H. Bevers, *Schengen Investigated* (London: Kluwer Law, 1996).

 99 Johnston, *supra* note 47 at 112–13.

100 J.P. Brodeur, 'Transnational Policing and Human Rights: A Case Study,' in Sheptycki, *supra* note 67 at 43–66. See also Mann and Lee, *supra* note 75.

101 Johnston, *supra* note 47.

102 D. Bayley and Clifford Shearing, 'The Future of Policing' (1996) 30:3 Law and Society Review 585; Bayley and Shearing, *supra* note 94; Johnston, *supra* note 47; Loader, *supra* note 47.

103 Jones and Newburn, *supra* note 24; Clifford Shearing, 'Public and Private Policing,' in W. Saulsbury, J. Mott, and T. Newburn, eds, *Themes in Contemporary Policing* (London: Independent Committee of Inquiry into the Role and Responsibilities of the Police, 1996) 83; Clifford Shearing, 'The Relationship between Public and Private Policing,' in M. Tonry and N. Morris, eds, *Modern Policing*, vol 15. *Crime and Justice: A Review of Research* (Chicago: University of Chicago Press, 1992) 399.

104 Bayley and Shearing, *supra* note 94.

105 Noaks, *supra* note 65.

106 Campbell and Reingold, *supra* note 60.

107 Johnston, *supra* note 47.

108 Richard Ericson, A. Doyle, and D. Berry, *Insurance as Governance* (Toronto: University of Toronto Press, 2003).

109 George Rigakos, *The New Parapolice: Risk Markets and Commodified Social Control* (Toronto: University of Toronto Press, 2002); R. Carrier, 'Dissolving Boundaries: Private Security and Policing in South Africa' (1999) 8:6 African Security Review, online: http://www.iss.co.za/Pubs/ASR/8No6/Contents.html; A. Wakefield, 'Situational Crime Prevention in Mass Private Property,' in A. Von Hirsch, David Garland, and A. Wakefield, eds, *Ethical and Social Perspectives on Situational Crime Prevention* (Oxford and Portland, Ore.: Hart Publishing, 2000) 125; Noaks, *supra* note 65.

110 Richard Ericson and Kevin Haggerty, *Policing the Risk Society* (Toronto: University of Toronto Press, 1997).

111 Clifford Shearing, 'Dial-a-Cop: A Study of Police Mobilization,' in R. Akers and E. Sagarin, eds, *Prevention and Social Defense* (New York: Praeger, 1974) 77; M. Farnell, Clifford Shearing, and Philip Stenning, *Contract Security in Ontario* (Toronto: Centre of Criminology, University of Toronto, 1980); for more recent analyses along these lines, see Noaks, *supra* note 65; Wakefield, *supra* note 109.

112 Wakefield, *supra* note 109; Caldeira, *supra* note 81; Huggins, *supra* note 81.

113 Johnston, *supra* note 47; Rigakos and Greener, *supra* note 8.

114 The McDonald and Keable inquiries into activities of the RCMP Security Service during the 1970s unearthed evidence that the force had hired non-state policing personnel to illegally break into the Montreal offices of the APLQ, a dissident group, and steal or copy its membership/mailing list. Canada, Commission of Inquiry concerning Certain Activities of the RCMP (Chair, Mr Justice D. McDonald) *Second Report* (Ottawa: Minister of Supply and Services Canada, 1981); Quebec, Commission d'enquête sur des operations policières en territoire québécois (M. Jean Keable, Commissaire) *Rapport* (Quebec: Gouvernement du Québec, Ministère de la Justice, 1981).

115 Huggins, *supra* note 81; Hillyard, *supra* note 80.

116 Wakefield , *supra* note 109.

117 Anand, *supra* note 26.

118 Shearing, *supra* note 64.

119 Rigakos and Greener, *supra* note 8; Rigakos, *supra* note 109.

120 For a description of the sterile nature of such fortified residential spaces in the context of Brazil, see Caldeira, *supra* note 81. While our own interviews in Vancouver's Downtown Eastside support the notion that enclaves do not develop much in the way of internal community 'culture,' there are insufficient data on this topic: future research in this area is required in the Canadian context.

121 S. Sheerer, personal communication, 1997.

122 R. Castel, 'From Dangerousness to Risk' in Burchell et al., supra note 48, 281 at 289.

123 Caldeira, *supra* note 81; L. Johnston, 'Crime, Fear and Civil Policing' (forthcoming: author's draft, cited with permission); Garland, *supra* note 46.

124 Clifford Shearing and Philip Stenning, 'Private Security: Implications for Social Control' (1983) 30 Social Problems 493; Bayley and Shearing, *supra* note 102.

125 Loader, *supra* note 47; Susan Eng, 'Policing for the Public Good: A Commentary,' Law Commission of Canada Study Panel on Order and Security (October 2001), in this book.

126 A. Von Hirsch and Clifford Shearing, 'Exclusion from Public Space,' in Von Hirsch et al., eds, *supra* note 109 at 94. These authors advance the notion of 'common spaces' in order to address the need to 'stop thinking of the new emerging spaces as either quasi-public or quasi-private and develop new spatial categorizations and a new normative framework appropriate to them ...'

127 C. Reinarman, 'The Social Construction of an Alcohol Problem: The Case

of Mothers Against Drunk Drivers and Social Control in the 80's' (1988) 17 Theory and Society 91.

128 In his book *Buildings and Power* (New York: Routledge, 1993), Thomas Markus demonstrates how a functionalist view of space (that the intentional design of built environments defines the character of spaces) is completely insufficient to understand the social character of architecture, including spaces such as malls and streetscapes.

129 S. Ruddick, 'Metamorphosis Revisited: Restricting Discourses of Citizenship,' in J. Hermer and J. Mosher, eds, *Disorderly People: Law and the Politics of Exclusion in Ontario* (Halifax: Fernwood Press, 2002).

130 H. Lefebvre, *Le Droit de la ville* (Paris: Editions Anthropos, 1972).

131 R. Sennett, *The Uses of Disorder: Personal Identity and City Life* (Harmondsworth: Penguin Books, 1970).

132 Shearing and Stenning, *supra* note 124.

133 Organizations such as the Toronto Disaster Relief Organization argue that homelessness should be considered an ongoing national emergency to the extent that the strategic use of public buildings and resources should not be limited to particularly severe, 'emergency' conditions.

134 J. Hermer, *Regulating Eden: The Nature of Order in North American Parks* (Toronto: University of Toronto Press, 2002).

135 Ibid. See Hermer's discussion on how parks are spatialized to police a state of permanent transience.

136 M. Augé, *Non-Places: Introduction to an Anthropology of Supermodernity*, trans. John Howe (London: Verso, 1995).

137 E. Goffman, *Relations in Public: Microstudies in Public Order* (London: Verso, 1971) at 63.

138 E. Goffman, *Encounters: Two Studies in the Sociology of Interaction* (Chicago: Bobbs-Merrill, 1961) at 7.

139 Shearing and Stenning, *supra* note 24.

140 Von Hirsch and Shearing, *supra* note 126.

141 Shearing and Stenning, *supra* note 24. This is not to suggest that policing within such 'communal spaces' is always and exclusively aligned with profit maximization. See, for example, the comments in *supra* note 4.

142 Clifford Shearing and Philip Stenning, 'From the Panopticon to Disney World: The Development of Discipline,' in A. Doob and E. Greenspan, eds, *Perspectives in Criminal Law: Essays in Honour of John LL. J. Edwards* (Aurora, Ont.: Canada Law Book Co., 1985) 335.

143 Ibid.

144 David Garland, 'The Limits of the Sovereign State: Strategies of Crime Control in Contemporary Society' (1996) 36:4 British Journal of Criminology 445 at 451.

145 Clifford Shearing, 'Remarks of Professor Clifford Shearing [on Zero Tolerance policing]' (1999) 35:4 Criminal Law Bulletin 378.
146 Ibid.
147 Department of City and Regional Planning, University of North Carolina at Chapel Hill, 'Business Improvement Districts (BID's): A Practical Tool for the Evaluation of Downtown Neighborhoods' (1999), online: http://www.unc.edu/depts./dcrpweb/courses/261/actman/bidweb1.html; A. Stark, 'America the Gated?' Wilson Quarterly (Winter 1998) 58.
148 J. Connell, 'Beyond Manila: Walls, Malls, and Private Spaces' (1999) 31 Environment and Planning 417; A. Cuthbert, 'The Right to the City: Surveillance, Private Interest, and the Public Domain in Hong Kong' (1996) 12:5 Cities 293; A. Cuthbert and K. McKinnell, 'Ambiguous Space, Ambiguous Rights – Corporate Power and Social Control in Hong Kong' (1997) 14:4 Cities 295; L. Drummond, 'Street Scenes: Practices of Public and Private Space in Urban Vietnam' (2000) 37:12 Urban Studies 23.
149 M. Davis, City of Quartz: Excavating the Future in Los Angeles (London: Verso, 1992).
150 J. Wilson and G. Kelling, 'Broken Windows' Atlantic Monthly (March 1982) 29.
151 G. Kelling, 'Acquiring a Taste for Order: The Community and Police' (1987) 33:1 Crime and Delinquency 90 at 96.
152 David Garland, 'The Culture of High Crime Societies' (2000) 40 British Journal of Criminology 347 at 350. Garland highlights the need to examine both the expressive and the instrumental 'registers' of 'tough on crime' policies.
153 G. Hughes, Understanding Crime Prevention: Social Control, Risk and Late Modernity (Buckingham: Open University Press, 1998) at 108–10.
154 The democratic gap is so severe in the South African instance that observers have suggested the emergence of separate 'cities within cities' with regard to the distribution of security and life chances that are populated by different racial/economic groups. See M. Sutcliffe, 'The Fragmented City: Durban, South Africa' (1996) 147 International Social Science Journal 67.
155 Aitkenhead; Baker; Nina and Russell, supra note 80.
156 J. Waldron, 'Homelessness and the Issue of Freedom' (1991) 39 UCLA Law Review 295.
157 Ibid., at 296.
158 L. Rochon, 'Cityspace: Designs for Success Stories' Globe and Mail (2 January 2002) R5.
159 Safe Streets Act, S.O. 1999, c. 8.
160 The following analysis of the Safe Streets Act draws on J. Hermer and J. Mosher 'Introduction,' supra note 129.

161 The potential breadth of this section was illustrated by defence lawyers who argued (Defense Factum, 2000 at paragraph 65) that section 3 of the act would include a wide variety of everyday interactions such as: (a) ask a friend to re-pay a debt as you both leave an automated teller machine, s. 3 (2)(a); (b) ask a person for change for a dollar as you and she are waiting to use a public telephone, s. 3(2)(b); (c) ask a person waiting at a bus stop with you for change for a five-dollar bill, s. 3(2)(c); (d) ask a person to pay his fare on a bus, even if the person asking is the bus driver, s. 3(2)(d); (e) ask a driver waiting to exit a parking lot to pay the charge for parking, even if the person asking is the person employed by the lot owner for that purpose, s. 3(2)(e); (f) ask your spouse for change to put in a parking metre as you exit a car you have just parked while she remains in the car, s. 3(2)(f).

162 C. Foote, 'Vagrancy-Type Law and Its Administration' (1956) 104:5 University of Pennsylvania Law Review 603.

163 W. Douglas, 'Vagrancy and Arrest on Suspicion' (1960) 70:1 Yale Law Journal 1 at 13.

164 The act prescribes the following punishment for sections 2 and 3: (a) on first conviction, to a fine of not more than $500; (b) on each subsequent conviction, to a fine of not more than $1,000 or to imprisonment for a term of not more than six months, or to both.

165 The most obvious example of this is the not-uncommon sight of someone who is simply sitting or sleeping on the sidewalk, and who is given pocket change by passers-by who perceive the person's presence as evoking a request for assistance.

166 In the closing submission made by the City of Toronto to a hearing before the Ontario Municipal Board regarding the Yonge-Dundas development in downtown Toronto, the city reviewed the legal status of public streets in the context of controlling panhandlers, vagrants, and 'squeegee kids.' In particular, it cited the case of *R. v. Trabulsey*, (1995) 22 O.R. (3rd) 314 (C.A.), in which it was held that trespass legislation cannot be applied to 'the public realm' of streets and sidewalks. *Supra* note 41.

167 We have noted, too, that the 'enclavization,' that so often results from policing and the laws that support it have some negative implications for those who are included within enclaves of privilege, as well as for those who are excluded from them.

168 Within the concept of equity we would include not only non-discrimination in law enforcement, and so on, but also equal access to protection, safety, security, and justice.

169 I. Blair, 'Where Do Police Fit into Policing?' Unpublished speech delivered

to Annual Conference of the Association of Chief Police Officers (ACPO), United Kingdom (16 July 1998). A copy of this speech is available from the authors. Also available from the Association of Police Authorities (U.K.), Circular 58/98.

170 P. Stenning, 'Reclaiming Policing Back onto the Community and Municipal Agenda' (1999) 9:2 Currents 28–31.

171 K. Asbury, *Preserving a Safe Toronto – Consultation Highlights: Toronto Police Services Board* (report submitted to the Toronto Police Services Board, 29 November 2000, and adopted by the board – memorandum from the board chair to members of the board, 8 March 2001, on 'Framework – Governance and Business Plan 2002 to 2004,' in which it is stated that, at the board's meeting on 14 December 2000' 'The Board ... committed to using the results of the "Preserving a Safe Toronto" consultations as a foundation of the next business plan').

172 Von Hirsch and Shearing, *supra* note 126 at 80–1.

2 Policing in Vancouver's Downtown Eastside: A Case Study

MICHAEL MOPAS

Introduction

With the signing of the Vancouver Agreement in March 2000, the governments of Canada, British Columbia, and the City of Vancouver established a shared vision of 'creating healthy, safe, and sustainable communities' with an initial focus being the city's Downtown Eastside (DTES).[1] The Vancouver Agreement defines the DTES as the area 'bounded by the waterfront along the Burrard Inlet on the north, Richards Street on the west, Clark Drive on the east, and Pender and Terminal Streets on the south' but notes that these boundaries 'will not preclude initiatives that fall outside them yet which contribute to the goals and objectives' of the overall strategy.[2]

The Vancouver Agreement is one of a number of plans undertaken by the city to improve conditions in this area. Although the proposed strategies often treat the DTES as a single community of people connected by a common geography,[3] there exist many smaller communities with quite different physical and social features that are a part of, but remain quite distinct from, the larger district. Many of these 'subareas' have been created or reaffirmed through the remapping of this district by city planners, allowing them to form their own unique identities and become politically active in how they are governed and in their own self-government.[4]

This form of governance 'by community' has been unfolding throughout North America since the late 1960s[5] and is perhaps most evident in the area of policing. The current trend towards community-based policing relies heavily on the notion of active citizenship and participation where communities work in partnership with state and non-state agencies both to identify local concerns regarding safety and security and to provide solutions to them.[6] This approach is clearly being adopted by the City of Vancouver in an effort to revitalize the community of the DTES.

For instance, the DTES Community Crime Prevention/Revitalization Project, a five-year plan approved in 1999 and funded by the National Crime Prevention Centre of the Department of Justice, has recognized the 'overlapping neighbourhoods and communities within the Downtown Eastside' and focuses specifically on the four larger neighbourhoods of Chinatown, Gastown, Strathcona, and the central Downtown Eastside.[7] The project notes that these distinct regions are 'extremely diverse in terms of population makeup, ethnicity and socio-economic status' and that 'while there will be crime prevention goals for the community as a whole, there also exist unique crime prevention interests, needs and solutions within different neighbourhoods.'[8]

The overall aim of the project is to 'involve the neighbourhoods and the area collectively in such a way that each neighbourhood, in partnership with government and the private sector, decides which kinds of crime prevention strategies to pursue in the creation of a safe and healthy community.'[9] In order to meet this objective, the city has acknowledged the importance of facilitation and mediation processes that will connect the various subcommunities of the DTES that have already created 'their own structures, leadership and internal cohesiveness.'[10] However, with the adoption of this approach, the recognition of a particular area and its population as a 'community,' as well as the ability to speak 'on behalf' of the community, become as central to policing as the policing initiatives themselves.

This chapter addresses this issue by examining the community-based and private forms of policing that are taking place within the 'subcommunities' of Gastown, Chinatown, and the 'Hastings Street Corridor.' The focus is on how the policing of a particular community is often a reflection of how the community is identified as both a geographic location and a population. In this examination, I consider how the different perceptions regarding certain policing initiatives among these subcommunities, particularly with respect to the role of private security personnel, reflect different conceptions of community and are deeply rooted in the existing conflict over land and space in the DTES between low-income residents and local business, property owners, and development groups.

The data used in this study come in part from primary and secondary documents, including media and news articles, city reports, community newsletters and pamphlets, and existing academic research. In addition, the study relies on qualitative data obtained through in-depth interviews with representatives from the City of Vancouver, the Vancouver Police Department (VPD), the community policing centres and neighbourhood safety office, and a number of community-based organizations.

It must be noted at the outset that, while the two private security firms that operate in Gastown and Chinatown were contacted regarding the study, both companies declined to participate. A representative from Primcorp Security, the company hired by the Vancouver Chinatown Merchants' Association, stated that their legal department had advised them that it was not in their best interest to allow an interview, given the current political climate, citing both the recent provincial election and the current controversy surrounding the city's plans to open drug-treatment and harm-reduction centres in the Downtown Eastside.

Likewise, a representative from Securiguard, the company hired by the Gastown Business Improvement Society, stated that there were a 'myriad of confidentiality issues,' particularly the protection of their customers' privacy, that prevented them from participating in the study. The Securiguard representative also mentioned that the matter had been referred to the company's chief operating officer, who agreed with his decision not to be interviewed.

A Brief History of the DTES

The Downtown Eastside is one of the oldest communities in Vancouver. Located just east of the city core, the area was once the central commercial zone, with many head offices, banks, theatres, hotels, and department stores set up along Hastings Street.[11] In 1889, Market Hall, which served as City Hall from 1896 to 1929, was built near the intersection of Main and Hastings. Next door, the Carnegie library (now the Carnegie Community Centre) was later constructed in 1903.[12] At the turn of the century, however, business investment shifted westward.

Though the Eastside remained the vital centre for warehousing and transportation, it soon became home to immigrant and working-class families, as well as single men.[13] The 'dollar-a-day' hotels and cheap rooming houses made the Eastside attractive to loggers, miners, and railroad and other seasonal workers looking for a place to stay between jobs.[14] Those new to the city were also able to find inexpensive accommodation in this area.

The 'dollar-a-day' hotels in the Downtown Eastside as they exist today

The consolidation of corporate interests in western Canada and the unionization in the resource, transportation, and construction industries that stabilized the demand for mobile work after the Second World War saw the end of the migrant workers.[15] Nevertheless, the Downtown Eastside remained a traditionally low-income neighbourhood with a very diverse population. As in the past, the single resident occupancy (SRO) housing in many of the residential hotels found in the DTES offers the most affordable accommodation in the entire city.

In the 1970s, lack of public funding led to the eventual closure of Riverview Hospital and other institutions, forcing thousands of psychiatric patients to move into the 'only affordable and welcoming community' of the Downtown Eastside.[16] In preparation for Expo 86, cheap rooming houses throughout the city were 'converted to hotels or otherwise gentrified.'[17] By the late 1980s, affordable or single-room accommodation was even more deeply concentrated in the Downtown Eastside. This remains true today.

The 'Community' of the DTES

With the work of many community activists during the last half of the 1960s and the emergence of various social organizations such as the Downtown Eastside Residents' Association (DERA), the 'skid row' image of this area as a 'haven of derelicts and transients' was challenged.[18] As Blomley and Sommers write,

> Contrary to characterizations of the population as shiftless and mobile, activists reminded outsiders of the district's stability, of the loyalty of many elderly men to it, of the small minority who were transients and alcoholics. The Downtown Eastside, in other words, was a neighbourhood and a community to which residents could claim some collective attachment and entitlement. Although the population was (and is) largely made up of renters, the sense of a collective property claim to not only the housing but also the communal spaces of the Downtown Eastside is an important one.[19]

Residents of the DTES neighbourhood are joined by 'histories of shared occupation, struggle and production.'[20] Even with its tremendous diversity, the DTES community is seen as one of the most stable communities in all of Vancouver. A representative from the DTES Neighbourhood Safety Office observes, 'Where else in Vancouver could the government dump people out of Riverview and send them? It's an extremely tolerant community. It's very multicultural. That's why I like this community so much.'

Groups such as DERA have continued to advocate for improved housing conditions and more affordable units for residents of the DTES and have also managed to build a significant amount of social public and co-op housing.[21] DERA also maintains its perception of the Downtown Eastside as a much larger geographic area, extending the boundaries of their services well beyond those defined by the city. In so doing, they also continue to challenge the division and remapping of the DTES by city planners.

Increasingly, the process of gentrification has become a concern for this community of low-income residents. The depressed land values, in addition to the 'central city location, an overheated property market, a planning policy that encourages the densification of downtown space and the changing function of the central city within the international division of labour' have brought about further development in and around this area.[22]

According to the City of Vancouver's 2000 Downtown Eastside Community Monitoring Report, condominium housing stock increased in this area from 343 to 876 units between 1 January 1995 and 1 January 2000, resulting in a gain of 533 units.[23] Since 1986, a total of 17,786 units of market housing have been constructed around the Downtown Eastside.[24] While many of the condominiums that are being built are directly adjacent to the DTES, they often separate themselves from this neighbourhood and the negative stigma attached to it.

For example, a development south of the DTES beside Chinatown in what is now called the 'International Village District' has a number of billboards posted that proudly advertise, 'IT'S NOT A BUILDING, IT'S A NEIGHBOURHOOD.' However, some question whether or not condominium developers can make such a strong claim. As one community worker comments, 'They advertise this thing as a neighbourhood within a neighbourhood, so I don't know what kind of neighbourhood they've got there. They've got a bunch of people living there but to me, that's not a neighbourhood. If you want a neighbourhood, you have to work at developing it but I don't know if any of them are interested.' Underlying this statement is a quite different conception of neighbourhood as being something more than the ownership of property. He adds, 'They reside here, but they don't live here. They shop, eat, entertain elsewhere. To me it's their problem. As long as we've got a vital and stable community down here, we're going to concentrate on our stuff because we're determined not to go away because this is our community. Apart from anything else, we've got nowhere else to go because we can't afford to live anywhere else.' Yet the separation between International Village and the rest of the DTES is further reinforced in the physical design of this space.

This separation is most apparent in the layout of Tinseltown – a large enclosed shopping mall built in this area within the last two years. Again, according to a community worker,

> They just pretend we're not here. They call this the backdoor of their Tinseltown [the doors facing north towards Hastings Street] and they're trying to turn the face of the front door the other way, facing the stadium, which is why they have a sign on the door at the back that states: CLOSED AT 8 PM FOR SECURITY REASONS. So they don't want people from this side going in there and coming out of there ... So for them, this side of the street doesn't exist.

Another interesting feature of Tinseltown is that only four of the businesses in this mall have separate entrances that lead onto the street:

'It's not a building, it's a neighbourhood.'

7 Eleven, McDonald's, Quizno's Subs, and Starbucks. All other shops and stores can be accessed only through the main entranceway.

Some have argued that this is a way of controlling who can enter the mall through environmental design. Although many of the spaces inside are still vacant, the majority that have moved in are high-end designer clothing stores. Thus, the 'undesirable' residents of the DTES are perceived as having no real reason for being in the mall, as the businesses they can afford to frequent are accessible through separate entrances. Security guards positioned at the main entranceways are then able to monitor who enters and, according to a number of interviewees, openly discriminate against certain individuals by denying them entry. One person interviewed has heard of incidents where residents of the Portland Hotel (an SRO building in the DTES) have been denied access to the movie theatres without cause.

These types of conflict may be symptomatic of increasing gentrification and the tremendous polarization among those in the DTES. A city official clearly summarizes this division:

> There is a battle over the land in the DTES, the whole gentrification issue. The low-income community who feels they are about to be displaced at any moment by greater economic forces, so they are digging in and saying, 'If we get displaced there is nowhere to go' ... Meanwhile, the other side is saying, 'We want our businesses to prosper and we need more mixed-income people and middle-income people to come in and spend money in the community.'

Developers, merchants, and property owners see the DTES as in need of extensive 'clean up,' citing the 'perceived problems' of welfare dependency, transience, and crime that exist in the area.[25] New development and an influx of affluent and propertied residents are to be encouraged since it is thought that they will 'bring about physical improvements in the neighbourhood in that, as property owners, they have a particular interest in their surroundings.'[26]

In contrast, low-income residents rely on their 'legitimate entitlement to the physical space of the neighbourhood, based on histories of shared occupation, struggle and production' to remain in this part of the city.[27] Developers and business groups are vilified as profit-driven predators who want to push them out of their own communities.[28]

Crime and Public Disorder in the DTES

The conflict between residents has also translated into concerns over the problems of crime and public disorder and the direction of public policy. Throughout its history, the Downtown Eastside has retained its status as a 'district of dubious morality.'[29] The area was (and is) commonly referred to as 'skid row' and is perceived as the home of 'supposedly rootless single men, classified as chronic alcoholics, drug addicts, perverts, drifters and outcasts of various hues.'[30]

Quite clearly, many of these same perceptions of the DTES continue today. The present drug problem is seen as being at critical levels, with Vancouver mayor Philip Owen calling this an 'unprecedented drug crisis in which people are dying by the hundreds, while many more are getting hepatitis C and HIV through intravenous-injection drug use.'[31] Media reports suggest that the city spends more money per person on dealing with illicit drugs than any other place in Canada.[32] In 1997, an estimated $96 million was spent in direct costs for law enforcement and health care.[33]

According to the City of Vancouver's 2000 Downtown Eastside Community Monitoring Report, the number of 'crimes against persons' (including homicide and attempted murder, assault and sexual assault, and robbery) in the DTES[34] for 1999 accounted for approximately 18 per cent (1,237 of a total 6,749) of the city's total.[35] While 'crimes against property' (including burglary and 'break and enter,' other theft and 'theft from auto,' motor vehicle theft, and mischief) showed a steady decline from 1995 to 1999, the DTES still accounted for 8 per cent (5,453 of 65,896) of the city's total.[36] Most striking is the high percentage of drug arrests in the DTES. In 1999, 61 per cent of the city's drug arrests were in the DTES (1,189 of 1,963).[37]

The negative perception of this area, however, often overshadows the fact that the overall level of crime in the DTES has continuously decreased. In the last decade, Vancouver's crime rate has fallen to 146 from 187 Criminal Code offences per 1,000 people.[38] Even crimes traditionally associated with drug addiction, such as robbery, break and enter, and theft of auto, have also dropped.[39] In spite of these numbers, there is still a belief among some members of the DTES, particularly business owners and market housing residents, that more law enforcement is needed.

The Revitalization of the Downtown Eastside

With an influx of problems such as drug addiction and dealing, HIV infection, the sex trade, crime, high unemployment, the loss of adequate housing, and the loss of many legitimate businesses, the City of Vancouver has undertaken a revitalization program for the DTES that adopts a multifaceted approach to help 'restore the area to a healthy, safe and liveable neighbourhood for all.'[40] As part of the revitalization, partnerships at various levels have formed to reduce crime and improve safety in the DTES.

Many of these initiatives are the product of the Vancouver Agreement – a commitment made between the federal government, the Province of British Columbia, and the City of Vancouver to 'work together to support sustainable economic, social and community development in

Vancouver.' Although the agreement is to affect the entire city, the initial focus of work is in the DTES. The Vancouver Agreement addresses three main themes: community health and safety, economic and social development, and community capacity building.

At the present time, the Vancouver Agreement partners have taken the first steps towards implementing the Four Pillars Approach to 'solving' Vancouver's drug problem. The Four Pillars Approach is a comprehensive strategy that combines prevention, treatment, enforcement, and harm-reduction initiatives. The proposed projects include an increase in the number of police on the street, the redesign of the physical space in front of the Carnegie Community Centre to reduce the open drug market on the corner of Main and Hastings, and the expansion of drug treatment and health services.[41] However, these proposals have led to an ongoing debate between 'those who seek to improve the Downtown Eastside by flooding it with help against others who believe expanded services would only lure drug users and the problems they bring.'[42]

A new group of residents, merchants, and property owners called the Community Alliance has formed to protest against government plans to introduce new facilities and programs for drug users, urging, instead, tougher law enforcement. In a newspaper article, Jon Stovell, president of the Gastown Business Improvement Society, is quoted as saying,

> In part, the changes are a result of changes in drug culture itself, the change from heroin to crack ... But equally to blame is how we've responded to that and how we've just reinforced that behaviour as acceptable in this neighbourhood and as a city sought to contain it down here. It's a process of containment, ghetto-ization and creating a social services-industrial complex that feeds off the unfortunate. It's a proven mistake.[43]

In contrast, community activists and low-income residents view this type of opposition as standing in the way of social programs and housing that will improve the lives of many disadvantaged people in the community.

Creating Borders in the DTES

While the Downtown Eastside is seen as one geographic location within the larger City of Vancouver, the area itself has been subdivided into seven distinct subareas. For city officials, the remapping of the DTES was a way to address various community concerns by 'defining a space which could be monitored and acted upon.'[44] These new communities were produced to help identify local concerns and create locally based solutions.[45] However, community activists objected to the introduction of these new maps, claiming that the Downtown Eastside neighbourhood was being 'mapped out of existence.'[46] The process was seen as a form of gentrification and dispossession that would 'dismember their community.'[47]

Though the threat of non-participation in the planning process by key Downtown Eastside groups was successful in reinstating the Downtown Eastside name,[48] the divided subareas still exist. As a result, many of the 'neighbourhoods' that form the Downtown Eastside have become their own political entities.[49] Neighbourhoods such as Chinatown that already existed through 'shared histories and memories that underpinned some collective identity'[50] were simply reaffirmed as distinct spaces. At the same time, the maps developed by city planners served to create new communities such as Gastown and Victory Square,[51] seen as 'invented spaces' produced 'from above' by the state.[52]

More importantly, these maps have become inextricably linked to the process of governing. Drawing on the work of Rose, Blomley and Sommers write that,

> Maps are more than 'mere' representations of reality or ways of 'acting upon the real' that enable the government of social life and human conduct. They are, in fact, constitutive of that reality, inscribing power on space, codifying, and thus privileging the meanings that make it recognizable and actionable. The ability to constitute space in this way is a crucial factor in the exercise of government power, for it makes possible the regularity, which is necessary for the motivation of self-rule. The extent to which governmental (and, indeed, other) authorities are able to mobilize 'the self-regulating capacities of subjects ... [as] key resources' is contingent largely on their ability to render space as transparent, fixed and predictable.[53]

Many of the neighbourhoods of the DTES have become politically active communities involved in how they are governed and in their own self-goverment, with various organizations, groups, and individuals acting on behalf of their respective communities.

Yet the differences between these neighbourhoods exist beyond the cartographic boundaries and borders drawn on city maps. Even with their close geographic proximity, many subareas maintain very different physical and social characteristics. While the DTES is often targeted as a single area by policy makers, this broad classification often obscures the

The northwest entrance to Gastown

fact that many problems and the way they are addressed vary drastically between locations. I address this issue in the following section by examining the community-based and private forms of policing that are developing in the 'subcommunities' of Gastown, Chinatown, and the 'Hastings Street Corridor.'

The Gastown Community

Gastown is one of Vancouver's best-known tourist destinations and is located in the north-east section of the Downtown Eastside at the edge of the Burrard Inlet. In 1971, the Province of British Columbia designated Gastown a historic site. In the years since then, Gastown has undergone continuous redevelopment by both the city and local property owners to restore this historic area.[54] The physical landscape of Gastown is lined with distinctive brick roads and vintage-style street lamps and features a number of tourist sites such as the Steam Clock and the 'Gassy Jack' statue. Daily historic walking tours are also offered in this district.

Because of its status as a tourist attraction, the area of Gastown is home to a number of art galleries, souvenir shops, and a variety of restaurants and bars that cater to this market. In the 1980s, the City of Vancouver recognized Gastown as a Business Improvement Area, requiring all businesses to be assessed an annual levy to fund the Gastown Business Improvement Society (GBIS).[55]

The brick road and vintage-style street lamps of Gastown

The GBIS, like other business improvement associations, is a 'self-help mechanism designed to assist local business people, property owners and city councillors in upgrading and promoting their business and shopping district to further trade and commerce in their area.'[56] The GBIS provides a forum for discussions over planning and the spending of funds contributed by all its members and also serves as a lobby for the interests of businesses.[57]

In addition to its designation as a business area, Gastown is also home to various residents. In particular, the area contains many SRO housing units. While the total number of units slowly dropped between 1994 and 1999, the Gastown area had approximately 1,137 (approximately 21 per cent) of the total 5,187 SRO units for all of the DTES in 1999.[58] However, the same time period saw a substantial growth in condominium housing, from 142 units in 1994 to 492 in 1999.

Blomley and Sommers note that the incoming residents occupying these condominium developments have 'organized and allied themselves with business groups to advance residential development in the area and to claim neighbourhood and community status.'[59] As a result, businesses and local property owners have established a sense of legitimized ownership of Gastown and the ability to represent and 'speak on behalf of the community' through the GBIS.

This claim to ownership by merchants and property owners has led to a clear separation of Gastown from the rest of the DTES and its residents. As Blomley and Sommers write, 'In comparing itself to the image of a deteriorating, burnt-out "ghetto," Gastown has been successfully able to claim the status of a neighbourhood and community and, in so doing, inscribe on to the landscape a space where the poor are outsiders and property-owners are those with rights of representation and voice.'[60] In many ways, the efforts of the GBIS to revitalize Gastown have both directly and indirectly made the area distinct and separate from the rest of the Downtown Eastside.

By refusing to be labelled as or associated with the Downtown Eastside, Gastown interests have 'asserted their right to map, name and regulate the space within the boundaries of the Gastown historical area.'[61] Many of the physical features of Gastown make anyone who enters well aware that he or she is no longer in the Downtown Eastside. The historic feel of the architecture and the street banners that demarcate the district all serve to create a very distinctive environment.

In addition, the GBIS has introduced various social programs that deal specifically with issues such as homelessness, panhandling, safety, and security. Because of its relatively close proximity to the Hastings Street Corridor and the problems associated with that section of the city, many of these initiatives reflect an attempt by businesses to improve the conditions for tourism and the general economic viability of Gastown. However, these efforts often promote an image of the poor as 'undesirables,' criminals, and drug addicts who do not belong in this heritage area.

An information leaflet produced by the GBIS, in association with the Robson Street Business Association, the Downtown Vancouver Business Association, and the Safe City Solutions Task Force, addresses how individuals should deal with panhandlers.[62] The leaflet, headed by the phrase, 'Real Change. Not Spare Change,' clearly assumes that those living on the street are addicted to drugs or alcohol with no evidence to substantiate this claim. It also appears to suggest that there are many services available that already provide assistance to these individuals. It reads, 'We know that most people on the street suffer from drug or alcohol addictions. Your loose change only feeds their addiction. Don't be fooled by signs saying they want food and shelter. There are agencies that provide *free meals* and *shelter* **every day**.'[63] Instead of giving their spare change, readers of the pamphlet are urged to 'make a contribution to a charity of your choice, that offers food, shelter, counselling, professional assistance and a chance for real change.'[64] Printed on the other side of the leaflet is the City of Vancouver's By-law to Regulate and Control Panhandling that was unanimously passed by City Council on 30 April 1998.

Private Policing in Gastown

In 1996, the Gastown Business Improvement Society contracted Concord Security Corporation, a private security company, to supply uniformed patrols in Gastown.[65] The major function of the private security personnel was to provide low-level public order maintenance. The physical presence of security was to offer an increased sense of safety and was viewed as a way of deterring disorderly behaviour and preventing crime.[66] The private security company currently contracted by the GBIS is Securiguard Services Limited.

According to the website of the Industrial Wood and Allied Workers of Canada–Canadian Labour Congress (IWA–CLC), last updated 2 April 2001, Securiguard has 503 licensed guards and 720 employees in total, making it the largest private security company in this union and in the entire province.[67] Originally started in 1974 to provide security services for the Brinco Mining Corporation in Cassiar, British Columbia, Securiguard has expanded its operations throughout Vancouver, Victoria, and Nanaimo, providing various security functions to more than sixty permanent sites.[68]

Securiguard is the first private security force in Canada to assume RCMP responsibilities at an international airport.[69] In 1997, when the Ports Canada Police were disbanded, the company was selected to take over the patrol function for the Vancouver Port Corporation and to liaise with both the Municipal Police and the RCMP.[70] Securiguard is also the primary security provider for major labour disruptions and strike actions in British Columbia and has worked some of Vancouver's major events including the APEC Summit and Y2K First Night.[71]

Securiguard also provides a number of specialized services. It is the first private security firm in British Columbia to implement bike patrols certified by the Vancouver Police Department.[72] The bike patrol operates twenty-four hours a day, year round, patrolling parking lots in downtown Vancouver to deter theft from automobiles, remove undesirable persons from client property, enforce parking regulations, and provide customer assistance.[73]

Securiguard is also the first private security company in British Columbia to receive RCMP certification for K-9 (canine) Teams. According to the company website, this unit is to 'provide a physical deterrence only and [the dogs] are *not trained for attack purposes.*'[74] The site also notes that the company is 'very cognizant of [its] role in private protection and the limitations and liabilities inherent in providing canine protection. Since incorporating canine teams in 1998 we are proud to state no criminal or civil litigation has developed against any Securiguard canine team.'[75]

Finally, Securiguard is one of a number of security training schools in British Columbia approved by the Ministry of the Attorney General. According to its website, all Securiguard officers 'receive extensive training in verbal judo, access control, legal limitations, safety and emergency procedures, and most importantly, public relations.'[76]

Securiguard is said to play a supplemental role in maintaining safety and security in Gastown. As an inspector with the Vancouver Police Department explains,

> They have a very professional company down there called Securiguard and they have a high presence. The way they dress in their yellow jackets, they have a very high presence. And that's reassuring to the tourist because we can never afford that number of police officers down there ... They're paying them less than half what you would pay a police officer and, for us, we estimate to put one full-time police officer on the street, it would be about $100,000 a year because of equipment, support, logistics, everything.

As well, Securiguard officers act on behalf of the businesses and merchants in the area by removing unwanted persons from their property and detaining shoplifters until police arrive at the scene.

The private security personnel also give additional assistance to the public police whenever possible. A Neighbourhood Police Officer in Gastown claims that there is a good working relationship between the Gastown Community Policing Centre and Securiguard. In particular, the officer mentions that information regarding crime or other problems in the area is commonly shared between the two agencies. He states that Securiguard personnel even use the Community Policing Centre to write their reports.

The officer gives high praise to the professionalism of the company and its personnel, noting that 'they treat everybody with respect.' He notes that personnel primarily respond to the problems of the local businesses and will either go to him or contact him on his cell phone when situations arise that they themselves cannot directly handle and/or do not have the authority to deal with. In general, the officer sees the work of private security personnel as having a very positive effect on the reduction of crime and public disorder in Gastown.

Community Policing in Gastown

Located at 219 Abbott Street, the Gastown Community Policing Centre (CPC) has been in operation for approximately ten years and is seen as a way for the police to connect directly with the neighbourhood they serve. The office is headed by a board of directors composed of representatives from the community, to ensure that the office is accountable and responsive to community needs.

Funding for the office is provided primarily through a joint City of Vancouver and Ministry of the Attorney General Community Safety Funding Program (with costs shared on a fifty-fifty basis). All grants are to be used 'for the implementation of crime prevention and safety related programs proposed by the CPC's and are not for providing core support to the offices.' The office must apply for this funding, and grants are made based on established program criteria that include the merit of the application, community need for the activities, and effective outcomes of ongoing program services.

In explaining the major function of the office, a Neighbourhood Police Officer assigned to the Gastown CPC states that

> Policing had gotten away from [being] community-based, being in contact with people. So they wanted to come back to more personal policing where you know your neighbours, you know the people you deal with, you know their needs and wants. And because Gastown is a fairly unique area, we have social housing here, we have businesses here, we have market housing, we wanted to put a police office down here that could try to meet the needs of the community.

The officer defines the community of Gastown as a very 'diverse population' made up of people who live and work in the area, visiting tourists, and the 'down and outers' on social assistance. The officer is also quick to point out the separation of the Gastown community from the rest of the DTES: 'We are a part of the Downtown Eastside, but we're separate. Because, unlike, say, skid row, we have a lot of business community here. And we have a lot of market housing here. So we're a separate community. We're a very diverse community.'

According to the officer, relatively few crimes take place in Gastown. The majority of offences that do occur, however, are said to be property related. At the present time, the major concerns for the CPC office include panhandling and some drug use and drug-related activities such as theft from auto. This is compared with the mandate of the nearby Downtown Eastside Neighbourhood Safety Office (discussed later in the chapter):

They deal with a different type of clientele in a different neighbourhood. And they have a different coordinator in their office and a different direction they want to take. So our office doesn't always marry up with the type of things that they want to do. They've got a different mandate than we have here in Gastown. So it's hard for us to get together sometimes to do coordinated projects but it doesn't mean we don't communicate.

Furthermore, the officer notes that the boundaries of Gastown insulate the area from many of the drug problems that exist in the adjacent Hastings Street Corridor:

Fortunately, here in Gastown, we have a little section out by the Army and Navy, Pigeon Park and around the block in the Army and Navy lane, that is our only real problem in here for drugs. It stays away from Water Street. It's not too bad on Cordova Street, although if you go up a block to Hastings Street and Abbott, it's a big problem. I'm not trying to say I'm passing the buck. It's just not in Gastown. People in Gastown are separate from that. As in Chinatown, Chinatown has a big drug problem over by the Carnegie. It's not all of Chinatown that's a problem, but it's a part of it. So, if there's a problem in Gastown that I need to take care of, then I'll try to do my best.

The office appears to operate on a conception of policing that involves reinforcing the community's ownership over its territorial space and establishing a sense of who does and does not belong in this area:

One of the basic principles of community policing is, Eyes on the street. So when you have a community police office and you go out and do presentations to the local community, you tell them, 'The more you use the street, the less problems you'll have on the street.' You still might have problems on the street, but if you're out there using the street and being neighbours on the street and you know your neighbour on your left and right, you know who belongs there.

This approach is in keeping with the use of citizen volunteer patrols. The office runs a citizens' patrol program where groups of trained volunteers, equipped with cell phones to contact 911 in cases of emergency, act as additional 'eyes and ears' for the police. Although the volunteers on patrol are instructed to remain 'hands off,' their presence is believed to act as a form of deterrence against public disorder and criminal activity.

In many ways, this program appears to be a 'foot patrol' offshoot of the Vancouver Police Department's Citizens' Crime Watch that has been in operation since 1987.[77] Volunteers are coordinated and trained by two police constables and patrol the streets and alleys of Vancouver in their own cars.[78] According to the Vancouver Police Department website, volunteers of this program must be over the age of nineteen, have no criminal record, be 'of suitable character, have good driving skills and access to a vehicle for patrols, have good English verbal skills, have good observation skills, and have the ability to assess on-view situations and relay details over a radio efficiently.'[79]

Once accepted into the program, volunteers must pass a security clearance and criminal record check that requires them to be fingerprinted.[80] Volunteers must also attend a two-hour training class before being able to take part in patrols where they, with their co-ordinator, review the contents of the procedure manual and discuss rules and regulations, basic surveillance techniques, radio procedures, legal responsibilities, and patrol and observation techniques.[81]

The volunteer patrol program run by the Gastown CPC, in partnership with the Insurance Corporation of British Columbia (ICBC), also works to promote crime prevention awareness. The volunteers, for instance, run periodic vehicle audits that are aimed at making people aware of how to make their cars more secure and less attractive to thieves (e.g., taking all valuable items, leaving the ashtray open, using security devices to lock the steering wheel, etc.).

Lastly, the Gastown CPC is a member of a Neighbourhood Integrated Services (NIS) Team. Created in 1996, the NIS Team coordinates the efforts of several city and provincial departments (such as Licensing, Engineering, City Planning, etc.) to reduce the impact of crime and disorder and improve living conditions in the various Vancouver communities. The NIS Team works to improve the liveability in SRO hotels, reduce crime-related business, keep vacant sites free of debris, and secure vacant buildings.

The Chinatown Community

Located in the south-west section of the Downtown Eastside, Vancouver's Chinatown is one of the city's oldest commercial and residential districts.[82] The community was established in the 1880s, a few years before the city's incorporation in 1886, by Chinese immigrants who moved to Vancouver to work as labourers in local industries.[83] It is the largest Chinatown in all of Canada, and in North America is second in size only to San Francisco.[84] Throughout the years, the community has been able to retain its cultural identity in the face of racial discrimination, economic hardship, and the decline of areas around it.[85] In the 1950s, residents of this community rallied against a proposal to run a highway through the Chinatown area, forcing the government to abandon the project.[86]

Much like Gastown, the area is seen as a tourist attraction and has also been designated by the province as a historic site. The physical design of the area emphasizes its distinctively Chinese heritage and sets it apart from the rest of the Downtown Eastside. Chinatown is home to many different businesses, with an array of restaurants, bakeries, clothing shops, and produce markets. In addition, other sites such as the Dr Sun Yat-Sen Classical Chinese Gardens are located here.

A number of city initiatives have been undertaken to promote the distinct identity of Chinatown and encourage tourism into the area. As part of the Vancouver Agreement, the city has helped to fund the construction of the Chinatown Millennium Gate.[87] This gate over Pender Street is seen as a way of promoting community pride and attracting shoppers and tourists to Chinatown.[88] According to member of the legislative assembly Jenny Kwan, the 'traditional gate will allow Chinatown to announce itself, and complement the other unique attractions of historic Chinatown.'[89]

In addition, the Silk Road project has been undertaken to 'make visible the ties between Chinatown and Downtown.'[90] The walking route from Gore Avenue to Robson Street – marked by street banners along the way – leads to many tourist attractions in both Chinatown and the downtown core. These initiatives may also be seen as a way of improving the economic viability of this particular section of the city.

Since the 1980s, Chinatown businesses have had to compete with large shopping malls developed in other parts of Vancouver and surrounding municipalities that cater mostly to the Chinese community.[91] In this

An intersection at the foot of Chinatown

regard, the Vancouver Chinatown Merchants' Association has been politically active, claiming that the current conditions of the DTES have
diverted business away from this area, making it extremely difficult to
compete with the new developments.

The association speaks on behalf of many of the businesses in the area
and the relatively small number of (predominantly Chinese) residents as
well. As a representative from this association claims, 'Chinatown is not
just the shops on the main streets. There are a lot of people living on the
second or third levels and many of these people are scared stiff to go out
at night ... So we sympathize with them. We share their concerns to
initiate change.'

Many of these concerns are directed towards the drug activity and
related offences that have been allowed to continue in the DTES and in
Chinatown. According to a representative from the Chinatown Merchants' Association, many merchants see themselves as victims:

> We're sick of it. All the problems are being pushed down here, whether it's
> drugs, mental illness, homelessness, prostitution ... It's called a containment
> policy. When I first started being active, they used to deny it. Now it's pretty

The Silk Road Walking Route street banners

common knowledge that they did have the containment policy that the problems are to be concentrated down here. And this is the unfairness of it all. We're the whipping boys for the people in City Hall.

He further suggests that the city has had a history of 'disregarding the historic value and the livelihood of the people in Chinatown.' He recalls that in the 1970s, the city wanted to put up a freeway that would run right through Chinatown. Then, in the 1980s, there was a proposal to tear down Strathcona (located just east of Chinatown) and turn it into a huge public housing project and, later, to build a garbage-processing plant in that area. Although they, with other members of the larger DTES community, have been successful in lobbying against these plans, he feels that those in Chinatown are still 'the defenceless' and 'voiceless.'

Referring to a 'golden past,' he sees the problems in Chinatown on the rise with the increasing level of drug activity. Acknowledging that Chinatown is a traditionally low-income neighbourhood that caters mostly to the average working-class family, he points to a real change that has taken place within the last thirty years: 'Look around and look at the bars in the windows, those were never there in my days. Shoplifting is phenomenal. There were businesses that went out of business simply due to shoplifting. It was very difficult and it was very emotional for a lot of people who see this as heritage, as a historical area. That is why crime and drugs is such a sensitive issue in Chinatown and why people react so strongly.' In response to many of these concerns, the Merchants' Association took it upon itself to hire private security guards to patrol the public streets in Chinatown in 1994.[92] The current contract holder is Primcorp Security.

At a cost of approximately $180,000 a year, the Merchants' Association hires the company to provide additional presence on the streets of Chinatown and to offer extra assistance to local business owners. A representative from the Merchants' Association explains that the private security personnel are 'goodwill ambassadors' who will 'lend a helping hand' to those in need. Their uniformed presence in Chinatown is said to deter petty criminals and 'give passers-by and shopkeepers peace of mind.' He further explains that the private security company is able to meet the needs of the community when limited resources prevent the public police from effectively doing so, stating that, 'The police are doing what they can, giving good service,' but that 'there is definitely a role for private security.'

Community Policing in Chinatown

Once known as the 'Chinatown Community Policing Centre,' the office has changed its name to the 'Chinese Community Policing Centre' (CPC) to reflect its expanding mandate. The Chinese CPC provides assistance not only to the residents of Chinatown but also to the larger Chinese population within the city as a whole. The office acts as a liaison between the Chinese community and the Vancouver Police Department by attempting to break down existing cultural and language barriers.

The office, for instance, provides Chinese translators and interpreters for those requiring these services. The CPC also offers a victim assistance program aimed at the Chinese community and gives more general help to those unfamiliar with the Canadian criminal justice system. With an increasing profile and growing public awareness of the type of services provided, the CPC receives many referrals from those within the police force and other agencies in the city.

However, as part of its mandate, the CPC also addresses local safety and security concerns within Chinatown. One of the major goals has been to promote and improve the image of Chinatown as a 'safe place' that, in turn, can restore confidence in the public police within this community, particularly among business owners. As a representative for the Chinese CPC states, the office is there to 'let Chinatown businesses know that everybody cares. That the office cares, the volunteers care, everybody cares.'

The office operates in much the same way as the Gastown CPC. The office is headed by a board of directors, comprising various members from the community, that oversees the general operations. As well, much of its funding is provided though the joint City of Vancouver and Ministry of the Attorney General Community Safety Funding Program. The office, like the Gastown CPC, also works in partnership with ICBC to promote crime prevention awareness.

As part of the Vancouver Agreement, the Chinese Community Policing Centre has had two new officers assigned to this location, bringing the number of its uniformed officers to eight. According to a City of Vancouver News Release, the move was a 'response to the needs of the Chinese community and based on consultation since October with various business, residential groups, and associations in Chinatown.'[93]

Since 2000, the Chinese CPC has coordinated 'Chinatown Watch,' a volunteer citizen patrol program much like the one in Gastown. The program currently has fifteen volunteers on three different patrolling shifts and provides an increased physical presence within the community. Volunteers remain hands-off and act as the 'eyes and ears' for the police by reporting and recording any incidents they may witness.

The Chinese CPC also works closely with the private security personnel assigned to Chinatown. The office coordinator for the Chinese CPC states that there is a very good working relationship between the office and Primcorp Security. He notes that,

[Primcorp] needs to work with the police. And that's the trend that I've seen in the past years. The security officers are often in touch with the police officers here and, sometimes, they patrol with each other ... [They]

also pass on information to each other. I can show you, we have dozens of pictures [of possible suspects and those known to the police] posted on the wall and [we] facilitate the security members to come around and have a look at them, to try and educate them in helping them do a good job.

With these initiatives in place, a representative from the Chinatown Merchants' Association sees a much better future ahead for the neighbourhood, attributing many of these changes to the increased visibility of public, private, and volunteer patrols: 'The fiscal indicators, things like blatant purse snatching, shoplifting, threatening of business operators and tourists, that type of thing, have decreased. There's not as much visible drug activity, so by those parameters I think we've come a long way. I would attribute it to, number one, the increased police presence as well as the hard work of our security.'

The Hastings Street Corridor

Although the Hastings Street Corridor is not officially recognized on city maps as a separate neighbourhood within the DTES, it is commonly seen and identified as the central location for the low-income resident community of the area. The 'skid row' image that has historically characterized this section of the city is still often associated with this stretch of land along Hastings Street between Gore Avenue and Cambie Street. As such, it is also the area that both the adjacent neighbourhoods of Gastown and Chinatown separate themselves from, reinforcing this clear division and the general distinctiveness of this space. The Carnegie Community Centre, located on the corner of Main and Hastings, is the heart of this communal space and has been described as the neighbourhood's 'living room.'[94]

The Hastings Street Corridor has become a location that is occupied by a very separate and distinct community of people who have been left off official city maps. This community is built around notions of shared struggle and common history among residents of this area. As a representative from the DTES Neighbourhood Safety Office explains,

This community is, by and large, quite cohesive. And the majority of people work together quite well. And we've taken on bigger battles before. The casino being one ... So there have been a lot of battles, and people really pull together. This is the poorest place in Canada. To somehow think that people don't matter and this isn't a community? This is a community. Even

A recently painted mural on the front of an SRO hotel in the Downtown Eastside

with all the kinds of press it gets, it really is a community. And real people live here and a lot of people don't want to leave here.

Members of this community have also been active in the area's revitalization. Citing the construction taking place at many of the SRO hotels, a member of a local community group reports that,

> There's been significant new housing development. Walk by the Sunrise (an SRO hotel) and check out the main floor ... There's going to be a free dental clinic in there. Co-op radio has moved in. They've restored the heritage character of the front of the streetscape along Sunrise. It's amazing. The Washington Hotel [an SRO hotel] across the street is great. They've restored the neon sign, they've put a historical mural on the front.

These developments, however, have been overshadowed by many of the negative characteristics of the location.

Indeed, the physical and social make-up of the Hastings Street Corridor is quite different from that of both Gastown and Chinatown and is most apparent in the lack of businesses in the area. A survey of a seven-block stretch of Hastings Street from Richards to Gore conducted by the

Hastings east of Cambie Street

city in April 2000 revealed a 29 per cent vacant storefront rate (1,784 feet of 6,170 feet of total frontage).[95]

Many of the businesses that do exist in this area – specifically, the pawnshops and convenience stores – have been seen as either facilitating and/or committing illegal activity. As an inspector with the Vancouver Police Department explains,

> There's the odd business. There's the odd restaurant. But many of these businesses down there, some of the businesses down there cater to the by-product of that disorder [like] the pawnshops. If you go and look at the places that sell food, you and I could not afford to buy some groceries there it's so high in price. But, they may be dealing in other things. They may be taking stolen property for drugs. And we do arrest shopkeepers and employees that do that kind of nonsense and a lot of businesses are closed.

From January to December 1999, thirty-one businesses had actions taken against them, most of which were directly or indirectly related to the drug trade.[96] As a way of further addressing this problem, the city has enacted a by-law that regulates the hours of operation of several classes of businesses that are believed to have negative impacts on the DTES and surrounding communities.[97]

The problems of crime and public disorder that are often related to the open drug trade appear most concentrated and visible in this part of the city. As a result, the types of activity that are taking place are seen as attracting many people to the DTES. According to a representative from the City of Vancouver, 'I think another dynamic is that we have a regional drug market. You see a lot of taxis rolling through. There are a lot of people coming from all over the lower mainland to buy drugs. There are a lot of people coming from the lower mainland to buy alcohol. There are a lot of people coming from the lower mainland to buy sex. So there's both this local phenomenon and a regional problem.' The situation may also be a product of the strategies adopted by the City of Vancouver and the Vancouver Police Department to 'contain' the problem within this one region.

Although a high percentage of all drug arrests for the city are within the Downtown Eastside, the major focus for law enforcement has been on drug dealing and trafficking. As an inspector with the Vancouver Police Department explains, 'Our philosophy has always been that people who are addicted to drugs need treatment. If they persist in committing criminal acts, they have to go to jail. But we focus on drug dealers, particularly those for-profit dealers ... We want them not only to be arrested [but] to receive substantive sentences to send a message ... That is our focus.' This approach appears to go hand in hand with the city's plans to reconstruct the exterior of the Carnegie Community Centre to allow the police to 'more effectively target drug dealers.'

The Main Street side of the building will feature a raised patio with low fencing attached to the Carnegie that will provide an outdoor smoking area with controlled access through the building, barring entry to people who are under the influence of alcohol or drugs.[98] In addition, bus stops on both Main Street and Hastings Street will be moved.[99] The public space in front of the Carnegie Community Centre on Main Street will also be substantially reduced to discourage illegal activities, and the cement structure above the washrooms will be altered to provide better visibility for the police and greater overall security.[100]

While drug dealing has become the major focus for law enforcement, the problem of drug use and addiction is generally viewed as a public health issue. In describing the dilemma faced by police, a representative from the City of Vancouver explains that, 'I think the police have been stuck for a long time. Their role has been limited because they can't really do much with the situation. It's not an enforcement issue. I think in 1993 when the Chief Coroner released his report, he was the first one that clearly said that this is not an issue for the criminal justice system. This is an issue for the health care system.' By containing the problem

The Carnegie Community Centre

and developing treatment and detox facilities within this neighbourhood, officials hope that those with addictions can be quickly diverted to these services. As an inspector with the VPD states,

> That whole area, we call it the Hastings Corridor, from Gore to Cambie. We're intentionally containing it there because if we put too much pressure on there, it will go back into Gastown and Chinatown, complaints will go up, and we don't want that. So, until these health initiatives come on board in the fall, which will give an outlet for the police to start to divert people into treatment, until that happens, we're containing. And we have said that publicly to the Police Board and in the media.

A representative from the City of Vancouver describes this strategy, outlined in the Four Pillars Approach, as short-term goals for long-term eradication:

> This is actually opening doors so people can move out of that lifestyle and move out of the DTES ... You're building a continuum of services. People aren't going to leave the corner of Main and Hastings and move towards an abstinence-oriented drug treatment facility in Richmond or Surrey ... Maybe one in a hundred. Most folks are too far gone. They can't get into treatment so they need a bunch of stepping-stones to get there. And those stepping-stones should ideally lead them, not necessarily away from the community, but away from the streets. And that's what we're trying to do. We're trying to

provide some open doors in the DTES for those people who can't access abstinence-oriented treatment services.

Though there has been considerable opposition to these initiatives from many of the businesses in both Gastown and Chinatown, the lack of any business organization and development interests in the Hastings Street Corridor has allowed these problems to be tolerated in this area.

There seems to be far less pressure from businesses within the Hastings Street Corridor to 'clean up' the visible problems often associated with drug use. In fact, many of the businesses here are often seen as profiting from the problems that exist in this section of the city. As a result, there are no private security companies directed at protecting the area and eradicating the presence of certain activities as there are in both Gastown and Chinatown.

With the absence of safe injection sites, the tolerance for visible drug use in the Hastings Street Corridor has actually had a positive effect on improving safety for many people in this community. The recent efforts of the Vancouver police to move a lot of the drug activity out of the SROs and bars has pushed much of this activity back onto the street. But, because this activity is taking place in more visible public spaces, problems such as drug overdoses and violence are responded to much more quickly.

The lack of investment and the problems of this area have also protected the community from increasing gentrification. As a community worker explains, 'The irony of it is, the only thing that has saved us from gentrification is the drug activity on the street, which scares people out. It doesn't do us any good, but it buys some time in an ugly sort of a way.' Nevertheless, most participants acknowledge that more businesses would be beneficial but that future development must be sensitive to the needs of the community. As one community worker observes,

> No one in this community is thrilled that there are no stores on Hastings Street. It's not just the rest of the city that is so offended by this disinvestment on Hastings Street. People are consumers of good and services as much as any other community ... So the neighbourhood wants to see some change in terms of what's going on the street. We want a safe neighbourhood. We want to improve quality of life ... But how we get there is very important in terms of ensuring that in 'revitalizing' this neighbourhood we don't shoot ourselves in the foot or find ourselves drifting eastward further into the industrial area, which is somewhat happening.

The Downtown Eastside Neighbourhood Safety Office

The Hastings Street Corridor is serviced by the Downtown Eastside Neighbourhood Safety Office (NSO), which operates differently from the other community policing centres in the city. More specifically, the office works on a much broader conception of community and attempts to work closely with the more marginalized populations, including drug addicts, the mentally ill, sex trade workers, and street youth, both within and beyond the defined borders of the DTES. A representative from this office explains:

> We work wherever we're being asked. Our child protection strategy will work in Grandview-Woodlands, Hastings North, and Strathcona around that issue. I had the sergeant in charge of community policing say, 'Well, that's not in the Downtown Eastside. That's not in your area. Why are you working with those groups?' Well, I thought, maybe the question you should be asking is, 'Why aren't they working with their own office and why are they working here. What do we offer that they want?'

The representative clearly sees the NSO as being far different from the other Vancouver CPCs. She argues that the office refuses to be called a 'policing centre' because so much of what they do is seen as being more than just policing. She further asserts that the office works outside what she describes as 'the narrow little box' of community policing that is currently being adopted by the Vancouver Police Department.

The NSO has refused to sign the operating agreement with the city and the department and is not an incorporated society, but instead is run by a coalition of community agencies. On the advisory committee are groups such as Ray-Cam Community Centre, Carnegie Community Centre, Strathcona Community Centre, the Downtown Eastside Youth Activities Societies (DEYAS), the Tradeworks Training Society (a job-training organization aimed at helping youth in the Downtown Eastside), and DERA.

This approach brings the community infrastructure in to direct the office. While the office has considered becoming an incorporated society, it was thought that this would become very limiting because 'it's whoever decides to drop in and become a member.' The NSO representative explains that, 'that kind of situation opens up [the office] to be taken over by one issue group or people who don't want to service the whole community, and that's not our philosophy.'

By making these partnerships, the office is able to draw on various resources and work with other agencies that operate within the community to provide solutions to local concerns. She asserts that the office 'looks at providing services' from a 'community development perspective.' Claiming that the other community policing centres are far too limited in their approach, the NSO representative explains that,

> The programs they offer are 'police programs' like block watch, block community, that kind of stuff. Where we look at broader initiatives. And we're more based on a problem-solving model. So let's get people to the table. If this is an issue, who needs to be here? What do we need to do? Which demands some real commitment from the players, which demands some real flexibility from us and the ability to connect with resources ... We're truly community-based and we work with people who actually live here. And we don't look at 'good people' and 'bad people' ... And we don't see people as 'less desirable' or 'less deserving.' So we work with local communities and make particular effort to work with people who are quite marginalized and who don't normally seek assistance. So we look at ways to bridge that gap.

Some of the activities that the NSO is currently working on include hard-targeting of high-risk youth who tend to gravitate to the area, public education around child protection, and safety meetings with women in the sex trade. The office is also working with other agencies in the area on how to deal with people with mental illness.

A number of community members note a very good relationship with one of the officers assigned to the DTES NSO. Special demands were even made by a number of community groups to keep the officer assigned to this office. They point to his proactive approach and problem-solving strategies as examples of 'real' community policing. As one interviewee comments,

> There's a lot of intervention in terms of trying to get things settled down before they develop into full-scale problems ... That's the kind of social element to the police that isn't just street law enforcement, but it short-circuits a lot of problems that could develop later on which end up costing more money, more resources, and ends up being handled in a messier way. And I guess that's essentially how community policing is supposed to work. Its proactive rather than reactive, and I think they're effective in doing that.

Other policing initiatives undertaken through this office have also been viewed as positive responses to community concerns. For instance, one community worker notes that cooperation between the community and the Vancouver Police Department has been successful in eliminating bar-related knife incidents.

Unlike the other CPCs in the city, the NSO does not receive its funding from the joint City of Vancouver and Ministry of the Attorney General Community Safety Funding Program. Rather, it receives support from the Ministry of Children and Families and from other sources such as the Vancouver Foundation and gaming money. While the relationship between the NSO and the Vancouver Police Department is described as amicable by both parties, the inspector for the DTES raised some concern over the approach that is taken by this office and would like to see them 'get on board' with the other twenty-one CPCs in the city: 'The DTES Safety Office is out of synch with us and they truly believe that they are the true representatives of the poor and impoverished, and I don't share that. I think there are a lot of agencies that do that. But we're working hard to get them to come closer to being on stream, but it's a challenge.'

Finally, the DTES Neighbourhood Safety Office has no working relationship with any security companies that operate in the neighbouring areas and appears to be quite critical of what they do. A representative from this office notes that the only relationship she has with these companies is limited to the 'odd complaint from people in the neighbourhood who get pushed out of those areas because they're not presentable.'

Other Forms of Policing Technology

It must be noted that the discussion presented above looks at only some of the public and private policing that is presently taking place in Vancouver's Downtown Eastside. Compiling an inventory of all the various crime-prevention techniques and strategies that are being employed in this area would be both an interesting and an important undertaking but is well beyond the limited scope of this study. Nevertheless, it is important to recognize some of the ways in which businesses and residents of Gastown, Chinatown, and the Hastings Street Corridor have provided their own systems of security.

For instance, a number of the banks located in Chinatown have contracted their own in-house security personnel, who are often posted at the main doorways. In a similar capacity, many of the bars and nightclubs found throughout the DTES, particularly in Gastown, employ bouncers who control entry and often handle disruptions that take place both inside and outside these establishments. Because these businesses commonly have line-ups that run outside and onto the public sidewalks, it is not uncommon to witness panhandlers asking those in line for spare change. In some instances, bouncers have told panhandlers to stop disrupting their patrons and have asked them to 'move on.'

Various forms of technology are also being used to deter crime and 'disorderly' conduct. Many of the businesses located in the DTES have stickers displayed on their doors and windows that indicate that the premises are being protected by a private security company and/or are equipped with an alarm system. Other common features include metal fencing and bars placed in front of stores and buildings, protective film over windows, electronic key cards and other high-tech locking devices, and the installation of closed-circuit television (CCTV) cameras.

CCTV cameras can be found in many of the banks and businesses in the Downtown Eastside. Some of these cameras are located inside the buildings and visually monitor, and sometimes record, those who enter. Other cameras, particularly those installed at some of the nightclubs, bars, and SRO hotels in the area, are aimed at the public streets and spaces just adjacent to these establishments, allowing those inside to watch what is taking place outside. Some might also claim that these cameras serve as a form of deterrence to those who might be involved in illegal or otherwise 'disruptive' activities.

While the use of video surveillance by private businesses has become relatively common in the Downtown Eastside, a proposal by the Vancouver Police Department to install CCTV cameras has been met with some resistance. The Vancouver Police Department has recently announced that it plans to make a formal request to the city's police board to fund the installation and operation of twenty-three surveillance cameras in the Downtown Eastside, Strathcona, Gastown, and Chinatown neighbourhoods.[101]

Similar to the programs in place in several cities in the United Kingdom, the United States, and eastern Canada, the CCTV cameras will monitor activity on the sidewalks, in alleyways, and in other public spaces.[102] These cameras will be operated from a remote site and have the capability of tracking an individual's movements over a particular area. A draft report prepared by the Vancouver Police Department states that CCTV is designed to have a 'deterrent effect of knowing that there is observation' and also to be used to alert police at an early stage to stop dangerous situations from escalating.[103] These cameras are said to provide operational assistance to police in evaluating a situation, safer convictions, savings in court time, and, most importantly, renewed public confidence.[104]

However, various groups have directly opposed the use of CCTV by police. The British Columbia Civil Liberties Association (BCCLA), for instance, has questioned the rationale for this proposal at a time when crime rates in Vancouver are actually on the decline, citing both the change in demographics (i.e., fewer males between the ages of sixteen and thirty) and the 'success' of certain community policing strategies at present in use as possible explanations for this decrease.[105] The BCCLA has also expressed concern over the potential infringement of personal privacy, and it questions whether the 'motivation for CCTV is the control of such legal but annoying activities such as panhandling.'[106]

The Carnegie Community Action Project (CCAP) has also made similar arguments against CCTV in the Downtown Eastside. Through an information booklet distributed in July 1999, CCAP has offered what it calls the 'first step in a community-initiated critical discussion about CCTV and its potential effects on the Downtown Eastside and the entire city.'[107] Again, one of the major arguments made is that the Vancouver Police Department has already been successful in responding to problems identified *by* the community by working *with* the community.[108] CCAP points to the success of the police in working with health and licensing authorities to eliminate bar-related knife incidents and to improve the conditions in some of the SRO hotels as evidence of this type of work.[109]

CCAP also appears to be quite critical of the motivation behind the installation of CCTV. Specifically, they see the possibility that these cameras will be used to displace some of the people in the DTES to serve the interests of those with the 'most social power,' in much the same way that private security has been used in Gastown and Chinatown.[110] The booklet states that,

> The use of CCTV ... provides no new housing or employment opportunities to the people who live in the neighbourhood. It offers no means of improving living conditions inside SRO hotels ... It focuses on the behaviour of those individuals who do not fit the expectations or mores of the camera monitors. In so doing, it bolsters those elements in the city who promote gentrification and displacement as the solutions to social problems in the Downtown Eastside by increasing pressure to expel individuals whose behaviour does not fit the model of the residential property-owner, the shopper or tourist.[111]

Clearly, the use of CCTV by the public police will continue to be the subject of debate within the context of a much larger conflict over space and land in Vancouver's Downtown Eastside.

Addressing Community Concerns

The general findings obtained in this study illustrate how the policing initiatives directed towards a particular community are a reflection of how the community is defined. In the Downtown Eastside, a number of subareas or neighbourhoods have been able to separate themselves and remain distinct from the larger community.

Although Gastown and Chinatown are located within the borders of the Downtown Eastside, they have both become quite separate and distinct areas. Their designation as historical districts and tourist attractions have made Gastown and Chinatown home to many local businesses that require the flow of 'desirable' traffic (i.e., tourists and shoppers) in order for these areas to prosper. This has led to policing initiatives that are aimed at improving the perceptions of safety, while keeping criminal or otherwise 'undesirable' activities out.

The initiatives undertaken by the Gastown and Chinese Community Policing Centres are clearly in keeping with these goals. The offices focus heavily on the notion of community ownership over territorial space and increasing physical presence to further establish a sense of who belongs in these neighbourhoods and who does not. The patrolling of the public streets in Gastown and Chinatown by citizen volunteers is one example of how this approach has been put into practice.

In addition, private security personnel hired by both the Gastown Business Improvement Society and the Vancouver Chinatown Merchants' Association are also seen as a means of maintaining the distinct identity of these areas. The cooperation and partnership that exist between these agencies illustrates how the protection of space has become a shared goal for both public and private police in Gastown and Chinatown.

In some respects, this approach to 'community policing' is consistent with the major principles of Crime Prevention through Environmental Design (CPTED) that are also being adopted by the Vancouver Police Department as a way of reducing the risk and actual incidents of crime, as well as of affecting 'the behaviour that calls for law enforcement.'[112]

According to the Vancouver Police Department website, there are five major principles of CPTED: (1) Territoriality (taking measures to make private, semi-private, and public space dynamic that will 'visually cue people that "this is my space"'); (2) Access Control (restricting entry into certain areas and locations); (3) Natural Surveillance (keeping an eye on a certain space to reduce the negative use of that space); (4) Image Maintenance (maintaining a good image to project responsibility and ownership); and (5) Environment (assessing land uses around certain development sites).

On one level, the design of both Gastown and Chinatown is in keeping with these principles. The visible street banners, the historic spatial landscape, and other physical features serve as visual cues that signal these areas as distinct 'territories'; this, in turn, establishes an image of these spaces as being specifically geared towards shoppers and tourists. At the same time, the presence of public, private, and volunteer policing patrols provides surveillance of these areas that creates a sense of responsibility and ownership and thus further reinforces their division from the rest of the DTES.

While the Downtown Eastside encompasses a very large geographic area that includes both Gastown and Chinatown, the notion of the 'Downtown Eastside community' often refers to the low-income and marginalized population of this area. The Downtown Eastside Neighbourhood Safety Office operates on this definition of community and regularly extends its services to those beyond the defined cartographic borders of the DTES. Although it cannot be properly located on a map of the DTES, this community is also commonly associated with the geographic location known as the Hastings Street Corridor.

Unlike Gastown and Chinatown, this stretch of Hastings Street between Gore Avenue and Cambie Street lacks the same type of business and development pressures that have translated into policing efforts directed towards the protection of a distinctive territory. At the same time, a containment policy adopted by the Vancouver Police Department has concentrated the various problems of the 'DTES community' in this corridor, away from Gastown and Chinatown.

One could argue that this process has served to reconstitute the Hastings Street Corridor as a space in the DTES that can be acted upon by the police and various social service agencies. The proposed plans for this area see the 'drug problem' as both a law enforcement and a public health issue. On one hand, police are to focus their efforts on drug dealing and trafficking, while those addicted to drugs are to be diverted into treatment facilities to be established right in this area.

In identifying the striking differences in policing initiatives, it is important to note how certain groups have gained the status of speaking 'on behalf' of a community. In Gastown and Chinatown, for instance, the local business associations have been able to stake their claim as a legitimate voice for their respective 'communities.' As a result, they have been able to establish these locations as predominantly historic districts and tourist attractions that require a substantial police presence (public, private, or voluntary) to increase perceptions of safety and deter criminal activity and general disorder that might harm the economic viability of these areas.

In the Hastings Street Corridor, community organizations such as the Carnegie Community Centre, the Carnegie Community Action Project, the Main and Hastings Community Development Society, and DERA are seen as advocates for the low-income and marginalized residents of the DTES. According to one City of Vancouver report, there are more than 200 social, health, education, and recreation services delivered by a number of agencies that focus solely on the Downtown Eastside, as well as those that are connected to organizations serving the city as a whole.[113]

Some of these organizations perceive many of the problems with respect to drug use and crime as the product of the conditions within this area and have lobbied for solutions, such as improved affordable housing and increased social services, that are directly aimed at the root causes. Other groups have been specifically involved in promoting harm-reduction programs for local drug users.

For instance, the Vancouver Area Network of Drug Users (VANDU), formed in 1998 and based primarily in the DTES, is a non-profit organization made of active and past hard drug users and supporting members who are 'dedicated to improving the quality of life for drug users, their families and our communities.'[114] While not condoning or promoting drug use, VANDU has continuously advocated for harm-reduction programs such as safe fixing sites and heroin maintenance, low-threshold methadone, and methadone and alternative treatment programs.[115] VANDU has been actively working with various levels of government and participating in public meetings, committees, boards, and forums and has also staged public demonstrations and awareness campaigns to push for large-scale system change.[116]

While these organizations do not always reflect the concerns of the entire community, they are seen as having a tremendous influence on how the area is governed. Thus, many of those interviewed were often quite sceptical about any group's claim to speak on behalf of a particular community and the motivation behind it. When asked if there was any conflict between the community and the business associations, one community worker noted,

We assume there is, but we don't know how widespread that is because the information from the business community gets filtered through the Business Associations. A lot of the time, they're crying 'the sky is falling' and we don't know how many businesses they represent because one of the problems with the Business Associations is that once they're established in the neighbourhood and you've got a business, you have to belong to it whether you want to or not ... So when they put out a press release that says, 'on behalf of the merchants' we don't know if they're talking about three businesses or four hundred and forty-three.

Conversely, a representative from the Vancouver Chinatown Merchants' Association often disregards what are perceived as 'community concerns' as a product of certain interest groups that would like to see a continuation of the status quo. In addressing the complaints regarding private security, he argues, 'I think a lot of the complaints you hear are exaggerated. There are vested interests among some groups to see security being lax in Chinatown. For example, a drug dealer would not be happy if a security officer is strolling constantly past him ... You have to be careful in differentiating who's doing the complaining and what's behind it.' He further suggests that those who are not involved in any sort of wrongdoing would have no reason to be concerned about the presence of private security personnel.

Communities in Conflict

While the community-based policing initiatives and the activities of private security may address the needs of a particular community, they sometimes conflict with the interests of the other communities in the DTES. As a result, the battles over 'ownership' of the Downtown Eastside have simply manifested at the community level. For some of the residents of the DTES, the presence of private security in Gastown and Chinatown has reduced the boundaries of communal space that is open to them. The fears of displacement and dispossession are thus being realized in a much different context. Conversely, for many of the merchants and property owners in Gastown and Chinatown, the social policies aimed at providing increased services are seen as having a negative impact on their economic sustainability.

The patrolling of public streets by private security personnel is perceived by some residents of the DTES as a way of excluding those deemed 'undesirable' from certain parts of this area. A number of the participants interviewed in this study have witnessed incidents where, without having the authority or legal grounds to do so, private security personnel in both Gastown and Chinatown have asked (and, in some instances, physically forced) certain 'undesirable' individuals (i.e., pan-handlers, the mentally ill, drug users, etc.) to leave the area.

Moreover, a number of interviewees said that they had heard, anec-dotally, that private security personnel had physically abused some indi-viduals. On this issue, according to one community worker,

> We have eyewitness reports by very reliable people of physical assaults. We have various anecdotal evidence of physical assault. We have photographs of a well-known guy in the neighbourhood who has mental health issues being literally led by the arms by a security guard, leading him to Water Street to get him out of Gastown. But the guy lives right here, and this is his neighbourhood, but he's being escorted away by this guy who has no authority to do it.

The community worker goes on to state that many residents have simply chosen to stay away from Gastown and Chinatown to avoid confronta-tion with and harassment from private security personnel.

However, the issue is not merely the presence of private security but the way in which they have exercised authority in what are perceived as being public places. For low-income residents, the ability to use public space is seen as a valuable commodity and a democratic right that is being taken away by those without any legal power to do so. As a community worker comments,

> If they're going to patrol stores and tell people they can't stay here, you can't sit on the ledge, you can't do all that inside somebody's store, or they catch you 'graffitiing' somebody's window and they want to hold you for the police, that's fine. If they want to patrol parkades, that's great. That's a good thing to do. Patrol parkades and make sure cars don't get broken into. But more often than not, they find their mandate is to walk up and down Gastown, seek people who look slovenly dressed or scruffy looking, and they take it upon themselves to tell them they don't belong on the street, get off the street ... They have no business telling people to get off the street. They have no business going up and down lanes telling people they can't stand here and smoke a cigarette ... As soon as they see someone that looks like they don't belong here, they come right out and say, 'You don't belong here and get moving.'

Many also question the underlying motivation behind private security, as most of these guards are seen as acting on behalf of the local BIA or Merchants' Association.

Some have also questioned the authority of private security personnel. One of the major concerns in Chinatown relates to the uniforms worn by security personnel, in that they closely resemble the uniforms of the public police, and thus violate the *Private Investigators and Security Agencies Act of British Columbia*. Other general concerns over private security personnel relate to their training (or lack thereof) in dealing with the public. Given both the nature of the area and the manner in which these guards operate, many of them are likely to confront people with mental illness or in a drug-induced state. Yet they have little training in dealing with such situations. As one interviewee asked, 'How long before somebody, a member of the public or the guards, gets badly hurt because the confrontation of that nature gets out of hand?'

Finally, concern was also raised about the accountability of private security personnel. As one community worker stated, 'My standpoint is that if they want to send people down there, have them conform to the same rules and regulations as police are, which is, have a number on your chest so when you are in violation of what you are supposed to be doing, you can report it and have people be able to come in and report them to their superiors.' Another interviewee compares the accountability of public and private police:

> There is no accountability. In the sense that, if you have an issue with the cops, there's somewhere to go. Whether it's the police complaints commission, et cetera. We can argue how effective that is, but there is a process. And, at the end of the day, police are accountable to City Hall ... And you can seek redress in a number of ways. With the guards, complaints have been lodged and what tends to happen is the lone guard gets cast away as some kind of 'bad apple' that gets kicked out of the barrel and that's that. And then somebody else is hired to fill his or her boots, as the case may be, so what do you do?

In order to address these concerns about the increasing presence of private security in public space, two community workers were able to obtain a small public education grant from the B.C. Legal Services Society. The grant was used to conduct preliminary research in this area and led to the publication of a pocket-sized leaflet (designed to be portable) that was distributed to residents of the DTES and that clearly explains their rights with respect to private security. In addition, public workshops were also held to raise awareness and educate residents about this issue. Despite this initiative, however, there is some doubt about whether individuals will stand up for their rights when confronted by security personnel.

When asked about the type of impact he thought this 'public awareness campaign' might have had, one interviewee responded as follows: 'I don't think it's had a huge impact at all. When you get down to the street level, with a couple of guys telling you to move, you can stand for your rights or you can say, "Whatever, I'll go around the corner and then come back when they've cleared off." It's one thing to know your rights. It's another to be in a position to insist on them ... How big of an issue do you make it?' Similar concerns were raised by the representative from the DTES Neighbourhood Safety Office with respect to the difficulty of making a formal complaint:

> It's very hard when you've got people, especially the victims, who are the least capable of pursuing something like that, to really pursue something formally. The last thing was a woman who had come in, and she's an addict, and she's in the sex trade, but she saw some poor guy from the Portland who has got some very obvious mental health problems beat up by a security guard ... Now, how do you get him to go forward with that? We've tried, it's just not possible.

Whether or not these information pamphlets have been useful, the fact that it was necessary to publish them highlights the concern over this issue felt by some people in the Downtown Eastside.

In contrast, business groups that claim to speak on behalf of the communities in Gastown and Chinatown have shown strong opposition to an increase in social services within the DTES. Evidence of this can be found in an appeal launched by the Community Alliance to the city's Board of Variance to stop the development of treatment facilities in the area, claiming that these services would be harmful to the neighbourhood.

This opposition appears to be directly linked to the use of communal space in the DTES and the impact that increasing social services is said to have on this area. The argument that is often made is that the creation of new services will simply attract more people who need them and, consequently, bring more problems into the DTES. The fear expressed by business groups in Gastown and Chinatown is that these problems will then enter their neighbourhoods and negatively impact their economic viability. Instead of an increase in social services, these groups would like to see more law enforcement.

These groups often perceive themselves as the victims of a containment policy that has allowed the continued ghettoization of the area. They often suggest that this type of situation would not exist in other parts of the city. A representative from the Vancouver Chinatown Merchants' Association has argued that,

> Our big concern or anger is, why is this type of situation only acceptable down here? If there were drug dealers standing on the corner of Forty-first and Yew, there would be blood on the streets. So why is it openly accepted here and not anywhere else?
>
> The city government is always proud to say that they're putting so much in Chinatown's physical structure. And they're right. They've done a lot. For example, the Millennium Gate is going to cost a million dollars. But the question is, 'What good is it if nobody dares to come down here?' Exactly where they put the Millennium Gate will be the new methadone clinic.

Conclusion

This chapter has identified how community-based approaches to policing are inextricably linked to definitions of space and citizenship. The process of governing 'by community' that has been embraced over the last forty years has clearly required a reconceptualization of how power is exercised. As we have seen, the mapping of communities by city planners and the designation of certain spaces become as integral to policing as the policing initiatives themselves.

The discussion presented in this chapter does not seek to deny the complexity of the social, political, and economic environment that currently exists within the Downtown Eastside. Instead, my general findings are intended to illustrate the difficulty of applying community-based initiatives in highly diverse areas such as the Downtown Eastside, where any claim to speak 'on behalf' of a community is viewed as a source of political power. It is true that the community initiatives directed towards this section of the city have addressed the need for participation and consultation by bringing members of this community together. However, the fact that certain 'subareas' or 'neighbourhoods' have actively influenced how they are governed and have assumed a self-governing function by separating themselves from the rest of the area and the impact that this has had on the larger political process have not been fully addressed.

The division of the Downtown Eastside into separate and diverse subcommunities has led to differing policing initiatives that, at times, have reinforced the existing conflicts over land and the use of space. This is perhaps most evident in the different perceptions that are held regarding the patrolling of public streets by private security personnel. On the one hand, some members of the larger Downtown Eastside community are quite pleased with the increasing presence of private security personnel and view them as an additional form of deterrence that can enhance feelings of safety and security within this area.

Others, however, are quite critical of these companies, claiming that they unfairly remove individuals deemed 'undesirable' from certain sections of the Downtown Eastside, or deny them entry, without any legal authority to do so. Charges of brutality and physical abuse by private security personnel were also raised, but could not be substantiated in this study. We find it rather unfortunate that the two private security companies in question chose not to participate in this study and thus could not respond to these claims. Indeed, we clearly recognize that this is an important component that was not included and that must be examined in any future research that may be done on this topic.

Nevertheless, there appears to be general agreement among those in the DTES that changes are needed to improve conditions in this area. Yet even when goals are shared by members of the different subcommunities, it seems rather unlikely that the processes of mediation and facilitation will be successful in obtaining consensus and agreement over how these goals are to be achieved when the interests of the 'community players' are so diametrically opposed to each other. Future public policies directed towards this 'community' must seek to fully acknowledge this dilemma.

Notes

1 City of Vancouver, 'The Vancouver Agreement: Schedule A' (2000) 1.

2 Ibid., at 5.

3 Ibid.

4 Nick Blomley and Jeff Sommers, 'Mapping Urban Space: Governmentality and Cartographic Struggles in Inner City Vancouver,' in Russell Smandych, ed., *Governable Places: Readings on Governmentality and Crime Control* (Aldershot: Ashgate, 1999) 286.

5 Ibid., at 263.

6 Nikolas Rose, 'The Death of the Social? Re-figuring the Territory of Government' (1996) 22:3 Economy and Society 283.

7   City of Vancouver, 'Downtown Eastside Community Revitalization Program – Interim Report' (24 January 2000) Administrative Report to Vancouver City Council, online: http://www.city.vancouver.bc.ca/ctyclerk/cclerk/000201/a7.htm, accessed 21 August 2001.
8   Ibid.
9   Ibid.
10 City of Vancouver, 'Building a Sustainable Future Together: Part of the Downtown Eastside Community Revitalization Program' (1998) online: http://www.city.vancouver.bc.ca/commsvcs/planning/dtes/sustain.htm, accessed 25 August 2001.
11 City of Vancouver, 'Downtown Eastside Revitalization Program – Community History' (2001), online: http://www.city.vancouver.bc.ca/msvcs/planning/dtes/communityprofile.htm, accessed 11 April 2001.
12 Ibid.
13 Blomley and Sommers, *supra* note 4.
14 Ibid., at 269.
15 Ibid., at 270.
16 City of Vancouver, *supra* note 7.
17 'A Tragic Timeline' *Vancouver Sun* (20 Nov 2000), online: http:www.vancouversun.com/fix/02_02.htm, accessed 6 June 2001.
18 Blomley and Sommers, *supra* note 4 at 272.
19 Ibid., at 273–4.
20 Nick Blomley, 'Property, Pluralism and the Gentrification Frontier' (1997) 12:2 Canadian Journal of Law and Society 187 at 205.
21 Nicholas Blomley, 'Landscapes of Property' (1998) 32:3 Law and Society Review 567.
22 Blomley and Sommers, *supra* note 4 at 269.
23 City of Vancouver, *2000 Downtown Eastside Monitoring Report* (Vancouver: Planning Department, 2000) 11.
24 Ibid., at 21.
25 Blomley, *supra* note 20 at 198.
26 Ibid., at 198.
27 Ibid., at 205.
28 Ibid.
29 Blomley and Sommers, *supra* note 4 at 269.
30 Ibid., at 270.
31 Frances Bula, 'This Is an International Crisis' *Vancouver Sun* (21 November 2000), online: http://www.vancouversun.com/fix/03–01.html.
32 Ibid.
33 Ibid.
34 According to 1996 census data, the Downtown Eastside accounted for only

3.2 per cent (16,275 of 515,400) of the entire population of the City of Vancouver.

35 City of Vancouver, *supra* note 23 at 26.
36 Ibid., at 26.
37 Ibid., at 27.
38 Ian Mulgrew, 'Drugs: Symptom or Cause?' *Vancouver Sun* (20 November 2000), online: http://www.vancouversun.com/fix/02_01.html, accessed 11 June 2001.
39 Ibid.
40 City of Vancouver, *supra* note 7.
41 City of Vancouver, 'Vancouver Agreement: Implementing a Four Pillar Approach' (2000), online: http://www.city.vancouver.bc.ca/commsvcs/planning/dtes/fourpillars.htm, accessed 11 April 2001.
42 Mulgrew, *supra* note 38.
43 Ibid.
44 Blomley and Sommers, *supra* note 4 at 261–2.
45 Ibid., at 275.
46 Ibid., at 261.
47 Ibid., at 261.
48 Ibid., at 281.
49 Ibid., at 271.
50 Ibid., at 271.
51 Ibid., at 275.
52 Ibid., at 282.
53 Ibid., at 265.
54 City of Vancouver, 'Downtown Eastside Revitalization Program – DTES Neighbourhoods' (2000), online: www.city.vancouver.bc.ca/commsvcs/planning/dtes/neighbourhoods.htm, accessed 4 April 2001.
55 Blomley and Sommers, *supra* note 4 at 273.
56 BIABC, 'What Is a Business Improvement Area?' (information leaflet; copy with author).
57 Blomley and Sommers, *supra* note 4 at 273.
58 City of Vancouver, *supra* note 23 at 11.
59 Blomley and Sommers, *supra* note 4 at 278.
60 Ibid., at 279.
61 Ibid., at 278–9.
62 Robson Street Business Association, the Downtown Vancouver Business Improvement Association, the Gastown Business Improvement Society, and the Safe City Solutions Task Force, 'Real Change. Not Spare Change' (pamphlet; copy with author).
63 Ibid., emphasis in original.

64 Ibid.
65 Gary Greer, 'Public Police and Private Security: Substitutes or Comple-
   ments?' (MBA thesis, Simon Fraser University, 1998).
66 Ibid., at 72.
67 Industrial Wood and Allied Workers of Canada, 'Company Information'
   (2001), online: http://www.iwa.ca/securityguard/companyinfo.htm,
   accessed 26 August 2001.
68 Securiguard, 'Securiguard Home Page' (2001), online: http://www
   .securiguard.com, accessed 26 August 2001.
69 Ibid.
70 Ibid.
71 Ibid.
72 Ibid.
73 Ibid.
74 Ibid. emphasis in original.
75 Ibid.
76 Ibid.
77 Vancouver Police Department, 'Community Services Section: Citizens'
   Crime Watch' (2001), online: http://www.city.vancouver.bc.ca/police/
   opServDiv/comServ/ccw/ccw2.html, accessed 21 August 2001.
78 Ibid.
79 Ibid.
80 Ibid.
81 Ibid.
82 City of Vancouver, *supra* note 7.
83 Ibid.
84 Greer, *supra* note 65 at 65.
85 City of Vancouver, *supra* note 7.
86 Ibid.
87 City of Vancouver, 'Vancouver Agreement Funds Construction of the
   Chinatown Millennium Gate' (news release, 17 February 2001; copy with
   author).
88 Ibid.
89 Ibid.
90 Ibid.
91 Greer, *supra* note 65 at 65.
92 Greer, *supra* note 65 at 66.
93 City of Vancouver, 'Vancouver Police Department Adds Two More Officers
   to Chinatown Community Policing Centre' (news release, 21 February 2001;
   copy with author).

94 Blomley, *supra* note 21.

95 City of Vancouver, *supra* note 23 at 19.

96 City of Vancouver, *supra* note 23 at 38.

97 City of Vancouver, 'Downtown Eastside Revitalization Program' (2000), online: http//:www.city.vancouver.bc.ca/commsvcs/planning/dtes/safety.htm, accessed 21 August 2001.

98 City of Vancouver, 'Backgrounder: Vancouver Agreement Launches Four Pillar Approach for DTES Revitalization' (2000) (First Focus Vancouver Agreement news release; copy with author).

99 Ibid.

100 Ibid.

101 Robert Matas, 'Privacy versus Safety on Vancouver Streets' *Globe and Mail* (1 August 2001) A6.

102 British Columbia Civil Liberties Association, position paper, 'Video Surveillance in Public Places' (1999), online: http://www.bccla.org/positions/privacy/99videosurveillance.html, accessed 24 August 2001.

103 Ibid.

104 Ibid.

105 Ibid.

106 Ibid.

107 Carnegie Community Action Project (CCAP), 'Closed Circuit Television Surveillance of Public Space in Vancouver' (1999) (information handout; copy with author).

108 Ibid.

109 Ibid.

110 Ibid.

111 Ibid., at 6–7.

112 Vancouver Police Department, 'Crime Prevention through Environmental Design (CPTED)' (2001), online: http://www.city.vancouver.bc.ca/police/opServDiv/comServ/cpted.html, accessed 21 August 2001.

113 City of Vancouver, 'Building a Sustainable Future Together: Part of the Downtown Eastside Community Revitalization Program' (1998), online: http://www.city.vanouver.bc.ca/commsvcs/planning/dtes/sustain.htm, accessed 25 August 2001.

114 Vancouver Area Network of Drug Users (VANDU), 'What the Heck Is VANDU?' (2000) online: http://www.vaudu.org, accessed 23 September 2001.

115 Ibid.

116 Ibid.

3 Policing Fantasy City

LAURA J. HUEY, RICHARD V. ERICSON,
AND KEVIN D. HAGGERTY

In his book *Fantasy City*, John Hannigan[1] provides a detailed analysis of
the growth of spaces of consumption within postindustrial cities. These
spaces fuel consumption through linking commodities and services to
entertainment. Hannigan terms these spaces 'fantasy cities,' or 'urban
entertainment destinations.' He points to the success of Disney as being
pivotal in the development and proliferation of other sites that similarly
mix elements of the fantastic – in the form of simulated spaces and
'consumable experiences'[2] – with retail goods and services. Examples of
this phenomenon abound. There is South Korea's Kyongju World Tradition Folk Village, Hong Kong's Ocean Park, or Canal City, a $1.4 billion
urban entertainment district in Japan.[3] There is even a Tokyo Disneyland
and a Euro-Disney. However, aside from Disney's parks, which mix technology, entertainment, and retail to great financial success, no other
place would seem to represent this form of postmodern development
as well as Las Vegas. With such features as artificial lagoons, 'ancient'
Roman shopping arcades, Venetian gondoliers, and a Statue of Liberty,
Las Vegas planners utilize fashionably fake themed attractions as a means
of luring spenders to support a billion-dollar-a-year casino and tourism
industry.[4]

The development and proliferation of the fantasy city concept is
symptomatic of larger changes occurring in society. These changes reflect the rise of a new type of consumerism. Although, as Slater[5] con-
tends, consumerism is not of recent origin, clearly there is something
different currently taking place. In discussing this difference, Slater[6]
states that consumption is no longer based primarily on mass-produced
standardized goods but rather on the 'specialized production of goods
more specifically tailored for and targeted on precise consumer groups

who are defined by lifestyles rather than by broad demographic variables like class, gender or age.'[7] Mirroring the larger market-place, fantasy city and its constituent parts offer customized, or 'canned,' experiences for individuals within particular lifestyle groups. And, just as the larger market-place is becoming increasingly fragmented because of the desire of advertisers to target preselected groups of consumers,[8] so fantasy city is itself becoming increasingly fractured through attempts at drawing particular market niches.

The new consumer society is not just about dividing up populations into market segments, it is also about fundamental changes in social relationships. According to Lasch[9] mass consumption 'tend[s] to discourage initiative and self-reliance and to promote dependence, passivity, and a spectatorial state of mind both at work and at play.' This can be evidenced in how we relate to brand logos. As Lasn[10] explains, for many of us the brand has displaced other traditional forms of culture: 'Our stories, once passed from one generation to the next by parents, neighbors and teachers, are now told by distant corporations with "something to sell as well as to tell."'

The new consumerism is also about the creation and exploitation of individual crises in relation to questions of identity.[11] For example, the teen *angst* experienced during the search for identity becomes fodder for commercials that, by offering not only *a* solution to the question 'Who am I?' but a multiplicity of solutions, intensify and exacerbate the anxiety surrounding this search. These solutions are tied to brands: 'Brand X is not a product but a way of life, an attitude, a set of values, a look, an idea.'[12]

As both Klein[13] and Lasn[14] note, another feature of the new consumer society is that it is not only the consumer who is consuming; the purveyors of a variety of goods and services are also consuming – consuming culture. This consumption, which Klein[15] describes as a search for 'coolness' or 'hip-ness,' leads to the appropriation of those images that are popular or are associated with particular qualities or characteristics that we admire, and their use to sell a variety of items that are not intrinsically 'hip.'

Hannigan[16] and others[17] have identified a new urban reality that is connected not only to new forms of postindustrial consumption, but also to changing social patterns driven by urban redevelopment. The rise of the new urban environment as a postmodern hyper-reality[18] can be traced to attempts by urban areas to compete with suburban malls for retail business through one of two strategies: the development of unique shopping experiences such as public markets;[19] and the importation of many of the aspects of the ultimate in simulated postmodern environments – the suburban mall. The effect of the latter has been, as Goldberger[20] notes, 'a kind of blurring of traditional differences between the city and suburb.' The effect of the former has been the creation of sites where cultural themes that had been successful elsewhere have been appropriated and duplicated.[21] Still other urban redevelopment projects simply exploit historical neighbourhood associations.[22] In some cases, as occurred with Vancouver's Gastown, historical associations are 'sanitized.' In others – for example, Las Vegas – cultural and historical associations are manufactured outright.[23]

The importation of themed 'experiences,' in combination with aspects of the suburban mall, to urban streets is paradoxical. The paradox is that such sites, and the historical or cultural associations they attempt to evoke, are contrived. Indeed, they stand as exemplars of Baudrillard's[24] concept of 'simulacra,' serialized copies of objects that never existed. And yet, according to retail consultant Ian Thomas, retailers and consumers see street shopping as offering a 'more real' experience.[25]

The move from traditional suburban malls to 'Main Street' shopping has resulted in the development of a very lucrative trend[26]. This trend has been brought about as a result of efforts by retailers to capitalize on 'practical lessons [learned] in the psychology of commerce.'[27] Retailers consciously draw on our reaction to elements in the environment and our unconscious association of goods with social interaction and status hierarchies. For example, part of the success of urban shopping, according to retailer Thomas, lies in the fact that '[p]eople are social animals and do want to go out, and shopping is seen to be very much a mainstream activity for socializing.'[28] Retailers capitalize on this knowledge by sponsoring events that both act as an initial draw for consumers and simultaneously reinforce the idea that their private or quasi-private retail zone is a public space.

Historically, questions involving whether granite benches will encourage unwanted users, or whether trees and planters will detract from storefronts, have not been a significant concern of urban planners. This is because planners and architects have tended 'to see streets and sidewalks strictly as a civic realm' – a realm in which traditional conceptions of sociability have been promoted.[29] However, the new urban reality is increasingly geared towards a new mode of sociability, one that is intrinsically linked to consumption and consumption-oriented pastimes.

And yet, the inner city remains a typically chaotic social space encompassing dynamic systems as well as static structures.[30] Goldberger[31] refers to this chaos as 'disorganization,' and suggests that it is this characteristic that contributes directly to the unique vibrancy of the urban landscape. However, as Ley[32] points out, disorganization is also associated, both in urban sociology and in the popular imagination, with social pathology: poverty, delinquency, mental illness, crime, family breakdown, and addiction. That is, '[t]he white middle-class imagination, absent from any first-hand knowledge of inner-city conditions, magnifies the perceived threat through a demonological lens.'[33] Thus, in order for urban entertainment destinations to succeed financially, there is a strong incentive placed on business and government interests to dispel fears associated with urban spaces.

One means of dispelling fears associated with urban life is careful monitoring and control of space. Increasingly, signs of urban crime and decay are being managed through environmental design.[34] Cities such as Washington, New York, and San Francisco address urban problems by utilizing ideas associated with Wilson and Kelling's[35] 'broken windows' theory. This theory proposes that environmental cues signalling neglect and decay, such as graffiti, boarded windows, and broken lights, are criminogenic. This is because these physical cues not only contribute to perceptions of the relative risk of criminal victimization in an area but also advertise to would-be criminals that this is an area with few social controls. Wilson and Kelling argue that by addressing the cues that contribute to these perceptions, crime in an area can be reduced. The reduction occurs as the space becomes repopulated by non-offenders (increasing 'natural' surveillance), and the deterrent effect produced in potential offenders who interpret well-kept neighbourhoods as being subject to forms of social control. Kelling and Coles[36] also approvingly note programs in the United States where security guards are deployed by business interests to perform public beat patrol and to routinely ask the homeless to 'move along.' Private security is portrayed as an obvious extension of the 'broken windows' theory – using policing as a means of increasing perceptions of safety while regulating the behaviour of the 'disorderly.'

In short, the main premise behind these and similar ideas[37] is that we can achieve 'the good' – meaning a vision of the good life in public space – if we can control our physical environments and behaviour that does not conform to normative values associated with 'etiquette,' 'decorum,' or 'civility.' Of course, what such proponents fail to address adequately is that their conception of what constitutes 'the good' is neither universal nor devoid of class-rootedness. Indeed, what they are advocating is a means by which traditional, middle-class values, which are increasingly becoming 'consumer-class' values, can be privileged in public space. Often these values are imposed in neighbourhoods that have been traditionally occupied by those who hold different values.

There are many other criticisms that can be, and have been, directed at this theory and programs derived from it. For example, as Davis,[38] Harcourt,[39] and Lianos and Douglas[40] note, broken windows–style policing explicitly targets the most disadvantaged in society, with the result that the marginalized are pushed even farther to the periphery. This is because, as Lianos and Douglas[41] point out, the process of '"rehabilitating" inner city spaces,' in order to permit groups to 'reclaim space as managed territory where safety is guaranteed,' involves 'erasing the *signs* of peripheral excluded cultures' (italics added). Another criticism is that broken windows policing deals with surface issues only. The underlying causes of crime, those embedded deeply in our social structures, are not addressed, and therefore crime and disorder can never truly be affected by such measures alone.[42] Yet another criticism is that the theory creates categories of 'order' and 'disorder' that collapse upon close scrutiny. As Harcourt[43] notes, the fixation with a meaning of order that focuses narrowly on aesthetics, cleanliness, and sobriety minimizes other offences that may have significant personal and economic impacts and ignores the fact that 'disorder' crimes are often committed by those of middle or upper-class standing.[44] The theory thus recasts traditional class-based divisions by creating a model purporting to show how crime in neighbourhoods is generated and regenerated almost exclusively by those of the lower class – the squeegee workers, the panhandlers, and so on.

As a policing philosophy, the ideas found in the broken windows theory are clearly gaining ground among North American police departments. This is undoubtedly because many of its promises – decreased police commitment to order maintenance issues through increased community involvement – are similar to those offered by the community policing model that was enthusiastically adopted by departments across North America in the 1980s and 1990s. Saunders,[45] in a study of community policing in Boston, looked at the application of this model in the field. In particular, he examined the gap between the promise of community policing and the actual practice. He found that the Boston program failed to address even the most basic criticisms offered of the department. The police were no more accountable to the public than previously, nor was policing made more equitable. Similarly, mechanisms for solving community problems or for determining local needs were not implemented. This led Saunders to conclude that critiques of community policing that label it as a 'triumph of style over substance' are well founded because 'community policing is primarily concerned with producing certain appearances that police hope will win back the political support of selected communities.'[46] As will become apparent later on, this too is a criticism that can be directed at broken windows policing, with its near-exclusive focus on aesthetic concerns.

Loader[47] similarly views community policing as largely rhetorical, but suggests that it is part of the rhetoric of consumerism. There is 'a discursive re-presentation of the police as deliverers of a professional service (rather than a force) and of "the public" as "consumers" of that service.'[48] That police agencies should embrace consumer rhetoric is seen to be paradoxical in that the promotion of the police as service providers is occurring at the same time that policing agencies are attempting to reduce the number of public services that they perform and to shift some of the responsibility for crime prevention back onto the citizenry.[49]

Garland[50] suggests that the apparent willingness of public agencies to divest themselves of some of the responsibilities that they formerly included within their mandates may be seen as the result of a recognition of the capacity limits of the state and its systems. He terms this process a 'responsibilization strategy' and defines it as 'involv[ing] the central government seeking to act upon crime not in a direct fashion through state agencies (police, courts, prisons, social work, etc.) but instead by acting indirectly, seeking to activate action on the part of non-state agencies and organizations.'[51] Garland[52] cites several means by which the state encourages citizen participation in crime prevention, but perhaps what is singularly motivating for citizens is an underlying 'sense of the failure of criminal justice agencies, and a more limited sense of the state's powers to regulate conduct and prohibit deviance.' On a local level, this process is spurred by municipal councils that are unwilling, or unable, to draw from public funds in order to finance increased policing services. While citizens may decry the policing services they receive, they often seem strangely unwilling to pay for enhanced services or new programs. Knowing this, many local governments see private security as a cheaper alternative.[53]

Clearly, there has been a growth in non-public policing and crime prevention measures. Spitzer and Scull[54] note the phenomenal growth of private security, which they suggest results from the overwhelming demands placed upon the police to meet citizen needs, demands that leave only a small portion of police resources available for responding to what are perceived to be low-level threats to property. Others, notably Shearing and Stenning,[55] attribute the rise of private security to the emergence of mass property, which includes both private and quasi-public spaces such as shopping malls and market sites. They suggest that reliance on private security by the private sector occurs for two reasons: 'public police [have] traditionally been confined to publicly owned property ... [and] those who own and control mass private property have commonly preferred to retain and exercise their traditional right to preserve order on their own property and to maintain control over the policing of it.'[56] Regardless, the use of private security is seen to be, to some extent, predicated on the belief that the public police have failed to sufficiently meet the needs of citizens with means to employ their own security.

Loader[57] sees the increasing commodification of policing services as resulting in a fragmentation of public policing, with a possibility of serious impairment to the public police mandate. As will become evident during the examination of aspects of private-public policing programs in the sites studied here, Stenson[58] appears to be closer to the mark when he suggests that the public police will resist a reduction of their role through increased alliances with private sector groups, alliances that may have the effect of instituting dual- or triple-tiered levels of policing based on the economic means of consumers of policing services.

In *Fantasy City*, one of Hannigan's[59] principal theses is that theme parks and entertainment sites are directly linked to the middle classes' historical pursuit of entertainment in the form of 'riskless risk': '[t]he "riskless risk" so evident in the themed environments of Fantasy City is part of a wider trend in which foreign cultures and domestic subcultures are appropriated, disemboweled and then marketed as safe, sanitized versions of the original.' As Hannigan[60] notes of the consumers of experience who seek spaces that have been replicated and rendered 'safer,' '[f]ew, if any, among the clientele for these attractions have the desire to embrace the actual risks posed by inner-city life, any more than Disney World patrons want to encounter the dangers of a genuine jungle cruise with its disease-bearing mosquitoes and monsoon floods.' Unfortunately, what is missing from Hannigan's account is a more thorough examination of strategies employed by site operators to provide 'safety,' or the perception of safety, for consumers.

Others, notably Shearing and Stenning,[61] Parenti,[62] and Davis[63] provide some information on the means by which urban and other entertainment spaces are rendered 'safer' for patrons. Shearing and Stenning[64] have looked at the use of private forms of discipline in Disney World and demonstrated the high degree of control that Disney World exerts over its patrons in order to regulate behaviour, thus reducing opportunities for 'disorder.' These forms range from attractive physical barriers and signs that control access to areas, to ever-present employees who guide patrons, correcting them when they behave contrary to Disney's rules. However, because these instruments of discipline also serve aesthetic, entertainment, and other functions, control is both pervasive and largely undetected by patrons. As Shearing and Stenning[65] note, 'a critical consequence of this process of embedding control in other structures is that control becomes consensual.'

What separates Disney's parks from other forms of fantasy city, and thus permits this high degree of control tied to pleasure, is that Disneyland and Disney World are privately owned, self-contained pieces of property outside of urban centres. The question of how to create order, and thus limit disorder, becomes significantly more problematic when the site of a fantasy space is within an urban centre. Owners of mass private property can erect barriers to exclude undesirables, instal video surveillance anywhere on their site to monitor rule breaking, and use the threat of expulsion to gain compliance. While businesses may use some of these measures within the confines of their private property, they usually have limited control over the public spaces that abut their business. One solution, as Parenti[66] discusses in relation to New York's redevelopment of Times Square, is privately sponsored policing of public space.

Urban policing is being transformed in the context of downtown retail development as a result of private investment in policing of public space. Some essayists have touched upon this new form of policing;[67] however, no one has linked the literatures of consumer culture, policing, and urban geography in order to explore the nature of 'urban entertainment destination' (UED) policing, its genesis, and its influence on the urban landscape. This is an important omission that is remedied here.

The link among these literatures is explored through an interconnecting thread: the cultural importance of signs. While the importance of signification is readily apparent in relation to consumerism, particularly with respect to branding and status consumption, the uses and meanings of signs are also of growing interest to police practitioners and urban planners. The adoption of Wilson and Kelling's[68] 'broken windows' theory by police and retail groups offers a prime example. The paramount concern of 'broken windows' is signification – the regulation of signs of disorder. Symbols and meanings are also becoming a focus in the work of urban planners who seek to maximize the economic potential of a space by increasing aesthetic appeal while simultaneously reducing signs of urban blight that have come to mean crime and danger in the popular imagination. The increased importance of signs – particularly with respect to the relationship between popular aesthetic sensibilities, as defined by consumer culture, and crime prevention practices – will be analysed. A simultaneous critique of both the 'broken windows' theory and modern consumer culture is offered, and the argument is advanced that the greatest effect of our culture's preoccupation with 'signs,' 'symbols,' and marketable 'identities' is to intensify class-based divisions within urban neighbourhoods. Ultimately, this leads to fractured rather than stable and cohesive communities.

The concept of fantasy city is central to this thesis. Whereas previous work has detailed aspects of the relationship between policing and modern consumer culture by exploring the ways in which the street has borrowed from the technology of the mall in order to move along the 'riff-raff,'[69] what we describe here is the influence of urban entertainment destinations – a street-level marketing phenomenon – on urban policing. We argue that the formation of such sites and their success have led to the development of certain forms of image-oriented policing. Fantasy city is not simply another marketing strategy employed as an alternative to the mall; it is an economic and cultural phenomenon that is being replicated across North America.[70]

We also explore the relationship between the 'broken windows' theory and retail economics. While there have been several studies of 'broken windows' policing, some utilizing crime trend data,[71] others employing an ethnographic approach (notably Wilson and Kelling's[72] original study), there has remained a need for more fine-grained empirical research in this area. In particular, what has been lacking to date is research and analysis of how business improvement associations (BIAs), in cooperation with local government and public police, facilitate these new forms of policing based on 'broken windows' concepts. Research is seen as an especially critical task because of the continuing growth of BIA-sponsored urban entertainment destinations. This gap in research is addressed here through an empirical study of two neighbourhoods within the city of Vancouver. The patterns revealed in these contexts are generalizable, since many of the programs and practices in Vancouver imitate those found in other North American, Asian, and European cities.

In the following sections, details are provided on the research setting and the methodology used. The urban spaces studied, and the governance of those spaces by BIAs, are also described. Then various forms of public and private policing that occur within the study areas are analysed. Following this, levels of community support for and resistance to the practices identified are assessed. There is also an analysis of wider trends in consumer market segmentation and the role that these trends play in determining policing practices. Then three propositions are advanced. First, that a major concern of urban entertainment destination operators is control of the image that their spaces project. Second, that much of the policing occurring in Vancouver's urban entertainment destinations is not a response to actual crime but is more properly thought of as related to this task of image management. Third, that the preoccupation of retailers and consumers with image is linked to market forces and the increasingly consumption-oriented nature of our culture. Finally, the main findings of this study are summarized.

Methodology

Forty-eight interviews with sixty subjects were conducted over several months.[73] Some subjects were first identified as a result of a preliminary study of textual materials. Others were identified through the use of snowball sampling, or were approached in public areas. Subjects included members of community groups (6), public police personnel (9), community residents (2), outreach workers (2), private security guards or security representatives (11), business owners, managers, and representatives (6), street youth (7), adult panhandlers (3), local area workers (2), street vendors (2), municipal personnel (2), and tourists (8). Although those interviewed have been identified as belonging to a particular group, many fall within multiple categories. For example, individuals identified here as street youth may also have spoken about their experiences as panhandlers or as area residents. This is also true of some business owners/managers, area workers, and community group members who are also local residents. In those situations where a role shift occurred during an interview, and the content of the interview is included here, the individual is identified as belonging to the group he or she was identifying with at that time.

The interview format was open-focused;[74] principally, because the nature of the questions necessarily changed from participant to participant in order to capture the beliefs, thoughts, and experiences of differently situated subjects more fully. Open-focused interviews allowed discussions to flow in a conversation-like manner. This fluidity was especially important for those subjects who may have been experiencing some anxiety during the interview. It also allowed flexibility in asking questions.

All interviews were taped with the subject's consent. All subjects were guaranteed confidentiality. Two means were selected to facilitate this. First, identifying information was omitted during the transcription process or masked. Second, where quoted, subjects are identified as belonging to one of the generic categories, or are listed as an unnamed 'subject,' 'respondent,' or 'individual.' Some exceptions have been made where extra description does not compromise the identity of the subject.

Primary and secondary documents were gathered and analysed in order to provide an understanding of some aspects of the political, economic, and geographical nature of the city's downtown environs. Document sources varied and included both hard-copy text and web-based materials.

Hard-copy texts included the following: news articles from Canadian newspapers and magazines; materials from the city archives and from community groups; BIA monthly newsletters and annual reports; provincial legislation and city by-laws; and city Community Monitoring reports. Some materials were obtained from government bodies through Freedom of Information requests. This process included documents relating to the Carrall Street deployment centre and the Crime Alert Pager program from the Police Department, and information on private security from the Attorney General's Office.

Web-based information was obtained from various BIA associations, the Police Department, and the city online archives. Non-text–based supplementary sources include the documentary 'Private Security, Public Places.'[75]

An Introduction to BIAs

Provincial and state legislation allows municipalities to create non-profit business improvement associations, organizations with the mandate of improving a designated area.[76] New York, Ottawa, Washington, D.C., and Philadelphia provide examples of cities that have such organizations.

In Vancouver, sections 233 of the *Municipal Act*[77] and 456 of the *Vancouver Charter*[78] give City Council the authority to create a BIA and to grant recoverable start-up costs to potential BIAs.[79] Designation of an area as a business improvement district (BID) is reviewable upon terms set by Council.[80] Once Council's approval has been received, the BIA can develop and implement programs that improve the area.[81] Such programs include '[t]ree planting, street furniture, improved parking, flower boxes and street banners.'[82] The philosophy of the BIA movement is that '[t]he cumulative effect of BIA activities will attract and maintain customers, clients, and shoppers to the commercial area as well as attracting new business to the community.'[83]

The costs of maintaining business improvements are generally met through the imposition of a special levy that is assessed by local government.[84] In Vancouver, the city's policy is to assess property owners proportionate to their share of the total taxable value of their property within the BIA boundaries.[85] However, an amendment in 1998 permits Council to levy 'a rate based on any factor determined by the Council,' and to levy rates differently 'for different classes of business.'[86]

BIA annual budgets must be submitted to Council for approval each year, following BIA membership approval at a general meeting.[87] Each April, Vancouver City Council advances money to the BIAs for operating costs.[88] The money is subsequently recovered at the time that annual property taxes are paid.

The selected research sites – Gastown and Granville Mall – are each designated BIDs. The Gastown Business Improvement Society (GBIS) operates within Gastown, and the Downtown Vancouver Business Improvement Association (DVBIA) is responsible for a significant portion of the downtown core.

Downtown Vancouver Business Improvement Association

The DVBIA was created by City Council in 1990. It encompasses approximately ninety blocks of the city's core. These blocks include more than 8,000 businesses comprising a mix of office, retail, and entertainment properties; this makes the DVBIA one of the largest business improvement districts in Canada.[89]

The organization is made up of staff positions, an elected board, and volunteer committees run by tenants and property owners. Staff positions include Executive Director, Director of Marketing and Communications, Director of Crime Prevention Services, Administrative

Assistant, and Office Assistant.[90] There are five volunteer committees: Entertainment/Retail; Maintenance and Security; Marketing and Communications; Business Community Interests (formerly Office Space Promotion); and Transportation and Parking.[91]

Through a series of partnerships with private agencies and the city, the DVBIA also indirectly employs other personnel such as the Downtown Clean Team – a group of young people hired to remove graffiti, posters, stickers, and other litter and debris from the city's streets.[92] Security services are contracted to agencies that operate under the direction of the director of Crime Prevention Services.[93] The director oversees a variety of programs including Citizens' Foot Patrol, Safety Fairs, and Security Audits, organizes crime prevention lectures for member businesses, and serves as a liaison to the public police.[94]

The DVBIA's budget for 2000–2001 was $1.8 million[95] which represents a significant increase from the $705,000 budgeted the year before.[96] According to the city,[97] projected expenditures for the year 2000–2001 were estimated as follows:

Entertainment and Retail Development	$80,079
Marketing, Promotion, and Access	$268,917
Maintenance and Security	$1,077,937
Research and Communications	$137,000
Office Expenses and Administrative Costs	$205,184
Contingency	$48,883

According to the DVBIA,[98] $835,000 of the increase in operating expenses over the previous year is due to the implementation of two new security programs: the Downtown Ambassadors and the Loss Prevention Officers.

Gastown Business Improvement Society

As early as 1979, Gastown redevelopers and local businesses were lobbying both the city and the province for the right to create an organization that would meet needs ranging from daily area maintenance to long-range planning and programming.[99] They were unsuccessful until 1989, when the Gastown Business Improvement Society was created.[100] The GBIS's role is to 'maintain and market the residential, retail and commercial opportunities in Gastown.'[101] In this capacity, it represents the interests of seventy of the area's property owners and 400 businesses.[102]

The structure of the organization is similar to that of other BIAs. There is an elected president and Board of Directors, and member-run committees such as the Safety and Security Committee. There is also one staff position – the 'GBIS Manager.' However, because of the GBIS's smaller size, its annual budget is significantly less than that of the neighbouring DVBIA. For the year 2000–2001, the GBIS requested a recoverable grant of $304,000 in order to meet the following expenditures:

Marketing, Promotion, and Public Relations	$78,000
Street Enhancement, Litter Removal, Safety, and Security	$134,000
Salaries, Fees, and Operating Expenses	$87,000
Contingency	$5,000[103]

Research Context

In selecting sites within Vancouver, we were careful to choose spaces that exemplify differing stages of redevelopment. In order to clarify the nature of these sites, we have provided a condensed history.

Granville Street runs the entire length of the city from north (downtown core) to south (into the neighbouring municipality of Richmond). Within the northern end of the street are businesses, shops, and restaurants including the Vancouver Stock Exchange and the Pacific Centre Mall. As pedestrians walk south, through what is termed the Mall, they move into an area filled with stores and services that cater primarily to the young and the hip. Here we find the Underground, which offers dog collars and body piercing, the Beauty Bar, where self-styled 'hipsters' can don pink afros and study themselves in mirrors, and a variety of 'hot' night clubs where young beautiful bodies line up to get inside.

As Granville Mall is not recognized as a community separate from the larger downtown south area, census data specific to the Mall are not available. Thus, in order to understand the demographics of the site, we relied on information obtained through interviews, observational data, and other research on the local population.[104] Based on these sources, it appears that Granville Mall's population is primarily a street population, one that is made up of older residents of the area's low-income housing, street youth, and transient adults. Since the area's street youth are a significant feature of life on the Mall, we were particularly interested in obtaining demographic data on this population. A study conducted for the City of Vancouver's Social Planning Department[105] found that on average there are 205 youth existing in and around the Mall. Researchers estimate that 15 per cent of these youth are Native, 5 per cent are classified as non-white (Asian, black, Hispanic, East Indian, and South East Asian), and 80 per cent are Caucasian. Of the street youth located and interviewed for this study, all but one were Caucasian.[106]

In earlier years, Granville Street was a major site for shopping and entertainment. Photographs of the street taken at night in the 1940s and 1950s show it ablaze with lights, as entertainment seekers enter the Vogue Movie Theatre or wait outside the Orpheum Theatre or the Commodore Ballroom. However, with the mass exodus to the suburbs in the mid- to late 1950s, Granville became increasingly deserted of shoppers and entertainment seekers. In order to attract lost revenues back into the area, the indoor underground Pacific Centre Mall opened on Granville Street in the early 1970s. Unfortunately, it had an unintended consequence that was detrimental for the purpose of reviving Granville: it pulled people off the street.[107]

In order to undo the damage caused by Pacific Centre, in 1974 City Council re-created a portion of Granville Street into a pedestrian mall.[108] According to critics, this was the 'worst planning blunder in the city's history and the root cause of the present malaise.'[109] Shoppers still stayed away, and stores continued to go underground into Pacific Centre.[110] As a result, the area south of the central-most business core became 'run down.' Business languished, and the street was populated with sex stores, panhandlers, street kids, and other symbols commonly associated with 'urban blight.' In the 1990s, two forces of redevelopment began work on improving Granville. The city rezoned the area surrounding Granville in 1991 to facilitate the building of residential high-rises. And property owners, seeing signs of increased tourism in Vancouver as a whole, began to redevelop area businesses to attract tourist dollars to Granville. A number of hotels that had formerly offered single resident occupancy (SRO) rooms were converted into tourist accommodations, leading to evictions of a number of the city's poor and elderly.

Some business owners along the Mall also sought to re-establish the area by re-creating its identity. Underlying this effort was a view of the Mall's problems as being linked to an undesirable image. As one developer explained, 'The problem is its negative identity. It's created by some of these adult stores plus the arcades.'[111] Briefly, the area became 'Theatre Row'; however, when Granville's merchants joined the DVBIA in 1998 this gave way to the 'Great Granville' concept,[112] which has now been replaced by the area's latest identity: 'The Entertainment District'

(TED). TED is an attempt by retailers to fuse the Mall's past with its present by evoking Granville's heyday as an entertainment destination through restoring nostalgic elements, such as the neon signs that run the length of the street, as well as by updating its image with a mix of funky and eclectic shops and services and a wide array of cabarets and pubs.

To achieve the transformation necessary, the city has commissioned a façade design concept for Granville Street, and removed a moratorium on liquor seats[113] in the area.[114] The DVBIA, in conjunction with the city, has been beautifying the area. Among other initiatives, the DVBIA has worked with shop owners on improving appearances, has created the Downtown Clean Team to remove surface debris, and has hung planters.[115] Colourful banners, which the DVBIA has hung along the 700 to 1300 blocks of Granville Street, 'define The Entertainment District.'[116]

However, not all residents of the community accept the TED identity. When a long-time resident of the area was asked if the TED banners reflect the community as a whole, the response was an emphatic no. The question of whether Granville Mall is a community was posed to a local street youth who similarly pointed out that the Mall is more than TED: 'For some people this is their home, their street.'

Gastown is another of the neighbourhoods that make up the city's downtown. It is situated along the waterfront of Vancouver, wedged between the central business district and the Downtown Eastside (the city's poorest neighbourhood). For a variety of political reasons, residents of Gastown and the Downtown Eastside lay claim to be either a part of or apart from the Downtown Eastside. In its Community Profile for Downtown proper, the city recognizes Gastown as distinct from the Downtown Eastside.[117] For this and other methodological reasons, we have elected to treat Gastown as separate from the Downtown Eastside.

Demographic information for Gastown was obtained from the City of Vancouver's Community Monitoring report, which utilizes 1996 census data. The median income of area residents is staggeringly low: $7,564 (males) and $11,180 (females),[118] with approximately 77 per cent of Gastown's residents being defined as 'low income.'[119] With respect to the area's ethnic composition, one piece of information that is important to note is that the popular notion that Gastown and the neighbouring Downtown Eastside are composed primarily of Aboriginal residents is false. Census figures for 1996 show that Aboriginal persons made up only 9 per cent of the population of the Downtown Eastside and 10 per cent of the population of Gastown.[120] Furthermore, despite the proximity of

Chinatown, individuals speaking Chinese as their home language made up only 6 per cent of Gastown's population.[121]

Within the fourteen blocks that encompass Gastown there are more than 100 street-level retailers and service providers, including antique dealers, Native art galleries, furniture stores, and souvenir shops featuring Canadian kitsch and tacky T-shirts. The area also includes a variety of eateries, nightclubs, and a microbrewery. Gastown is, however, a multiuse neighbourhood that also incorporates office space, privately owned condominium complexes, and social housing.

Gastown is the site on which the City of Vancouver was founded in 1867. Its name comes from one of the city's earliest entrepreneurs, Captain 'Gassy' Jack Deighton, who operated a saloon in the area to serve mill workers. For many years Gastown was a commercial and warehousing district, but, as the city expanded westwards, the area increasingly fell into disuse. By the 1950s Gastown formed part of the city's skid road.

In the mid-1960s plans were in progress to bulldoze Gastown.[122] Ley[123] states that preservation of the area as a heritage site initially began as a grass-roots movement of small businesses and counter-culture groups who resisted the city's plans to turn the district into a freeway. The freeway project was eventually abandoned in the face of public outcry over the destruction of the heritage buildings occupying the space. In 1969, the Gastown Rehabilitation Project, a partnership among a wide range of business and community interests and various levels of government, was formed in order to rescue the site. The city coordinated a five-year restoration program involving investment, renovations, and rezoning. Public sector investment consisted primarily of capital expenditures in the form of improvements to public lands and necessary zoning and by-law changes, with the private sector investing heavily in renovations of heritage buildings.[124] In 1971, the provincial government designated Gastown a heritage area. This is Gastown's primary identity, and it is this identity that forms the basis of its tourist trade.

Geographer David Ley[125] has noted what he terms 'the postmodern face of Gastown' – a face that he suggests is attributable to a 'public intervention' that resulted in 'spontaneity increasingly becoming staged' so as to make the site a prime tourist destination. Ley[126] states that 'as early as 1973 and the beautification schemes, an architectural historian saw the new Water Street landscape as made in the image of Disney.'

It is an imperfect copy of Disney, however, as Gastown cannot completely rid itself of its historic past as embodied in the presence of many of its 'unsanitary' elements: the poor, the mentally ill, the addicted, panhandlers, and other long-time low-income residents who inhabit the area and the nearby Downtown Eastside. Thus a palpable tension exists: as businesses and recently arrived, higher-income residents struggle to maintain their newer, more elegant image of 'historical' Gastown, they are met with resistance by community groups and their clienteles, who perceive this new vision as excluding them. The result is a fractured community. As one area resident stated unequivocally, 'The neighbourhood is ... kind of a disgusting parody of a neighbourhood.'

The Public Police in Urban Vancouver

For policing purposes, the city is divided into four districts. Of particular interest here are Districts One and Two.

District One encompasses most of Vancouver's inner urban core. It is subdivided into four policing areas: Waterfront, the West End, North False Creek, and Granville Downtown South.[127] Officers in this district patrol on bicycles or in squad cars, or are assigned as liaison officers to a Community Policing Centre (CPC) – a neighbourhood policing office. In Vancouver, CPCs are administered by a volunteer citizen advisory council in conjunction with the district's area management team.[128] There are several CPCs within District One, including Granville, Waterfront, and Davie.[129]

The Granville Downtown South CPC is located on the Mall. The office is staffed with a paid volunteer coordinator and several volunteers. The centre operates a number of programs, many of which are directed primarily at disorder prevention through the reduction of forms of 'nuisance.' For example, there is Bar Watch, a program in which bar and club operators work with the police in order to minimize problems associated with liquor licence seats, and the Vending/Busker/Window-Washer Enforcement Program, aimed at removing 'illegal and/or problematic street vendors and buskers and dealing with street window washers,' among others.[130]

District Two encompasses Gastown and the more easterly sections of Vancouver, including the Downtown Eastside, Strathcona/Chinatown, Grandview-Woodland and Hastings-Sunrise areas.[131] There are approximately 200 police officers assigned to patrol this district, on foot or in squad cars. Officers may also be assigned to one of the area's CPCs, which include Grandview-Woodland, Strathcona, and Gastown.

The smaller Gastown CPC is staffed with two full-time officers, a paid volunteer coordinator, and volunteers. The Gastown CPC runs fewer programs than its Granville Mall counterpart; programs include a Citizen's Foot Patrol, BlockWatch, and BarWatch. And, as will be discussed later, Gastown CPC's officers also provide informal support to local private security who engage in disorder prevention activities in the neighbourhood.

Private Security

As of 14 April 2000 there were 6,363 licensed security patrol personnel in the province of British Columbia compared to 4,762 in 1994.[132] This figure represents an increase of approximately 33 per cent in just over a five-year period, signifying the rapid growth of this industry in British Columbia.[133]

A large number of businesses within both of the BIDs studied utilize the services of licensed and unlicensed private security. Licensed personnel include armed guards and individuals engaged in patrol work who are regulated through the *Private Investigators and Security Agencies Act.*[134] This act gives authority to the Security Programs Division of the Ministry of the Attorney General, which administers the granting and holding of security professional licences. Among unlicensed security, businesses employ 'in-house' retail loss prevention staff and 'bouncers' or door staff.

Both the DVBIA and the GBIS utilize licensed private security services, although they do so in qualitatively different ways than other business interests. The following subsections explore the use of these services.

Granville Mall: The Downtown Ambassadors

In the spring of 2000, the DVBIA announced with some fanfare that it had revamped its Downtown Ambassadors (DAs)[135] program. The program originated in 1994 when the DVBIA hired a group of postsecondary students to operate information booths and to patrol the BID each summer.[136] Aside from assisting area visitors and merchants by providing general information and directions, their primary duties included '[liaising] with the community police officers and offices ... documenting any graffiti, aggressive panhandlers or removing any illegally posted bills within the DVBIA boundaries.'[137] As one former Ambassador proudly stated in the BIA's newsletter, 'it is our role to ensure that the tourists' and locals' impressions of the city are positive.'[138]

The new program replaced the part-time students with sixteen full-time Alliance Security (of the Inter Tech Group) patrol persons on foot and in bike patrols. Patrols now operate within the ninety-block BID from 7:00 a.m. to 10:30 p.m. daily on a year-round basis.[139] The contracting of private security services to fulfil the Ambassadors' function clearly represents a change in the direction of the program. In its literature, the DVBIA makes explicit this change of focus to crime and disorder prevention by stating that 'all other goals ... are subservient to the ultimate ambition of public safety and security.'[140] This change is also reflected in the adoption of 'broken windows'-style policing. In its 1996–1997 Annual Report, the DVBIA acknowledges the influence of the 'broken windows' theory on its crime prevention programs. Included is a discussion of a visit to Vancouver by George Kelling, sponsored by the Association: 'this past spring, a powerful metaphor [broken windows] was impressed upon the minds of many prominent members of the business community, civic officials, police ... a philosophical message that became one of the highlights of the DVBIA's year.'[141]

Despite the fact that the Ambassadors program is clearly dedicated to crime and disorder prevention and its members are employed by a private security firm and are provincially licensed as security patrol, the DVBIA is careful to characterize the Ambassadors program not as a private security program but rather as a tourism and hospitality service. One subject spoke directly to this issue: 'I think the Association's been careful not to conceptualize the Ambassadors program as a security force.' It was also noted that police interviewees avoided referring to the Ambassadors as private security. One officer looked increasingly uncomfortable when the question of the Ambassadors as private security arose, and attempted to redefine their role by emphasizing the tourism aspects of their duties. This discomfort is likely due to the fact that the regulatory functions that the Ambassadors perform are embedded in a carefully marketed guise: that of the friendly tourist service. To openly contradict this guise is to call into question the functions that they serve in the public sphere and the role of the police and City Hall in facilitating those functions.

Ambassadors are immediately recognizable to observers as a result of the vivid, distinguishing uniforms they wear and the trademark logo on their backs, which reads, in reflective white block letters, DOWNTOWN AMBASSADORS. They are garbed in varying uniforms of red and black. Differing styles of uniforms are related to differing functions and weather conditions. Ambassadors also carry radios for remote contact, notepads for recording observations, and first-aid packs.

The primary advantage of this vivid clothing is that it stands out in a crowd. This not only benefits tourists and shopkeepers who may be seeking assistance but is also intended to function as a crime deterrent. In the vernacular of 'broken windows,' the clothing assists in signalling to would-be offenders that the space is being observed. As one police officer suggested, 'as ugly as the uniform is, they are visible. And if you have a perception that somebody's watching, that affects behaviour.'

Among the duties that Ambassadors are expected to perform is to be '"eyes and ears" monitoring problems related to safety, security, cleanliness, graffiti, panhandling and illegal vending.'[142] The 'eyes and ears' concept is a recurring theme, although one that is employed cautiously. For instance, one senior officer initially responded to a question on ways in which public police work with private security by replying, 'I've got a bunch of eyes and ears walking down Granville Street, in the DVBIA area, phoning the police when they see problems.' However, he later reacted defensively to a question about whether Ambassadors may be at risk as a result of performing solo patrols at night in the downtown core. The response, spoken with noticeable exasperation, was, 'This eyes and ears stuff seems to always creep to the front, but they're supposed to approach a tourist and offer them assistance.'

Aside from those duties that are directly related to crime prevention, the Ambassadors also engage in order maintenance activities by either demanding that those defined as the 'disorderly' – panhandlers, squeegee workers, and other street persons – desist from certain behaviours, or by asking them to 'move along.' According to the DVBIA's own statistics, they are particularly successful at this second task: in the period from 15 May 2000 to 31 March 2001, the Ambassadors had '6,911 interactions with street persons ... achieving a 90 per cent compliance rate to "move along" when requested.'[143] In 'broken windows' terms, such activities are seen as important because, as Wilson and Kelling[144] posit, there is a direct link between order maintenance in the form of 'managing panhandlers' and crime prevention: 'the unchecked panhandler is, in effect, the first broken window.' Thus, the presence of panhandlers signifies a neighbourhood with few social controls, one that will offer little resistance to would-be criminals.[145]

Part of the Ambassadors' mandate is to ensure that any such messages are countered, both through their physical presence and through actions directed at the 'disorderly.' For example, street youth and outreach workers informed me that Ambassadors, armed with the knowledge of the existence of the city's anti-panhandling by-law,[146] and the right of property owners to remove people from their property, routinely tell panhandlers and street youth to move along. Property rights, for example, are enforced in dealing with panhandlers in public space who are touching a wall belonging to a property owner. This contact is used as justification to order them to move along. They also 'order' the 'disorderly' by telling panhandlers and others who are sitting on the street to stand up, or to remove their personal property from public sidewalks.[147] The creeping nature of the Ambassadors' mandate is made obvious when one considers that these are activities more commonly seen as the responsibility of the public police.[148]

Some youth and community group members alleged that Ambassadors use force in order to move youth who are sleeping on sidewalks or behind buildings. They stated that Ambassadors kick them or use other means that they perceive to be assaultive. We discussed these allegations in general terms with a senior officer, who advised that the police and private security use their feet to tap people awake, and that this is done for safety reasons.

A number of subjects advised me that street people would be uncomfortable with complaining to the police about incidents of abuse by security guards. This is because they see the police as working cooperatively with guards, and do not feel that they can trust the police to act on their complaints. In an interview with a senior officer this issue was raised, as was the more general question of whether police informally keep watch over the activities of security guards within District One. This individual's response was

> Informally? I think we've actually had a formal eye on some of them. We've charged a number of security guards for excessive force. Assault. Three of them actually. Sorry, two and warned another one.[149]

It is important to note that the Ambassadors do serve in a multidimensional role. Aside from performing tasks related to crime and disorder prevention, they also engage in activities related to 'tourism and hospitality.' Thus their duties include providing information to tourists, participating in safe walks, and assisting tourists and other visitors in a variety of ways. Such activities are undertaken in order to provide visitors with a positive image of the downtown core. To this end, Ambassadors are also responsible for assisting in the regulation of visible signs of physical decay and disorder. They do this through participation in a program called Best Foot Forward, in which Ambassadors and shopkeepers patrol designated zones within the city and report graffiti and other forms of vandalism, posters on street furniture, overflowing garbage cans, problems with street lighting, and anything else that is seen to detract from an area's visual appeal. These reports are received by both the DVBIA, which monitors street cleanliness and order carefully, and by City Hall officials or private companies who are responsible for responding to the given problem. To ensure that Ambassadors are carrying out these patrols, they are armed with diester wands that they use to swipe on designated bar code readers throughout patrol zones. These readers advise the DVBIA as to whether patrols are being performed.

Granville Mall: The Loss Prevention Officers

To augment the work of both the Ambassadors and various retail loss prevention officers and other site security employed by member businesses within the downtown core, in 2000 the DVBIA also announced the formation of a completely new security enterprise: the Loss Prevention Officers (LPO) program. This program consists of approximately six licensed security guards, also retained through Alliance Security, whose mandate is to target individuals committing crimes against private property.

What makes this program particularly noteworthy is that it has resulted in the creation of a strange hybrid, with private and public functions embedded in the body of a privately controlled individual who actively works with the public police and other private security. In describing the successes of the program, the DVBIA[150] indirectly notes this hybrid nature: '151 individuals have been arrested for theft within the DVBIA area through joint co-operation, communication and partnership with police, member businesses and in-house and contract security personnel.' LPOs essentially perform many of the same functions as the classic store detective; however, there are notable differences between the LPO and the traditional models. For instance, while both models utilize many of the same traditional policing methods, the objective of the LPOs is not simply crime prevention or detection but the policing of signs that may serve to deter would-be consumers or space users. Thus, while the means employed by actors within both of the models may be the same, motives for actions often vary.

As part of their daily activities, LPOs perform covert surveillance on suspect individuals. In observing and trailing suspects, they are not bounded by the perimeter of a particular building or space; rather, they work within the entire ninety blocks of the BID. According to one subject, 'the concept is to provide a number of roving people on different shifts ...'

Information on suspect persons is collected by LPOs and placed in reports, copies of which are forwarded to the DVBIA for 'tracking purposes.' These reports require LPOs to provide a suspect's name, known aliases, a full description (including hair, weight, and height), notable features such as scarring or tattoos, and other notes that may include no-go information, dates of previous arrests, and so on. These reports are also supplemented with photographs of the individual that are often taken by LPOs, who carry digital cameras for this purpose. However, photographs can come from other sources, including store video surveillance cameras and police mug shots.[151]

Walking the streets is a significant part of their work; this provides LPOs with the opportunity to spot known criminals or suspicious activity. One individual described this process as follows:

> So, the guys are walking the street and they would say, 'Hey, that's John Doe. He's an active booster. We could set up on him, and actually surveil [sic] him.' And they'd follow him for a period and see if he went into a store. And so he would sit down ... and he would begin to line a shopping bag with tin foil. Then you know that the guy's going into one of the stores. The tin foil is, of course, to beat the detectors. So we'd follow him and actually make an arrest.

Like the store detective who holds shoplifters and vandals for the police, the LPOs employ the citizen's power of arrest. Where this program also differs from the more traditional model of private security is that after an arrest is made the LPOs also fill out Crown reports[152] for attending police officers.[153] The rationale for performing this task is simple: it engenders cooperation between the LPOs and public police members who may otherwise be unwilling to provide assistance to DVBIA private security. As one subject explained, 'You don't want to make work for the police officer. You don't want to arrest somebody and turn him over, and nail the [officer] with three hours of paper.'

Another significant difference is that LPOs will sometimes work, in tandem with police[154] or solo, on 'sting' operations in both public and private space. As one subject advised, 'We'll have businesses come to us sometimes and say, "Our parkade is being hit, so can you set up on it?" We'll go ahead and do it.' An example of such a 'set up' is placing a truck in a parking lot and monitoring a video feed obtained from discreetly placed cameras in the target area. As one individual described it, 'We'll park a truck in there and set up and see what happens.'

Aside from differences between the LPO program and more traditional loss prevention programs, as based on the store detective model, it is important to note that the LPO program is also different from that of the Ambassadors. Unlike the Ambassadors, who are visible deterrents and whose presence is intended to invoke feelings of security in space users, the LPOs work undercover and their actions are generally focused on dealing with known or suspected offenders rather than with the general public. This, coupled with the fact that much of their work is in the area of retail, office, and auto-related theft, suggests that the presence of LPOs on the city's streets would have little or no effect on the overall aesthetics or dynamics of the space, and thus no effect on tourists and other space users. However, this is not the case.

Again, following Wilson and Kelling's ideas on 'fixing broken windows,' the DVBIA requires members in both of its security programs to perform activities centred on reducing signs of crime and disorder that may deter the consumer classes from using a space. Thus, while they differ from the Ambassadors with respect to the means they may employ to achieve BIA objectives, LPOs share the same mandate: to control the physical space by regulating visible signs of crime and disorder.[155] For instance, while the LPOs are largely invisible to space users downtown, they do have an impact on the environment through their work on minimizing graffiti and vandalism. This is done through conducting surveillance on known vandals and monitoring areas where vandalism is likely to occur in order to apprehend those whose activities damage property and detract from an area's aesthetics. Furthermore, while a significant portion of their work is directed at retail and office theft, LPOs also perform crime prevention services in the area of property offences that largely impact the consumer classes, such as bag snatchings and thefts from autos.[156] Their activities in this respect serve to protect tourists' and other consumers' experiences. And, as one subject advised, the LPOs have received directives from the DVBIA to assist the Ambassadors in 'controlling' panhandlers, which is certainly a task more closely related to image protection than crime prevention. This individual explained the process to be employed by the LPOs as follows:

If a guy was aggressive, I had the okay from the police. We could phone the police and they would move in and take some of those who were aggressive out. If they were passive beggars, we could hand them out the information. Various agencies, food sources, that sort of thing.

Gastown: The Gastown Security Patrol

The use of private security personnel to patrol public streets within Vancouver originated in Gastown in the early 1990s as a result of business concerns with security issues. These concerns can be traced back to the early days of the BIA's existence. Hartford,[157] in his study of downtown revitalization programs, reveals that a former owner of a restaurant in the area told him that the owner's 'main concern was the security problem and he gave up his involvement in the BIA when it became clear there simply was not a sufficient budget to address this problem.'

Gastown's security patrol program utilizes the services of contract personnel from the Securiguard company. Securiguard employees, who work in shifts of two, patrol the fourteen-block area on foot, seven days a week. The guards are immediately recognizable in uniforms consisting of white shirts, yellow jackets, and black pants with reflective trim and stripes. Their visibility clearly serves a deterrent function. They carry radios for remote contact and notepads for documenting observations.

Gastown's private security patrols perform a number of tasks, including providing assistance to tourists and responding to calls for service from local businesses. Such calls can range from asking people to leave premises to holding shoplifters. In a statement that echoes the view of many within the policing profession, a police subject stated that, 'Basically, the private security ... does all the stuff that the cops don't have time to do, and don't want to do.' A scenario offered by this individual to illustrate the type of calls that guards may receive also illustrates the linking of order with aesthetic concerns: 'You have somebody who comes into your store and they're reeking like a garbage can and they're talking to themselves and muttering. And they're obviously a junkie ... you want them out of your store because they're either going to shoplift or scare the tourists, or maybe get violent.'

As the GBIS is also a supporter of 'broken windows' thinking – they were also one of the sponsors of Kelling's visit to Vancouver – Gastown's guards spend a significant portion of their time preserving physical and symbolic forms of order and minimizing opportunities for disorder. As occurs on Granville Mall, GBIS guards approach one of the more visible signs of 'disorder' on the street – panhandlers. One subject described the means employed to move panhandlers along as follows: 'We're trying to use persuasion and common sense and things like that.' However, unlike the Ambassadors, who have been observed moving panhandlers along by directing them to shelters or by simply standing in front of them (thus forcing panhandlers to 'choose' to move away from a site), Gastown security guards actively work to 'push' panhandlers and other street persons out of the area as a whole by using intimidation tactics. For example, guards will overtly follow individuals who arouse their suspicions in order to signal to the individual that they are being watched. They will continue following such individuals until they have left the BID. The technique is clearly intended as preventative in nature in that it provokes departure from the area rather than facilitating covert surveillance.

The guards, like the Ambassadors, also record observations in notebooks. The guards will follow suspected panhandlers or other 'suspicious persons' and take notes, or will stop these individuals to ask questions, recording responses in their notebooks. This practice prompted some discussion with respondents who had been the subject of guards' notes. It is evident in speaking to these people that they experienced this note taking as a form of intimidation:

QUESTION: What do you think the purpose of the note taking is?
ANSWER 1: I think [the guard] wants me out of this part of town.
ANSWER 2: I think that taking the notes would be 'Look, we've got a file on you and you'd better be careful. You'd better watch out, I can take notes. I can put it in a database and we know all about you.'

Like the LPOs, Gastown guards also photograph individuals who have been caught shoplifting, an activity that is performed with the full knowledge and cooperation of local police. These pictures are then distributed to business owners within the GBIS district. One individual who had been caught shoplifting recently in Gastown spoke about the experience:

QUESTION: Has a guard or a policeman ever taken your picture?
ANSWER: Actually one of the security took my picture here.
QUESTION: How was that done? Did they walk up and take a Polaroid? ...
ANSWER: Right in front of everyone they took a picture of me.
QUESTION: Were you asked for your permission or they just did it?
ANSWER: No permission. Just taking your picture is what they told me.
QUESTION: And did the policeman watch them take your picture?

ANSWER: Yep.

QUESTION: Did you find it unusual that they would want to take your picture?

ANSWER: They wanted to take my picture so they could put it on every store on Water Street. That's what I heard.

QUESTION: Did you hear that from them or ... ?

ANSWER: The police officer.

One of the questions posed to police personnel in and around the Gastown area concerned the extent to which public police perform formal or informal supervision of the guards and their activities while on the street. One respondent answered, 'I know that [police officers] watch the security very closely ... They can watch the security guards and say, "You know what, you really should not be going up and saying ... mouthing off to this guy because ... he just got out of prison for assault. So you want to be careful yourself."' This protectiveness towards the guards is also manifest in other, more unsettling ways. On one occasion a police officer in Gastown was observed yelling at a local street person while a security guard stood watching. The officer was advising the street person that 'he [pointing to the guard] works with me,' thus indicating that the man was to offer the guard respect because of his professional association with a 'real cop.' This was an important scene to witness. As Wilson and Kelling[158] note, the mere presence of private security is not always sufficient to control or deter someone who is 'challenging community standards' because private security lack the 'aura of authority necessary to perform this difficult task.' Because of this, it is often necessary that the 'real' police are seen to be openly supportive of private security.

In relation to Wilson and Kelling's[159] comment that private security lack the authority of police, it is worth noting that security guards in the sites studied frequently behave like public police officers as a means of conferring the benefits of an association with legitimate authority upon themselves. For example, security guards often carry themselves in a similar manner to the public police: brisk, erect, and confident, sometimes to the point of arrogance or aggressiveness. One local resident, referring to a Gastown security guard, stated, 'She's a problem. She's very proud that she gets to wear a uniform ... [to] parade around.'

Guards may also employ the clipped tones of the police officer, and have indeed been trained to punctuate their speech with policing terms. As one subject noted, some guards consciously refer to themselves as 'officers,' which is not only 'an attempt at authority ... [but] indicative of the way they think of themselves.' Their note taking, which occurs in public and often in the presence of the individual who is the subject of the record, can certainly be seen as akin to the reporting and paperwork filing of the police patrol officer, as well as a mechanism for power and control. Both the security guard and the suspect understand that such records may be evidence in a potential prosecution.

The BIAs derive benefits from having guards act like public police. For example, as a result of taking on the role of 'law enforcement,' the guards may become more willing to engage in actions that maintain the BIA's view of what constitutes public order, because preserving social order is a mandate of the public police whom they seek to emulate. This can translate into having guards remove undesirable individuals from public spaces by asking someone to 'move on,' stating that it is 'against the law' to be in a particular space when it is not, physically escorting someone, and, in extreme cases, issuing threats of violence and engaging in physical assaults.[160]

Another, more obvious benefit to the BIAs is that the guards' overt presence serves to deter undesirable elements who detract from the area's physical charms and lead to perceptions of crime. As one area worker suggested, 'if there's a lot of people who could be a problem, they see the security guards and think okay, I'd better not do anything or these guys are going to come after me with their walkie-talkies.'

For the police, aside from the crime deterrent value that the physical presence of security guards in public may have, the primary benefit they receive comes from the willingness of guards to perform 'dirty work.'[161] Typically, dirty work includes rousting vagrants from private property and dealing with 'petty crimes' such as shoplifting, although one guard did advise that police informally ask guards to enforce a provision of the panhandling by-law that is no longer in effect. Thus, guards continue to tell panhandlers and other street people that they must stand up. In the case of the Loss Prevention Officers, dirty work also encompasses 'tedious work' such as the filling out of Crown reports and the gathering of basic information to expedite charging and to reduce the paperwork of the attending police officer.

Sharing the Job of Crime Prevention

The DVBIA, as its newsletters make clear, has directed extensive energies at developing mutually cooperative relationships with the public police. The result has been the development of both formal and informal processes of information sharing between the private and public sectors.

Operation Cooperation began in 1991 as a result of a meeting between senior members of the Vancouver Police Department and representatives of private security working within the downtown core. These two groups met to discuss ways in which the public and private sectors could work cooperatively on crime prevention issues.[162] Operation Cooperation is coordinated through the Waterfront CPC, with members meeting monthly to discuss relevant issues such as 'improving the working relationship with the Vancouver Police Department; Police/Security evaluation discussions; theft from autos, office theft, shoplifting; vagrants/panhandlers, [and] emergency procedures.'[163] As one security company representative advised, the most common problems that Operation Cooperation members face are 'graffiti and property damage,' followed by thefts from offices and autos. However, the stated rationale for this program is contained in a pamphlet obtained from the Waterfront CPC that makes explicit the link between entertainment, retail economics, and anti-crime and disorder measures:

> Tourism employs 72,000 jobs in Greater Vancouver and contributes more than $2.5 billion into the local economy. By getting involved and utilizing this resource group, it will maintain the safety and stability of the area.[164]

The CAPP paging program grew out of Operation Cooperation. A subscriber to the paging service fills out a report sheet that asks for specific information to be relayed through the paging network. The subscriber calls the Dispatch Centre and provides the information to be transmitted. The message is then broadcast in text to all pager holders in a specified call group.[165] Messages are also sent by the police to subscriber businesses. All CAPP messages are subsequently stored and archived.[166]

According to the Vancouver Police Department, 'selective [sic] police & security officers carry pagers from the Operation Cooperation network, providing timely suspect description and pertinent information directly to the officers'; the program is described as being 'an information exchange between police, private security and Business.'[167] At present, there are approximately sixty pagers carried by VPD officers.[168] Other CAPP members include the DVBIA, the city, the Vancouver Hotel Association, and the Retail Loss Prevention Association.[169]

The CAPP program and Dispatch Centre are not part of the E-comm 911 system, but are instead supported by TeleLink Paging Network. Subscribers pay fees to join the service and are provided with a pager, manual, and access to the service. TeleLink advertises that businesses that participate will 'have a direct link to the police and other businesses by a central Pager Dispatch Centre.'[170] This enables businesses to inform the police, and each other, about 'a crime or suspicious activity.'[171] The type of activities that TeleLink suggests warrant a paging alert include armed robbery, stolen credit cards and fraudulent cheques, shoplifting, auto-related thefts, property theft, missing persons, vandalism and mischief, other non-violent crimes, and suspicious persons. Internal police department records[172] obtained through a Freedom of Information request reveal the nature of some of the dispatches sent over the pager system:

DISPATCH [information deleted]. Aggressive mentally insatiable [sic] male violent, 35+ yrs, 5'10: 150–160 lbs, collar length brn hair, pale skin, beard & moustache smells, gray jeans and off gray suede jacket, brn cowboy.

DISPATCH [information deleted]. Panhandling, Male, 45 yrs., 5'9" tall, 160 lbs, collar length white hair, Caucasian skin, White moustache and white beard about chest length, Bagpipes, Blue hat, green checked Scottish outfit.

Other similar entries suggest that the bulk of the transmissions have more to do with order maintenance issues relevant to member businesses than with actual crime prevention or public policing matters.

While the CAPP program may give member businesses the impression that they are 'connected' to the police, this is a false image. Officers are not required to respond to a page and may seldom do so. In relation to actual crime prevention benefits, it would appear that the police actually have little practical use for the pager. As one police subject from outside of District One stated, 'It sounds, no offence, kind of dorky ... [officers are] listening to radios, and their own cell phones, and their own pagers. I mean, how many modes of light communication do you really need?' The efficacy of the program in relation to increasing arrests is also doubtful. During the course of an interview, an officer who supports the pager program was asked for the number of arrests that have resulted from its use. He replied that there had been several, but when pressed could cite only one instance.

A possible explanation for police involvement in a program that would seem to net them little benefit in the way of actual crime prevention is that the paging program has a particular symbolic purpose. As was the case in Saunders's[173] study of community policing in Boston, this program is about producing appearances that signal community involvement. In effect, the pagers say to the business community, 'We are here for you, we listen to you, we value you,' although this is belied by the fact that officers can and do ignore the messages they receive.

For the DVBIA, cooperative relations with the public police in programs such as CAPP can be used to demonstrate to its membership that the association is actively addressing the crime and safety issues that always seem to be at the forefront of retailers' concerns. Furthermore, messages found in the association's literature, such as 'the DVBIA prides itself on an effective working relationship with Vancouver Police,'[174] assist in conferring legitimacy and status on the DVBIA's crime prevention efforts.

While formal programs such as Operation Cooperation provide avenues through which police and private security concerns can share information and relay problems that are occurring downtown, information sharing also takes place at an informal level. The LPOs actively work with the public police, and to a lesser extent this is also true of the Ambassadors and their relationship with the police. Generally, this 'working together' takes the form of reciprocal information sharing between the DVBIA and its program members and the public police.

For example, DVBIA staff record and analyse incidents of crime and vandalism in their district, and information concerning possible trends is routinely passed along. The LPOs also share information with and receive information from members of the property crimes unit of the Vancouver Police Department. As one subject advised, when the program first began '[the property crimes unit] assisted us with identifying booster groups.' Not all information provided is specifically in relation to identifying crime or criminals; the LPOs have also been provided with training by members of the public police in areas such as conducting surveillance.

Information sharing is fostered by the prior existence or the development of interpersonal relations between members of the DVBIA and the public police. This developing of ties is a deliberate process, as one individual makes clear: 'We met daily with [the police] ... [we] made sure that the guys knew each other, and as I say, they worked together a couple of times so if they did see somebody or they had something going on, they knew who to contact.'

As was previously noted, in some cases bonds are fostered as a result of awareness by police officers that private security can provide assistance in performing tasks that the police do not have time or other resources to deal with. A subject made this clear during a discussion of the LPO program:

I think it was the frontline officers that we were a little bit more concerned about. But I think that the program and the individuals who did the programs proved that they were professionals that belong in this together, in partnerships. Now the information exchange and intelligence exchange has been nothing but awesome. [The police] come to [the LPOs] and say, 'Hey we are looking for so and so, if you see so and so contact us.' Or they might say, 'So and so is active in this area or doing this. Keep an eye out for so and so.' And we do the same thing. We say, 'So and so has been seen going into this business. He seems to be going in with product, coming out with nothing. We believe that that business might be buying stolen property.'

In Gastown, information sharing occurs between the police and the GBIS security guards through routine contact rather than through formal mechanisms. As one police subject stated 'We have security, and the security, like I've said, really liaises and works very closely with the constables if they're on duty ...'

While it does not appear that the GBIS has made formal attempts to become involved in the provision of crime prevention services outside its security patrol program, local businesses in Gastown have privately funded a police deployment centre in the neighbourhood.[175] What makes the Carrall Street site even more remarkable is its close proximity to four community policing centres[176] and the department's headquarters on Main Street. According to the notes of one officer, obtained through a Freedom of Information request, the justification for another police office in this area was that the centre 'will bring the police officers much closer to the community and will enable the police to get ahead of problems ...'[177] Yet, as another memo makes clear, 'the public will not be invited ... There will be no volunteers, no community programs, and no public meetings in the premises.'[178] Another stated purpose of the site is that it will be 'where members can write reports, have a cup of coffee, meet to discuss operational beat issues, or use a washroom.'[179] The centre 'will also provide a central location for coordinated enforcement activities to operate.'[180] However, the deployment centre may have yet another use: '[i]t will also provide space and resources for both Chinatown and Gastown security to Liaise [sic] and cooperate with police working the area.'[181] To this end, '[b]oth Chinatown and Gastown Security will be encouraged to use this facility.'[182]

Confirmation as to whether private security use this space was difficult to obtain. When the issue was raised with a senior officer, the response

was, 'I don't think so. I could be wrong there, but I'm not aware of that ...
We try to have a very good relationship with all the security companies
that work within all our areas ... the deployment centre, I'm not sure that
they have access to that because we have police stuff in there.' A member
of a community group stated that GBIS security guards have been seen
entering the building on multiple occasions.

At first glance, the centre would seem to serve little practical purpose
from a community crime prevention standpoint. Its location is not well
marked, the blinds are drawn, and the police seldom, if ever, linger
outside the doors. As one area resident suggested, '[It] doesn't make a
lot of sense to me ... I think it's just a token gesture.'

The deployment centre, however, is not just a token gesture; rather, it
serves specific purposes. For the business community, it is a means by
which they can exert pressure on the police to use the facility in a way
that justifies their expenditure. The contents of an internal memo
obtained from the police department[183] make this evident. The memo
discusses a complaint by a local business owner that the deployment
centre is having little effect in curbing neighbourhood drug trafficking.
The recipient of the memo is advised to work on 'developing some
enforcement "High Profile" programs to work out of that centre.'[184]

The centre is also symbolic on multiple levels. The deployment centre
represents an attempt by the business community in this area to bridge
what has often been an antagonistic relationship with police management in District Two. For the police, the building conveys two messages
to the community that are evidenced by a small old-fashioned glass globe
marked with the word 'Police' over the centre's entrance. First, it deliberately evokes an association with Robert Peel's 1829 London bobbies
and the first rise of community policing. Second, it is intended to fit in
with the heritage character of the Gastown site. Thus, this adornment,
like the CAPP pager program, is intended to produce the appearance of
community involvement.

Supporting Private Sector Policing Initiatives

As was noted previously, public 'civility' is a recurring theme found in
much of the literature of 'broken windows.' The essence of this theme,
which, when coupled with rhetoric on public safety and conceptions of
public good becomes the discourse of 'broken windows,' is perhaps best
explained by Ellickson.[185] For Ellickson 'reclaiming' public space is
central to fulfilling a variety of needs of urban communities. For ex-

ample, 'open-access public spaces are precious because they enable city residents to move about and engage in recreation and face-to-face communication.'[186] Ellickson[187] thus sees BIAs and other 'third-party' sources of order as enforcing formal and informal rules of 'proper street behavior,' activities that permit the flow of speech that might otherwise be curtailed by 'disruptive forces.'

What Ellickson and other proponents of 'broken windows' policing are actually advocating is the reproduction of class-based distinctions in the form of a conception of a public good/ideal republic that is intricately tied to retail economics, commercialization, and pro-consumption messages. This conception of the ideal public life as a series of 'consumer lifestyles' can be seen in at least three places. First, Ellickson[188] makes the prioritization of consumer lifestyles explicit when he discusses public disorder as 'the tragedy of the agora' ('agora' being the Greek word for market-place). Second, pro-civility advocates generally urge the reclaiming of public spaces from the disorderly, who are portrayed as limiting the potential for expression and exchange in these spaces.[189] When one looks at the spaces from which the 'disorderly' are being removed, it is apparent that these are urban centres where expression is becoming increasingly exclusive to commercial speech.[190] Third, retail economics and community well-being are typically linked by supporters of BIA policing.

That Vancouver City Council actively supports the BIA process is apparent, not only from their willingness to listen to the BIAs but also in the changes that they have made in order to streamline the BIA approval process. The effect of this streamlining is to encourage the forming of BIAs within the city.

One municipal worker informed us that Council's support for the BIA process is predicated on the belief that BIAs make 'the city more healthy economically, more healthy in terms of helping the community.' According to this individual, a 'healthy community has a healthy business district. A healthy community means that people can go and *shop* and do other things inside their community.' A healthy community is also one that does not 'attract crime.' In short, by supporting the BIAs and their area improvement and order maintenance efforts, Council believes that it is facilitating means by which crime can be reduced and communities can be made economically viable – at little cost to the city. Indeed, at the recent opening of the Carrall Street deployment centre, the city's mayor, Philip Owen, stated that he hoped the new centre would result in increased collaborations on similar projects by the private sector and public police because 'This is what's happening in the world... It's the right way to go.'[191] While Owen did not expand on why he perceives such measures as being 'the right way to go,' it is clear that 'collaborations' such as the deployment centre offer support for Garland's[192] 'responsibilization' thesis, and that it is the use of private funds to support public services that is a significant factor behind Mayor Owen's approval.

Police officers interviewed generally supported the BIAs and their willingness to fund policing programs and/or private crime prevention initiatives. This support was particularly evident among department management. For example, the contents of an internal Vancouver Police Department memo on the CAPP pager program, written by a department manager, reveals this individual's views on the benefits of supporting public-private policing relationships: 'I remain convinced that this is the way to go, linking security and police for a common community interest.' An interview with a senior officer revealed a similar attitude. This person advised, 'I am prepared to work with anybody in that area that wants to engage in a real partnership.'

In relation to the question of how members of the rank and file view private security, those interviewed tended to see the presence of private security as providing benefits for the police. During interviews it became apparent that support for private security and public-private partnerships is likely due to the fact that private security releases police from some forms of lower-level duties, or 'dirty work.' One officer discussed this in relation to community policing, a program she depicted as providing means by which the police can divest themselves of some of the responsibility for dealing with nuisance issues. Private security is part of this solution because it enables property owners to direct service calls for nuisance issues to security rather than to the police.

Some officers who support redevelopment of urban areas see private security patrols and the work of the BIAs as beneficial in assisting this process. As one officer stated, 'We look around at the decay and the disorder and we wish we could fix it and make it a nice place to live. And the idea with broken windows, and dealing with it from the ground level up instead of the reverse, I like it.' Then, in a comment indicative of the tendency of proponents of the 'broken windows' theory to equate order with commercialization, this officer proceeded to tell us his vision of a redeveloped space within the Downtown Eastside (of which Gastown is a part): 'a Starbucks on the corner and maybe some secretaries on these benches having lunches, feeding birds.' Unfortunately, the majority of inhabitants of this area cannot afford the three dollars for a cup of coffee.

The civility discourse also comes through in the comments of business owners and business representatives. For example, one representative of the business community illustrated the success of security-based programs in the downtown area by noting that the number of 'squeegees' has been substantially reduced, and stated that 'we look at victories where we've sort of taken back the public realm from individuals [such as squeegee workers] who were creating havoc.' A business owner, in giving support to the DVBIA's crime prevention efforts, made the link between retail economics and the Ambassadors program: 'I think the Ambassadors do a good job in that it's nice to have people who have their eyes focused on the street. And it's nice having them be able to help people. We've had a lot more tourism this year, so the economy is coming back ... [The Ambassadors] help.'

The majority of non-business individuals interviewed were unaware of specific programs of the BIAs aside from the security patrols. Of those who discussed the DVBIA patrols, several saw the program as a positive development. One street vendor related a story in which a local woman – 'a street person' – had her stolen handbag retrieved from a dumpster by three Ambassadors. In describing their actions, the vendor repeatedly stressed their 'effectiveness.' An outreach worker, who was somewhat critical of aspects of the Ambassadors program, spoke of why she was not wholly opposed to the program. She spoke of witnessing an Ambassador escorting an individual to a detox facility in the Downtown Eastside at night. This episode convinced the worker that 'It's not all about "You can't pan here." There are some of them that are helping people in a good way.'

In relation to Gastown's security patrols, one business representative advised that the area's merchants were supportive of the program because it made them feel safer in their stores. Such programs are also perceived to be necessary by property owners and merchants, this individual explained, because there was empty retail space on Water Street, attributing this to what he perceived to be a deterioration in public civility in this neighbourhood:

What you see is the downward spiral. The businesses move out ... And this is all due to this kind of behaviour that has been allowed, and the bureaucrats dictating to us about what is and is not allowed and should be acceptable in our neighbourhood. And I'm saying, no. There should be no difference. I don't care if you're in Kerrisdale[193] or you're on Water Street. Why does the code of behaviour have to change? The people aren't behaving like this because they're poor.

It is worth noting that it was difficult to locate individuals other than GBIS members who hold favourable views of its security patrol program. In part, this is because of the nature of the program and what it represents to many within the community: the guards symbolize the socioeconomic disparity of the neighbourhood and its creeping gentrification. However, one representative of a community group did advise that some elderly people feel safer because of the guards.

Areas of Tension and/or Resistance

SECURITY GUARD: 'I feel that police ... they think that they are more over us, you know.'
SENIOR OFFICER: 'Getting police officers to accept [working with private security] is difficult.'

It was apparent from speaking to different sources that, while many police officers accept the presence of private security and are willing to work with them in a limited capacity, not all officers hold private security guards in high esteem. Of those interviewed, some viewed private security guards as a form of nuisance. This was first raised by a non-police subject who has had extensive contacts with the police in District Two:

> We've always raised our concerns about ... private security guards, and the police are sort of keeping their head down. They've tried to stay out of the politics ... But on the Q-T some of them have actually told us that 'This is really a problem and they tend to actually cause more trouble' – the security guards tend to cause more trouble than they actually alleviate.

A police officer subsequently confirmed that mistreatment of members of the public by private security creates problems for police. According to this individual, 'We deal with a lot of victims that become victims because of dealings they've had with private security people, and they've been negative dealings.'

Police subjects were generally concerned about a lack of appropriate training for guards on patrol. This training deficiency was perceived as posing a threat to the safety and rights of the public. As one officer expressed it, 'You always hear of this about the police, but certainly I think that from private police you'll find with more frequency you get more people that complain that their rights have been violated.' Another officer noted that guards lack an 'awareness of a person's rights ... different municipal by-laws or provincial statutes, federal laws, [and the] Criminal Code.'

The subject of private and private-public cooperative policing programs is one on which the communities studied are divided. Some members of community groups approve of these programs or, perhaps more accurately, do not view themselves as being opposed to aspects of these programs (such as the outreach worker who applauded an Ambassador for taking an individual to detox). Other groups, however, are in total opposition to having private security perform public patrols.

Of the latter, some view the presence of private security in public places as part of a general 'poor-bashing' trend, one with disturbing implications. According to this perception, security patrol programs are equivalent to privately owned occupation forces.[194] Security is seen as the arm of businesses that are not above using coercion as a means of imposing an identity on a space that is beneficial for business but is at odds with the community's present and historical reality. The idea of using guards to protect a site and its image for the benefit of businesses and shoppers is viewed as offensive to traditional notions of public space and community. The concerns this raises are brought into focus by a member of a local community group:

> The idea of putting security guards out in order to make the place feel safer for shoppers implies that the public spaces, the streets, are circulation areas between the private spaces – the businesses – [and] are valuable only insofar as they serve to channel people into private businesses ... many people have a weightier view of public space than that ...

The issue of a lack of public accountability for private guards on public patrol was raised by several community group members who expressed concern about the potential for civil rights abuses. As was noted by one subject, the governing legislation – the *Private Investigators and Security Agencies Act*[195] – contains no reference to their use in public. This is viewed as problematic because, without appropriate enforcement mechanisms built into the act, infringements by guards on the rights of citizens go largely unanswered, or are dealt with solely as private disciplinary matters.[196] It is worth noting that a number of residents of Gastown, in discussing both the BIA's previous and present security patrol companies, spoke of harassment of street people and other members of the urban poor as an ongoing concern. As one community group member stated, 'I just hear of really rough treatment of some of our folks [in Gastown] ... I think basically [the guards are] there as a thuggish presence.'

Another criticism directed at security guards in general is in relation to their style of uniforms. One subject suggested that militaristic uniforms, coupled with the affectations that guards often adopt, may confuse or mislead people into believing that guards are police officers. The supposed effect of this would be to render it more likely that people will mistakenly obey a guard's direction. However, individuals interviewed stated that they were easily able to distinguish between security guards and police officers. In particular, subjects were aware that private security guards, unlike public police, have no more legal right to enforce public laws than other citizens. While street youth sometimes referred to police scornfully as 'pigs,' they recognized that police hold a legitimate state-sanctioned form of authority, unlike Ambassadors, who were variously described by youth as 'snitches,' 'street rats,' and 'bitches.'[197] This recognition of the difference in powers leads to small acts of resistance. Both street youth and outreach workers described how kids would disobey Ambassadors' directions to 'move along' by sitting down as soon as an Ambassador's back was turned. Other individuals, when told to move along because they are violating property rights by leaning on a privately owned wall, will sometimes respond by removing their body from the wall, but otherwise remain in place.

Two of the business owners/managers[198] interviewed are opposed to the Gastown patrols. These individuals raised many of the same concerns previously noted. Gastown workers interviewed about the security program were either ambivalent or expressed opposition. One employee of a local business, when asked if he would ever use the services of the GBIS's security patrols, stated that he routinely chooses to deal with conflicts on his own because he feels that the guards are too confrontational.

In relation to the Ambassadors program, a community group member who is also a long-time resident of the Granville area, informed us that 'I know the owners of a couple of businesses that don't support [the Ambassadors] at all. They don't approve of what they're doing, they don't approve of their tactics ...' One business owner, while in the main supportive of the Ambassadors' work, expressed his concern over the philosophy underpinning the program when asked if he would be willing to participate in citizen crime prevention patrols:

> No, I wouldn't do that ... Maybe if we're dealing with Sarajevo outside or Herzegovina. I mean come on here, it's just a bunch of panhandlers and a bunch of kids ... If that's the world you want, you should privatize it and hire security guards ...

Balancing Competing Future Visions: The Problem of Market Segmentation

Competing views of the sites studied, and the role of policing within them, also arise as a direct result of street-level market forces. Retailers and service providers increasingly target their products and services to specially created aggregates within the marketplace.[199] These aggregates are described as the products of advertisers and corporations that create 'lifestyle' or 'niche' submarkets based on a variety of demographic characteristics that are seen to be more closely associated with the image that corporations wish to project for their product.[200] While there have been a number of analyses of market segmentation as it relates to the marketing of products to large-scale audiences through mass communication,[201] what has been neglected is the role that the technology of market segmentation plays in shaping smaller-scale market venues such as specialized shopping districts. Indeed, we are increasingly seeing a 'market segmentation of the street,' as local street-level retailers (BIAs) organize their attempts to draw customers who fit desired demographics.

Lifestyles are not simply abstractions created at the whim of advertisers, as Turow[202] seems to suggest, but very real divisions that can have a significant impact on urban streetscapes. This point was raised during an interview with a local businessperson when the discussion turned to tensions that exist along Granville Mall due to competing visions among retailers of what the site should look like, and what purposes it should ultimately serve. The Entertainment District (TED) concept, which is in the process of being implemented along Granville Mall, is about nightlife. It is about concentrating the number of liquor licence seats in the area to a few blocks within the downtown core, and increasing the number and diversity of bars and cabarets available to serve patrons who are seeking an 'experience.' For this reason, its proponents seek to attract a younger, hipper, 'edgier' type of customer from among the city's tourists

and from its outlying urban and suburban areas, individuals with dispos-
able income who will be drawn to the clubs and bars, as well as to the
funky clothes stores, tattoo parlours, and body-piercing boutiques that
litter the Mall. These stores fit nicely into a vision of homogenized
counter-culture that can be packaged and sold to those seeking 'riskless
risk.' Therefore, in a perverse way, the envisioned 'edginess' of the TED
space would seem to be enhanced through the presence, within 'toler-
able' limits, of the street's youth. Their being in the space, in conjunction with the prophylactic presence of police and security, adds an
authentic touch to the 'slumming' experience while allowing space users
also to feel a measure of safety and security. However, if individuals are
seen to cross the boundary of what is considered acceptable behaviour
in public space – by, for example, displaying signs of active addiction or
being in a particularly 'shabby' or unkempt state – then pressure is
brought to bear on them to move along, as their presence then begins to
detract from the 'experience.'

Not all site operators on Granville fit within the TED concept, and the
markets they cater to reflect widely divergent tastes. For example, businesses on the Mall run the gamut from sex shops to family hotels, from
nightclubs to the Vancouver Symphony. This mix draws disparate consumers, with different personal comfort levels. In the long run, some
businesses may be forced to relocate as their 'up-market' clientele or
'family values' goods and services become increasingly incompatible
with the 'down-market' clientele that TED sponsors will attract. This is
an important point because, although the primary focus here is on how
the imposition of a marketable 'identity' on an urban neighbourhood
can create divisions between residents and businesses, this process can
also foster divisions among retailers and other business interests.

At present, attempts are being made to balance competing market
needs and interests as much as possible. For example, the Orpheum
Theatre has moved its front entrance from Granville Street, so that
symphony patrons may now enter on Smithe[203] Street and avoid
Granville's club-goers and panhandlers. Another problem facing merchants on the street has been the over-representation of sex shops,
which are apparently a little too 'edgy' for the homogenized identity of
TED.[204] In order to reduce this glut of sex shops, the city has pledged to
use strategies involving licensing and municipal by-laws.[205]

Policing remains the primary method used on Granville Mall to bridge
divisions that have resulted from the competing demands of a seg-
mented market space. As a local businessperson advised, 'We find that

people ... that like going to the Orpheum, to the VSO, they don't like the street. The only way that we can make them feel more comfortable is to have a physical presence on the street. Police. The Downtown Ambassadors.' The importance of policing to area businesses in terms of managing the transition from what the street is now to what it could be under the TED concept cannot be overstated. Again, comments by this businessperson make this clear:

> We're going to have entertainment businesses that are going to attract a different type of crowd ... But at some point we have to find a balance ... we have to have a police presence. You have to have Ambassadors doing patrols. You have to try to minimize, again, unruly behaviour. I think that by just having a mere presence of the Ambassadors and the police that does sort of say ... people can have fun but within confines. And if something does get out of those confines there's action that's taken to take it under control. Panhandlers ... they can be on the street if they want to be, but they have to be within the by-law. They can't be aggressive. They can't bother people. Everyone's allowed on the street. We have no right to force people off the street. But at the same time property rights have to be respected ... So it's going to be achieving that delicate balance between all the different users ...

Gastown stands in sharp contrast to Granville Mall, in that there is seen to be less reason for concern among the businesses about balancing space to meet the needs of differing market 'lifestyles.' This is primarily because of the uniform nature of the businesses in the area. While there are a number of artists and dot.com companies present, Gastown operates principally to service day tourists. Many of these tourists disembark from cruise ship terminals seeking 'experience' in the form of a pleasant visit to the historically picturesque sites offered in guidebooks. Their needs and desires are different from those of Mall patrons; 'riskless risk' is not part of the desired experience.

Tensions in Gastown are between long-time lower-income residents (and the community groups who serve them) and area retailers. Business owners appear to agree on a common desire to create and maintain Gastown as a completely 'riskless' environment for tourists. Therefore, while businesses along the Mall seem to have a *marginally* higher tolerance for the presence of 'disorder,' Gastown's security patrols direct their efforts almost exclusively at ensuring that persons or things that project 'disorder,' 'crime,' 'danger,' or anything 'unpleasant' to consumers are completely excluded from the site.

However, given the dynamics of the neighbourhood, and its history and geography, recreating Gastown as a pristine fantasy city completely free from crime-related risk and disorder is an impossible task. There are practical limits to what the GBIS and its patrols can do. These limits are set not only in terms of available money and resources that can be directed towards 'solving the problem,' but also when consideration is given to what the net effect of increased policing would have on the space. As one representative of a security company noted, 'You can't put the guards all up and down there to protect the tourists ... it just starts to look like a police state then.'

Retail Policing in Fantasy City

One of the more interesting stories in Gastown is about the steam clock on Water Street, built in 1977 to replicate an 1875 design. Its claim to fame is that on the quarter-hour it blasts puffs of air to the tune of Westminster chimes, providing endless amusement to the crowds that gather around to take its picture.

It is a fake. It is powered by electricity, although a rather cunning design gives it the appearance of being steam powered. The majority of tourists, and even some locals, are fooled by its appearance. Somehow it seems appropriate that the clock stands as a symbol of Gastown. As a 'genuine reproduction' it not only falsely conjures historical associations to a past that never quite existed in as genteel a fashion as the clock suggests, but it also represents a present that is equally contrived. Gastown is postmodern redevelopment – a pastiche of fake historicism, crass commercialism, and chocolate-box appeal.

Granville Mall, which is itself undergoing redevelopment, is clearly in danger of becoming similarly transmogrified. While terms such as 'fake' and 'contrived' are used to describe the urban entertainment landscape of Vancouver, it is important to remember that fantasy city *is* deception. These sites deceive people into believing that their feelings of nostalgia, their need to be entertained, their desire for 'otherness' or for the exotic, can be fulfilled by a few hours of consumerism disguised as legitimate 'experience.' The deception is perpetrated through the imposition of an 'identity' on a space, and through the use of marketable 'images' associated with that identity that are produced for consumption and are not ultimately 'real' products. And, to be clear, this deception is perpetrated solely as a means of generating revenue. Close examination suggests that the policing that occurs in fantasy city parallels aspects of the environment to the extent that policing in these sites is increasingly focused on producing and preserving images.

In the sections that follow, three arguments are presented. First, that a primary concern of urban entertainment destination operators is control of the image that their spaces project. Second, that much of the policing occurring in Vancouver's urban entertainment destinations is not a response to actual crime but is more properly thought of as related to this task of image management. Third, that the preoccupation of retailers and consumers with image is linked to market forces and specific aspects of consumer culture. Image and profits are entwined.

'Crime Problems'

It is difficult to tell the extent of criminal activity in the sites studied. The Vancouver Police Department does not keep statistics on a neighbourhood-by-neighbourhood basis. And even if it did, such figures would not necessarily be good indicators of levels of crime, as crime is likely to be under-reported in areas where victims are of a low socio-economic status. For this reason, during interviews we asked subjects for their perceptions about problems relating to crime and disorder.

Interestingly, both the police and other respondents acknowledge that a primary, if not the main, task of both public and private police in Gastown is to deal with order maintenance issues rather than crime. Respondents also overwhelmingly agreed that violent crime is not a significant problem in Gastown, that the bulk of offences committed are property crimes associated with drug and alcohol addiction. Auto-related theft is an especially frequent occurrence, with, as one officer described it, 'cars being smashed and ransacked.' Area workers and business owners similarly spoke of businesses being victimized through property crime, especially 'smash and grab' burglaries perpetrated by addicts who often take items of little value. Other common offences include shoplifting, drug dealing, and thefts of tourist luggage and bags.

Perceptions related to crime are especially salient in Gastown. In particular, issues commonly associated with 'urban blight' or 'social decay' were repeatedly raised by respondents when the subject of crime and safety was introduced. The majority of those interviewed acknowledged that Gastown's problems were largely social problems and not criminal matters *per se*. However, the effect of 'nuisance-related' problems on the site's image was cited by many as a significant cause for concern. As one police subject noted, 'I think this neighbourhood ... It looks horrible. I mean you see somebody picking scabs off their face who weighs eighty pounds, you think this neighbourhood is Armageddon.'

Perceptions of crime and danger associated with the presence of panhandlers and the mentally ill are sometimes fed by their behaviour. Incidents in which panhandlers harass people on the street – following behind and shouting, refusing to accept a negative response, and simply the sheer volume of requests for money – have all been observed. As a police subject stated, 'Tourists get very freaked out when they come down here because the aggressive panhandling makes them feel very uncomfortable. I think they're worried that they're going to get mugged right on the street ...' Local retailers are worried that such perceptions, whether accurate or not, will undermine business. In speaking of the subject of panhandling to a vendor, this person opined, 'There's a lot of panhandling and [it] is reaching proportions beyond damage control in the name of our tourism.'

As with Gastown, crime along Granville Mall tends to be low-level property and drug offences. Respondents interviewed stated that serious violent crimes are relatively infrequent, and those that do occur are generally out of the sight of tourists. As one community group member offered, 'We know there's drugs down here. We know there's marijuana and whatever. But ... you don't see people being robbed down here. I mean, we know people are getting robbed, but it's the lower, lower, lower echelon.' While tourists and shoppers have been victimized through purse snatchings and other forms of theft, incidents of robbery or assault tend to occur on 'cheque issue days' and involve individuals 'rolling' other low-income people for welfare money. Thus, contrary to what the presence of private security might suggest, violent crime in this neighbourhood is seen to impact primarily on those who are tradition-ally constituted as the 'disorderly.'

In speaking to the police, it is clear that they also recognize that most issues affecting the community are not Criminal Code offences. One police officer stated unequivocally that the nature of the problems in that area has 'less to do with crime and much more to do with the so-called public order maintenance issue[s]. Things that are irritating to people because people are not respecting each other's rights to be in that public space at the same time. So that's one person's perceptions of their rights to skateboard down the sidewalk, and there's another person's right to not have to listen to the noise and have to constantly look to dodge them. Likewise somebody's right to lie on the sidewalk interferes with somebody else's right to run a business that's attractive.'

This is again reminiscent of the 'civility' theme found in much of the 'broken windows' literature: formal rules and agents of enforcement are necessary to ensure civility in public space because informal rules of 'etiquette' and 'decorum' are not always observed.[206]

As in Gastown, panhandling is seen to be a primary threat to businesses along the Mall. As one business owner explained, 'Panhandling isn't a big problem, it's what you call a visible nuisance problem. For people who want tourist money into the street, particularly retailers and business people in general, property owners, it's a blight because they know people don't like it.' While some panhandlers are older local residents, and include addicts and the mentally ill, many are street youth. Based on observation and comments made by service providers, the youth are significantly less aggressive in their tactics. They tend to be quiet, polite, friendly, and do not harass, follow, or obstruct the path of others, as commonly occurs in Gastown.

Image-Management Projects

In order to combat negative perceptions that result from the presence of various forms of 'social decay,' and, more generally, in response to market dictates and the desire for lifestyle-based consumerism, image management is a central preoccupation in fantasy city. Vancouver's UEDs attempt to project a façade of safety and security while simultaneously offering consumption-oriented pleasure for the consumer classes. This is done through a targeted use of policing.

In a fashion similar to Disney World's use of seductive, informal techniques of control,[207] the police presence in these spaces, both public and private, is experienced by rule-observing tourists and consumers as either non-existent, as blending seamlessly into the space, or as openly friendly or perhaps simply benign. Among tourists in Gastown, some individuals interviewed did not realize that the guards were in fact private security, while others did not notice the guards at all. The focus of the guards' attention is on those who break the formal and informal rules of the space – panhandlers and other street people – rather than on interacting directly and routinely with the area's visitors.

The DVBIA's approach is slightly different from that of Gastown. For the DVBIA, the Ambassadors are themselves a marketable product, a service that it offers to potential consumers, consumers not only of that particular service but also of the other products and services that the site offers. To this end, the Ambassadors are actively marketed through an advertising campaign that signals to would-be space users that this is a helpful, friendly, and approachable service that provides them with safety and well-being, at least in the form of assistance, while visiting the city's downtown core. In order to propagate this image of the Ambassadors, the DVBIA has recently begun placing advertising posters at bus stops across the city. These posters show smiling Ambassadors underneath a caption that reads, 'Wireless, mobile & user friendly.' We are also informed that the Ambassadors are 'Your personal connection to Vancouver's Downtown.'

There are many ways in which the public police also participate in this image-management project. Perhaps the most obvious form of participation is their selective enforcement of 'nuisance' by-laws during tourist season. The issue of whether there was a noticeable difference in levels of police enforcement of the former panhandling by-law between the tourist season and the off season was raised with both panhandlers and community group members. Both groups were generally quick to agree that there is an observable difference. One community group member noted that, 'with the panning laws, cops are tightening up. More so in the summer because of the tourists ... In the wintertime, it eases up a little bit ...' A young panhandler linked increased enforcement to specific public events: 'They'll leave panhandlers alone say like a week or so, but when something like Symphony of Fire or something else [comes along], they're really cracking down.'

Merely having a police presence, regardless of how active this presence is, is not, however, sufficient in terms of assisting the BIAs to achieve their goals. Considerable private and public police attention must also be spent on issues that are directly related to enhancing the areas' images and projecting the appearance of a 'clean' and 'controlled' environment. Previously, the Best Foot Forward program was discussed and the role of the Ambassadors in ensuring that visual signs of dirt and decay are removed from downtown sites, as well as the means by which LPOs attempt to eliminate graffiti. Thus, it is worth noting that GBIS security patrols also perform 'cleaning' functions centred on preserving aesthetics and managing the perceptions of people using the space. An illustration of their activities can be found in an incident witnessed by one of the authors and two members of a community group during a walk through Gastown. Someone had placed posters advertising a march in support of efforts at locating women missing from the Downtown Eastside on various city-owned street poles. A security guard was observed tearing these posters down in order to enforce the city's anti-postering by-law.[208] That this action was clearly tied to managing perceptions was immediately apparent when one considers both the space in which this action occurred and the content of the posters. The posters were put up in a neighbourhood that caters largely to tourists, and advertised a planned protest on behalf of local prostitutes who are believed to have been murdered. By removing these posters, security guards were reinforcing a contrived image of Gastown as a 'safe' or 'crime-free' zone. This interpretation is supported in that the guards are highly selective in relation to which posters they tear down. Posters that relay information concerning homeowners' meetings are usually left in place, while those of local activists and poverty-related community groups are frequently removed.

Moving It Along: One Effect of Image-Management Policing

Although the primary concern here is with the effect that the new policing practices are having on the neighbourhoods studied, it is also worth briefly addressing their effects on other communities. Within the past couple of years, suburbanites within the Lower Mainland (Vancouver and surrounding municipalities) have begun to experience something that was largely unknown to them outside of the downtown core, or known to a significantly lesser extent: panhandling. There are two ready explanations available for understanding the rise of panhandling in nearby communities. First, the increase could reasonably be attributed to gentrification in urban neighbourhoods that formerly housed the poor. As was previously noted, areas such as Granville Mall have seen inexpensive housing stocks decline as SRO hotels and other cheap lodgings were converted into tourist accommodations and/or expensive condominiums. This has 'pushed' some low-income people into other communities where they can find affordable rental properties. Second, and equally likely, is that much of the image-oriented policing described here is producing its intended effect: petty criminals and visible signs of 'disorder' (such as panhandlers) are being 'pushed' into neighbouring areas.

Various interviewees who represented security interests similarly noted changes taking place as a result of what they perceived to be a 'pushing' of crime and disorder out of downtown neighbourhoods. Their insights are worth briefly recording here in light of the lack of available data in the criminological literature on the displacement effect produced by 'broken windows'-style policing.[209] For example, in relation to a discussion on the efficacy of the DVBIA's programs, a subject advised that,

> We know [bad] guys who've said, 'You know you guys are just too much for
> me.' They get on a bus and move out to Metrotown [an area in Burnaby] ...
> Are we having an impact? Yeah, we are, we're having an impact. Are we
> displacing some of that stuff? You bet we are doing some of that.

One security agent, also speaking about the effectiveness of the LPO
program, stated that '[bad guys] know all of a sudden that another
group of loss prevention officers are watching them and they found that
it was not profitable for them to steal in this area and [they] move onto
another one ... Just like prostitution. You go in and you move it out of
the area, you know that it's going to go somewhere else.' This sentiment
was echoed by yet another security representative: 'It's a complex thing
because you're never going to stop crime, you're just going to displace it.'

Why Fantasy City Generates Demand for Image-Oriented Policing

In order to understand more fully why it is that fantasy city generates
demands for new forms of 'image-oriented' policing, it is imperative that
we understand its place in consumer culture.

At its most elemental, today's consumerism is about status consumption and the search for social identity.[210] To this end, retailers and
brands have a vested interest in creating desire through manufacturing
'exclusivity'; that is, through associating products with certain images
that carry cultural cachet, and then marketing them as exclusive products to those willing to pay for the status that being 'exclusive' carries.[211]
Lasn[212] explains how this works:

> The most powerful narcotic in the world is the promise of belonging. And
> belonging is best achieved by conforming to the prescriptions of America ...
> In this way a perverted sense of cool takes hold of the imaginations of our
> children. And thus a heavily manipulative corporate ethos drives our cul-
> ture.

The importance of cultural capital[213] and its accumulation was a
subject that was raised during interviews by individuals of lower socio-
economic status and by community group members. Individuals who
participate in the accumulation of 'stuff' may be less aware of the
processes involved than are those who are unable to participate.

In discussing their experiences as the objects of exclusionary tactics practised by public and private police who enforce laws and policies directed at preserving 'images,' a number of interviewees noted the role of clothing as indicative of social status, and thus of negative or positive ascribed attributes. The difference in attribution of characteristics based on apparel is made explicit in the comments of a local outreach worker. In discussing whether street kids in groups on Granville Mall project an intimidating image to other space users, he stated,

> We have suburbanites come down here and they're standing in a group ... People are walking by [and] they don't seem to be intimidated by the suburbanites dressed in nice FUBU shirts ... But you have our youth standing there with raggedy jeans and holes in them, with skateboards, and that poses a threat.

This perceived threat clearly relates to the fears that urban centres are seen to evoke. Fears are precipitated over the presence of those who are not like us, and are heightened through repeated conflating of panhandling, and other forms of street involvement, with crime.[214] That such perceptions can be mistaken ones, on multiple levels, is evidenced in the following statement of a local street youth:

> I've met a lot more dangerous people wearing rich, expensive clothes ... I'm just saying people dressed in normal as a disguise. ... I used to dress really good and hang around with bad people. Hanging out with people that robbed people, and they looked just like everybody else. [Now] I usually wear all black and scary looking sometimes. And I don't do anything.

These comments offer support for one of Harcourt's[215] criticisms of 'broken windows' thinking: the categories used in order maintenance policing, those of 'order' and 'disorder,' are ultimately useless in facilitating crime prevention because they require individuals to make attributions based on class-based conceptions of what a 'criminal' looks like or how a 'criminal' behaves. As the young panhandler makes clear, these attributions are often erroneous.

For years now, the mall has held a special place in our social life. The mall is also an exclusive space because of the presence of security; it is the mandate of mall security to make sure that people are behaving 'civilly,' which means, in this space, according to consumption-oriented scripts. Thus, you are unlikely to see 'bag ladies' in the Gap, or people panhandling in front of the Eddie Bauer store. The work of the guards ensures that you will only see people like yourself, people with the means to purchase and to wear the products that the mall offers. However, when the street becomes the mall, as is occurring in cities across North America, the problem of how to maintain exclusivity arises. The answer, of course, is to import the technology of the mall onto the street and to apply the same screening processes to ensure that coolness does not become contaminated through contact with the 'uncool.'

How is it that we come to see people as objects to be 'moved along' and otherwise manipulated at our whim? Lasch[216] offers a cogent explanation:

> Commodity production and consumerism alter perceptions not just of the self but of the world outside the self. They create a world of mirrors ... the mirror effect makes the subject an object; at the same time, it makes the world of objects an extension or projection of the self. It is misleading to characterize the culture of consumption as a culture dominated by things. The consumer lives surrounded not so much by things as by fantasies. He lives in a world that has no objective or independent existence and seems to exist only to gratify or thwart his desires.

Extending Lasch's thoughts, we see that fantasy city isn't just about offering patrons consumable 'experiences,' or even about offering consumable products and services; it is also about providing a site where consumers can consume images, including their own. Like the hall of mirrors in the amusement park funhouse, fantasy city is an attempt at escaping reality, where everything, including ourselves, becomes a series of fantastic images reflected off the mirrors that the site provides. In entering this space, we enter the world of the hyper-unreal. Strolling along cobble-stoned pathways to visit a shop that offers 'genuine' reproductions, dancing on tabletops in *faux*-Mexican cantinas, throwing darts in an 'English-style' pub, or experimenting with pink afros and tongue rings in the most oxymoronic of places – the trendy counter-culture shop – we try out new identities for ourselves and others to see and experience.

Lasch[217] also argues that 'the state of mind promoted by consumerism is better described as a state of uneasiness and chronic anxiety.' Our ever-increasing preoccupation with fantasy, as evidenced by our desire for fun (at almost any cost) is the result of a state of anxiety provoked by mass-media entertainment outlets, product manufacturers, and retailers who all have a vested interest in presenting idealized versions of the 'ultimate self' – selves that can never be achieved because they are simulacra, images of images that do not exist.

For most of us, poverty, mental illness, and addiction are not the stuff of fantasy. The presence of poverty in spaces of pleasure serves not only as a reminder of what can happen to the less fortunate of us – fears we would like to be protected from – but it also has no intrinsic amusement value. In fact, quite the opposite; it is alternately depressing, fear-inducing, boring, guilt-provoking, sad, frustrating, anxiety-producing, confusing, and so on – all unpleasant feelings that we seek to escape by going to a site intended to offer us pleasure and distraction. Wardhaugh[218] sums up this nexus well: 'there is something dangerously pre-modern about the poverty and apparent disarray of beggars and other street people that sits uncomfortably with the struggle for identity and a sense of place engaged in by the inhabitants of the postmodern city.'

It is not only our struggle for identity that causes our reaction towards those we seek to dispossess from spaces; it is also our belief that they lack identity and, more dangerously still, that they have given up, or are in the process of giving up, the struggle that we may find ourselves engaged in. Douglas[219] clearly speaks to this in discussing the relationship between 'dirt,' 'disorder,' and 'identity':

> In the course of any imposing of order, whether in the mind or in the external world, the attitude to rejected bits and pieces goes through two stages. First they are recognizably out of place, a threat to good order, and so are regarded as objectionable and vigorously brushed away. At this stage they have some identity: they can be seen to be unwanted bits of whatever it was they came from ... this is the state at which they are dangerous; their half-identity still clings to them and the clarity of the scene in which they obtrude is impaired by their presence.

These 'unwanted bits' represent disorder because they are abandoned, derelict, and 'dirty' (visually or otherwise aesthetically unappealing – at least by the standards of the consumer culture's aesthetics). And, because 'dirt offends against order,' we can thus perceive the actions of the BIAs, in concert with the city and the public police, as representing a move towards restoring order: '[eliminating dirt] is not a negative movement, but a positive effort to organize the environment.'[220]

Where the urban poor are tolerated to some degree is in those spaces that utilize their presence for 'image management' purposes related to the 'experience' offered. However, even then, risk in the form of human or other physical symbols associated with poverty, crime, and danger is only tolerated if it is 'riskless risk,' risk that is managed, sterilized, contained, or otherwise rendered 'harmless' for general consumption.

What Fantasy City Tells Us

Fantasy city is a physical manifestation of social changes that are occurring on a global basis. Analysis of this physical space reveals the extent to which we have become mired in a consumerism that is seductive for those with means but retains a strong coercive element directed at excluding those without. This consumerism, fuelled by a multibillion-dollar advertising and entertainment industry, is seductive because it plays on twin desires: to belong, and to experience pleasure without pain.

Advertising and media increasingly dictate the manner and style of our social interactions. 'Shopping is good'[221] because it provides fulfilment of social needs. Primarily, the need is to be part of a community, with a common purpose involving others and identification with a group. However, in a consumer-oriented society this need becomes perverted so that the primary messages sent and received are those associated with status and hierarchy based on consumption of material goods. Belonging in a more encompassing sense is replaced with a form of belonging that has multiple forms of inclusion and exclusion.

The nature of some of the divisions that are being created and maintained in the public realm has been explored here through an examination of policing strategies used by retailers in order to preserve the integrity of the consumer's 'experience.' The targets of these strategies include the homeless and other urban poor, who are told to 'move along' in order to assist in the presentation of desired images to be sold and packaged to fun-seekers. Reminders of poverty, inequality, difference, and/or anything that does not fit the desired image are similarly removed from these sites.

In order to assist the objective of image maintenance, the city has borrowed from its counterparts across North America and enacted a series of 'public order' or 'quality of life' by-laws that disproportionately affect the poor, and are used as instruments by both public and private police to expunge their presence from public space or to regulate their behaviour. Proponents of the enforcement of such by-laws, principally Kelling and Coles[222] and Ellickson,[223] have argued that individuals should be judged on their behaviour and not on their status. This is a disingenuous argument, and one that calls to mind de Tocqueville's famous comment on the poor and rich alike being prohibited from stealing bread and sleeping under bridges. The acts that each cite as 'disorderly,' such as panhandling, bench squatting, or sitting on sidewalks, cannot be isolated from the actor's status since individuals who perform such actions often do so for reasons related to their status. For example, low-income individuals in the neighbourhoods studied view adjacent areas of public space as a type of 'living room,' a place where they can visit with their neighbours and participate in their community. This occurs because the tiny, squalid, SRO rooms that many live in do not facilitate social interaction. Individuals who defecate and urinate in public spaces, acts particularly viewed as offensive by 'broken windows' proponents,[224] often do so because they have limited or no access to washrooms. Open-access public restrooms are limited in the city, and the majority of 'public' facilities are only available to paying consumers of products and services. Finally, what Kelling and others neglect to address satisfactorily when insisting on the necessity of enforcing codes of public behaviour that reflect dominant middle-class values is the degree to which standards are being imposed on areas where other values have traditionally held sway. This imposition comes about through the 'reclamation' of desirable urban property from the urban poor by redevelopers and others.

In some instances, such as on Granville Mall, the urban poor are more likely to be tolerated by retail and other interests because they serve as 'props' on a site that caters to a young and hip market, a clientele that is searching for 'riskless risk.' In such cases, 'quality of life' by-laws assist private security and police by providing a means by which any 'danger' that these props may signal to others is reasonably contained. In still other situations, notably in Gastown, by-laws similarly assist in the image-management project, although the project is a markedly different one. In Gastown, 'quality of life' by-laws are used simply to effect removal of those things that do not project the desired image of quaintness and heritage, or that offer competing visions of the space.

These projects, and similar ones across North America, have led to the creation of 'image-oriented policing,' a form of public-private policing modelled on the 'broken windows' theory. Such policing is primarily directed at the creation and maintenance of images through the regulation of signs of disorder. Image-oriented policing has as its goal the re-creation of public space as 'orderly' commercialized sites. This link between order and commercialization is evidenced in multiple sources: from the City Hall person who advised us that a 'healthy community' is one where people shop, to the police officer who envisioned progress as a Starbucks in the middle of a ghetto. It can also be found in the underlying connection between 'quality of life' policies and policing and conceptions of public space as commercial space. This link is also made explicit in the work of Ellickson,[225] who views public disorder as 'the tragedy of the marketplace.' 'Broken windows' and other such image-oriented forms of policing that have as their aim the regulation of signs of disorder are, and are intended to be, exclusionary. Exclusion is based largely on surface appearance, including appearing to possess the means to consume.

This study has also revealed, in part, the extent to which policing is becoming commodified and the way in which this process is blurring the traditional boundaries between public and private policing. Security guards now patrol public streets on behalf of retailers, and are used to provide services that the public police no longer have the time, money, or inclination to carry out. This is best exemplified by the Loss Prevention Officers, who not only conduct surveillance and set up covert 'sting' operations for retail and auto-related thefts but, on a more mundane level, routinely fill out Crown reports – a task that was formerly conducted only by peace officers.

It is not only the private police who are a commodity to be purchased and used. Increasingly, the services of the public police are being bought by retail and other business interests. The deployment centre and the CAPP pager program are cases in point. What is particularly interesting about such transactions is that they are most often conducted under the guise of community policing, a set of practices that carry with them egalitarian principles that are never truly realized. Nor can they be, because most citizens and citizen groups lack similar means to purchase buildings and high-tech equipment in order to ensure police cooperation for ordinary community efforts.

This buying and selling of policing has had a serious impact on the urban environment itself and, particularly, in relation to our understanding of public space. Urban geographers and others have been decrying for years the changing face of the urban landscape resulting from increasing losses of public space through privatization. What they have noted is that privatization has largely been a result of local and/or provincial or state efforts to increase revenues in urban centres. What has largely escaped undetected is the role of the police in facilitating this process. Whereas the city remains heavily involved in privatization through its planning committees and its BIA development program, the police assist by actively supporting the efforts of business interests in their order maintenance efforts. They do this, for example, by lending some of their authority to BIA programs, and specifically to the guards, and they do so knowing that the guards routinely push people off the public streets at the behest of the BIAs. The message that is conveyed by such activities is that the streets belong not to the public but to retailers and consumers. This message is reinforced during tourist season and special events, when the police initiate 'public order' crackdowns on street people. It is not coincidental that such times are the most profitable for retailers.

The Politics of Community Identity

What is taking place in both of the spaces studied is a struggle for identity that in many ways reflects contemporary identity crises occurring within, and spurred by, the consumer market-place. In today's society, in order to be successful at their enterprise, entities must have a socially desirable identity.[226] This identity must be a whole image because, as Douglas[227] rightly suggests, we seem unable to tolerate ambiguities. The politics of identity, as applied to community, necessarily revolves around those questions that are also seen to apply to individuals, to companies, to market-places, and even to countries: What should the community look like? What vision should it have for itself? How ought its members to feel about it? What steps should be taken to achieve its goals? What image does it wish to project to outsiders? What and whose interests will it ultimately serve? These are questions that many inner-city dwellers, community groups, space users, politicians, and business interests face, and will continue to struggle with, as redevelopers continue to promote the economic benefits of establishing urban entertainment destinations and other spaces that import the consumer classes to low-income neighbourhoods.

Political, economic, social, and cultural issues surrounding community identity threaten to undermine the ability to achieve the wholeness desired by site operators and redevelopers. These issues speak to divisions within market segments, local neighbourhoods, and the larger society, and particularly to those divisions that centre on the question of what conception of 'the good' neighbourhoods and other spaces ought to be striving for. Wholeness in identity, in image, can be achieved, but this means exorcising those parts that are not perceived to fit. It means the silencing of voices within a community in order to preserve an aesthetic that, superficially at least, appears to have seamlessness and unity of form.

Does it have to be that way? Of course not. There is nothing inevitable or particularly necessary about creating and maintaining whole images and presenting them as identities. This is a fiction of the market-place, and one that speaks to a shallow preoccupation with surface and a lack of imagination and adventure. Its effects are dangerous, and they clearly threaten to destroy fragile or faltering communities by erasing or weakening the diversity, and thus the vibrancy, that can exist within them. Furthermore, it exacerbates tensions among groups, and thus can threaten to undermine further the stability of a neighbourhood.

Notes

1 John Hannigan, *Fantasy City: Pleasure and Profit in the Postmodern Metropolis* (New York: Routledge, 1998).
2 'Consumable experiences' refers to the use of entertainment and cultural themes as a means of selling retail products and services. A consumer is not merely purchasing a product; he or she is also buying an 'experience.'
3 Hannigan, *supra* note 1.
4 Ibid.
5 Don Slater, *Consumer Culture and Modernity* (Cambridge: Polity Press, 1997).
6 Ibid., at 174.
7 Joseph Turow, *Breaking Up America: Advertisers and the New Media World* (Chicago: University of Chicago Press, 1997) at 3. He describes lifestyle marketing as the blending of variables (income, generation, gender, etc.) into *geographical and psychological profiles* that advertisers can use to target their desired audience.
8 Ibid.
9 Christopher Lasch, *The Minimal Self: Psychic Survival in Troubled Times* (New York: W.W. Norton and Co., 1984).
10 Kalle Lasn, *Culture Jam: How to Reverse America's Suicidal Consumer Binge – and Why We Must* (New York: HarperCollins, 1999).
11 Slater, *supra* note 5.
12 Naomi Klein, *No Logo: Taking Aim at the Brand Bullies* (Toronto: Random, 2000) at 23.
13 Ibid.
14 Lasn, *supra* note 10.

15 Klein, *supra* note 12.
16 Hannigan, *supra* note 1.
17 Margaret Crawford, 'The World in a Shopping Mall,' in Michael Sorkin, ed., *Variations on a Theme Park: The New American City and the End of Public Space* (New York: Hill and Wang, 1992); Paul Goldberger, 'The Rise of the Private City,' in Julia Vitullo-Martin, ed., *Breaking Away: The Future of Cities* (New York: Twentieth Century Fund Press, 1996) at 135–47; and David Ley, *The New Middle Class and the Remaking of the Central City* (Oxford: Oxford University Press, 1996).
18 Hannigan, *supra* note 1.
19 Marc V. Levine, 'The Politics of Partnership: Urban Redevelopment since 1949,' in Gregory D. Squires, ed., *Unequal Partnerships: The Political Economy of Urban Redevelopment in Postwar America* (New Brunswick, N.J.: Rutgers University Press, 1989) at 12–34.
20 Goldberger, *supra* note 17 at 138.
21 Hannigan, *supra* note 1.
22 Ken Jones, 'The Urban Retail Landscape,' in Trudi Bunting and Pierre Filion, eds, *Canadian Cities in Transition* (Toronto: Oxford University Press, 1991) at 379–400.
23 Umberto Eco, *Travels in Hyperreality*, trans. Walter Weaver (New York: Harvest Books, 1986).
24 Jean Baudrillard, *Simulacra and Simulation*, trans. S.F. Glaser (Ann Arbor: University of Michigan Press, 1992).
25 John Mackie, 'Back to the Streets: Shoppers across North America Are Leaving the Small Malls for the Funky Atmosphere of Street Shopping,' *Vancouver Sun* (15 November 1997) B6.
26 Steven Lagerfeld, 'What Main Street Can Learn from the Mall,' *Atlantic Monthly* (November 1995). See also Mackie, *supra* note 25.
27 Ibid.
28 Mackie, *supra* note 25 at B6.
29 Lagerfeld, *supra* note 26.
30 Goldberger, *supra* note 17.
31 Ibid.
32 Ley, *supra* note 17.
33 Mike Davis, *City of Quartz: Excavating the Future in Los Angeles* (New York: Vintage Books, 1992).
34 Richard V. Ericson and Kevin D. Haggerty, *Policing the Risk Society* (Toronto: University of Toronto Press, 1997). See also George L. Kelling and Catherine M. Coles, *Fixing Broken Windows: Restoring Order and Reducing Crime in our Communities* (New York: Martin Kessler Books, 1996).

35 James Q. Wilson and George L. Kelling, 'Broken Windows: The Police and Neighborhood Safety,' *Atlantic Monthly* (March 1982).

36 Kelling and Coles, *supra* note 34.

37 Albert J. Reiss, 'The Legitimacy of Intrusion into Private Space,' in Clifford D. Shearing and Philip C. Stenning, eds, *Private Policing* (Newbury Park: Sage Publications, 1987) at 19–44; Robert C. Ellickson, 'Controlling Chronic Misconduct in City Spaces: Of Panhandlers, Skid Rows, and Public-space Zoning' (1996) 105:5 The Yale Law Journal 1165.

38 Davis, *supra* note 33.

39 Harcourt (1998) makes this point perfectly clear through a deconstruction of Zimbardo's (1969) famous car-vandalism study, a study frequently cited as offering support for 'broken windows.' Zimbardo found that many of the *vandals* who stripped and destroyed the abandoned car, were *well-dressed, apparently clean-cut whites*, including one family of four. Bernard C. Harcourt, 'Reflecting on the Subject: A Critique of the Social Influence Conception of Deterrence, the Broken Windows Theory and Order-maintenance Policing New York Style' (1998) 97:2 Michigan Law Review 291–390.

40 Mary Douglas and Michalis Lianos, 'Dangerization and the End of Deviance: The Institutional Environment' (2000) 40 British Journal of Criminology 261.

41 Ibid., at 273.

42 Roger Hopkins Burke, 'Begging, Vagrancy and Disorder,' in Roger Hopkins Burke, ed., *Zero Tolerance Policing* (Leicester: Perpetuity Press, 1998) at 82–90.

43 Harcourt, *supra* note 39.

44 Ibid.

45 Ralph H. Saunders, 'The Politics and Practice of Community Policing in Boston' (1999) 20:5 Urban Geography 461.

46 Ibid., at 461–3.

47 Ian Loader, 'Consumer Culture and the Commodification of Policing and Security' (1999) 33:2 Sociology 373.

48 Ibid., at 376.

49 Loader, *supra* note 47.

50 David Garland, 'The Limits of the Sovereign State' (1996) 36:4 The British Journal of Criminology 445.

51 Ibid., at 452.

52 Ibid., at 447.

53 Local governments not only utilize the services of private security through BIA and other programs, they also retain private security services directly. For example, Vancouver City Hall contracts a security service to patrol its main library. Private security has also replaced former federal officers: a private company now performs security functions at the Vancouver Interna-

tional Airport in place of RCMP members, and does security patrols on the
Vancouver waterfront that were formerly conducted by Ports Canada police.

54 Steven Spitzer and Andrew T. Scull, 'Privatization and Capitalist Development: The Case of the Private Police,' in Kevin R.E. McCormick and Livy
Visano, eds, *Understanding Policing* (Toronto: Canadian Scholars' Press,
1992) 545.

55 Clifford D. Shearing and Philip C. Stenning, 'From the Panopticon to
Disney World: The Development of Discipline,' in Anthony Doob and
Edward Greenspan, eds, *Perspectives in Criminal Law* (Aurora: Canada Law
Book, 1984).

56 Ibid., at 527.

57 Loader, *supra* note 47.

58 Kevin Stenson, 'Community Policing as a Governmental Technology' (1993)
22:3 Economy and Society 373.

59 Hannigan, *supra* note 1 at 71.

60 Ibid.

61 Shearing and Stenning, *supra* note 55.

62 Christian Parenti, *Lockdown America* (London: Verso, 1999).

63 Davis, *supra* note 33.

64 Shearing and Stenning, *supra* note 55.

65 Ibid., at 344.

66 Parenti, *supra* note 62.

67 Davis, *supra* note 33; Hannigan, *supra* note 1; Zygmunt Bauman, *Work,
Consumerism and the New Poor* (Buckingham: Open University Press, 1998);
and Parenti, *supra* note 62.

68 Wilson and Kelling, *supra* note 35.

69 Mike Davis, *Ecology of Fear: Los Angeles and the Imagination of Disaster* (New
York: Vintage Books, 1999). See also Davis, *supra* note 33, and Crawford,
supra note 17.

70 The success of fantasy city is leading to a reverse trend – elements of UEDs
are now being imported into the mall. We witnessed the growth of this trend
recently in a suburb of Vancouver when a mall – the Metrotown shopping
complex – recently rechristened itself Metropolis and began to lease space
to 'experience' retailers such as the Rainforest Café (mechanical jungle),
Coast Mountain Sports (rock-climbing walls), and Superstar Sports (*faux*
indoor running track).

71 Harcourt, *supra* note 39; Wesley G. Skogan, *Disorder and Decline: Crime and the
Spiral of Decay in American Neighborhoods* (New York: Free Press, 1990); Dan
Macallair and Khaled Taqi-Eddin, *Shattering 'Broken Windows': An Analysis of
San Francisco's Alternative Crime Policies* (San Francisco: The Justice Policy
Institute, 1999).

72 Wilson and Kelling, *supra* note 35.
73 Interviews by Kevin Haggerty and Laura Huey. Fieldwork by Laura Huey.
74 By open-focused, it is meant that interviewers did not use a set of pre-prepared questions but rather raised a set of general concerns that subjects spoke to. Keeping the interview style very open and loose permitted subjects to raise issues that they had not previously considered.
75 TKO Productions, video, *Private Security, Public Places*, produced and directed by Todd Keller, 1998.
76 Business Improvement Area of British Columbia (BIABC) (27 February 2000), online: http://www.biabc.com.
77 *Municipal Act*, R.S.B.C. 1996, c. 323, s.233.
78 *Vancouver Charter*, S.B.C. 1953, c. 55, s. 456.
79 City of Vancouver, 2000c, 'Approval of Business Improvement Area (BIA) Budgets,' *Administrative Report* (15 March 2000) C File No. 8300, online: http://www.city.vancouver.bc.ca/ctyclerk/cclerk/000330/pe4.htm.
80 Ibid.
81 BIABC, *supra* note 76.
82 Ibid.
83 Ibid.
84 Ibid.
85 City of Vancouver, 'Business Improvement Area Program,' *Policy Report: Urban Structure* (14 October 1997) CC File No. 8000, online: http://www.city.vancouver.bc.ca/ ctyclerk/cclerk/971030/pe1.htm.
86 City of Vancouver, 'Business Improvement Area (BIA) Program,' *Administrative Report* (18 December 1998) CC File No. 8300, online: http://www.city.vancouver.bc.ca/ctyclerk/cclerk/971030/pe1a.htm.
87 City of Vancouver, *supra* note 79.
88 Ibid.
89 Downtown Vancouver Business Improvement Association, 'Annual Report to the Members: 1998/99,' *Annual Report* (1999a).
90 Downtown Vancouver Business Improvement Association, 'Downtown: News from the Downtown Vancouver Business Improvement Association Newsletter' (May 2000).
91 *Supra* note 89; See also ibid.
92 *Supra* note 89.
93 Ibid.
94 Downtown Vancouver Business Improvement Association, 2000c (2 July 2000), online: http://downtownvancouver.net.
95 Downtown Vancouver Business Improvement Association, *supra* note 89.
96 Ibid.
97 Ibid.

 98 Ibid.
 99 Michael Hartford, 'Downtown Revitalization Program: Issues and Experiences' (1993) Province of British Columbia, Ministry of Municipal Affairs, Recreation and Housing.
100 Ibid.
101 'Discover Gastown' (1 July 2000), online: http://www.gastown.org.
102 Ibid.
103 City of Vancouver, *supra* note 79.
104 Verdant, *Homeless Street Youth in Downtown South: A Snapshot Study*, City of Vancouver Social Planning Department report (June 2000).
105 Ibid.
106 Our observations did not uncover anything significant on the issue of ethnic relations in the areas studied. This is most likely because the sites studied are in varying stages of gentrification, and thus are becoming predominantly white neighbourhoods.
107 Robin Ward, 'New Name for Granville Won't Solve Its Problems,' *Vancouver Sun* (9 April 1997) C6 and C8.
108 Ibid.
109 Ibid.
110 Ibid.
111 Doug Ward, 'Vancouver's Last Frontiers: Granville Strip Transforming a Dysfunctional Main Drag,' *Vancouver Sun* (2 March 1996) D1.
112 Charles Gauthier, 'Subtle Changes to Granville,' *Vancouver Province* (1 September 1998) A19.
113 Liquor seats refers to the number of patrons that can be served in an establishment that operates to sell alcohol.
114 City of Vancouver, 'Pending or Current Policy Development Plans' (26 May 2000), online: http://www.city.vancouver.bc.ca.
115 Downtown Vancouver Business Improvement Association, 'Renewal 2000: A Special Report,' *Downtown Vancouver Business Improvement Association Newsletter* (1999b).
116 Downtown Vancouver Business Improvement Association, 'Annual Report to the Members: 1999/00,' *Annual Report* (2000g).
117 City of Vancouver, 'Community Profiles: This Is Downtown' 20 September 2001, online: http://www.city.vancouver.bc.ca/commsvcs/profiles/Downtown.html.
118 City of Vancouver, 'Community Monitoring Report: Downtown Eastside' (2000). Income levels and other demographic data from the Gastown 2001 census are likely to show the extent to which gentrification has occurred in the neighbourhood.

119 Ibid.
120 Ibid.
121 Ibid.
122 Gastown Rehabilitation Project, 'Newsletter,' Vancouver City Archives Pamphlets, 1977–49.
123 Ley, *supra* note 17 at 238.
124 Gastown, *supra* note 122.
125 Ley, *supra* note 17 at 238.
126 Ibid.
127 City of Vancouver, Vancouver Police Department: Operations Division, District One (30 June 2000) 2000d, online: http://www.city.vancouver. bc.ca/police/structure/operations/patrol.d1.htm.
128 Ibid.
129 Ibid.
130 Ibid.
131 City of Vancouver, *supra* note 117.
132 Attorney General of British Columbia, 'Materials on Private Security Released under FOI Request ATG-00-212' (2000).
133 Ibid.
134 R.S.B.C. 1992, chapter 34.
135 The current style of Ambassador program owes much to similar programs found in other North American cities, such as Philadelphia, Washington, D.C., Winnipeg, and Ottawa.
136 Downtown Vancouver Business Improvement Association, *supra* note 89.
137 Ibid.
138 Ibid.
139 Ibid.
140 Ibid.
141 Downtown Vancouver Business Improvement Association, 'Annual Report to the Members: 1996/97,' *Annual Report* (1997).
142 Downtown Vancouver Business Improvement Association, *supra* note 89.
143 Downtown Vancouver Business Improvement Association, 2001a, Newsletter, 'Downtown Bulletin' (May 2001). According to the DVBIA, not all of these interactions involved requests to 'move along.' Interactions also included exchanges of information, with Ambassadors advising individuals on where to obtain meals and shelter.
144 Wilson and Kelling, *supra* note 35.
145 Ibid.
146 The panhandling by-law was legally amended by City Council in early March of 2001, as a result of a successful challenge to a similar by-law in

Winnipeg and court action in Vancouver by anti-poverty groups scheduled for March of 2001. The amendments substantially loosen some of the restrictions on panhandling but still place limits on people's ability to beg on Vancouver's city streets.

147 This was in keeping with a provision of the panhandling by-law that prohibited begging while sitting or lying down.

148 Much attention was given by the media to the statements of public police that they seldom, if ever, enforced the panhandling by-law. Such statements were misleading. The public police may not have given out tickets to pan-handlers, but the police routinely told panhandlers to 'get up' or 'to move along,' using the threat of a ticket under the by-law as a means of ensuring compliance. During the course of interviewing a subject on Granville Mall, researcher Laura Huey and her interview subject were directed by a police officer to 'get up' from the sidewalk, even though neither was in the act of soliciting money. The mere appearance of individuals sitting or crouching on the sidewalk was sufficient to trigger the order.

149 The question asked of a senior officer about security guard abuses, and the answer quoted above, were not specific to the Ambassadors program.

150 Downtown Vancouver Business Improvement Association, *supra* note 89.

151 The use of police mug-shots in these files was noted during an interview. The actual source of the mug-shot is not known. In response to a question on this point the interviewee advised that 'You can always scan pictures in on a scanner.'

152 In Canada, charges are filed by Crown counsel upon the recommendations of police. Police officers must fill out a Crown report that provides details of the alleged crime and information on evidence gathered.

153 This involves filling out the first two pages of the Crown report and providing a narrative of what occurred.

154 The degree to which public police and the LPOs work jointly on 'sting' operations is not known. However, at least two subjects advised that public police 'cooperate' in such endeavours.

155 To be clear, one of the objectives of the LPOs is to police signs; however, they do fulfil other functions that further distinguish this program from the Ambassadors. But the overall objective of both programs is the same: to provide a functional environment for the profitable transaction of business.

156 Tourists and local shoppers are likely more affected by thefts from autos than other groups because thieves looking for quick and easy cash will target cars with consumer goods, cameras, and so on, lying visible within a car's interior.

157 Hartford, *supra* note 99 at 73.

158 Wilson and Kelling, *supra* note 35 at 38.

159 Ibid.

160 For examples of documented cases of violent acts committed by security guards, see TKO, *supra* note 75. See also Barbara Waldern, 1998a, 'Civic Rights and Policing Jurisdiction Issues Regarding Private Security Guards Patrolling Public Areas,' Brief submitted to the Attorney General for British Columbia, Ujjal Dosanjh (18 November 1998); and, Barbara Waldern, 1998b, 'When Crime Prevention Becomes Criminal: Growing Use of Private Security Guards Alarming,' *The CCPA Monitor* (December 1997/ 30 January 1998). Although allegations of security guard violence were raised during interviews, no attempt was made to substantiate these stories, as this issue was not a primary focus of this study.

161 Everett C. Hughes, *The Sociological Eye: Selected Papers* (New York: Aldine, 1971).

162 Vancouver Police Department, Pamphlet, 2000c, 'Operation Cooperation.'

163 Ibid.

164 Ibid.

165 Vancouver Police Department, Pamphlet, 2000d, 'Crime Alert Pager Program.'

166 Ibid.

167 Vancouver Police Department, *supra* note 162.

168 It is worth noting that the initial CAPP program start-up costs for the Police Department were significantly underwritten by outside interests. Of the roughly $5,750 operating cost for the initial fifty designated police pagers, the police committed only $1,000; the remaining money was secured from external sources. Vancouver Police Department, 2000e, 'Materials on Crime Alert Pager Program and Business Links Released under FOI Request 00-0785A.'

169 Vancouver Police Department, *supra* note 165.

170 TeleLink Paging Network (31 January 2000), online: http://www.telelink. com.

171 Ibid.

172 Vancouver Police Department, 2000e, *supra* note 168.

173 Ralph H. Saunders, 'The Politics and Practice of Community Policing in Boston' (1999) 20:5 Urban Geography 461.

174 Vancouver Police Department, *supra* note 165.

175 Vancouver Police Department, 2000a, 'Materials on Deployment Centre Released under FOI Request 00-0573A.'

176 The Vancouver Police and Native Liaison Society, the Chinese Community

Policing Centre, the Gastown Community Policing Centre, and the Downtown Eastside Neighbourhood Safety Office.

177 Vancouver Police Board, 'Written Response to the Coalition against Police Brutality and Harassment' (26 April 2000).

178 Ibid.

179 Ibid.

180 Ibid.

181 Ibid.

182 Ibid.

183 Vancouver Police Department, *supra* note 175.

184 Ibid.

185 Ellickson, *supra* note 37.

186 Ibid., at 1179.

187 Ibid., at 1188.

188 Ibid.

189 Ibid.; Kelling and Coles, *supra* note 34.

190 The presence of the panhandlers in such spaces can be seen as personifying powerful social messages with distinct anticapitalist overtones – messages that conservative thinkers tend to portray as socially insignificant, or as rabble-rousing that occurs at the expense of others (usually the mythical 'honest taxpayer').

191 Shane McCune, 'Private Cash Pays for Police Station,' *Vancouver Province* (9 December 1999) A39.

192 Garland, *supra* note 50.

193 Kerrisdale is a relatively wealthy community in Vancouver's west side.

194 Conversely, in District Two, some business owners view the police as 'doing nothing,' or as 'not doing enough' to alleviate problems of social disorder and crime. This has led to a frequently rocky relationship between police management in this district and local business interests. The extent of the anger felt by members of the Strathcona, Gastown, and Chinatown business communities towards the police department for its perceived failings was evidenced recently by the formation of the Community Alliance group, which has been outspoken in its criticisms of the department and its drug confiscation policy. Shane McCune, 'Fed-up Merchants Tell City to Arrest Junkies,' *Vancouver Province* (10 August 2000) A6.

195 *Private Investigators and Security Agencies Act, supra* note 134.

196 What is particularly disturbing about the *Private Investigators and Security Agencies Act* is that it favours the concerns of private security service providers over those of the public. This is suggested because individual complainants are not allowed input during any stage of the process. Nor

are they made aware of the ultimate disposition of their case. This is because the act treats investigations confidentially. Thus, the act does not allow for publication of the names of offender agencies, so that those agencies or individuals with particularly bad track records in dealing with the public are never subjected to public scrutiny.

197 A street slang term to denote someone who is weak or lacking in power.

198 We have not provided any identifying information concerning the two business owners who are opposed to the patrols because Gastown is a very small space. To do so would risk compromising their anonymity.

199 Turow, *supra* note 7.

200 Ibid.

201 Ibid.

202 Ibid.

203 Many references to the Orpheum's location list the theatre as being on Smithe and Seymour rather than Smithe and Granville.

204 Elizabeth Aird, 'Attempts to Regulate the City's Porn Shops: Uncovering a Can of Worms,' *Vancouver Sun* (24 November 1994) B1.

205 Frances Bula, 'Bid to Clean Up Porn Shops Faces Opposition,' *Vancouver Sun* (10 February 1995) B2. See also Andy Ivens, 'Planned Sex-shop Law Riles Citizens and Store Owners,' *Vancouver Province* (11 January 1995) A8.

206 Kelling and Coles, *supra* note 34; Albert Reiss, 'The Legitimacy of Intrusion into Private Space,' in Shearing and Stenning, eds, *supra* note 37, at 19; and Ellickson, *supra* note 37.

207 Shearing and Stenning, *supra* note 55.

208 Vancouver has an anti-postering by-law that prohibits the placement of posters on city or private property. Posters are permitted in 'kiosks' that are provided by the city in designated places. The enforcement of this by-law, including removal of the posters, is rightfully the jurisdiction of city by-law enforcers. However, one individual from City Hall advised in a conversation that there is nothing to prevent private citizens, including guards, from enforcing the by-law by tearing down posters placed on city property.

209 Bernard Cohen, 'Police Enforcement of Quality-of-life Offending: A Critique,' in William S. Laufer and Freda Adler, eds, *The Criminology of Criminal Law* (New Brunswick, N.J.: Transaction Publ., 1999) 107; Eli B. Silverman, 'Below Zero Tolerance: The New York Experience,' in Roger Hopkins Burke, ed., *Zero Tolerance Policing* (Leicester: Perpetuity Press, 1998) 57.

210 Lasch, supra note 9; Lasn, *supra* note 10; and Klein, *supra* note 12. See also Juliet B. Schor, *The Overspent American* (New York: Basic Books, 1998).

211 Schor, ibid.

212 Lasn, *supra* note 10 at xiii.
213 Pierre Bourdieu, *The Logic of Practice*, trans. Richard Nice (Cambridge: Polity Press, 1990).
214 Julia Wardhaugh, 'Homeless in Chinatown: Deviance and Social Control in Cardboard City' (1996) 30:4 Sociology 701.
215 Harcourt, *supra* note 39.
216 Lasch, *supra* note 9 at 30.
217 Lasch, *supra* note 9 at 28.
218 Wardhaugh, *supra* note 214 at 709.
219 Mary Douglas, *Purity and Danger: An Analysis of Concepts of Pollution and Taboo* (London: Routledge, 1979).
220 Ibid., at 2.
221 This is a slogan taken from an advertising campaign of the Bay department stores.
222 Kelling and Coles, *supra* note 34.
223 Ellickson, *supra* note 37.
224 Kelling and Coles, *supra* note 34.
225 Ellickson, *supra* note 37.
226 Lasch, *supra* note 9.
227 Douglas, *supra* note 219.

4 Policing Communities and Communities of Policing: A Comparative Study of Policing and Security in Two Canadian Communities

CHRISTOPHER MURPHY AND CURTIS CLARKE

Introduction

> Policing is being transformed and restructured in the modern world. This involves much more than reforming the institution regarded as the police, although that is occurring as well. The key to the transformation is that policing, meaning the activity of making societies safe, is no longer carried out exclusively by governments. Indeed, it is an open question as to whether governments are even the primary providers. Gradually, almost imperceptibly, policing has been 'multilateralized': a host of non-governmental groups have assumed responsibility for their own protection, and a host of nongovernmental agencies have undertaken to provide security services. Policing has entered a new era, an era characterized by a transformation in the governance of security.[1]

A body of recent policing literature suggests that the policing in Western societies is in a period of dramatic transition, change, and development.[2] In societies increasingly dominated by global market forces and neoliberal political values, governments have been forced to rationalize public services such as policing. As a result the public police have adopted various strategies of managerial and organizational reform. O'Malley states that policing has begun to reflect 'the ascendance of neo-liberal rationalities and related social technology of new managerialism.'[3] Shearing argues that, at the level of internal discourse, police services are emulating the new market language, as articulated in terms such as 'the police industry, customers, products and market share.'[4] Operationally this has meant 'eliminating, shifting, sharing, and privatizing' various types of police services.

The resulting elimination or downloading of some traditional police services coupled with an inability or reluctance to meet 'new' policing and security demands has created a new market for services previously provided by public police. The rapid growth of mass private property and space[5] as well as the development of new models of business technology have created a range of new policing and security needs that cannot be satisfied by the public police. As a result of this expanding demand, a mix of public and private police are increasingly providing alternative policing and security services. In the public domain, individual citizens, community groups, agencies, and police-sponsored or '-partnered' community policing groups are adopting different modes of preventive policing and protection. Governments, private companies, and citizens who desire more personalized and/or sophisticated policing/security are increasingly creating their own in-house police and security services or are hiring from an expanding number of private security or hybrid public-private policing services. Policing thus increasingly becomes decoupled from or loosely linked to governments and public service, and more oriented to private services and market principles.

The resulting fragmentation and diffusion of policing activities and responsibilities is consistent with neoliberal government strategies for reducing public spending, adopting fiscal restraint, and decentralizing and transferring non-core government services and responsibilities. It also signals a shift from 'modern' expansive and expensive government and state-based crime control[6] to a late-modern, commodified, and market-driven security and risk management environment.[7] In this kind of polycentric policing market environment the centrality and nature of the government and the public police role in providing policing and security services are increasingly called into question.

This transformation of policing and security in the postmodern or late-modern era raises a number of theoretical and public policy questions that need to be empirically addressed: To what extent is this theorized transformation actually taking place? Can it be detected and described empirically? Does it operate differently at the local level? How is it rationalized by the agencies and actors involved? Who provides what kinds of policing and security services, with what success, and accountable to whom? And what market, legal, or justice principles govern the provision of services? This kind of research can also address questions critical to understanding the new role of the public police and governments in this new late-modern policing and security environment. Of particular interest are the nature and pattern of relationships developed between various policing and security agencies, the kinds of policing and security networks that develop, and the public governance of those policing networks.[8]

Without adequate local, comparative data it is difficult to answer these questions and test or refine the largely hypothetical thesis of macro changes in policing and security. As Jones and Newburn[9] suggest, 'There are few if any rigorous studies of the private security industry's actual structure and functions, and how relationships with the public police actually work in practice.' The following research monographs present two detailed, empirically based, descriptive case studies of local policing and security institutions, patterns, and relationships in two Canadian urban environments: Halifax and Edmonton. Both case studies focus on the role and activities of public policing and its changing relationship with the broader policing and security environment in which it operates. While essentially local in orientation and scope, the studies allow analysis of the broader postmodern policing hypothesis to be grounded in empirically based examples. Both case studies address the same topic using essentially the same methodology but utilize differing analytic and presentational strategies. The Halifax case study represents a descriptive portrait or map of the various agencies, activities, and relationships involved in policing and security in the Halifax area and then examines their broader theoretical and policy implications. The Edmonton case study reports a different configuration or mix of public and private policing patterns and relationships and explains it as a product of the particular political economy and history of Alberta.

Methodology

The following were the primary research objectives of this comparative policing study:

1. Collect original and existing data in order to describe the range of agencies, services, and activities involved in policing and security in two urban areas, Halifax and Edmonton.
2. Examine the growth and evolving relationships between public, private, and community policing and security institutions in two urban policing environments, especially regarding issues of policing roles, governance, and rationalization patterns.
3. Compare and explain the similarities and differences found in the

general policing and security trends and patterns in both case studies and examine their relationship to broader trends in policing and security change.
4. Identify potential research and public policy issues as result of the research.

The research strategy adopted in this comparative study encouraged breadth over depth, mapping agency relationships and activities rather than focusing on a single agency case study. This is appropriate when the purpose is a preliminary exploratory overview of previously unresearched terrain and is necessary when trying to document the hypothesized expansion, diversity, networking, and loose governance relationships in a changing policing and security environment. Both studies employed a variety of research methods, including document analysis, semi-structured interviews, and some limited field observation. The primary research strategy consisted of semi-structured interviews designed to elicit information and knowledge of analytically relevant qualities and characteristics on various policing and security institutions in both Edmonton and Halifax. Collection of common core information elements on various police and security institutions/agencies and their policed communities/clientele supported the construction of an empirically based descriptive portrait or a map of policing and security agencies and activities in both urban communities. The data collected allowed us to analytically categorize institutions by type, locations, activities, and relationships, and to create a detailed composite description of policing and security[10] in both Halifax and Edmonton.

Part I Policing Halifax: Diversity and Deregulation

Any understanding of contemporary developments in policing requires recognition of its 'indivisibility': the fact that public and private forms, far from being distinct, are increasingly connected. More and more, policing is undertaken by a complex and diverse network of public, private and hybrid agencies. To refer to policing as a 'network' does not imply that its components are yet coordinated – in that respect 'patchwork' might be a better term – but does suggest that the actions and reactions of one part will impact on the others. For that reason, any rigorous analysis of contemporary policing has to focus upon what one might call its 'diverse totality.'[11]

The following case study provides a comprehensive descriptive portrait of the 'diverse totality' of public and private policing and security agency activities and relationships that exist currently in one urban area – Halifax, Nova Scotia. This research not only provides valuable empirical data on a concrete policing and security environment but is a basis for an empirically based examination of broader and largely theorized policing trends such as the pluralization of policing,[12] the rationalization of public police services,[13] the commodification and expansion of private policing and security,[14] the development of hybrid policing,[15] and governance problems and equity issues.[16]

The Social and Political Context of Local Policing and Security

Halifax is the largest city in eastern Canada and the capital of Nova Scotia, one of Canada's oldest and poorest provinces. Halifax Regional Municipality (HRM) is an amalgamation of three communities, a sprawling suburban and rural area with a population of approximately 400,000 people. The Halifax-Dartmouth urban core is built around its historic harbour, the location of several private and public shipyards, container ports, dry docks, a major waterfront public entertainment and tourist recreation area, a naval dockyard, a cruise ship terminal, and two toll bridges. Halifax has a socially and economically varied population in its urban core, distributed in clearly understood, income-based neighbourhoods with different policing and security needs. In addition, Halifax is the major public and commercial centre in the region and has a number of public and private institutions and facilities, including an international airport, container ports, five hospitals, five universities (with more than 30,000 students), numerous federal and provincial government buildings, a movie studio, and a number of Department of National Defence (DND) residential and military areas. As a commercial and service sector, it has numerous bars and restaurants, hotels, and shopping malls, and a large casino. This business-service combination brings in approximately 3 million visitors or tourists a year to the city. In short, though similar in many respects to most urban centres, Halifax has a surprisingly varied and diverse mix of public, institutional, residential, commercial, and entertainment sectors, all with different security and policing needs.

The environment for the governance of policing in Nova Scotia can perhaps be best described as traditional and conservative. Structurally this has meant a politically decentralized and highly regionalized province, with a relatively weak central government. Municipally based police services and strong local government traditions have created a diversified public policing environment. A number of embarrassing 'local' policing problems have recently highlighted the problems of weak central or provincial governance and supported a move to more centrally administered policing standards and regulations. As a result, over the last ten years the provincial government has reluctantly but gradually begun to exercise more authority and influence over local policing. This has become particularly evident in its support for the rationalization of small-town police services, through regionalization and the creation of province-wide recruiting and training standards. However, the province's desire to become more active and to manage or regulate municipal policing has been restrained by conservative fiscal politics and jealously guarded traditions of local political autonomy.

While public policing in Nova Scotia has been somewhat insulated from recent fiscal pressures to drastically rationalize government services, its growth over the last ten years has been limited. But during this same period there has been considerable growth and use of alternative policing and security agents, such as special constables, commissioners, extra-duty police, and private security. And while these agencies have been relatively free of regulation and governance,[17] there is now growing government recognition of the need for more government involvement. The Provincial Police and Public Safety bureaucracy is involved in promoting and rewriting legislation to enhance the regulatory policing role of the province. The proposed legislation expands the current act (the *Private Invetigators and Private Guards Act*) to cover more elements of private security, create minimum training and education standards, enhance legal accountability, and provide more resources for compliance enforcement.

Public Policing

Both the Halifax Regional Police (HRP) and the Royal Canadian Mounted Police (RCMP) provide public policing services in Halifax. This unique shared policing responsibility is a result of the recent amalgamation of the three individually policed urban communities and the incorporation of RCMP-policed rural areas. For political reasons, the amalgamation process declined to create one municipal police service, preferring to create a regionalized urban Halifax Regional Police and retain the RCMP to police the rural or county perimeter. According to local government and police officials, the current dual agency situation has created occasional communication problems, jurisdictional confusion, conflict, competition, cost inefficiency, and governance problems. A municipal government study is now underway to assess the desirability of the current shared mandate and the feasibility of creating a single municipal police service.

HALIFAX REGIONAL POLICE (HRP)

By national measures of police per population, Halifax would seem to be a well-resourced city. The police per population ratio in pre-amalgamation Halifax (1995) was 1 per 479,[18] the second lowest in the country. After amalgamation in 1998, the combined RCMP and municipal police rate rose to 1 per 510, or about eighth in the country[19]. But while conventional measures of police resources show a modest decline in personnel, they also, like the national trend, show an increase in actual municipal policing expenditures. Nevertheless, Halifax police have long argued that they need more police officers, given a high rate of violent crime and Halifax's location as a regional port and entertainment centre. Limited or inadequate resources are regularly used by both services as an explanation for not being able to respond adequately to varied community demands for more or better police service.

While HRP provides a range of conventional public policing services, there appears to have been a significant shift in the distribution and focus of police resources and services over the last few years. A more fiscally conservative political environment, changing management philosophy, and new policing demands have resulted in a gradual shift away from discretionary, resource-consuming, community-oriented policing activities to more reactive 'serious' crime, order, and enforcement functions. For example, a high-profile police mini-station in a high crime area is closed, a downtown foot patrol program is curtailed, while the detective division is increased, and a 'cold files' squad is created. It is therefore not surprising that inadequate or limited police response or presence has become a media and political issue, especially in predominantly poor, minority neighbourhoods and in the high-demand downtown business and entertainment area. Community meetings, councillors' debates, and newspaper articles have made police response and resources a political issue. Community leaders and merchant associations complain about the lack of police presence, slow response times, and limited police efforts. Interviews indicated that one merchant association was so dissatisfied with what they described as inadequate police presence and visibility and slow response times that they hired private security guards to patrol the 'public' streets outside and around their stores.

Another HRP response to the resource-demand problem has been to define their policing responsibilities more narrowly or selectively. For example, Halifax does not proactively patrol public parks in the region. Instead, regional government created a Parks Police service to police its most popular city park. Areas, properties, or events that require 'additional' policing increasingly pay extra for those services, by contracting for 'extra-duty' police officers. Thus what is a legitimate core or a discretionary 'public' police function seems to be increasingly defined by its resource implications. Faced with increasing service demand, reorganization and amalgamation pressures, and limited budget growth, the Halifax Regional Police have thus chosen to 'rationalize' their services by adopting service consolidation and a 'core' policing strategy. While there is some recognition that this may need to change in the future, under current operating philosophies far more resources would be required to make a significant difference in service delivery patterns.

THE ROYAL CANADIAN MOUNTED POLICE

The RCMP police the rural areas and communities around urban Halifax that are now incorporated within the new regional municipality. Approximately 160 RCMP officers (and 40 civilian and 24 auxiliary members) police a number of communities and villages with a population of approximately 100,000. RCMP officers per population ratios across Canada are generally lower than municipal police ratios, in part because of the rural nature of their policing environment, in part because of more flexible and efficient use of police personnel. In addition, the RCMP can occasionally call on provincial and federal police personnel, thus allowing them to enhance their level of expertise without adding new municipal resources. Despite this, the RCMP report their current Halifax police per population ratio of 1 per 1,000 is higher than the desired national RCMP average of 1 per 625, and that they also need more officers in order to improve services.

To stretch limited resources, the RCMP have adopted a number of rationalizing organizational and operational strategies. They utilize one-man cars and flexible shift schedules, operate as constable-generalists, and make extensive use of civilians and auxiliary police officers. Another resource-driven strategy has been to aggressively pursue community policing as a means of using community resources. Locally recruited 'community constables' are utilized in a predominantly black community, citizen volunteers are employed in victims and Neighbourhood Watch programs, and more than 300 citizen volunteers are involved in the patrol and surveillance of their own communities in thirteen Community on Patrol programs. Without more detailed research, it is difficult to evaluate whether these measures have been successful in meeting public demand. However, a lack of public or political complaint and the spread of community policing programs suggest public support for the RCMP's community-based policing strategy.

In summary, the findings suggest that, for a variety of fiscal, political, and economic reasons, there has been a considerable rationalization of public police services in the Halifax region. This is especially true in high-demand neighbourhoods and downtown commercial areas and is evident in a lack of visible patrol presence, slow response to minor crime, limited investigative resources, and the growing use of alternative community policing resources. Police have responded to resource problems by limiting and re-prioritizing existing services into a core service policing model, improving the internal efficiency of their operations, and expanding the use of alternative private and community policing resources. The resulting rationalization in police services has contributed to the growing need for more cost-effective and specialized alternative policing and security services.

Community Policing and Security

The community or public can be seen as a distinct resource for policing and security. In this context, community can be understood in a range of ways: for example, as a formally organized group of stakeholders, as individual citizens, or as distinct community sectors (residential or commercial ratepayers). The common link is their efforts to create a safe environment either through collaborative initiatives with the public police or by contracting to private service providers. Regardless of the method, the outcome is one of co-producing public safety and order maintenance.

DOMESTIC OR RESIDENTIAL COMMUNITY POLICING AND SECURITY

As in most cities, the level of actual crime and crime risk in Halifax varies significantly by neighbourhood location, income, and social composition. The city's violent crime rate is higher than average, while its property crime rate is comparable to that of other Canadian cities. The most common household or business response to crime risk is to invest in crime prevention hardware such as locks and alarms. While the pervasive use of electronic alarm systems has become a visible feature of most city neighbourhoods in the last few years, to date no residential neighbourhood has hired private security guards. Some condominium complexes and apartment buildings have done so, and some high-end suburban developments are reported to be considering it.

Until recently, HRP prided themselves on being a community-based policing service, but since regionalization, they have rationalized their community-based service delivery by moving away from broad community involvement to a more reactive core policing. Despite public and political support for more collaborative community policing efforts, HRP have tended to see community policing as a drain on critical or core police resources and have done little more than offer conventional crime prevention programs such as Neighbourhood Watch. This limited response has failed to satisfy poor and minority community demands for more police involvement and response to their elevated crime and public order problems. There is now increasing discussion with HRP about the need to revitalize community policing through more effective and resource-limited target community policing strategies such as problem-solving teams.

On the other hand, the RCMP, rather than see community policing as a resource problem, have turned it into a resource opportunity. They have aggressively promoted community policing programs in rural communities as a way of enlisting the support, efforts, and energies of the community on their behalf. In addition to the usual crime prevention programs such as Neighbourhood Watch, they have initiated thirteen Communities on Patrol programs (COP), involving more than 300 volunteers who actively patrol their own communities. They argue that this level of community policing allows them to provide more coverage and better response with limited resources, especially in the rural areas that they tend to police. While the effectiveness and impact of community policing programs are difficult to assess, they do demonstrate at least a limited desire among the public to play a more active part in their own policing.[20]

THE BUSINESS COMMUNITY

Halifax has a range of types of businesses, in diverse locations, with a variety of policing and security needs. The financially stratified and private nature of the business community also means that it receives highly varied levels and types of policing and security. Businesses that can afford to do so use both private security and the public police, while others must rely solely on the public police. Though the nature of the business and its location often dictates how much and what kind of security is required or desired, the ability to pay for 'alternatives or additions' to pubic policing ultimately determines the final security mix. While investment in various forms of security is a significant cost for all forms of business, the degree to which this is possible is again dependent on the ability of the business to pay. This results in a varied and highly stratified and uneven distribution of policing and security within the business community.

The degree of tension and conflict between the public police and two downtown business/merchant associations is striking in urban Halifax. Both groups have been publicly critical of the lack of police presence on 'their' busy public shopping areas or streets. Amid much publicity and debate, one business group has hired private security to do aggressive foot patrolling on the public street around the shopping area; the other is considering doing the same. Both groups feel that they should be getting more police services 'for their high business taxes' and resent having to hire private security to do what they perceive to be a public police responsibility. This critical attitude is more characteristic of small business, as big stores and businesses meet most of their policing and security needs through in-house and private security, while smaller businesses must rely on public police and their competing service priorities. The police argue that people's policing needs take precedence over property and that they simply don't have the resources to provide the level of property protection and investigation that the business community desires.

Hybrid Police

The following section describes the provision of specialized policing and security services for public purposes by agencies other than the full-time public police. Usually these policing activities have a strong 'public-interest' component and are done in collaboration with or instead of the public police.

MILITARY POLICE

Halifax has one of Canada's largest urban military populations. Approximately fifty full-time military police officers are responsible for policing approximately 5,000 civilians and military personnel and several domestic residential areas, military bases, and port facilities. They also contract about 150 commissionaires to provide additional security and support in these locations. Military police have the mandate to police all persons on

Department of National Defence (DND) property. This includes shared policing of DND personnel off DND property, and of all personnel on DND property. Military police possess the same Criminal Code powers as the public police and can exercise these powers over DND personnel overseas. When DND personnel commit an offence off the base in the public police domain, military police open a shadow file, but the case is normally handled by the public police. Offences that happen on DND property are first dealt with by military police, and only sometimes do they call in public police. In addition to doing all the regular public policing functions, including responding to persons or property calls, criminal investigations, and preventive patrol, military police also have security and intelligence responsibilities for the protection of personnel and property (ships) at home and abroad. Military police are part of the regular command structure; they report directly to the commander of the base and thus have no civilian oversight responsibilities.[21] Though operating independently of local police, they report a close working relationship with local police and are routinely in contact with them on cases and issues of mutual interest. There have been some coordinated, joint policing operations for the policing of visiting Navy ships from Canada and other countries. In summary, the military police have an important but selective public policing function in the Halifax area, providing a high level of policing and security for designated military and residential areas, people, and property under their limited jurisdictions and serving as a valuable backup for Halifax public police.

THE COMMISSIONAIRES

The Canadian Corps of Commissionaires (CCC) are a unique policing and security organization. Originally created in 1937 by the federal government in order to provide employment for decommissioned war veterans, the modern corps has become a large and ambitious general police and security organization that is a major presence in both public and private policing and security (P&S) in Halifax. A non-profit public organization with a specially legislated mandate, the corps provides broad police and security services to both public and private contractors. In Nova Scotia, the corps has 1,110 full-time members, of whom 800 work in the Halifax region. They provide about 50 per cent of their services to various government contract locations such as the provincial legislature, the Department of National Defence, Halifax Regional Municipality police stations, and government buildings. The remaining 50 per cent of services are to private or commercial clients. The corps generated approximately $20 million in revenues last year in Nova Scotia. Though its hourly rates are higher than those of most private commercial companies, they remain competitive for high-end security clients. Typically, it supplies guards for property protection and personnel surveillance for public and government buildings, hospitals, bridges, and so on.[22] The Commissionaires also perform more ambitious policing and security functions at the newly privatized Halifax International Airport. A detachment of Commissionaires recently won the contract over the HRP and RCMP to provide all physical security functions at the airport. Commissionaires, prior to 11 September 2001, performed most airport security duties, with the exception of a required RCMP armed-response capability, pre-boarding security, and occasional customs and immigration requirements. A detachment of twenty-six RCMP members has been reduced to six as a result of this arrangement.[23] The Commissionaires suggest that this kind of unique 'policing' role may be an expanding part of their future mandate. Because most of its members must have military or police backgrounds, the corps offers a well-organized, efficiently managed, comparatively well-trained, stable, mature workforce. These organizational and service qualities are unusual for a private security agency and attractive to its many clients, for whom these benefits are worth the extra cost. Indeed, the growth of demand for its services is now outstripping its capacity to provide personnel, and it is being forced to be more selective with contracts while also attempting to expand the pool of recruits. Though Commissionaires are neither regulated under the provincial police act nor directly accountable to local government, their military tradition, training, and backgrounds seem to provide adequate assurance of service competence and internal accountability to those who contract their services. The ongoing expansion and growth of the corps suggest that it offers some of the virtues of public policing (organizational stability and reliability) at a fraction of the cost, making it likely it will remain the preferred government and institutional response to meeting non-core policing and security needs.

However, the ambitious and ambiguous mandate of the corps as a non-profit, quasi-private policing and security agency that actively competes for private and public contracts may present some problems. Private security companies complain that it's an unfairly favoured public and protected organization that violates the normal market rules of competition. As the corps expands its private contract policing activities, its potentially conflicting public and private obligations may also become more problematic. In addition, its status as a quasi-public policing agency raises questions about its lack of accountability to governments and the public. So while the Corps of Commissionaires currently offers a well-trained, reliable, and cheap alternative to public police, its rapid growth and expansion in the new policing and security market-place will inevitably invite more public and market scrutiny and perhaps government regulation.

SPECIAL CONSTABLES

In 2000, there were more than 1,476 special constables licensed by the Province of Nova Scotia. Special constables perform a variety of restricted policing functions, and their restricted policing and investigative powers are limited by task, time frame, and jurisdiction. Typically, special constables enforce particular government statutes or by-laws, and their status as peace officers grants them limited powers of arrest and power to issue a court summons. For example, By-law Enforcement Officers are special constables who have been granted limited powers to enforce municipal by-laws. By-laws are increasingly being used by urban governments as a means of social regulation and governance, through by-laws governing parking, noise, alarms, pesticides, animal control, traffic, smoking, housing standards, and so on. While public police at one time enforced all municipal by-laws and still have authority and ultimate responsibility to enforce them, it is now cheaper and often more effective to use full-time by-law enforcement officers to do by-law enforcement exclusively.[24] In general, it would appear that the increasing use of special constables rather than public police to do a growing number of low-level regulatory and enforcement tasks has evolved in Nova Scotia as a response to the fiscally motivated need to rationalize and diversify policing and security services in the province.

'EXTRA-DUTY' PUBLIC POLICE

Extra-duty police are public police officers who are paid to perform selected policing functions by someone (public or private) who contracts them to provide 'extra' policing for a particular location, event, or area. While previously only HRP personnel have performed this role, the RCMP in Nova Scotia have also recently begun to do selective extra-duty services. While extra-duty policing can also be listed as form of private policing, the research for this study suggests that public police, even when serving in a private capacity, are increasingly an important part of the 'public' policing response in urban Halifax. The 'extra-duty' program co-coordinator confirmed that on many Friday or Saturday nights in the Halifax downtown area there are often more extra-duty public police doing extra paid duty than there are regular public police actively policing the same area. Fully uniformed and armed public police are visible outside bars, in liquor commission shops, at public concerts and sporting events, and directing traffic at movie sets throughout the city. Extra-duty police are often used to police public events or properties that require more than the reactive, core policing levels available. In many cases, these are occasions and locations that might have previously relied on regular police service. However, even when extra-duty police are used to protect private property or events, they still retain a public dimension, as these are often events or locations where the public are involved and there is a public interest in their order and security (e.g., high school dances, busy bars, etc.). The extra-duty personnel make the presence of regular public police unnecessary and facilitate more effective police action if required. Finally, as all extra-duty police are required to be available to assist regular public police in emergency situations, they give public police an additional presence and response capability. Thus, as police resources become more limited, extra-duty public police have become an essential part of the general police response to policing and security demands in downtown Halifax. However, despite its impressive operational and fiscal advantages, regular and extensive use of extra-duty police for quasi-public or private events does raise serious questions about the efficient management of existing police resources, public policing priorities, potential conflicts of interest, and growing service inequality between events and businesses that pay and those that can't or won't.

In summary, the category of 'hybrid' public policing illustrates the conceptual difficulty in drawing a clear distinction between public and private police. For example, how does one classify (1) 'extra-duty' public police working for privately run public events or locations (bars) who are technically employed by municipal government to provide paid private services, or (2) the Commissionaires, a non-profit government-created organization that competes with the private sector for security contracts? This quasi-public or grey zone is the intersection of the public and private police. This sector appears to be growing, since government and its agencies desire to provide low-cost and more narrowly directed policing services to meet the expansion of security and policing demands. While this growth may have enhanced the overall policing and security resources in the region, it has occurred piecemeal, with most policing agencies operating separately and independently of each other.

Private Security

This broad policing category refers typically to policing and security agencies, organizations, and individuals that are in the business of selling policing and security services on the open market to public and commercial enterprises for personnel and or organizational profit. In addition to private security guard companies and individual private investigators, this category includes private companies or organizations that create or hire their own internal 'in-house' policing and security services, and companies that sell monitored security alarm systems.

SECURITY GUARD COMPANIES

There are approximately ninety-five licensed private security guard companies, with more than 3,007 licensed employees in Nova Scotia; about 80 per cent of these service the Halifax area. These companies range from large multinationals such as Securitas, boasting more than 240,000 employees worldwide, to small locally owned security companies employing as few as 12 security guards. Private security guards are located throughout the city in a wide variety of locations such as shopping malls, large apartment buildings, car dealerships, business parks, public housing estates, and so on. While some specialize in a particular security service such as motorized armed transport, most companies provide a range of low-skill property and person protection and surveillance – security guard services. However, private security companies collectively provide a surprising range and variety of policing and security services. The following is a list of some policing and security activities done by the fifteen private security police agencies surveyed in the Halifax research.

Some Private Security Policing Activities

Mobile and foot patrol	Security surveillance
Property protection	Personal protection
Calls for service	Public order policing
Medical/ Emergency response	Traffic policing
Arrest (citizen's arrest powers)	Law enforcement (by-law, CCC)
Criminal investigations	Court and case preparation
Crime prevention consulting	Armed force (armoured car security)

Virtually all the surveyed companies indicated that they had increased the number of employees and the yearly value of their contracts in the last few years, and all expected the demand for their services to increase even more in the near future. This expansion is attributed in part to the declining ability of public police to provide certain traditional policing services and in part to the growth of new, specialized security and protection markets.

The security guard business in Halifax is highly competitive and requires little entry-level expertise or investment. This promotes competitive pricing, meaning that low personnel costs are required to make a profit. Private security personnel in Halifax are poorly paid. Hourly rates reported by respondents ranged from a minimum of $6 to a high of $15, and an industry average of $8. Low wages mean a limited and transient pool of labour to choose from. Most companies report high turnover rates, relatively low educational levels, and employees with limited skills and ambitions. Most of the fifteen security executives agreed that higher wages would improve the qualifications of the personnel attracted to private security but would also make the business less profitable and probably price their services out of the reach of some of their current customers and clients. All agencies reported some form of in-house training, though the quality, extent, and appropriateness of such training is unclear. Without externally required training standards, there is little market incentive to provide training, as low personnel cost wins most contracts. The competitive nature of the industry has therefore inhibited the development of an industry-based regulatory organization. However, most of the security executives interviewed supported the need for government-mandated minimum standards of training and education; standards would actually be good for business, some noted, as they would apply equally to everyone and allow companies to charge more for provincially licensed services.

Relationships between private security and public police are complex. On an official level, most private security companies claim to have positive and cooperative relationships with public police. It is important for private security to get along with the public police as they depend on public police to act on the results of their efforts (i.e., investigations, arrest, and charge). The effectiveness of security guards in many ways depends upon the responsiveness and cooperative support of public police. However, while senior executives and some individual operatives spoke of positive and collaborative relationships, they were also critical of the police response to their clients and their policing needs. Some security executives cited slow police response times, limited or inadequate investigative efforts, and sometimes hostile or contemptuous attitudes towards private security. However, most security executives said they would welcome a more formal and coordinated relationship with public police and felt they had something to contribute to the general policing efforts of the public police.[25]

CORPORATE 'IN-HOUSE' SECURITY

This section describes security services or individuals employed by non-governmental public or private organizations to provide security and policing services exclusively to that organization. The provincial Department of Justice estimates that there are more in-house security personnel in the Halifax area than there are licensed security guards. It is difficult to document accurately the size and growth of the private security industry, as personnel are regarded as employees of the company and do not have to be provincially licensed. Most commercial companies or large public organizations have some sort of in-house security force or expertise. For example, all Halifax universities employ some professional campus security. Dalhousie University has twenty-five full-time security officers (and up to 300 part-time students). The newly opened casino has a security force of thirty-five to forty people managed by a retired senior RCMP officer; one large chain store has two in-house security managers who subcontract four different security functions; and virtually all bank and financial institutions have a variety of security and loss prevention personnel. Bouncers or 'admittance control agents'[26] might also be classified as a form of in-house security. It is estimated that about 150 unlicensed bouncers work at various bars and nightclubs throughout the city, with some bars employing as many as 20 on a given night.

Though providing a wide range of general and highly specialized policing and security services, much in-house security appears to be focused on financial loss prevention and theft reduction. Most in-house security focuses exclusively on the specialized security needs of the employer. This private security relationship clearly determines how these personnel operate and their degree of involvement with public police or the justice system. As regular company employees, in-house security personnel tend to be better paid, more skilled, and better educated than 'contract' private security guards. Subject to neither government regulation nor political scrutiny, in-house security prefer to resolve many of their employers' policing and security problems internally. When they do deal with public police, some security executives seemed critical of either the limited police response or the relatively minor penalties accorded by the public justice system. They also noted a lack of police knowledge of their specialized security needs, limited police response to internal theft and fraud cases, or disagreement over the perceived seriousness of an offence or appropriate sanctions against it.

Thus the decision to invest in additional or specialized internal police and security services can be seen in part as a realistic recognition of the legal and practical limits of public policing and the criminal justice system as a means of addressing particular 'private' or special policing and security needs. It also explains a preference for discretionary 'private' control of the whole security, adjudication, and sanctioning process. As in-house security grows in size and scope and more aspects of our lives as consumers and employees fall under its jurisdiction, its purely private, unregulated, and non-accountable nature will also require far more research and public scrutiny.[27]

PRIVATE INVESTIGATORS

There are approximately 100 licensed private investigators in the Halifax area. Current legislation describes private security investigators as persons who search for people, information, and missing property, investigate insured financial claims, do personal background investigations, apply lie detector tests, and do surveillance. Many private investigators in Halifax do insurance-related investigations and fraud cases. 'Suspect' insurance claims are investigated by private investigators, and their findings allow the company to decide whether to pay or challenge a claim. As result of the prevalence of false claims, insurance companies spend a great deal on private investigators, but reportedly save more than that amount by successfully challenging fraudulent claims. While most cases are relatively simple and require limited skills, some fraud cases are expensive and complex and require a range of specialized investigative skills such as forensic accounting. Though investigators are often involved in sometimes intrusive personal surveillance and investigate 'criminal' frauds and theft, these cases seldom involve them with the formal criminal law, police, or the courts. Arguing that public police have neither the responsibility, the resources, nor the expertise to be involved in cases that can be regarded as 'private' disputes, private investigators are gatekeepers to what is essentially an alternative private justice system – one that often prefers to settle criminal fraud and theft cases privately, without involving the public police, the criminal law, or the justice system.

This situation is potentially problematic, as private investigators are as unregulated and un-monitored as private security guards. Investigators themselves complain about the number of suspect 'low-rent' investigators ('trunk slammers') who sometimes use unethical and illegal tactics to gain their information. Thus, most established investigators welcome the possibility of more stringent government regulations in the hope that it will eliminate the unethical but also the low-cost investigators who will 'do anything to get a file.' So while private investigators have key policing and security functions, they are clearly located in the private realm.

In summary, it appears that a varied mix of community policing and security has developed in the Halifax region.[28] This mix is most acceptable to those who can afford to combine both public and private P&S efforts. The most dissatisfied elements of the Halifax business and residential community are those that can't afford to supplement community policing and security with private or community self-policing measures.

Halifax in Summary

This policing and security mapping exercise describes Halifax as an active and complex policing and security environment, policed by a variety of public and private policing agencies. These include public police, private security guards, peace officers, police auxiliaries, private investigators, in-house security personnel, bouncers, special constables, by-law enforcement officers, and extra-duty public police officers. They are allocated and distributed variously but not consistently by law, geography, public and private designations, type of policing function, and market opportunities. Responding to a broad range of policing and security needs, these varied policing and security bodies possess a variety of policing powers and skills and operate in a relatively unregulated and un-integrated policing network, governed loosely and selectively by a mixture of government regulation, legal rules, and market forces. The end result is a patchwork of variously policed, protected, and secure spaces, activities, people, properties, and neighbourhoods, expressing varying degrees of satisfaction. In short, the Halifax regional policing environment has become a complex, varied, decentred, loosely linked, relatively open, and diversified policing and security environment.

Whether this new diverse policing and security environment is problematic depends in part on the policing paradigm used to evaluate it.[29] Argued from a neoliberal or postmodern market perspective,[30] this composite of public and private policing and security can be seen as an effective and efficient market solution to the growing need and demand for diverse policing and security services in the Halifax region. Given the increasingly expensive and limited response capacity of the public police, the current expansion of quasi-public, private, and community policing in Halifax is said to be cost-effective, as it allows public police to focus their limited resources on the priority concerns of the public, while those who desire more general or specialized policing and security services must pay for them. Thus the public do not have to pay for 'private, specialized, or extra' policing and security needs. An open, deregulated, and competitive policing and security market helps ensure that policing and security are highly responsive to customers' policing needs and are efficient providers of policing and security services. Neoliberals argue that, given the limited resources, organizational inefficiencies, and legally limited powers of public police, the growth of private security as an addition or alternative to public policing makes a city like Halifax ultimately a safer place to live and do business. Thus, private security and its public variations can be seen as a market-based solution to the complex and expanding policing and security needs of modern society.

However, the modern, liberal, welfare state perspective suggests a less positive analysis.[31] The rationalization of public policing signals a decline in the state's commitment to provide broad-based police services to all citizens. Rationalizing public policing and encouraging private security to grow as an alternative means a diminished role for both the police and government. Police argue that many of the functions being done by private security were once and still should be done by public police, and that their privatization results in inferior and publicly unaccountable service. Privatization also diminishes the ability of the state to protect the public interest and ensure the application of the liberal-democratic values of citizenship, equality, due process, and accountability to an increasingly expanding but vital arena of societal activity. Finally, pluralization and privatization increase the overall inequality of communities and societies with respect to safety and security[32] by treating these as marketable commodities, limited to the citizens, neighbourhoods, and businesses that can afford to pay extra for them. So while both private and public police protect some, others must rely on the increasingly limited services and resources of the public police.

While this research validates in varying degree both of these perspectives, the apparent choice between the current open, unregulated, uncoordinated policing and security market and a limited but expensive state-monopolized public policing model is an unnecessarily restrictive choice. In order to better address the policing and security concerns of the current Halifax policing environment, there is a need for more rational, aggressive policing and security governance and closer operational integration of both private and public policing activities. While the proposed new provincial private security legislation will in part meet many of the governance concerns raised, it will also inevitably legitimize and strengthen the participation of private security in the policing and security market-place. If this happens and the public police wish to maintain a dominant role and responsibility for the overall policing and security of the Halifax region, they will need to reconsider their current role in this new policing environment. A realistic postmodern policing role[33] will mean accepting and utilizing the presence of 'other' public and private policing and security agencies as part of the public policing mandate, not a separate category. Public police must find ways to be more knowledgeable about the policing and security operations and activities of other policing agencies in their jurisdiction and must secure their support and assistance in order to produce a more integrated and coordinated general policing response. In such a 'steering not rowing' role, the public police would oversee, coordinate, and regulate all the public and private policing and security activities in their environment. This new role would enhance the scope of the public police mandate and help ensure that public interests were being protected without necessarily requiring investment of more public resources in policing and security. In short, a more controlled, integrated, and coordinated policing and security effort with clear operational distinctions, formal protocols and protections, and accountability mechanisms would provide a more effective, accountable, and equitable policing and security environment for all citizens in the Halifax region.

Part 2 Policing Edmonton:[34] Regulating and Responsibilizing

At the time of writing, the city of Edmonton in Alberta had a population of 666,104 and an extended population of 937,845 in the greater Edmonton metropolitan region (a number that was expected to reach 972,000 in 2004). This projected growth was to be stimulated, in part, by the healthy oil and gas exploration and manufacturing sector, which is currently facing strong oil prices and falling extraction costs. But while Edmonton's economy benefits from oil and gas exploration, it also attributes part of its growth to strong public sector employment. Edmonton is the provincial capital of Alberta and also boasts fifteen postsecondary institutions, four acute-care hospitals, a regional psychiatric hospital, three federal correctional institutions, a Department of National Defence base, and an extended agricultural sector.

In terms of policing, the Edmonton Police Service (EPS) has a deployment of 1,535 members (a police per population ratio of 1:569). As in many Canadian cities, Edmonton's crime rates showed a continued decline from 1990 to 1999. This trend has begun to reverse, with an increase between 1999 and 2000 of 3.7 per cent for person-related crimes, 4 per cent for property-related crimes, and 15 per cent for morality-related crimes.

The fiscal and political climate of the 1990s in Alberta required a resource-efficient version of community policing, one that would limit rather than expand police efforts, allow police to use declining police resources more effectively, shift or share the responsibility for policing to others, and, more importantly, maintain the central role of public police in the governance of policing and security in Edmonton. In the shift to community-based policing, policy makers adopted community participation and the rhetoric of partnership in their engagement with the imperatives of post-welfare crime prevention. These new imperatives suggested that the state should respond to crime and disorder not in the traditional direct manner but indirectly through the resources and actions of individuals.[35] In the context of this arrangement, the role of community policing was to 'uncouple policing and police so that policing becomes everybody's business rather than exclusively or primarily the business of police.'[36] While the concept of post-welfare crime prevention has particular implications for policing and communities in general, there are unique consequences specific to each locale. In the following case study, we examine how Edmonton uncoupled itself from its responsibility as sole proprietor of crime prevention while maintaining a proactive leadership role. Moreover, Edmonton provides a good example of how multi-agency cooperation does in fact support greater access to community surveillance, organization, and intelligence. This study maps the layering of services, the division of labour, and the collaborative relationships that punctuate the problem-solving environment characteristic of Edmonton. Finally, this case study offers an example of how policing and community stakeholders have responded to the critique and realignment of neo-liberal reform. Furthermore, it examines the political, operational, and collaborative dynamics from which have evolved a model of an integrated policing and security continuum.

Political Context: Building the Framework for Responsibilization

At present, Alberta Justice is reconceptualizing police governance in an effort to reassert its regulatory authority over a wide array of police services in the province. The assistant deputy minister for the Public Security Division has been tasked with the development of a ten-year strategic blueprint for policing. In July 2002, a legislative committee, the Policing Alberta MLA Review Committee, tabled its sweeping analysis of Alberta's *Police Act.* This report[37] and current government rhetoric suggest a potential shift in the ministry's role from that of decentralized manager to that of architect/regulator of a continuum of security and enforcement. While on the surface this focus on the relationship between government and police practices may not appear uncharacteristic of a ministry responsible for policing operations, it is in fact, a dramatic shift from the previous decade of inattention.

With the 1993 election of Premier Ralph Klein's Conservative party, policing, like other municipal services, was swept into the vortex of budget restraint and restructuring. Under the banner of the Klein revolution, municipal policing suffered two direct hits. The first came from the Ministry of Justice in its attempt to put in place its required three-year business plan. In Alberta Justice's 1994–5 annual report, Deputy Minister of Justice Neil McCrank set out eleven business functions with a number of goals attached, 'some of [which] are related to budget, while others are related to increased efficiency or improvement of service.'[38] Topping the list of business functions was that of 'reducing crime through policing and prevention programs,' and the first goal related to this function was 'to provide high quality cost effective programs to prevent and control crime.' In order to achieve this goal, municipal policing grants were reduced by 50 per cent ($16 million) over the three years of the business plan. The achievement of this reduction was well under way within the first year of the business plan, and by 1 April 1994, Alberta Justice no longer awarded municipal policing grants, relinquishing this responsibility to the Ministry of Municipal Affairs. It was at this point that municipal policing took its second hit.

Municipal Affairs' disbursement and administration of municipal policing grants would prove problematic in that the funds were included in the lump sum grants allocated to the municipalities. The situation became even more precarious when the 1994–5 budget set out a $59-million cut in municipal grants. Further to this 'the1995/96 budget would see this grant reduced by 10 percent to $169 million and outlined plans to cut this grant in half again by 1996–97.'[39] Limited municipal grants nurtured a competitive relationship between municipal agencies and services as they vied for pieces of the shrinking budgetary pie. As in other municipalities, Edmontonians took on increased responsibility for order maintenance as a function of the service's fiscal constraints and adoption of community-based policing; this increased citizen responsibility would also serve to discipline them for a new era of global capitalism. And while this fiscal disciplining had the potential to create a competitive environment wherein services isolated themselves in order to consolidate resources, what emerged instead was a cooperative, multi-agency approach to order maintenance.

The Public Police: Edmonton's Response

Edmonton's solution to increased fiscal restraint and demands for efficient service took shape in the form of the 'Edmonton Police Plan.' The Police Plan was conceived as a guide by which Edmonton would set out clear service goals, boundaries of accountability, and methods of evaluation. As noted in the Police Plan's strategic vision,

> The creation of the Edmonton Police Plan is the first step in establishing a mutual and collective vision which guides the Service in the delivery of quality policing in this city for the next three years. The Edmonton Police Plan will evolve to include the principal components ordinarily associated with separate plans devoted to strategic issues, technology, communications, facilities, finances, and operations. It will not be shelf material.[40]

Interestingly, a similar process of strategic planning, accountability, and evaluation was taking shape in the provincial government with its implementation of three-year business plans. These business plans would serve as a mechanism of accountability; but, more importantly, they would empower departments and agencies to make decisions on how to implement reform objectives. Certainly, similar traits can be noted in the operational process guiding Edmonton's Police Plan. Furthermore, the underlying premise of this process was the objective of implementing a decentralized service structure, whereby the responsibility for service could be downloaded to the division and thus to the community. This same process influenced the governance and operational practices of the RCMP, Municipal By-law Services, and provincial enforcement and regulatory branches.

The operational premise of the Police Plan corresponds to Osborne and Gaebler's[41] concept of steering and rowing in which the executive sets the objective or goal for the organization (steering) and empowers those who are most capable of delivering the service (rowing). Similarly, Edmonton's Police Plan outlined a process of service delivery that required a bottom-up process wherein front-line officers, supervisors, and managers synthesized service-wide plans into actions and standards. These divisional actions and standards would be 'negotiated with the Chief's Committee for the purpose of planning, performance evaluation and accountability.'[42] The criteria by which these would be measured were based on whether or not they supported the goals of the EPS. One example of a bottom-up initiative is the Co-operative Police Program.

The program was initiated as a six-month pilot project to examine a more effective use of private security/loss prevention officers in an effort to reduce calls for service and lower the priority call overflow. The initial project included representatives from London Drugs, Sears, the Bay, Canadian Tire, Zellers, and Woodwards. EPS members from the Crime Prevention Unit facilitated a two-day workshop attended by loss prevention officers and managers with the objective of training these individuals in powers of arrest, search and seizure, report writing, evidence collection and retention, court proceedings, and witness preparation. The program was initially assessed using the criteria of increased convictions, reduced police time on scene, response time, and investigation time. Preliminary results indicated a decrease in response time, a reduction of investigation time from one hour to twenty-five minutes, an increased conviction rate, and overall cost savings to the service of $50,000 to $60,000 a year.[43]

As the Co-operative Police Program expanded, so too did its scope of activities. The program now facilitates a Merchant Crime Alert Program, wherein program partners meet on a monthly basis to share intelligence and target professional criminals. This initiative was assessed to ensure that it did not contravene the *Criminal Identification Act* or the *Freedom of Information and Protection of Privacy Act* (FOIPP) with respect to the privacy of suspected and charged criminals. As a result of these meetings, the arrest rates have risen dramatically, especially those for repeat offenders.[44]

As the program evolved, other organizations sought partnerships in the project. These include some from private industry, such as Caritas Health Group (Special Constables) and West Edmonton Mall Security, as well as municipal agencies such as the city's Light Rail Transit (LRT) and Transit inspectors. Because of their surveillance function within the municipal core, the LRT inspectors have a particularly significant role in the network of Edmonton policing, as they monitor an extensive CCTV system that links with numerous retail sites throughout the Light Rail corridor.

An interesting aspect of this program is the diversity of legal jurisdictions and powers held by the membership. While this jurisdictional diversity enhances the scope in which prevention initiatives may unfold, it also creates certain limitations. For example, because security guard/loss prevention officers do not have special constable status, they cannot release those they arrest under a 'promise to appear' notice but must release arrested individuals into the custody of a police officer. In this scenario, an officer is still required to attend the scene, albeit for a limited function and time, undermining the original premise of this program. In an effort to counter the inefficiency of this arrest process, an alternative method of release has been developed in collaboration with the Crown's office. A loss prevention officer or security guard can release under the alternative measures program if the detained individual agrees to participate in the program and has no prior record. Once an individual agrees to this process the security officer contacts EPS communications to confirm through the Canadian Police Information Centre (CPIC) that the individual does not have a record and thus is eligible. If confirmation of eligibility is received, the individual is released and a report is written up by the security officer and dropped off at a community station. To ensure equity and effectiveness, the release program is governed by a protocol that requires the Edmonton Police Service to review the operationalization of procedures set by the service and the Crown's office. In the review process, this program was deemed to have achieved the service objective of multi-agency team building; more interestingly, as well, it matched the provincial objectives of providing high-quality, cost-effective programs.[45]

In retrospect, Edmonton's Police Plan emulated practices and strategies that were being used in the realm of public sector restructuring. The broad service objectives of the Police Plan served as a directive for units and divisions, a directive that is very similar to that of the business plans outlined by provincial departments. As with provincial departments, the actions of each unit or division were evaluated in terms of their support for the broad objectives set by the executive. Similarly, decentralization shifted responsibility for the achievement of these broad objectives to the newly empowered units and departments.

Further analysis of Edmonton's Police Plan indicates that the service placed an increased importance upon the collection of performance indicators and standards in an effort to raise public service quality and provide ongoing evaluation. In more generic terms, the plan was a model that supported the basic principles of measuring results, putting the customer (the community) in the driver's seat, introducing a market orientation, and fostering decentralization. And while the rhetoric of customer service guided the actions of the service, citizen responsibility and a reliance on community partnerships were also key components of the reform initiative, corresponding with public service initiatives of responsibilization. The link between the public sector reform mantra of accountability, efficiency, and effectiveness and the service's objectives of decentralization and citizen responsibility is readily apparent.

Community involvement played an essential role in Edmonton's developing continuum of policing. Volunteers supply a valuable resource, both financially and substantively, through the numerous hours they spend assisting both EPS and their own communities. For example, between 1 November 1993 and 28 March 2001, the Ottewell Community Patrol Program logged 17,295 patrol hours and 146,043 kilometres. While the program is a joint initiative between EPS and members of the Ottewell community, citizens patrol using their own vehicles and fuel, and equipped with radios funded through various community leagues within the patrol's boundaries. The EPS commitment to the program is a designated patrol car and office space for a base operator located in the Ottewell Community Station. In the policing division of labour, the patrol offers the services of surveillance, intelligence gathering, and security presence, all of which augment existing EPS functions.

A further example of this division of labour supported by volunteer activity can be noted in the dedicated service of victim advocates associated with the Victim Services Unit. For the first five months of 2001, volunteers logged 8,411 hours, responded to 8,595 inquiries, and completed 3,746 follow-up reports, as well as attending crisis callouts and performing court-related functions. In addition to improving the quality of service provided to citizens, the volunteer contributions represent a significant financial saving to EPS. In a recent effort to assess the value of volunteerism within Alberta, the provincial government derived a formula which established a generic value of $10 an hour. According to this simple cost formula, the previous two examples of volunteerism have supplied EPS with a resource worth $257,060. A further acknowledgment of the important function volunteers serve comes by way of the 1999 provincial government's three-year $75,000 grant to EPS Victims Services to assist with advocate training and support.

In addition to cooperation between the EPS and community and business groups, current initiatives have involved partnerships between the RCMP and the EPS. The RCMP's K-Division (Alberta Region) headquarters is located within the city of Edmonton, and yet the role of the RCMP within the city has tended to be a limited one. This is not to suggest that there is little for the RCMP to do, for their mandate includes a variety of tasks that transcend the policing duties of the EPS. These include federal law enforcement, immigration, customs, national security investigations, and VIP security. Where there is an overlap of jurisdiction the trend is towards a sharing or teaming of resources. This teaming occurs in the areas of drug enforcement, various homicide investigations, and activities of the Criminal Intelligence Service of Alberta. Moreover, common policing tasks and teaming of resources satisfied a common set of restructuring goals.

An additional partnering of policing exists with the Canadian Forces Base (CFB) Garrison Military Police under the rubric of joint investigations, training, and enforcement initiatives. Both EPS and the Military Police suggest that clearly defined jurisdictional boundaries and responsibilities have facilitated the success of the partnership. The clarity of the enforcement boundary has proven beneficial when investigations and calls for service relate to military service members, as the behaviour and activities of military personnel are subsequently governed and sanctioned under the *National Defence Act.*

Canada Customs and Immigration also have an enforcement function within Edmonton. However, their collaborative relationship with other agencies is more appropriately characterized by a link to the RCMP, in part simply because the RCMP are the only other agency mandated to enforce the *Customs Act.* Moreover, there exists a national memorandum of agreement that stipulates that the RCMP are to be given the first right of refusal to prosecute and file drug offences initiated by customs activity. In a broader context of enforcement and collaboration, customs intelligence/investigationc units are active participants in the multi-agency network coordinated by the Criminal Intelligence Service of Alberta.

Federal immigration officers have a somewhat different partnership relationship. Because they have limited internal resources, they rely on other services to assist in their enforcement and intelligence functions. As one would expect, the EPS and the RCMP assist Immigration in both locating and removing individuals deemed to have contravened the *Immigration Act.* More interestingly, however, the task of locating offenders is also shared with the Military Police, University of Alberta Campus Security, and security agencies at various shopping malls. Moreover, immigration officers are further constrained by not having access to particular intelligence information, a restriction governed by Immigration's designation as a non-investigative agency under the *Freedom of Information and Protection of Privacy Act.* As such, Immigration is restricted in the type of information it can gather and share, and thus it must rely on other agencies' investigative services.

A final example of partnering corresponds with the mandate of the Canadian National Railway (CN) police. CN's position in the continuum of policing combines the roles of service provider and service recipient. CN police have a service provider's responsibility for a large portion of the municipality, because of the extensive track system running through the centre of the city (CN police jurisdictional boundaries include all CN property and 250 metres of adjoining property). Conversely, Canadian National Railways represents a corporate citizen of the city, and thus the EPS responds to the needs of CN police as they would with any other corporation. In this public-corporate relationship, the EPS supplies the services of specialized units such as identification, lock-up, and other investigative units.

Edmonton's implementation of collaborative relations is due, in part, to the service-wide manner in which restructuring was undertaken, an internal environment conducive to broad structural change, and an executive willing to utilize alternative managerial techniques. Moreover, Edmonton succeeded in soliciting wide-ranging support for empowerment, partnership, fiscal downloading, and responsibilization. The quick transition to a decentralized service structure, coupled with a negotiated relationship with Edmontonians and partnering agencies, supported a wholesale process of reform and development of a continuum of police service.

Hybrid Policing: A Further Division of Labour

The operational shift that Edmonton Police Service and other agencies undertook reflected the tone that many services were to adopt but, more importantly, laid the foundation for an environment conducive to problem solving, partnering, and collaborative programming. This orientation supported the development of a continuum of policing that included public policing, private security, and community partners. It was a blueprint for a policing division of labour.

While the preceding section focused on the Edmonton Police Service, it is essential to note that other agencies making up the mosaic of policing grappled with similar governance and budgetary concerns. What makes Edmonton unique is the willingness of public and private agencies to implement an interactive division of labour in a constructive and collaborative manner. This process is strengthened by a relationship wherein various services share the coordination of policing and security and, where jurisdictions overlap, actively negotiate the division of operational tasks. Rather than responding to the imposition of neoliberalism through isolation and competition, the EPS took an active, problem-solving approach, one that required partnering and the coordination of a policing division of labour.

And yet it was not only public policing that confronted the need for partnering and collaboration. The Alberta government's restructuring strategy was imposed on all Albertans. Provincial, municipal, and private layers of security and enforcement would be affected by government reform. The role of many of these agencies would either expand or be tightly woven into the matrix of security and enforcement, a weaving that was guided initially by the Police Service's pursuit of cost-effective operations. In the following section, we examine this extended matrix of policing by dissecting the operational jurisdiction of special constables. A continued interest of this analysis remains the concept of collaboration and the evolution of an expanded division of labour.

Special Constables: A Strange Brew

The category of special constable includes both private security personnel and public employees who perform a range of provincial and municipal enforcement and regulatory functions.[46] The common denominator among special constables is that they are governed under the provincial *Police Act* and funded from the public purse, either directly or through a contract relation. Alberta has approximately 2,900 special constables, between 500 and 600 of whom are used to supplement RCMP operations in rural communities. At present, Alberta Justice is considering the expansion of both the numbers and the functions of special constables. Within Alberta Justice there is a growing consensus that special constables should be utilized more for low-level enforcement functions to free police services and resources for other purposes. The province argues that this initiative would allow for a more equitable use of funds. Central to this debate however, is the question of how much authority special constables should be empowered to exercise. Their accountability, functions, training, and relationship to the state's regulatory arm need to be set out in legislation.[47] There is concern that if these elements are not clearly articulated special constables may take on increasingly advanced policing functions without adequate training or provisions for accountability. It is this very debate that the Policing Alberta MLA Review Committee has engaged through a province-wide consultation.

Provincial, municipal, and quasi-public organizations rely on special constables to enforce a wide array of statutes pertinent to their organizational mandates. Take, for example, the variety of statutes a provincial conservation officer must enforce. These include the Criminal Code, the *Canada Shipping Act*, the *Migratory Birds Convention Act*, the *Fisheries Act*, the *Wild Animal and Plant Protection and Regulation of Internal Trade Act*, the *Wildlife Act*, the *Off Highway Vehicle Regulation*, the *Highway Traffic Act*, the *Traffic Safety Act*, the *Environmental Protection and Enhancement Act*, the *Forests Act*, and the *Gaming and Liquor Act*. Clearly there is a jurisdictional overlap with many of the enforcement agencies in the municipality of Edmonton. For conservation officers, there is also a geographical overlap, in that they cover all municipal and rural lands (excluding federal lands), particularly bodies of water and adjacent lands, terrain that is also within the jurisdiction of the EPS Park Patrol and the Municipal Park Rangers.

Provincial Gaming and Liquor inspectors, on the other hand, have a limited enforcement function but play an essential regulatory role within the security matrix. Under the Provincial Casino Terms and Conditions and Operating Guidelines, security standards are both set and inspected by Gaming and Liquor. Furthermore, all security guards working within a casino must register with the provincial Gaming and Liquor Commission and, as a condition of employment within a casino, must hold a current licence under the provisions of the *Private Investigators and Security Guards Act* or the *Police Act*.[48] Gaming and Liquor inspectors oversee particular order maintenance issues corresponding to licensed premises. In Edmonton, Gaming and Liquor inspectors meet on a monthly basis with the City Planning Branch, Fire and Police Services, in an effort to address specific concerns relating to community disorder. This collaboration facilitates the mapping of various by-laws/statutes that can be utilized to effect long-term problem resolution. But, more importantly, it creates a layered organization with varied capacities to address community disorder.

Special constables are also utilized in municipal governance and the enforcement of by-laws. As with provincial regulatory/enforcement branches, Municipal By-law Services (MBS) offer a layer of options and resources that supplement or complement the matrix of security and enforcement. Municipal by-law officers bring to the problem-solving table a diversity of enforcement and regulatory tools. In the context of problem solving, MBS works with other regulatory agencies to develop joint initiatives. In addition, MBS actively gathers and shares intelligence about identified problem properties and businesses. This function is consistent with Ericson and Haggerty's[49] concept of community networks, wherein community policing and problem solving involve increased communication among various public institutions.

A final example of a service provider/special constable designation can be located in quasi-public organizations such as hospitals and universities.[50] One example is the Caritas Health Group, which oversees the operation of the Grey Nuns Hospital, the Misericordia Hospital, and the General Hospital. Under the governance of Caritas, special constables are responsible for the enforcement of a diverse set of statutes such as the *Gaming and Liquor Act*, the *Highway Traffic Act*, the *Mental Health Act*, the *Motor Vehicle Act*, the *Provincial Offences Procedures Act*, and the *Public Health Act*. And while the jurisdictional boundaries are specific to Caritas property, this does not suggest that the level of collaboration with other agencies is any less important. Caritas Health Group, in conjunction with the EPS and the RCMP, set out a Memorandum of Understanding outlining the expectations of each service. The rationale for this agreement was to avoid any confusion about enforcement and support responsibilities.

Similarly, the University of Alberta Campus Patrol has negotiated a protocol with the EPS clarifying each service's function, jurisdiction, and procedures for specific investigations, and outlining the framework for joint operations. As with the Caritas Group, University of Alberta Campus Patrol enforces a customized range of statutes within a jurisdictional boundary defined as university property and all boundary roads.

Within the continuum of enforcement in Alberta, special constables play a significant role. As the preceding examples suggest, they serve a variety of enforcement and regulatory functions; more importantly, however, they augment the efforts of the EPS and the RCMP. They also serve to fill specific gaps in problem-solving initiatives. Clearly, special constables are an additional resource layer that supports community objectives of enforcement and security. They build on the concept of a layered organization, a division of labour tied to the needs of crime prevention and enforcement.[51] And while Alberta Justice recognizes the value of this enforcement layer, the question remains whether or not the role will expand.

Private Security

In a province in which free-market ideology and the rhetoric of customer service take pride of place, one would expect private sector security to grow and to be matched by a corresponding decrease in the public police presence. And yet, for a variety of reasons this has not been the case in Edmonton. One of the more obvious reasons is that the security market environment, as characterized by numerous managers, is highly competitive, antagonistic, and lacking coordination. Industry insiders have suggested that this environment stifles any effort to self-regulate or to enhance the profile of the industry either within the community or, more importantly, in the eyes of provincial regulators. There is also continuing public concern about the need for accountability measures and stringent regulations to govern the private sector.[52]

While private security certainly plays a role in the continuum of crime prevention, its function remains limited. It has a narrow area of operations that includes access control, alarm response, surveillance, and limited patrol responsibilities. In many instances an expanded role has been facilitated by public agencies in an effort to enhance public safety initiatives or to expand the community network. In these circumstances, private security has been utilized as a resource, added to the layered organization of crime prevention. It is a role that blends the characteristics of service provider with those of collaborative partner.

THE CORPS OF COMMISSIONAIRES

This body provides one example of how private sector services are utilized in the publicly coordinated police matrix. More specifically, the Commissionaires demonstrate how a private sector provider can fulfil low-level enforcement and crime prevention tasks within the broader municipal jurisdiction. The Corps of Commissionaires has an interesting status within the continuum of crime prevention and security. First, with respect to its regulatory link to the province, under the provincial *Private Investigators and Security Guards Act* members of the Corps are not required to hold a licence as indicated in the act, even though they hold security guard status. Second, with respect to federal government contracts, the Commissionaires have a first-right-of-refusal agreement. At present, federal contracts consume 55 per cent of the workload of the Corps; the remaining 45 per cent of the Commissionaires' contracts consist of municipal and private sector agreements.[53] One of these contracts is with the City of Edmonton, for parking enforcement, photo radar operations, and arrest processing for the EPS. As a condition of their employment, the Commissionaires are given special constable status in order to enforce task-related statutes (such as the *Highway Traffic Act* and city parking by-laws). In a similar police-related contract, the Commissionaires are contracted by CFB Garrison and serve as police dispatchers, identification officers, evidence custodians, and court and victim services liaison. They also maintain a mobile patrol function responsible for the security of military property at various locations throughout the city (e.g., the Armouries).

IN-HOUSE SECURITY

The private, in-house security service for the West Edmonton Mall, on the other hand, illustrates the need for stakeholders to share the responsibility for crime prevention and order management, especially when their operations create risk environments. The West Edmonton Mall (WEM) is the largest mall in Canada, with two indoor amusement parks and a marine mammal park. The composition of the mall gives it the characteristics of a city. It has both liquor-licensed and retail establishments, an average population of 60,000 people per day, increasing to 200,000 on Saturdays, and on any given evening there are 10,000 people consuming alcohol within its environs. Not surprisingly, the security service receives, on average, 40,000 calls for service each year. The security service employs fifty officers with a range of operational tasks, including foot patrol, bike patrol, vehicle patrol, undercover surveillance, gang squad intelligence, communications, and CCTV surveillance.[54] WEM security officers enforce the *Trespass to Property Act*, specific municipal by-laws, and Criminal Code offences such as theft, assault, and impaired driving. They are involved in the cooperative policing program, participate in the alternative release program, and have a unique dispatch code with the EPS that allows them to set up occurrence files and access CPIC. They partner with the EPS on special projects on WEM property such as anti-theft programs, check-stop programs, sweeps for alcohol and drugs in the parking area, and so on.

SPECIAL-DUTY POLICE

Another layer of private sector security is, in fact, an extension of the service provided by the EPS Special Duty Unit. Although the unit operates as a provider to private interests, this function has evolved in response to private sector contractual relationships governed by city by-law requirements and public service privatization.

City by-laws state that if a for-profit organization hosts an event (such as an Edmonton Eskimos football game) and the activity results in the need for policing (e.g., traffic control), the city is not responsible for supplying police officers. Therefore, the organization must hire police officers to address the particular needs arising from the event. Athletic organizations such as the Canadian Football League (CFL) and the National Hockey League (NHL) require, as a condition of the franchise contract, that all games be attended by a security contingent consisting of one staff sergeant and nine constables. As this transcends the mandate requirements of the city, alternative contract arrangements are implemented utilizing officers from the Special Duty Unit.

Privatization of certain municipal services, such as roads and utilities, has created a particular service need. As these services are no longer municipal departments, they cannot utilize the direct services of the EPS for road closure and traffic-flow management but must contract to the Special Duty Unit. Anything beyond the organizational norm of the police service must be contracted out, as EPS operations will not take officers out of the roster to serve the needs of private industry.

Other examples of Special Duty functions are security at weddings where there are large cash gifts. Licensed establishments that have concerns about criminal activity, gang presence, or unruly clientele also contract with the unit. The role of these officers is not to act as bouncers or doormen but to offer a police presence and enforce laws. The service's philosophy is, 'You hire us; you don't buy us.' Officers are there to enforce the law not to turn a blind eye or to act as agents of the establishment.

One reason for the success of this option is that there are limitations to the services private security companies can offer, as outlined in the *Private Investigators and Security Guards Act* and the various statutes (e.g., the *Highway Traffic Act*) that allow only police officers to perform certain functions.[55]

The above section is by no means an exhaustive analysis of private security or the various functions the private industry serves, but it is an outline of the multilayered nature of private and public policing. As stated earlier, both the competitive market environment and legislative restrictions limit the role of private security. But yet another, and more compelling, reason why private security has not displaced public policing is the commitment of public policing to crime prevention. The EPS and other public agencies have not relinquished their stewardship; they have, in fact, maintained a proactive leadership role.

The question that Alberta Justice must ponder is the role that the private sector plays in the continuum of policing and whether this sector can be included in the enforcement blueprint in a meaningful way that addresses current shortcomings in the division of labour. If the present scenario is any evidence of what the future might hold, the private sector will continue to have a restricted role consistent with alarm response, access control, loss prevention, and surveillance tasks. And yet there are examples of innovative agencies that have forged productive and collaborative relationships with public policing, and in doing so have inserted themselves into the multilayered organization of public crime prevention and enforcement.

Edmonton in Summary

Underlying Edmonton's current integrated division of labour is the central strategic principle of seeking a 'full partnership between the community and their police.'[56] In the context of Edmonton's continuum of policing and Alberta Justice's neoliberal agenda, full partnership assumes that the community is an active negotiator, not a passive recipient of police policy. Full partnership, understood in these terms, is meant to 'empower the community to bring it onto a more equal footing with the police in terms of joint ownership of local crime and disorder problems and as co-producers of peace, order and security at the local level.'[57]

The emphasis on partnership set the parameters for a new contractual relationship between police and community. It did so by first constructing an alternative identity of community, countering the image of dependence and helplessness as perpetuated by the professional model.

Second, the partnership focus forced a realignment of responsibility and authority, which in turn created a network of alliances between various communities, agencies, and the EPS. Third, this approach established criteria for measuring effectiveness based on the successful inclusion of community partners in the process of problem solving rather than on numbers of arrests and clearance rates that reflect a narrow concept of law enforcement.

Edmonton's operationalization of community policing displaced the community's reliance on police services to resolve all issues of crime control, a step that required a shift in the roles of both the community and the police. This has meant a realignment of both the responsibility and the role of the EPS in maintaining order – a new role in which police figure more and more as 'knowledge brokers, expert advisers and security managers.'[58] This image is dramatically different from that of the crime fighter and law enforcer of the professional model. As for the community, its responsibility becomes to apprise the police 'of the services it requires in its specific locale,' and 'to advise its police on what are locally regarded as problems of order and security' as well as to 'stress a correlative adaptability and accountability of police to local communities.'[59]

With the growth of community policing, the EPS is no longer the sole initiator of action, but this has not necessarily undermined its locus of control. The EPS continues to possess the attributes (resources and knowledge) required to resolve identified problems.[60] Though the EPS remains a locus of control, its role has changed from providing a reactive response to criminal events, to what O'Malley refers to as 'a proactive leadership role.'[61] O'Malley goes on to suggest that this leadership role is one of an 'accountable professional practitioner ... a community leader harnessing community resources to tackle the problems which give rise to crime and disorder.'[62] In this designation, the EPS has become not only a crime prevention resource but also a catalyst prompting neighbourhoods and communities to take the initiative for problem solving.[63] The task of the EPS, as proactive manager, has therefore been to facilitate crime prevention and help communities help themselves. This articulation of crime prevention and the role of the police supports the neoliberal principle of empowering citizens, of ensuring that individuals and various stakeholders play an active role in their own governance – a role consistently reinforced by the provincial government's efforts to prepare Albertans for a new era of capitalism.

The goals of the Police Plan were achieved by a concerted effort to operationalize a process of consultation wherein citizens and various agencies would be empowered. Consultation put in place a mechanism whereby the EPS could discuss priorities and formulate strategies with the community and policing partners.[64] Consultation further served as a platform from which the EPS established its proactive leadership in managing the required resources of crime prevention. Finally, this consultative process assisted community representatives in setting their agenda for safety and security while facilitating a better understanding of the problems associated with public policing.[65] Consultation therefore was the means by which the various sectors of the community were engaged and motivated, while the EPS interacted simultaneously as service provider managing the commodity of crime prevention and order maintenance.

As in other public services, the perspectives of policy makers and police leaders have shifted over time. Policy analysts emphasize a shift towards a language drawn from private sector management. Police service reform, like public sector reform generally, has reflected a critique of existing services from a perspective that imports ideas associated with management in profit-oriented sectors. Leishman, Cope, and Starie draw attention to a 'new policing order' framed by what they refer to as 'new public management.'[66] Moreover, new public management 'is now deeply ingrained within the management structures of the police service.'[67] As Chris Murphy notes,

> The previously insular and organizational culture of public policing is being increasingly colonized by business concepts, values and terminology. New management training frequently uses business analogies and cases to illustrate proper police management principles. Police are encouraged to see themselves in the 'business' of supplying policing services to clients, customers and consumers.[68]

The current trend of police leaders is to increasingly address the problem of service performance and work to decrease operational costs by appealing to private sector strategies of efficiency and fiscal restraint. Others argue that, 'the structural forms gathered under the community policing umbrella are precisely those *au courant* among progressive corporations and management consultants.'[69] In retrospect, it would appear that such approaches have not been ignored by Edmonton. Moreover, one might suggest that Edmonton has been an astute student of the political environment and has not shied away from embracing 'neo-liberal rationalities and the related social technology of new man-gerialism.'[70]

Comparative Analysis

The Edmonton and Halifax case studies reveal both similar and distinct patterns in the growth and diversification of policing and security. And while each of these case studies can be read as a stand-alone portrait of policing networks, activities, relationships, and governance issues, they are comparable in that they provide an empirical basis to examine micro and macro patterns in different 'localized' social and political contexts. There is little doubt that this analysis of policing in Edmonton and Halifax raises particular questions about the general growth and diversi-fication of policing, the changing role of public police, and the problem-atic governance of pluralistic policing.

Explaining Policing Growth and Diversification

By adopting a broad definition of policing and security, this research was able to encompass 'all' of the public and private and community agen-cies involved in the provision of security and policing services in both communities. As a result, both case studies reveal surprising growth in the number and variety of alternative or non-government policing and security services involved in policing. In Halifax and Edmonton the research shows not only that the number and types of private security agencies have increased dramatically but also that the use of hybrid or specialized public police (such as special constables and commissionaires) has also increased. In addition the case studies show that a growing diversity of policing functions are being undertaken by private, hybrid, or specialized police to deal with a range of 'new' policing tasks such as forensic accounting, by-law enforcement, low-level patrol, and property protection. This growth and diversification in policing can be explained by a variety of macro-level policing trends operating at the local level.

The rapidly growing cost of public policing coupled with limited budget growth in the 1990s led to a ten-year decline (1989–2000) in police per population rates in Canada. This decline, coupled with new and more complex service demands, forced public police throughout Canada to begin to rationalize their services in a variety of resource-saving ways.[71] In both Edmonton and Halifax, for example, public police had to find ways to rationalize or limit their traditional service response.

This meant eliminating and limiting some traditional police services, sharing some service responsibility with or downloading it to other partners, and ignoring or encouraging the growth of private policing. In urban Halifax, for example, it is clear that the police can no longer satisfactorily respond to increasing community and business requests for more patrol presence, policing at public events, minor property and person protection, and complex theft and fraud investigations. In Edmonton we find a concerted effort to utilize the services of various partners while attempting to maintain a position of stewardship over the continuum of policing. Both case studies indicate that some public policing functions are being done by a range of alternative service providers, such as extra-duty police, by-law enforcement officers, special constables, private security guards, security consultants, and forensic investigators. These developments suggest that the growth of private security is in some measure related to the declining response capacity and priorities of public policing and the growing demand or market for private specialized policing and security services.

But public police rationalization only partially explains the growth of private and hybrid forms of policing and security. During this growth period there has also been an expansion of new demands for conventional policing and security services. Changing socio-economic conditions and behavioural norms appear to have increased crime opportunities and thus the actual incidence of crime in both Halifax and Edmonton. Even a sceptical reading of the official crime statistics reveals a significant and consistent increase in particular forms of recorded crime in both cities over the last twenty years. This increasing level of real crime and disorder, communicated and magnified by daily media accounts, has combined to create a perception of elevated risk of personal property victimization. This perception, though perhaps exaggerated, has nevertheless contributed to an increased demand for more policing and security. Thus demand for more police and security has escalated in response to both real and perceived policing and security needs.

In addition to the increase in crime and public feelings of insecurity, there has been a tangible expansion of private business and 'mass private space'[72] in both Halifax and Edmonton. In Halifax there has been considerable new commercial development. Since 1990 two new business parks have been established, several large shopping centres and strip malls have been built, and numerous stores, bars, restaurants, office buildings, and condominium complexes have opened for business. In Edmonton the economy continues to grow at an unprecedented rate,

fed by increased oil exploration and related development. This economic boom has also fed adjoining communities, thus increasing the
Edmonton regional population to well over a million. This population
growth has stimulated an increase in housing and construction of 24 per
cent in 2002 over the previous year. In both locales, the growth of mass
private space[73] during this period has certainly created new policing and
security needs, requiring enhanced security forces. For example, the
West Edmonton Mall has fifty security officers at its disposal, and in
Halifax the new Casino Nova Scotia has an in-house security force of
thirty-five. While most private security functions remain focused on
typical 'security guard' activities such as passive surveillance, security
presence, and so on, there is evidence in both case studies of the gradual
expansion of the static guard's role into areas of enforcement, patrol,
community policing, and minor investigations, and also into more
sophisticated, high-end, forensic and financial investigations for both
government and private business clients.

Policing and Security: Changing Roles and Relationships

Conventional analysis of policing conceptualizes public police as the
primary and often exclusive provider of police and security services in an
area. Based on a modern liberal welfare state's conception of government and governance, this approach sustains the fiction that public
police have responsibility for and therefore a monopoly of most policing
services. As a result, the public police are portrayed as the authoritative
and effective source of policing and security. Both case studies provide
compelling evidence that the dominance and centrality of the public
police in the delivery of policing and security services is changing and
suggest a need to radically revise the conventional public police-centric
notion of contemporary policing.

Both Edmonton and Halifax demonstrate that public police no longer
provide the broad array of policing and security services that they once
did and have limited resources to meet new and specialized policing and
security demands. However, while both Edmonton and Halifax public
police have rationalized their services, there are significant differences
in how their rationalization strategies have affected their role and importance in the delivery of policing and security services in their jurisdictions. In Halifax, the public police have responded to increased demand
by reducing the scope and reach of their service role – specifically, by
cutting, limiting, or sharing police services. A priority emphasis on

serious crime, emergency, and crisis policing functions and a downgrading of less serious community demands signals the emergence of a limited, 'core' public policing role. The end result is that a growing number of people and businesses in Halifax no longer look to the public police for property or personal protection. The resulting diverse mix of policing and security agencies and services is not formally or centrally networked or coordinated. In Edmonton, it would appear that the police have accepted the reality, legitimacy, and utility of private and community security. Through partnership and collaboration, the EPS has been able to retain its traditional broad policing and security mandate. This rationalization and regulation strategy means that the public police gain considerable operational and political benefits by enlisting the expertise and resources of private security as partners and co-producers of public safety and law and order.[74]

Governance Patterns

The declining role of public police as the direct provider of broad policing and security services and the growth in the number and importance of alternative or non-government police and security agencies/services make the question of the public governance of modern or late-modern policing especially problematic. In a diverse or polycentric policing environment, the decentralization or diffusion of policing powers and responsibilities to a growing diversity of policing agents and agencies makes the issues of public accountability and public good difficult to operationalize.[75] Our two case studies suggest that different governance responses to the growth of diversity in policing are possible, with different consequences for both police and public governance.

The different policing and governance responses in this study are reflections of two different provincial political governance cultures. In Nova Scotia, a traditionally limited provincial role in local municipal governance has meant a lack of strong centralized policing and security planning, regulation, and direction. Limited governance is especially evident in the lack of regulation of private security policing in Nova Scotia. Regarded initially as a business and taxation issue and not one of public safety and security, the growth of private security in Nova Scotia has taken place with minimal government regulation. In addition, limited government has meant that there has been little effort to rationalize or integrate public and private policing. Thus policing and security in this environment are in effect self-regulated, loosely networked, largely beyond public scrutiny, and guided primarily by market forces and values. In contrast, the Alberta government's restructuring strategy was imposed on all Albertans. Provincial, municipal, and private layers of security and enforcement were affected by government reform. As a result, the role of many of these agencies either expanded or was tightly woven into the matrix of security and enforcement. Interestingly, these shifts occurred not by way of police and security-related legislation but as a result of neoliberal political and economic ideology and policies imposed by the provincial government. For Edmonton, concepts of empowerment, decentralization, partnering, and business planning were key to the successful navigation of various fiscal and political obstacles that Alberta's transition to neoliberalism created. Furthermore, the EPS adapted to municipal and provincial downloading by instituting ownership and community and business partnerships. Although its restructuring is not fully integrated or rationalized and is still more policy than practice, Edmonton has laid a foundation for an integrated division of labour in which the EPS continues to assert its broad policing and security mandate.

Conclusion

This comparison of two local urban policing and security networks has produced a number of findings and observations that validate and refine the hypotheses about global policing trends and patterns that inform this research. In particular, we were interested in empirically examining, at the local level, late-modern policing trends such as pluralization, rationalization, privatization, commodification, and neoliberal governance. The pluralization[76] of modern policing was clearly evident in both case studies, as policing in both Halifax and Edmonton has grown to encompass a broad range of activities conducted by an increasingly diverse network of public, private, and community agencies, companies, and groups. The rationalization[77] of public policing was also evident, albeit in different ways. In both cities the role of the public police as the central provider of broad policing services and service rationalization has diminished. This has been accomplished through a combination of community responsibilization and role redefinition. The commodification and privatization[78] of some existing and some new policing activities is demonstrated by the significant growth in the amount and diversity of private and hybrid security policing in both cities. These broad policing trends have combined so that a rapidly increasing number of people and properties in both cities are routinely being policed and protected by a combination of alternative police agencies and arrangements.

However, while both case studies by and large reflect late-modern macro-level policing patterns, they also reveal variations that at least clarify some of the general trends. The governance of policing in our case studies clearly varies by location and political culture. In Edmonton, an active government regime motivated by neoliberal ideals aggressively pursued its role as a regulatory agency protecting the role of government and public police in the governance of policing and public safety. As a result of this governance philosophy, private security and the community are a regulated and integrated element in a diverse policing network, with the Edmonton public police as the central hub of its operations. This suggests that the government has the option of remaining a dominant and aggressive player in the governance and delivery of policing and security. The Halifax case study demonstrates that *laissez-faire* governance and an unregulated policing and security environment produces a diverse but loosely linked policing and security network, one that allows market influences rather than public principles to dominate and gives governments and the public police a limited role. So, while macro-level governance patterns and trends operate, the study of specific 'local' contexts and unique situational demands can reveal instructive variations on a common theme.

Notes

1 David Bayley and Clifford Shearing, *The New Structure of Policing: Description, Conceptualization and Research Agenda, Research Report* (Washington, D.C.: National Institute of Justice, 2001) 1.

2 Les Johnston, *The Rebirth of Private Policing* (London: Routledge, 1992); I. Loader and N. Walker, 'Policing as a Public Good: Reconstituting the Connections between Policing and the State' (2001) 5:1 Theoretical Criminology 9–35.; T. Jones and T. Newburn, eds, *Private Security and Public Policing* (Oxford: Clarendon Press, 1998); and Robert Reiner, *The Politics of the Police* (Toronto: University of Toronto Press, 1992).

3 Pat O'Malley, 'Risk, Power and Crime Prevention' (1992) 21:3 Economy and Society.

4 Clifford Shearing, 'Reinventing Policing: Policing as Governance,' in Otwin Marewin, ed., *Policing Change, Changing Police, International Perspectives* (New York: Garland Publishing, 1996).

5 Clifford Shearing and Philip Stenning, *Private Security and Private Justice: The*

Challenge of the Eighties (Montreal: Institute for Research on Public Policy, 1982).

6 David Garland, 'The Limits of the Sovereign State: Strategies of Crime Control in Contemporary Society' (1996) 36:4 British Journal of Criminology, 27 at 445. See also, David Garland, *The Culture of Control* (Chicago: University of Chicago Press, 2001).

7 Richard Ericson and Kevin Haggerty, *Policing the Risk Society* (Toronto: University of Toronto Press, 1997).

8 Loader and Walker, *supra* note 2.

9 Ibid., at 26.

10 Operational Definitions: Given the considerable debate (Jones and Newburn, *supra* note 2 at 24–52) over the range of terminology used to describe the agencies and individuals involved in both public and private policing and security, it is important to describe the operational definitions used in this case study. The definitions used were designed to be broad enough to encompass all or most of the agencies and organizations, whether public, private, or a hybrid, formally involved in some aspect of delivering 'policing and security' services in Halifax and Edmonton. *Policing* is loosely defined as activities related to the active enforcement, through threat or force, of public rules and laws concerning order, crime, and security. *Security* encompasses a range of actions designed to prevent, reduce, and eliminate risk, loss, or damage to persons or property, including activities such as guarding, surveillance, installation of security devices, and so on. *Public police* in various forms are distinguished as direct agents of government, specially empowered by the criminal law, who usually operate for public purposes. *Private security* are agencies or companies that sell their policing and security services, usually but not exclusively to private interests, for private purposes and profit.

11 Johnston, *supra* note 2

12 Loader and Walker, *supra* note 2; Johnston, *supra* note 2.

13 Jones and Newburn, *supra* note 2; Chris Murphy, 'Policing Postmodern Canada' (1998) 13:2 Canadian Journal of Law and Society 1.

14 Shearing and Stenning, *supra* note 5; Jones and Newburn, *supra* note 2; Loader and Walker, *supra* note 2.

15 Jones and Newburn, *supra* note 2; Johnston, *supra* note 2.

16 Loader and Walker, *supra* note 2; Bayley and Shearing, *supra* note 1.

17 In Nova Scotia, the governance of private *security* is done through the provincial Department of Justice and its Police and Public Safety Division, under the *Private Investigators and Private Guards Act* (1989) R.S., c. 356, s.1. The current regulatory approach is one of business licensing rather than

public safety. Regulations regarding credit ratings, insurance, and licensing fees take precedence over education, security training, or experience requirements. As one security executive put it, 'anyone can be in this business if they can pay for a licence.' Administrative staff have limited resources, and there is little if any monitoring or enforcement of the limited regulations that do exist. The legislation, if enacted, will signal a greater governmental role in the regulation and standardization of private and community security in Nova Scotia.

18 K. Swol, 'Private Security and Public Policing in Canada,' *Juristat* 18:3 (Ottawa: Statistics Canada, Canadian Centre for Justice Statistics, 1998, catalogue no. 85-002-XPE98013).

19 Ibid.

20 It would also appear that because of location, income, or community composition, some communities have been responsibilized more effectively than others and adopt different levels of participation in community policing programs. This higher but uneven level of community policing involvement may improve community safety in some communities but may also be increasing the overall level of inequality of safety and security.

21 For example, the Military Police employ 100 Commissionaires to assist with security on National Defence property. HRM has hired 11 Commissionaires to do traffic and parking by-law enforcement, and a number work at the HRMP front desk.

22 Recent public investigations of military policing and justice initiated a series of internal reforms designed to make police more operationally independent of the command structure and to upgrade training and policing skills.

23 This situation is being re-evaluated in response to '9/11.'

24 As by-laws address a number of potential areas of social conflict, their effective enforcement often requires both public and by-law enforcement officers. Their separate operating relationship and different enforcement philosophies and priorities have made this problematic.

25 Legal Powers: The limits and the limiting of private security's legal powers were matters of concern to both public and private police. Some private security want more legal police powers, such as the powers of search and seizure, arrest, the use of force, and greater access to police information (e.g., from the Canadian Police Information Centre). However, this desire is tempered by a reluctance to become subject to the constraints and limits of public accountability, liability, and the courts. Most private security executives recognize that by having a more limited role, with limited public and legal responsibilities, they actually may have more operational freedom than public police. The key complaint of private security seems to be their

operational dependency on the public police to provide legal responses to their policing and security problems. While granting private security more legal powers is a complex and serious public policy question, it is also a pressing one, as more and more of the policing and security of everyday life comes under private jurisdiction. Accountability concerns about the abuse and use of existing private security powers, while voiced by public police and some community representatives, were not directly researched in this study. The absence of clear public accountability mechanisms and oversight bodies also makes the issue of legal powers and public accountability a key policy issue. While private security argue that the competitive market-place makes them more accountable for satisfactory service than the public police are, these claims have not yet been seriously examined.

26 See Nova Scotia's *Private Investigators and Private Guards Act* (1989) R.S., c. 356, s.1.

27 Specialized Corporate Security: Because of limitations of time, resources, and access, this research did not examine the role and influence of what can be described as 'high-end' corporate private security consisting of either in-house security consultants and experts or highly specialized contract consultants who perform a variety of specialized security functions, including forensic accounting and investigations, risk and loss prevention, and information technology and online security. Various consulting companies in Halifax, such as KPMG and Deloitte and Touche, offer security and forensic investigation services.

28 It should be noted that there are more than sixty companies listed in the Halifax telephone book offering a range of electronic security services, but specializing in multi-purpose monitored alarm systems. These companies act as an intermediary between alarm users and police, fire, and ambulance services. The recent growth and proliferation of these companies in the Halifax area suggest that the market for risk reduction and security is greater than the public police can satisfy. While it is impossible to get accurate industry data, it was estimated that in Halifax about 80 per cent of all businesses and 20 to 40 per cent of all households are electronically alarmed. Though concerned about the proliferation of companies and some of their sales methods and services, most in the industry predict a healthy future for the electronic security industry .

29 Jones and Newburn, *supra* note 2.

30 B. Forst and P. Manning, *The Privatization of Policing: Two Views* (Washington, D.C.: Georgetown University Press, 1999).

31 Ibid.; Reiner, *supra* note 2; Loader and Walker, *supra* note 2.

32 Bayley and Shearing, *supra* note 1.

33 Ian Blair, 'Where Do the Police Fit In?' (speech to Association of Chief Police Officers [ACPO] Conference, 16 July 1998); Loader and Walker, *supra* note 2.

34 The diversification and pluralization of policing and security in the late-modern era is in part a response to the fiscal crisis of the liberal welfare state and the ideological desire to limit state expenditure and involvement in the provision of public services such as public policing.

35 David Garland, 'The Limits of the Sovereign State: Strategies of Crime Control in Contemporary Society' (1996) 36:4 British Journal of Criminology 445.

36 Shearing, *supra* note 4

37 Alberta, Solicitor General, 'Report of the Policing Alberta MLA Review Committee' (Edmonton: Alberta Justice, 2002).

38 Alberta Justice, 'Annual Report 1994–5' (Edmonton: Alberta Justice, 1995).

39 Mark Lisac, *The Klein Revolution* (Edmonton: NeWest Press, 1995).

40 Edmonton Police Service, 'The Edmonton Police Plan 1996–1998' (Edmonton: EPS).

41 David Osborne and Ted Gaebler, *Reinventing Government: How the Entrepreneurial Spirit Is Transforming the Public Sector* (New York: Penguin Books, 1993).

42 John Lindsay, 'Notes from the Chief' (April 1997), Edmonton Police Service.

43 Interview with Sgt B. Adams, Edmonton Police Service, 2002.

44 Ibid.

45 Alberta Justice, '1991–1999 Departmental Budget Expenditures' (Edmonton: Alberta Justice, 1999).

46 Jones and Newburn (*supra* note 2) have characterized this category of policing as hybrid in that it is not clearly demarcated by a public-private sectoral divide.

47 While the *Special Constable Regulation* (2003) set out various requirements and procedures related to the employment and use of special constables, there are concerns related to governance and accountability. The regulation outlines a process whereby complaints and disciplinary action are the responsibility of the employer, not Alberta Justice. Within the regulation the onus is upon the employer to respond to issues of misconduct and abuse of authority, a process removed from the regulatory arm of the province. (See sections 9(1), (2) and section 10.)

48 Alberta Gaming and Liquor Commission, *Casino Terms and Conditions and Operating Guidelines*, Section 6.3.12 (2003).

49 Ericson and Haggerty, *supra* note 7.

50 The category 'quasi-public' is used in reference to organizations funded through public formulas but governed by internal boards of governors.

51 David Bayley, *Police for the Future* (New York: Oxford University Press, 1994).

52 In an effort to address these concerns, the 2002 MLA review of the Alberta *Police Act* recommended that the solicitor general 'initiate a comprehensive review of the private security industry in order to modernize legislation and to determine how the industry can be integrated into the overall strategy of public safety' (MLA Review of the Alberta *Police Act*, 2002, Rec. 8), *supra* note 37, at 19.

53 An example of the diversity of the corps can be illustrated in its current pilot project between the Edmonton branch and an Edmonton-based software company to test CCTV use that will give real-time images of building interiors once an alarm system has been activated. The real-time images are beamed to monitors within the responding vehicle or to palm pilots held by the security officer *en route*. The alarm system, once activated, locks down a site and supplies digitalized photos of suspects. Currently, the project is being piloted with 7 Eleven stores and Burger Kings throughout Edmonton, with future interest in a similar pilot from Imperial Oil.

54 Hiring criteria for WEM security are extremely rigorous. Potential applicants must have at least a two-year diploma in police foundations or law and security, a degree in criminology, or five years of police experience. Police Services frequently recruit from WEM security.

55 The unit is funded completely by the services supplied on a cost-recovery basis. Billing has increased in the past four years from $400,000 to more than half a million dollars annually. The fee schedule is set out in the following manner: Constable $42/hr, Detective $47/hr, and S/Sgt $52/hr, out of which comes a $9 administration fee that goes back to the operation of the unit.

56 Andre Normandeau and Barry Leighton, *A Vision of the Future of Policing in Canada: Police Challenge 2000* (Ottawa: Solicitor General of Canada, 1990) at 487.

57 Ibid., at 49.

58 Ericson and Haggerty, *supra* note 7 at 164.

59 Pat O'Malley and Darren Palmer, 'Post-Keynesian Policing' (1996) 25:2 Economy and Society.

60 Shearing, *supra* note 4 at 142.

61 O'Malley, *supra* note 3 at 18.

62 Ibid.

63 R. Trojanowicz and B. Bucqueroux, *Community Policing: A Contemporary*

Perspective (Cincinnati: Anderson Publishing Co., 1990); Ericson and Haggerty, *supra* note 7.

64 Bayley and Shearing, *supra* note 1; Normandeau and Leighton, *supra* note 56; Barry Leighton, 'Visions of Community Policing: Rhetoric and Reality in Canada' (1991) 33 (3–4) Canadian Journal of Criminology 485–522.

65 Normandeau and Leighton, ibid.

66 Frank Leishman, S. Cope, and P. Starie, 'Reinventing and Restructuring: Towards a New Policing Order,' in Frank Leishman, Barry Loveday, and Stephen Savage, eds, *Core Issues in Policing* (London: Longman, 1996).

67 Stephen Savage and Sarah Chapman, 'Managing Change,' in Frank Leishman, Barry Loveday, and Stephen Savage, eds, *Core Issues in Policing* (London: Longman, 1996).

68 Chris Murphy, *supra* note 13.

69 Stephen Mastrofski, 'Community Policing and Police Organization Structure,' in Jean-Paul Brodeur, ed., *How to Recognize Good Policing: Problems and Issues* (Thousand Oaks: Sage Publications, 1998).

70 O'Malley, *supra* note 3 at 10.

71 Murphy, *supra* note 13.

72 Shearing and Stenning, *supra* note 5.

73 Ibid.

74 Blair, *supra* note 33; R. Morgan and T. Newborn, *The Future of Policing* (Oxford: Clarion Press, 1997).

75 J. Sheptycki, 'Postmodern Power and Transnational Policing: Democracy, the Constabulary Ethic and the Response to Global Insecurity' (Geneva: Geneva Centre for the Democratic Control of Armed Forces [DCAF], April 2002).

76 Johnston, *supra* note 2.

77 Murphy, *supra* note 13.

78 Johnston, *supra* note 2.

5 Beyond Public-Private:
Towards a New Typology of Policing

GEORGE S. RIGAKOS

Introduction

It is now common sociolegal knowledge that the once-accepted categories of 'public' and 'private' are becoming a less and less effective conceptual rubric from which to mount serious intellectual inquiries into policing. Something quite important has been happening to the configuration of policing in the last three decades. This fundamental transformation involves the steady growth of private security, most notably in North America,[1] but also in Britain[2] and other European nations.[3] In Canada, private security employment matched and then surpassed public police employment in the late 1960s to early 1970s.[4] Today, private security employment is at least twice that in public policing.[5] This process of increased reliance on the private sector for security provision is mirrored in the general privatization of other core state endeavours including education, welfare, and medical care. But in no other sphere of creeping neoliberalism[6] are the stakes so potentially high. If the *fictio juris* liberal foundation for the modern state is to retain even its symbolic meaning, captured in the Hobbesian notion of each surrendering part of his or her liberty for the greater good in order 'to live peaceably amongst themselves, and be protected against other men,'[7] then the continued advance of private security is the gravest threat to Western democracy of all privatization trends. If even the semblance of public accountability[8] and a 'greater good' is lost, then the rationale for the state itself, manifested in its presumed monopoly over the use of legitimate violence,[9] is compromised.[10] In some quarters, this has resulted in exploring what can be salvaged from 'public good' policing.[11] What is often forgotten in our recent attempts to theorize these trends in policing – sometimes considered 'postmodern'[12] or post-Keynesian[13] – is that it was only a revolutionary conceptual leap in our notion of what constitutes 'policing'[14] in the first place that made possible many contemporary advances in police theory. Once the historical antecedents of policing had been rediscovered by sociologists and once they began taking heed of the exponential growth of private security,[15] new branches of inquiry sprouted forth and the conceptual map of 'policing' was transformed.[16] By the time Shearing and Stenning[17] produced their edited collection *Private Policing*, all that remained was to articulate what was fast becoming an accepted sociolegal truism: policing was an activity engaged in by various public, private, and quasi-public bodies encompassing organizations from IBM computer fraud investigators[18] to insurance companies,[19] municipal police forces, and so forth.

For all the tremendously important empirical and theoretical work that has taken place since then – most of which accepts implicitly (and sometimes explicitly) that the boundary between public and private policing is 'blurred' – there has yet to be any analytic development of our categorizations of policing based on this new conceptual underpinning. This is the thrust of this chapter – to develop a typology of policing that transcends the public-private dichotomy already long problematized by most researchers as a viable and meaningful basis for differentiating between forms of security activity. I will take as my premise, therefore, the idea that it is now time for serious conceptual rigour, for the identification and categorization of policing in a manner that meets the needs of our broadening notions of security provision. The focus of analysis in this project is *policing labour types* (activities), not only because this flows directly from the original empirical basis for contemporary public and private policing research (i.e., they appear to be *doing* similar things), but because, as I will demonstrate, it is the most fruitful and conceptually robust analytic category at our disposal. What is planned herein is thus very much a typology of *policing* rather than a typology of police.

The remainder of this chapter is divided into four general parts. The first part, 'On the Art of Typology Construction,' examines what it means to engage in typology construction in the first place – a typology of typologies, if you will – and sets the groundwork for the examination of previous police typologies in the section immediately following it. In that section, 'Previous Typologies of Police and Policing,' I consider prior categorical treatments of policing, discussing their relative strengths and weaknesses in relation to their utility for informing a general typology of public and private policing activities. This general overview is followed by a description of my chosen 'method' for constructing a typology of policing, in the process making reference to what has been learned in the previous two sections. The fourth and last section (not-withstanding the conclusions) finally posits a typology of policing that purposefully seeks to overcome the public-private dichotomy.

On the Art of Typology Construction

To talk of typology construction usually means a first step towards theory construction – the two in any case are eventually bound to intersect. This is fundamentally the case because, in the end, typology construction is a heuristic, explanatory exercise. While there appears to be general agree-ment among sociologists about the purpose of typology construction – that is, to elucidate, explore, teach, construct theory, and so on – there are very few who would agree on how this is to be accomplished.[20] Preferred methods of typology construction range from non-existent or purely heuristic 'ideal types'[21] to empirically based categorizations de-duced from multivariate statistics.[22] That social scientists rely heavily on typologies without a standardized method for their construction is un-derstandable given that, as human beings, we are always engaged in what McKinney[23] describes as 'existential typing.' But this *pragmatic* form of reduction routinely employed by members of a social system to develop short-hand knowledge about their surroundings – a process we all en-gage in – should be distinguished from the *social scientific* enterprise of 'constructed types.' The latter is also ubiquitous and open to much debate, but in the end relates back to a process of logical, theoretical 'typifications of typifications.'[24] The distinction is thus between *first-* and *second-*order constructs.[25]

Despite the formality of social scientific 'second-order' constructs, they none the less are dependent on raw experiences and selection. As McKinney[26] puts it, 'all concepts are generalizations and all generaliza-tion implies abstraction and reduction, and one aspect of this is the process of typification.' The fool's question to be raised at this point might therefore be, 'But what reality do typologies reflect?' Any at-tempted answer embroils one in a metaphysical game from which any 'resolution' reflects an empirically unassailable contention about ontol-ogy. Of course, the *reality* of anything can be questioned, but social scientists have little recourse other than to make their deductions ex-plicit, their analyses transparent, and in the end, whether implicitly or explicitly, to accept that there is some order in the cosmos and that this constitutes some generally agreed-upon 'reality.' The real questions are therefore not metaphysical but rather methodological, at least for intellectually mature social scientists.

Of course, we know that there is no single method, but rather multiple techniques for the construction of typologies in the social sciences.[27] It should be little surprise that those scholars most committed to understanding typology construction in the social sciences have conveniently created typologies of typology construction. As I see it, the central dichotomy within typology construction mirrors the dichotomy of deductive versus inductive reasoning that methodologists ask social scientists to reckon with in general theory construction. Bailey[28] argues that this core dichotomy in typology construction can be expressed as the heuristic-empirical distinction. He cites others who have made similar observations: Hempel's[29] ideal versus classificatory types, Cappechi's[30] abstract versus non-abstract types, and McKinney's[31] ideal versus extracted types.

The finest example of a purely heuristic typology is Weber's notion of the 'ideal type,' wherein he makes very clear that this categorization has very little to do with any 'description' in an empirical sense: 'It is not a *description* of reality but it aims to give unambiguous means of expression to such a description ... In its conceptual purity, this mental construct (Gendenkenbild) cannot be found empirically anywhere in reality. It is utopia.'[32] Weber engages in a process of 'classification' without 'identification.'[33] The former relates to an ordering into groups on the basis of comparable units of analysis, or units within one object of analysis, on purely conceptual grounds; the latter requires measurement of a specimen before assigning it to a cell in a supposed typological table. In a purely heuristic typology, there is classification but no identification. In an empirical typology there is *first* identification and then classification. The empirical, measurable method for typology construction is in heavy use in quantitative social scientific research, and in particular in the field of psychology.

Very early on, statistical analysis, as a method for typology construction, was embraced by social scientists as a more 'scientific' and exacting procedure.[34] Winch,[35] for example, argued that typology construction was a job for factor analysis. Somewhere in between 'ideal types' and factor analysis lies what Bailey[36] considers the 'classical' method of typology construction: erecting a model and then exploring whether it fits with nature, refining the model, and so on. In other words, a hypothetico-deductive treatment but, unlike ideal types, clearly in search of empirical exemplars.[37] What conditions a researcher's decision to employ any one of these three approaches is less a conscious metatheoretical standpoint than simply the goal of achieving a certain end given the parameters of the task she has set out for herself. The most fundamental aspect of typology construction is the object of analysis – not all objects of analysis lend themselves equally to typology construction using heuristic or empirical or classical approaches. This will also be mediated by the chosen *unit* of analysis.[38] This has been the case for the creation of typologies of the police (or policing). Previous typologies have varied considerably depending upon what aspect of policing the author found most salient (the chosen unit) and how 'police' was originally conceptualized as an object of investigation. Decisions made about both the object and unit of analysis then come to lay the foundation for the heuristic purpose of such a classification.

Previous Typologies of Police and Policing

I want to point out certain key distinctions in the police typology literature at the very outset of this section. These are core distinctions that frame the context for this project and the typologies I will proffer in the following section. First, we must distinguish between typologies of public versus typologies of private police. The key contribution imagined for this chapter stems from overcoming what many now consider to be the largely problematic dichotomy of public versus private classifications. I can make this claim only in the context of what I view as the second core distinction in previous typologies, that is, the difference between typologies of police versus typologies of policing. I have chosen the latter in order to conceptually negate the salience of the former. In a nutshell, this is already the crux of most writing on the organization of policing: first, that the duties and responsibilities of public and private police are ever more overlapping,[39] and second, that reliance on their public or private nature (as legally defined) is not only difficult to determine[40] but in any case tells us very little about what these different policing bodies actually do.

There have been five implicit units of analysis for constructing types of police or policing in the academic literature: the first three relate to police and the remaining two to policing. They are (1) historical epochs; (2) nation-states; (3) officers; (4) deployment styles; and (5) activities.

1. *Historical typologies* are an embedded part of the common stock of

knowledge in police textbooks. These constructions fall into three general categories based on the political sensibilities of the historiographer and the relative attention given either to official, expert accounts about the development of the police or to popular dissent about their formation in early-nineteenth-century Britain. This debate is often characterized as a difference between more conservative[41] and more revisionist[42] historians – the former assuming a consensual, evolutionary development and the latter a conflictual, revolutionary imposition of the 'new' British police in 1830.[43] Despite these differences of ideology, including their attempted intellectual reconciliation, all of these positions subscribe to a certain general macro-historiography of the development of the English police that itself is another type – in this case perhaps purely historical rather than ideological. These are presented as general epochs: feudal policing arrangements were local, uncompensated, and non-specialized, while capitalist formations tend towards centralized, compensated, and specialized bodies. Spitzer[44] maintains that this political economy of policing can be extended to other national contexts beyond Britain that developed economically on slightly different tracks but none the less employed similar security arrangements during their transition from agrarian-based economies. This time-based police typology is now common textbook wisdom.[45] To the best of my knowledge, there have been no historical accounts of private police bodies that ascribe some typological-historiographical sequence.

More recently, however, theorists have begun to add more epochs to developmental accounts of police. The most well-known and controversial one stems from the 'mass private property' thesis,[46] which argued that a 'new feudalism' was taking place in policing as private security was growing at a rapid rate. Later, Bayley and Shearing[47] would extend the argument even further by claiming that a revolutionary break was occurring in contemporary policing, profoundly affecting the relationship between public and private space and the deployment and structure of policing. Similar arguments are made by O'Malley and Palmer,[48] who label comparable tendencies as 'post-Keynesian,' and by Ericson and Haggerty,[49] who conceptualize similar institutional surveillance strategies as the arrival of a 'risk society' for policing. A Marxian, economically informed perspective is advanced by Spitzer and Scull[50] as they point to the crisis of state budgets and an increasing transference of power to elites for policing.

What all of these perspectives have in common is the proffering of some variation on a third type of police organization attributable to neoliberalism or 'postmodern' social trends.[51] This transition point is often ascribed to somewhere between 1965 and 1975,[52] not coincidentally the period when private security overtook public police employment in North America. The benefit to this theorizing has been an infusion into the literature of the long overdue entreaty to take developments in private security more seriously, to reckon with the private sector in typology construction and theoretical modelling. But if there is any trap that these perspectives fall into, it is that they sometimes obscure far more than they illuminate. Both modern and feudal organizations of policing can be far more varied within epochs than between them. Artificial historical ruptures are, of course, only guideposts telling us more about economic relationships than about changes in policing or strategies of government.[53] The potential use of historiographical typing of police organizations, however, is still very valuable within the parameters of our particular project. They are a rich source of historical examples of divergent policing activities in various contexts.

2. My second type of typology of police centres on the *nation-state*. This unit of analysis is obviously wide ranging, much like that of historical types. In fact, these two units of analysis often overlap as theorists confine their constructs to a particular historical period or particular national territories. Emsley[54] creates a typology of the nineteenth-century police in Europe. His typology is based on the formative logics and original constituent strategies of police bodies in different nations (e.g., England, France, Italy, Prussia). He posits three basic forms of public police: state civilian, state military, and civilian municipal. Emsley's typology is decidedly structural, and he excludes private police from consideration.[55]

Bayley[56] offers a similar state-centred typology of police, but in a contemporary context. He argues that national structures, relative centralization, and the number of police bodies in any given country can be organized into a world classification of types of police structures. Bayley[57] considers Canada a decentralized-coordinated-multiple system because 'in any one place policing is overwhelmingly the responsibility of a single force – though that force may be variously national, provincial, or municipal.' When a contracted provincial force (or the RCMP) is removed, another fills its place with limited jurisdictional overlap.[58]

For Brewer,[59] any structural typology of police must take into account whether the society is divided. He argues that in societies such as Northern Ireland, Lebanon, Israel, Sri Lanka, Fiji, and South Africa – where conflict is endemic and violent – policing takes on a form distinct from that of integrated societies. Divided societies encourage police to engage in selective enforcement, discriminatory practices, political partisanship, and dependency on the political system. There is typically an absence of accountability, relatively unrestrained use of force, a conflation of duties with military state security, and so on. Unlike Emsley and Bayley, Brewer includes consideration of volunteer groups, vigilante organizations, and other reserve or private forces.

Where these structural typologies of the public police end is where Johnston's[60] work begins: that is, with the important role of non-state or private police organizations. But while Johnston does an exceptional job of covering developments in the overlapping roles of the public and private police, particularly in the United Kingdom, his attempt at creating a 'model' from which we might differentiate between policing bodies eschews any notion of creating strict or mutually exclusive categorical representations.[61] The result is a scalelike representation of parallel spatial and sectoral continua with lines indicating interaction between these two axes: on one side, supranational to local, and on the other public to private. From the perspective of a typology of policing, we must ask, 'What, if anything, does the fact that there may be very little to distinguish the activities of say a supranational armed contract security firm policing a local gated community in some U.S. jurisdiction from the activities of a neighbouring local public police service mean for knowing more about policing?' In other words, what more do we know than before? Or, more importantly, how has what we now know about private and public policing impacted our typology other than, in the end, to say 'various levels of policing may be more or less likely to be public or private'? In any case, I am now being unfair to Johnston, who had no intention of building the sort of typology of policing intended herein. But what Johnston accomplishes in his book cannot be ignored: the very idea of the relative importance of the state as the sole arbiter of policing (in both a structural and an activity-based sense) is questioned.

Jones and Newburn[62] further problematize the use of particular national contexts to explain developments in private and public policing by invoking data from Britain questioning the cross-national applicability of the 'mass private property' thesis. They argue that it may be a purely North American phenomenon. State-centred, structural typologies of police, therefore, begin to unravel when the private sector is added to the equation. This is because the object of analysis is misapplied (police versus policing), and because, by privileging the state as the unit of analysis, these typologies ignore what amounts to at least two-thirds of all policing activity.[63]

3. The third type of police typology is the categorical representation of *officers* themselves. I want to deal rather summarily with this form of police typology because, as a unit of analysis, it has the least bearing on the project at hand. Without doubt, there is a very rich and important literature on public police subculture,[64] in some cases resulting in 'types' of police officers (see Muir's[65] typology of police as professionals, reciprocators, enforcers, and avoiders). More recently, some ethnographic work has been done on private police agency subculture, such as campus security officers[66] or contract parapolice.[67] Even more likely are statistical classification systems based on entrance exams, psychological tests, and tests to ascertain corruption.[68] Typologies of officers are of limited assistance to us in the construction of a general typology of policing because the unit of analysis describes types of people rather than considering the types of things people do within policing organizations that we might consider a type of policing activity.

4. The fourth type of police typology is *deployment styles* – most clearly related to our preferred unit of analysis to be discussed in the next section. If one includes the literature on community-based policing under this section – and there is every reason to do so – the literature on deployment styles is vast. This is partially due to what Klockars[69] correctly identifies as a tendency towards circumlocution in the institutional rhetorics of policing.

Other well-known typologies of public policing deployment styles include Black's[70] styles of social control, including the penal style, the conciliatory style, the therapeutic style, and the compensatory style, or Wilson's[71] watchman style, law enforcement style, and service style. Both are well-known descriptors of police deployment, widely found in most police textbooks; however, for the same reasons stated above, they do not help us. Typologies of public police deployment styles include Baldwin and Kinney's[72] description of police tactics (fire-brigade policing, local intelligence policing, and community policing) or Dell Porta and Reiter's[73] model of protest policing.

The closest any analysis has come to creating a typology of police deployment styles while including both private and public policing is Shearing and Stenning's[74] 'Snowflakes or Good Pinches?' article. But even here, the authors are not so much concerned with describing policing activities *per se* as with describing the different operating logics of private and public policing: loss prevention (later managerial or 'actuarial') versus crime control (later penal or 'retributive'). The idea was that the private police followed a managerial mindset while the public police followed a crime-control mindset. Shearing himself appears to later disregard this dichotomy,[75] since there is simply too much evidence to show the opposite: that public and private policing follow deeply overlapping logics.[76]

5. This leaves us with the fifth and final of my types of police typologies: *policing activities*. There have been very few attempts at categorizing police routine activities across the public-private dichotomy. The rare attempts at creating a typology of policing activity have been mutually exclusive of either the public[77] or the private[78] realm. Private security, for example, may engage in up to forty different types of activities,[79] ranging from airport security, alarm installation, bodyguards, investigations, and so forth. Jones and Newburn[80] have come as close as possible to a typology that transcends the public-private divide by conducting what amounts to a comprehensive security census of the London borough of Wandsworth. Theirs is a groundbreaking study for operationalizing the common stock of theoretical knowledge in policing and for systematically cataloguing all policing bodies, both private and public, while investigating the nexus in which they cohabit. Of course, their categorization of Wandsworth policing organizations[81] is not intended as a general typology of policing activities; nevertheless, built into their understanding of these distinctions is the notion that sectoral designations are not as relevant as what these bodies do. In their case, unfortunately, given that their study chronicles a circumscribed jurisdictional area, Jones and Newburn end up using spatial boundaries as one axis of categorization and retain public-private-hybrid designations as another typological axis.

In anticipation of the first-ever Canadian Conference on Police and Private Security in Toronto in 1999, Murray and McKim[82] tried to make some sense of the deeply overlapping domains of public and private security. They created a table of private security activities that demarcated levels of similarity to police functions. Level one refers to static guard duties, which they consider to be 'low risk activities' and thus the least like public policing. Level two is an ambiguous category called 'enhanced security services,' level three 'private investigation,' level four 'corporate security,' and level five 'forensic investigations' – supposedly the most similar to public police activities. I think Murray and McKim had the right idea, but they began from a deeply flawed assumption. The problem is twofold. First, they run contrary to the overwhelming theoretical and substantive literature on the overlap between public and private policing by trying to retain a division. Second, even though their unit of analysis is useful, their typology is impressionistic, tied to no empirical exemplars – it is unscientific. Had they researched the breadth of private security provision and the historical antecedents of modern public policing they could not have maintained a comparative distinction between public and private policing. Why is static guard duty (level one) unlike public policing? What of public-agency officers guarding federal buildings, military complexes, or working extra duty in private golf courses, gated communities, and so on? Why is forensic investigation (level five) most like public policing when the overwhelming majority of police officers have absolutely nothing to do with forensics? The public police category of 'inspector' was lifted from the private Bow Street Runners, and the public police were historically not allowed to engage in any undercover work in Britain. Perhaps an alternative table should be constructed to demarcate how similar public police activities are to those of the more established and historically rooted private sector. But such a table would only obfuscate and problematize any real discrepancies, and, of course, that is my point. We must begin by considering policing as an activity, regardless of its public or private (or hybrid) nature, if we are to create a workable typology.

Method

Even though I have already surveyed the limitations of other approaches in the previous section, I need to explain why, in my opinion, an activity/ labour-type unit of analysis for constructing a typology of policing is a better choice. I choose a labour-based unit of analysis because it follows directly from the concept of 'policing.' The contemporary theoretical cogency of the concept of policing originally stemmed from observations of criminologists and sociologists (first-order construct) that people in private security were far more abundant, making them the new major player in security provision. In addition, these academics also saw that these private operatives were physically *doing* things that the public police only used to do (in the contemporary late-modern sense). So, from the outset, the explicit impetus for the theoretical expansion of our notion of what constitutes the doing of police work was based on changes in labour organization, be they quantitative sectoral variances or qualitative work assignments. This is what I mean by theoretical coherence to an original conceptual break. It also seems natural that, as our object of analysis becomes broader (police to policing), our unit of analysis needs to reflect this by becoming more robust and inclusive.

Activity, for me, encompasses both deployment strategies and organizational logics that may result in differences in human output.

This is an important distinction. The rhetoric of deployment, tendencies towards 'professionalization,' 'community-based' policing, and so on, is in many ways only a slight variation on assessing the original 'style' or mandate that brought a particular agency into being, whether it be militaristic, or civil, or something different again. Either approach forces us to reckon with particular institutional histories and structural variations: we are compelled to deal with each policing body as a discrete unit of analysis rather than with the *activities* of any particular policing body as analytic units (in and of themselves) – that is, as activities within the broad spectrum of *all* policing labour regardless of particular organizational histories or structures, be they public or private. Thus, my approach is not to ask what each police organization does in order to adequately label individual agencies within a given typology, but rather to view the general practice of policing as constituted by a constellation of recurrent, persistent, basic human activities grouped into a new typology of policing with no conceptual allegiance to police structures.

My notion of policing and thus my object of analysis may be defined as follows: Any individual or organization acting legally on behalf of public or private organizations or person(s) to maintain security and/or social order while empowered by either public or private contract, regulations, or policies, whether written or verbal. This is a bit clumsier than other definitions, but I think necessary if we are to exclude vigilantism and other forms of illegal or thuggish protection racket-style operations in organized crime.[83]

My approach involved, first, examining contemporary materials on private policing activities, including previously published academic accounts, my own data from ongoing projects, online advertising by various security firms, industry reports, and yearly stockholder reports. Second, I use historical sources to uncover resilient activity patterns of both public and private police. There are a plethora of sources with rich descriptions of policing in early capitalism. The classic method, which is presumably hypothetico-deductive, should allow for modification of my typologies as determined by the data. After I applied my unit of analysis to the data, I found that I could construct some general types that I continued to modify throughout the research, until I was eventually satisfied. This is much like the process of theory construction described by Wallace[84] – the unavoidable interrelationship between induction and deduction.

I did, however, impose three additional criteria before finalizing any typology of policing. First, I wanted to identify activities that could not be confined to any one organizational structure or sector; that would be counter-intuitive and counter-productive to this project. Second, my typology would strive for mutual exclusivity. As much as possible one category should be definitionally, although not necessarily functionally, distinct from the others. Third, and finally, I tried to keep my types of police activity down to no more than five categories. No one remembers twenty categories, and they are rather unhelpful as a learning tool.

A Typology of Policing

A labour-based typology of policing activity for both the public and the private sector may be broken down into five categories. The terms I employ are based on the closest approximation to the phenomena I am trying to describe within each type. However, these can sometimes be misleading.[85] The original use of the term may refer to the essence of the category but not encapsulate it entirely, not in the way that I employ the label herein. The five types of policing activity are: (1) polemic; (2) sentry-dataveillant; (3) investigative; (4) patrol; and (5) civic-sumptuary. For the remainder of this chapter, when I say 'police' I am referring to both public police and private security.

It is important to remember that these types are not about categorizing police bodies but rather about the general activities that any, but not necessarily all, police bodies may engage in. This typology suggests that any given officer, regardless of his or her sectoral designation, may at a given moment be engaged in at least one of the types of activities described but in the next moment be engaged in another. Throughout what is to follow, I may variably refer to policing bodies and their formative logics, but I am not arguing that this is actually a determining factor in what they end up doing. Across time, this typology of policing activity is mostly relegated to forms present from 1750 onwards. I do not always stay within this temporal frame because there are certain policing antecedents that occasionally bear directly on my argument. For the most part, however, I stay away from pre-capitalist policing formations. Across space, I am inclined to make a rather bold claim – I think these typologies are applicable to all societies. However, given that my sources are predominantly European and North American, I would do so at the risk of extrapolating beyond my source information. Further research can challenge the veracity of this typology in other contexts.

When I say 'labour-based' policing activity, I merely mean the expenditure of human energy in the pursuit of doing security work. I use a labour-based approach for two reasons: First, because I believe that labour activity, as a unit of analysis, can eventually be most useful for theorizing transformations in the organization of policing, including the study of movements towards mechanization and the extraction of surplus value. Second, because I want to entrench through definition the difference between policing styles/deployment strategies and general labour activity. This distinction is important because I am not talking about general pursuits or mandates. Why should we consider 'patrol' or general policing activity and not 'arrest' or 'testify' or even 'train in the use of baton,' and so on? We are interested not in cataloguing the particular minutiae of a police officer's work day but rather in categorizing the general assigned labour tasks that may give rise to any assortment of such secondary security duties. To do otherwise would place us in the ridiculous position of considering every action, from talking to complainants to polishing one's gun or ironing one's shirt, as a possible category of policing labour. The typology presented herein thus treads below the level of institutional rhetorical devices (or reforms) and above that of a radical deconstructive particularism of policing labour at the level of human kinetics. We are interested in recurrent, persistent, general, and constitutive labour-based activities that make up the bedrock of what it is to do policing.

As M. Moncey, one of the first-ever police leaders of the French gendarmerie, wrote, 'Protecting good citizens, containing the malevolent, apprehending the guilty when it has not been possible to prevent the crime, these are the tasks of every hour and every moment.'[86] And thus, like others such as Mayne and Peel who followed, general mandates are declared and some reference activities are offered, but not in the way I cluster and employ 'activities' and then analyse them herein.

Polemic

Type one or polemic policing includes 'warlike' or paramilitary policing that places the people whom the police are assigned to safeguard at risk of losing either status, money, power, or their lives. The police act with subjugative or repressive tactics and are prepared to use lethal force in the protection of elite structures, citizens, or dignitaries. The more divided or unequal the society, the more likely type one policing will be deployed. This is otherwise known as the ideological 'iron fist.' This form of policing activity is hardly exclusive to capitalism. In fact, it may be argued that it is definitionally constitutive of the idea of having an armed protectorate in the first place.

Armed protective bodies, since long before the praetorian guard, served in this capacity under various modes of production. Under capitalism, the police can act as a buffer for the bourgeoisie while attempting to either defend against or crush (both are military decisions) labour unrest, popular dissent, peasant uprisings, race riots, and so on. Thus, the police are a physical arm of political coercion. Although polemic policing may be more likely to occur during times of war – as, for example, in the pacification of populations in newly acquired territories or the rounding up 'foreigners' on domestic soil – there need not be a state of war with any foreign power for the police to undertake polemic activities. Polemic policing may be colonial; it may involve the arrest and detention of dissidents or the suppression of labour unrest. Polemic policing is often an 'initial mode' for many forces, being created in times of political crisis to reinforce the status quo, but eventually becoming more diffuse and ubiquitous and undertaking many other types of policing activity. Today, typically, the police are uniformed and carry military hardware including chemical weapons, rubber bullets, batons, sniper rifles, riot gear, and so forth. There is a general trend towards the expansion of polemic policing as it blends in with other forms of policing activity and becomes a more common recourse.[87]

The classic examples of military-style policing are the various gendarmeries that have been made up of soldiers answerable to a ministry of war (or defence), while at the same time being available to civilian authorities to engage in the apprehension of criminals, control vagrancy, support local authorities during disorders, and generally suppress banditry in areas where the state had minimal reach.[88] In Canada, however, our Gendarmerie Royale du Canada (the RCMP) has never been under the purview of the Ministry of Defence, although right from the force's inception the Mounties were organized to fight civil insurrection. They were, for all intents and purposes, a military cavalry equipped with a wide array of weaponry, including a cannon. The 'great march west' of 1874 is often celebrated as the bringing of justice to the Northwest, but the long column that crossed the Canadian prairies was actually set up to do far more, including suppress Native unrest, by force if need be, and establish Canadian sovereignty.[89]

Other countries also kept similar forces to similarly engage in polemic-type policing. For example, the Habsburgs maintained a large company

in Brussels, the Prévôté de l'Hôtel, to deal with public order and suppress any uprising. When there were considerations for creating a national force similar to the early French *maréchaussée*, the military blocked
the idea. In Sardinia-Piedmont, Victor Amadeus III established the Corpo
Militare di Polizia in October 1774. The corps would later come to be
known as the '*carabini*' for the carbines they carried. This body would
later re-emerge as an Italian national police force – the *carabinieri* –
instrumental in the unification of the country in the mid-nineteenth
century[90] when the French had been pushed out of the northern territories. They were a militaristic force and, like the gendarmerie, were
initially central for pacifying new territories and agitators. The German
gendarmeries were organized as a rural force but were commonly drawn
into the cities during emergencies. The French gendarmes lived in
centralized barracks, but the German gendarmes did not.[91] Like the
RCMP before them, when the early Pennsylvania state police were formed,
they were modelled after the militaristic Royal Irish Constabulary. They
were mounted on horses and heavily armed, and they were housed in
barracks.[92]

During the Gordon Riots of 1780, London seemed at the mercy of
street mobs. They are considered to be the most frightening and the
most serious of the eighteenth-century uprisings, and they continued to
play a role in the formulation of the new police well into the nineteenth
century.[93] Babington strongly argues that the 'riots in 1780 must have
convinced every intelligent man and woman in Britain whose mind was
not addled by outworn prejudices or historical misconceptions that the
methods for preserving the peace in the country were in need of drastic
reform.'[94] Although the British police are set *against* this supposed
'continental' model and described as a civilian police agency, they were
just as likely to be deployed in cases of insurgency: 'Irrespective of
disavowals, the big city police forces in Britain have always had a paramilitary function available in emergency to be rushed to quash distant
troubles to the civil authorities.'[95] Other policing bodies sprang forth in
colonial contexts, or in competition with these early forces. While the
gendarmes quickly engaged themselves in all types of divergent policing
activity, their supposed opposites – ostensibly based on fundamentally
different principles (the 'bobbies' in Britain, Guardia in Italy, etc.) – also
conversely and immediately engaged in polemic activities.

Polemic policing sometimes, but not always, becomes more prominent during wartime or territorial expansion. The military, in early-
nineteenth-century Paris, worked alongside the police and maintained

their own patrols and garrison posts.[96] In Brittany, the *maréchaussée* were often seen as an occupation army.[97] The *maréchaussée* were actively involved in tracking down deserters from the French armed services right through the eighteenth century, or with dealing with soldiers who had committed civilian offences such as violent crime and theft. The Italian peninsula was almost impossible to police effectively until the French gendarmerie pacified it. Bands of brigands would shoot at the gendarmes, as bandit leaders adopted colourful names and looked forward to thwarting the efforts of their occupiers.[98] The *carabinieri* ran up against ferocious resistance in the south and especially in Sicily during the Brigands' War, which required the deployment of the army. During the unification years, the *carabinieri* played a vital role in creating the modern state of Italy.[99] During wartime, the gendarmes were the functionaries of the state even in the face of local resistance to conscription or when local officials tried to shelter deserters. The demands of the gendarmeries often brought them into confrontation with rural dignitaries who had no authority over their local gendarmes but were under the control of a centralized state.

By December 1859, the chairman of the Cheshire Police Committee in the English countryside was contemplating a significant degree of militarization by asking whether there 'would be any objection raised by the Home Office to the Police force of this Co. being instructed in the use of the Rifle, and if not, whether the Rifles could be supplied to the men from the Police Rate.'[100] Like the gendarmes of France in the new territories, the Irish Peace Preservation Force (IPPF) was to act as a reserve to the army, quelling local disorders and ensuring peace in a society where the majority resented the imperial imposition of the British state. This public order maintenance function on behalf of the occupying power was central to the initial formation of the force and of its eventual successor, the Royal Irish Constabulary.[101] Similar British imperial models were deployed in Bombay, Palestine, Madras, West Africa, Nigeria, Jamaica, Kenya, and throughout the empire. As noted previously, Canada and Ireland created state-centred police forces geared towards maintaining stability and order in new frontiers – whether suppressing Native and settler revolts or pacifying well-rooted nationalism. When certain states of the United States were contemplating their own police forces, they looked to the Irish and Canadian model.[102] The Texas Rangers, re-established in 1874, were responsible for protecting the border with Mexico and stemming Native uprisings to the west. As the threat of Native and Mexican incursion died out by 1880, the Rangers began to police their own population, handling situations that required a military presence beyond that available to local authorities.[103]

That a very important part of the activities of police organizations is to act as a mighty political arm of the state cannot be denied under the weight of historical evidence. The Gendarmerie Royale in Paris worked in the political centre of France and was regularly involved in putting down political unrest, including, most prominently, its bloody support of Charles X's brief reign. Only two weeks after the July Monarchy, Parisian residents celebrated the disbanding of the Gendarmerie Royale, which they rightly saw as a political body on the side of the monarchy. But soon its successor, the Garde Municipale, also gained a similar reputation for brutality.[104] For a short time, immediately after the Revolution of 1848, the Garde Municipale was also disbanded in favour of a short-lived civilian police (La Garde Rouge or Les Montagnards) recruited from those who had manned the barricades. Eventually, a more military Garde Républicaine was formed and fought alongside the army during the workers' revolt only a few months later.[105] When Louis Napoleon successfully carried out his *coup d'état* in December 1851, he relied heavily on the gendarmes in Paris. The gendarmerie assisted in taking the Ministry of the Interior and ejected ministers who assembled to protest the coup. Even after workers and peasants reassembled to restore the Republic, the gendarmerie sided with their prince-president and, joining with the army, spilled into the countryside to smash the popular unrest. They were swift and brutal. The gendarmerie were doted on by their new emperor, who saw their role as central to the maintenance of the new regime.[106]

A similar conservative political allegiance is to be found among the Italian *carabinieri*. The best example of the resolute dedication of the *carabinieri* came in February 1834 when, according to the tradition of the corps, Giovanni Battista Scapaccino came across a group of republican volunteers coming from Switzerland and France. When called upon to declare his allegiance to the republican cause, Scapaccino responded 'Long live the King!' Since that time, the lore and conservative proclamations of the force have made many Italians uneasy. As Emsley[107] puts it, 'after 1821 the loyalty of the Piedmontese Carabinieri to its monarch was never again in doubt, and the senior officers of the corps prided themselves on a personal bond between the Carabinieri and the king.' Eventually, the Italian government would become so concerned about the *carabinieri* that they created the Guardia di Pubblica Sicurezza on the supposed British model of a civilian police. In any case, predictably, the

Guardia too now take active polemic roles in public order maintenance and the suppression of unrest.[108] Throughout its history, the Greek gendarmerie acted at the behest of monarchist or right-wing and anti-Communist regimes. The national police had become so saturated with the ideals of 'political policing' reinforced by law that wholesale purges of senior staff were carried out by Venizelists and later socialists.[109]

One of the primary activities of polemic policing is to act to enforce the sensibilities of the elites whom they represent. The French gendarmerie, like other later gendarmeries, were stationed in the countryside. This placed them in a strategic position to move against peasant revolts or any other form of rural uprising. Yet they remained equally adept at sweeping into urban areas in support of city police during times of insurrection.

In divided societies, especially during class crises, polemic policing activities become pre-eminent. In England, legislation from the early sixteenth century onward had given constables responsibilities for the idle and wandering poor under the vagrancy acts. An act of 1576 required that constables apprehend and deliver to the next constable all vagrants defined as such by an act of 1572. The offenders were to be escorted from officer to officer to the gaol or a House of Correction. In 1598, the constables' duties were extended by an alteration in the punishment meted out to vagrants. Vagrants were to be apprehended, whipped, and then conveyed to the next constable, along with a pass directing them from officer to officer to their place of origin or last residence.[110] Such enactments for the control of the poor – a class-based war against a part of the population – would continue throughout the eighteenth and nineteenth centuries.[111]

In 1720, a French royal ordinance expressed concern that the *maréchaussée* (later to be amalgamated into the gendarmes) should be more vigilant against vagabonds, disreputable individuals, and all forms of beggars and vagrants (*gens sans aveu*).[112] So difficult was the task of policing and persecuting the dispossessed that, in 1770, the commander of the Auvergne company – a district with an isolated, poor, and stagnant economy – informed the minister of war that he would be suspending the apprehension of beggars because a strict enforcement could lead to the arrest of more than 4,000 people.[113] In order to spur the crackdown against the dispossessed, in 1767 the French government announced a reward for the arrest of beggars, and the cavaliers complied immediately in order to receive the bonus. Soon, however, the courts and new houses of correction could not keep up, and the intendants stopped paying the bounty.[114] The *maréchaussée* were unpopular with those they were meant to police. There is a litany of reports of verbal abuse of officers and of community members coming to the aid of vagrants who were being arrested, especially where the medieval perception of the beggar as sacred figure survived. In the same way, deserters often requested and received the support of their local countrymen against cavaliers who were trying to apprehend them.[115] Generally speaking, when conducting polemic activities against the poor, the gendarmerie were placed on alert during times of bad harvests, economic downturns, or political agitation. They targeted vagrants and vagabonds and broke up attempts to stop the movement of grain from their towns – also an arterial activity.

An important vehicle for class unrest and mobilization has been union activism. Polemic policing has always been about stifling union radicalism, whether the body orchestrating the attack was public, private, or some hybrid. In Britain, during the years of war against revolutionary and Napoleonic France, the provinces experienced food riots in 1795–6 and 1799–1801. As workers lost their jobs to mechanization, the Luddite industrial disorders spilled over in 1811–12. At the same time, many people with property feared insurrection of some sort by English Jacobins sympathetic to ideas espoused by the French revolutionaries.[116] 'By the 1830s and 1840s dread of the "dangerous classes" could be transformed into near hysteria.'[117] Storch argues that the upper classes were not in agreement about the administrative structure of the police or about their accountability, but few questioned that their attention should be focused on working-class districts.[118] In Mansfield, a detachment of Metropolitans forbade working men from talking in groups in the road.[119] The police also attempted to suppress Sunday meetings, but met with a violent response. In 1820, the Duke of Wellington was concerned enough about radical protests to urge that the government 'ought, without the loss of a moment's time, to adopt measures to form either a police in London or military corps, which should be of a different description from the regular military force, or both.'[120] There was considerable criticism of the new police because of their military character: the *Weekly Dispatch* protested about 'these military protectors of our civil liberties' and labelled them a 'gendarmerie,' while the *Monthly Magazine* labelled Colonel Rowan as 'a military retainer of the Duke [of Wellington].' The men were deployed as riot squads in both London and the rest of the country. In fact, during the 1830s, Metropolitan policemen appeared in the provinces at the request of local authorities to put down the first anti-poor law disturbances and later the Chartists.[121] As another example of the interchangeability of policing bodies engaged in polemic activity, Emsley reports that in Italy, 'a high percentage of police action against strikers and socialists by both the Carabinieri and the PS [Guardia] tended to be violent, brutal, and unrestrained.'[122]

When bourgeois hegemony appeared to be slackening, English legislation introduced in 1859 took the unprecedented step of seizing control of policing out of the hands of the local authorities of three large industrial cities: Birmingham, Bolton, and Manchester. The Whig government feared Chartist disorder and a sympathetic local government.[123] Chartist sympathies were very strong in Birmingham where the meeting for the national Chartist Convention in July 1859 took place. The move to a police force that would follow bourgeois demands would be repeated in Canada and the United States when local police failed to crush labour unrest or, in some cases, simply refused to deploy or joined the strike. Thus, during the 1919 Winnipeg General Strike, the local police resolved to join rather than fight the workers. The RCMP were summoned and, with the assistance of hastily sworn-in 'specials,' promptly and quite brutally smashed the strike. The RCMP were later involved in similar violent strike-breaking in Estevan, Saskatchewan, at the Souris coal field where they shot and killed three strikers and wounded eight others. A monument bearing the inscription 'murdered in Estevan, September 29, 1931, by the RCMP' was eventually removed by the town council. There is a litany of other examples of the RCMP being used as the police force of last resort throughout Canadian labour history. Of course, a reliance on public forces was by no means necessary for effective polemic deployments. U.S. elites were more likely to rely on private ruffians such as men rounded up by the Pinkerton Detective Agency or, in cases of emergency, the military. American industrialists eventually began to employ state police, and in many instances they would seek to legislate their own private forces.[124] Clashes between private police and strikers were violent and lethal. When the local sheriff, the local police, and a company's own private police appeared insufficient to control striking workers, the company would ask local authorities to demand state militia, but they often found that these militia were sympathetic to the strikers. Militia from Pittsburgh refused to act against their fellow citizens during the Great Railroad Strike of 1877. In Martinsburg, West Virginia, the local militia refused to ride a train operated by non-union labour.[125]

Like their French, English, and Irish brothers, the American labour movement was plainly aware of the role of these new state police. When the State of Illinois had before it a bill to create a similar force, the state labour organizations mobilized. The Illinois State Federation of Labor, under John H. Walker, sent a circular to all local unions: 'No more deadly menace to American institutions has ever crept into our government than the so-called "constabularies" that have been created in several states where the corporation interests dominate and control. They are really armed government strike-breakers, kept for the purpose of crushing the workers into submission, preventing their organizing or improving their wages, hours, conditions, or treatment, against the wishes of the despotic interests.'[126] Walker argued to the state legislature that the proposed state police were just another example of the 'science of camouflage' by which anti-labour measures were made to appear as though they were intended to serve the common good.[127] Beginning in 1917, eight attempts were made to establish a paramilitary police in Illinois, ostensibly to undertake polemic activities, but they all failed. The police in Buffalo during the late nineteenth century did everything they could to smash union organizing, including stopping strikes and breaking up workers' meetings. The Broadway Market Riot, in the heart of the Polish community, broke out after a police charge stopped a labour meeting. Police reinforcements were called to quiet the disturbance. Radical working-class meetings could not even start, as the police blocked the entrances to rented halls.[128]

It would be a great error indeed to assume that polemic policing belongs to a particular era or a particular police formation. First, as we have already seen, supposed 'civilian' forces were just as quick to perform polemic policing activities when the need arose, and where there were instances when they would not, any number of other policing bodies, either public or private, could be called upon to fill the void. This is because, as I have argued, polemic activity is a generic constitutive component of policing. Second, as I will now demonstrate, polemic policing has remained an omnipresent aspect of policing.

Since 1960, the number of police services with dedicated paramilitary units in the United States climbed from 0 per cent to 89 per cent in 1995.[129] The tumultuous anti-capitalist protests in Seattle, Quebec City, and Genoa demonstrate that police forces are well equipped and willing to use whatever force is necessary to disperse crowds. As they have throughout the history of policing, and in particular in the United States,[130] private policing agencies are just as willing to engage in polemic policing activities today. Wackenhut Services offers high-grade paramilitary security for American facilities. In Aiken, South Carolina, they hold a contract for protecting the Savannah nuclear facility run by the U.S. Department of Energy. The private police force (accredited by the Commission on Accreditation of Law Enforcement Agencies) operates special response teams and a helicopter. The officers are equipped with military rifles and uniforms. They are prepared for anti-nuclear protests.[131] More comprehensive contract security firms are also available that offer complete labour-suppression packages. Under the guise of 'asset protection,' Vance Security Services is a one-stop shopping pavilion for all the needs of an industrialist. This security firm offers riot squads armed with batons, shields, helmets, and so on, monitors labour picket lines by video surveillance, and even conducts private investigations on labourers. After Vance has secured your facility, infiltrated your workers, and begun 'photo-documenting,' it can even provide replacement workers. Its 'workforce staffing team' provides temporary labour such as manufacturing and assembly workers, heavy machinery and precision equipment operators, warehouse and other distribution workers, and forklift drivers who 'take pride in exceeding productivity standards set by regular employees.'[132] Other security firms, such as Intelligarde,[133] Scott Security,[134] and London Protection International,[135] regularly engage in strike 'protection' duties. Special Response corporation specializes in labour disputes and offers military- or police-trained 'disciplined' officers who may conduct photo surveillance and asset protection, including planning for confrontations with unlawful pickets, compensation or identification for property of non-striking employees damaged during the strike, and provisions for recording working time and collecting pay.[136] Gettier strike security offers similar services, including protecting perimeters, videotaping picket lines, deploying strike dogs, and making sure scab labourers get into the facility.[137]

Other security agencies bypass international laws by activating paramilitary and covert services to recapture corporate hostages in overseas countries. Covert Recovery Service has operatives who are former soldiers of special services such as the CIA, the Navy Seals, and MOSSAD. They brag that 'diplomatic efforts fail, we never fail!' during their human 'snatch' operations and specialized intelligence gathering.[138] In this particular case, colonial protection and military muscle have been undertaken by private contractors on behalf of international corporations. Jemsec International Security offers counter-piracy teams that will retrieve stolen cargo, escort ships, extract identified key figures, and destroy boats and other vital equipment needed for the pirates to succeed. They will thus wage naval sabotage on behalf of private interests.[139]

Sentry-Dataveillant

Sentry-dataveillant (or type two) policing roughly begins with the wide assortment of activities associated with the age-old activity of 'keeping the watch.' More broadly, however, I include here mostly 'static' forms of policing akin to sentry duty or modern-day access control. Part of sentry-dataveillant policing is passive intelligence gathering and monitoring at a distance, including alarm response, and adopting a regulatory or bureaucratic stance. This defensive, passive posture may also include privacy counter-measures such as debugging so as to deny access to private information through clandestine means. Of course, today dataveillance[140] is a common fact of life. Umpteen public and private agencies compile information on populations. People need to surrender information in exchange for the freedom to proceed into a facility, onto a plane, into a country, and so forth. Sentry-dataveillant policing is about monitoring flows of population through surveillance. Sentry duty or 'access control' may appear to be an activity quite different from that of scanning databases for biographical information on citizens, denizens, clients, outsiders, and insiders. However, the latter is merely the digital manifestation of the former. Both are activities designed to assess, vet, and decide on access. Moreover, in contemporary settings, human access control typically takes place in tandem with the assistance of identification terminals that scan passengers, employees, guests, and so on. Security agents (ranging from embassy police to night-club bouncers) size up those wishing access while examining their identification. Increasingly, the scrutinizing of people's identification and risk (or making them known and transparent) is assisted by card readers, databases, metal detectors, and X-rays. But this is only the confluence of human and digital vetting activities. While sentry-dataveillance policing may be passive intelligence gathering, it is highly proactive because everyone who wishes to pass comes under its gaze. Most recently, this form of policing has seen an explosion through digital read-outs and closed circuit television (CCTV). Technological development has fostered a transition in type two policing from human interaction to digital interface; from rudimentary sentry duty to more sophisticated electronic tagging and identification mechanisms. Sentry-dataveillant policing is now often accomplished remotely as officers are dispatched by a computerized monitoring system to check out an alarm or violation.

Of course, there are ample historical precedents for this form of policing activity. Legislation in 1285, the Statute of Winchester, ordered boroughs to provide watches of a dozen men, and the smaller towns of between four and six, depending upon the size of their population.[141] From the outset, governmental techniques for increasing prosperity and expanding wealth depended on tracking the population. 'Long before the Benthamite prison attempted to render the symbolic individual into something always panoptically transparent, manageable and contained, [Sir William] Petty had envisaged a similar panoptic format as economic necessity in the mid sixteenth century.'[142] Petty, the founder of statistics and political economy, planned to improve London by what Mykkänen[143] regards as a 'technical cluster' of actuarial ideologies. His 'London Wall' was to encircle the entire city and be '100^m foot in circumference, 11 foot high, 2 brick thick, in fortification figure, with 20 gates, worth 20^m£.'[144] The wall was to be a means for concentrating commerce through planned 'choke-points' where all movement of persons and goods would be made transparent. Petty's utopian city places the statistical and human grid in constant 'telematic'[145] as he is anxious to 'take in accompt of all persons and things going in and out of the Citty' so that 'Men for crimes may be put out of it,' and to 'Ban within the wall, who to beg or perish.'[146]

Mykkänen correctly identifies this as perhaps the first instance in which city gates were to be 'guarded not by sword but by pen.'[147] This sentry-dataveillant format would employ watchers whose primary activity would be to monitor and exclude on the basis of identification, and to produce a statistical account. But the wall was also to be a 'visible boundary of property and impositions.'[148] Save for the use of computers, how different is Petty's entreaty that men carry 'uncounterfitable' identification in 1650 from modern private and governmental access-control activities? 'In either case, the binary outcome reflects the need of the surveillance system to "know" who is coming into contact with it: one is either allowed in through the gate, door, lobby or sent on their way.'[149]

In late-sixteenth-century England, there were already attempts to control population mobility among the poor by requiring passports for travel. Village constables were responsible for issuing and inspecting vagrants' passes and for policing the whole 'passport system' through which travel was authorized. The purpose was not so much to safeguard travel as it was to monitor risky populations. The diseased poor, who under the law of 1598 were required to have licences to travel to the baths, had to submit their documents to constables.[150] At the same time, the hue-and-cry system, which dated back to the Middle Ages, operated by passing information about offences and offenders from village constable to village constable. The passing of information by word of mouth became slowly replaced by the circulation of written hue-and-cry warrants that carried descriptions of offenders and stolen property.[151] A form of private surveillance intersecting with public offices can be seen in the use of paid carriers and other travellers who would spread information in distant places, including especially to town criers and constables, both of whom continued to be in service through the eighteenth century. Constables' accounts indicate that the hue and cry was copied before being passed on for local consumption, possibly in the form of posted bills or by being publicly read by the town crier or bellman.[152]

Where crowds and commerce flourished, the comings and goings of the population needed to come under increased scrutiny. The French archives are littered with sentry-dataveillant plans and proposals to monitor the roadways into emerging commercial and industrial centres. It was always in the interests of the central government and local officials that stations were set up this way, both to stop robbery and brigandage and also to enable officials to carry out annual inspections. In 1768, the textile town of Elbeuf, which was also in the middle of an important agricultural district that supplied Paris, Rouen, and Versailles, requested and received a new brigade. The brigade was located at a strategic chokepoint for the movement of goods and persons and augmented the surveillance capacity of the state. Another proposal was made for the establishment of a brigade outside the town of Avignon, precisely where the main road divided, with one road to Orange and the other to Pont St Esprit.[153] A similar strategic use of monitoring flows of people was to be found on the English turnpikes. Toll-gates were instrumental in maintaining surveillance of those who travelled in and out of the city. Toll keepers would be paid to watch for stolen horses or suspicious characters.[154]

In France, following the Revolution of 1789, the French state began to rely more heavily upon surveillance than it had before. Part of the reason for this was that it could no longer act with impunity and coercion in dealing with its citizens, who now possessed new rights under the new Republic. This new 'tutelary administrative and judicial apparatus'[155] continued to grow unabated as a less coercive but far more penetrating system of social control. The post-Revolutionary rural communes were authorized to use gardes-champêtres, whose primary responsibility was to enforce the new rural code of 6 October 1791 to protect property and crops. For Emsley,[156] this body of men was 'in many respects ... a formalization of the customary village practice of recruiting crop watchers.'

Back in London, John Fielding drafted plans for the improvement of security on the highways by organizing the householders into bands of twenty for the purposes of supplying Bow Street with information about criminals.[157] Each of the conductors at Bow Street had to keep a journal in which he entered reports of accidents, crimes, or other events encountered during hours of duty.[158] Fielding also slowly turned Bow Street into a clearing-house for all crime information in England. He described the work of his brother Henry and his group of thief-takers while imploring all constables, jail-keepers, inn-keepers, and so forth, to send him information on known criminals. He published regular broadsheets entitled 'The Quarterly Pursuit of Criminals' and 'The Weekly Pursuit' with an occasional supplement entitled 'The Extraordinary Pursuit,' which were all forerunners of the modern-day *Police Gazette*. The descriptions of criminals published in these broadsheets were widely distributed and affixed to church doors, inns, and other public areas.[159] Long before the Fieldings' work, there had been gathering and distribution of information pertaining to victims, witnesses, suspects, pawnbrokers, justices of the peace, and the public; however, the Fieldings *did* 'systematize the gathering of information' and gave it a continuity and focus.[160] Chadwick envisaged that this system would help mount investigations on the basis of the information it contained as well as alert owners who had their property stolen about how they could take appropriate precautions.[161]

John Fielding's preoccupation with creating the most comprehensive and up-to-date compendium of criminality is understandable in light of his brother's view of lower-class inhabitants of London. At all costs, the secretive labyrinth of the city jungle had to become known. In 1751 Henry Fielding wrote, 'Whoever indeed considers the Cities of London and Westminster, with the late vast Addition of their Suburbs; the great irregularity of their Buildings, the immense Number of Lanes, Alleys, Courts and Bye places; must think, that, had they been intended for the very Purposes of Concealment, they could scarce have been better contrived. Upon such a View, the whole appears a vast Wood or Forest, in which a Thief may harbour with as great Security, as wild Beasts do in the Deserts of Africa or Arabia. For by wandering from one Part to another, and often shifting his quarters, he may almost avoid the Possibility of being discovered.'[162] Styles argues that it was not a deliberate state-run initiative that created a surveillance system in England; rather, 'it depended on public rather than on official action' in the general availability of 'the spread of commercial printing,' which therefore 'entailed a shift

away from a surveillance based on the official machinery of law enforcement towards a surveillance based on the market.'[163] Even from its inception, investigative policing was heavily dependent on an efficient system of
information dissemination found in sentry-dataveillant activities.

In both the English and French policing systems, accurate recording
and cataloguing of information were crucial to their operations. Police
positioned themselves in strategic areas to accomplish this task. In France,
during a period of concern about the spread of false rumours that might
instigate revolt, a circular of November 1810 mandated that the gendarmerie post themselves in areas where public coaches stopped for
respite in order to overhear the conversation of passengers and get the
name and address of anyone uttering such rumours.[164] During the early
years of the restoration of the monarchy, some company commanders of
the gendarmerie provided written monthly reports on the state of the
local economy, including grain prices in their main markets. So important were the tabulation of patrol statistics and record keeping to the
French gendarmerie command that failure to keep records in good
order could cost a man his promotion. In July 1841, Lieutenant Duschesne
was ordered back from the Garde Municipale in Paris to Vire at his own
expense in order to tidy up the mess in which he had left the records of
his former Calvados company.[165] In 1818, the Prussian gendarmes also
collected statistical information for the government.[166]

Sentry-dataveillant policing includes general protective or static guarding. During the epidemic in 1832, while the efficacy of Scotland's 'cholera police' was lauded in other countries, the most acute 'problem'
confronting the rural authorities in this period was vagrancy.[167] In the
early nineteenth century, Spain consolidated most of its municipal police forces, responsible chiefly for guarding municipal buildings and
maintaining civic order. These local police have remained a constant yet
marginal feature of policing in Spain.[168]

Starting in 1932, the Russian militsia employed a passport system that
forced citizens to notify their local branch about every stay exceeding
three days. This was admissible in a system with no legal notion of
privacy. The passport branch of the militsia was informed of a person's
birth and maintained a record of all his or her movements throughout
the person's lifetime. Since many citizens often ignored these strict
requirements, they easily became vulnerable to militsia intervention.
When youth gangs and marauders became a problem for the militsia in
the years leading up to collectivization, they vigorously deployed the
passport-control system to monitor and control urban migration and to

stop and detain suspicious persons.[169] The militsia were used to maintain security at government buildings and certain private homes, regulating access through passes. They also staffed embassies and consulates, keeping citizens away from foreign asylums. At larger and more sensitive state facilities, the spetsmilitsia safeguarded secret information and technology.[170] Troubled youth or children were registered at local militsia *Detskaia komnata*, attached to the militia post. These youth were monitored, and community members were asked to participate in delinquency prevention. Youths returning from labour camps were placed under even greater scrutiny. The militsia also maintained a detailed file on those deliberately unemployed: approximately 500,000 'parasites' and beggars were on police lists nationwide in the mid-1980s.[171]

Today, paperwork is seen as a pervasive and dominating aspect of policing – so much so that some authors have cited it as the most important aspect of policing in modern society.[172] Klare[173] has likened post-Second World War private security firms in the era of McCarthyism to 'private C.I.A.s' that collude with state interests in amassing information on organizations and persons deemed a security threat to the establishment. But it appears that even in 1863, police chiefs were complaining about the amount of 'non-police'–related reports for which they were responsible. The Bedfordshire chief constable protested that his superintendents took too much time out of their day to keep detailed records of public houses: 'I respectfully submit that much Book-keeping and Statistical Returns will occupy the officers more than is desirable or useful. The Books they now keep with the returns they have to make up weekly take up quite as much time as can be spared from their duty in looking after their men and in pursuing crime.'[174]

In any case, remote access control, general population surveillance,[175] and the collation of dataveillant information[176] in late capitalism[177] have greatly accelerated the dispersal of information under bureaucratic-based policing activities.[178] Today, public and private police agencies, especially in large corporate institutions, including insurance companies, operate a nexus of information sharing.[179] A remarkable amount of general access control is undertaken by private contract security firms or quasi-public bodies such as the Corps of Commissionaires in Canada. Increasingly, these activities are being accomplished remotely. When examining public and private police employment and alarm monitoring services in the United States, we see that no single sector has seen a decline, even when the numbers are adjusted as a rate per 100,000 population. The public police have seen a 7.1 per cent jump in employment numbers between 1994 and 1997, while the private security sector has grown more slowly at 3.9 per cent. Some of this growth might be explained by President Clinton's political intervention in hiring 10,000 more police officers. In any case, in 1997, those employed in private security still outnumbered public police by 47.9 per cent. The most astonishing growth was in alarm monitoring, a 73.3 per cent increase. There is a clear movement towards remote monitoring to replace human labour.

Most security services now have an alarm-response branch, and the police still respond to home and commercial alarms, although lack of public police effectiveness here has resulted in an enormous expansion in the private sector. Information systems are now big business, as are the information technology systems that monitor both outside populations and security staff.[180] Sentry-dataveillant policing activity is as much about knowing others as it is about convincing consumers that they know more about their watchers – that their security officers are transparent and accountable. Intelligarde accomplishes this by compiling a database on all persons issued NPEs (Notices Prohibiting Entry). When notices are issued against trespassers, they are filed with headquarters along with shift reports and other paperwork. Part of the regular duties of daytime communications officers is to input this information into a 'bannings' database. In effect, this 'Law Enforcement Company' dispenses thousands of NPEs and maintains an electronic case history of all individuals coming into confrontation with Intelligarde staff.

While the NPEs contain information regarding the names, addresses, and offences of banned individuals, they also record considerably more detail. These include the specifics of the offence, including the date and time; the exact section of the *Trespass to Property Act* enforced; specifically where the offence occurred (i.e., in what stairwell or hallway); and the offender's gender, height, weight, hair colour, hair style, and even attire. The banned individual's appearance is also noted, especially skin colour, possible ethnicity, tattoos, markings, and glasses. Perhaps most importantly, since much of the parapolice officer's time is spent interacting with the homeless (at least 35 per cent of individuals banned from Intelligarde properties are homeless), Intelligarde has the most comprehensive electronic registry of illegal or unofficial residences in Toronto.[181] These are the particular stairwells, alleys, and underground parking lots or entrances of the megacity. Much like its private police forbears, the 'Law Enforcement Company' comes to accumulate information on the movements and particulars of a city's underclass. Unlike the Thames police of 1800, Intelligarde, like other late-modern observation institutions, benefits from the power of computerization: 'computers differ from other machines because they possess "memory" and because they can "talk" with each other using telecommunications ... it does enable human beings to do more easily many tasks that require brainwork. Unlike the machines of early industrialism, which multiplied muscle-power, computers can be programmed to perform functions associated with mental power.'[182]

Sociologists continue to ponder whether the nature of surveillance has actually changed because of new technologies. While some argue that computers qualitatively transform the nature of surveillance,[183] others are more reserved but none the less intrigued by these developments.[184] But the simple ability to make populations known almost immediately, by merely employing common Free Text Retrieval to comb an organization's database, accelerates and widens nets of surveillance.[185] In one year (August 1996 to September 1997), Intelligarde personnel submitted approximately 56,400 written reports that ranged in importance from major occurrences to simple shift summaries or alarm responses. In this sense, 'knowing' means remembering previous incidents or interactions – and this is accomplished by a centralized computer system not unlike that of public police systems such as the Canadian Police Information Centre.

Other security companies have larger, international sentry-dataveillant systems that provide travel alerts to executives, or 'snitch' lines that allow employees to report other malfeasance. Pinkerton's Alertline[186] is a phone-based system that encourages workers to call in tips to a toll-free number. Wackenhut has a similar system. Thousands of telephone calls per year come into these centres. Each one is logged, after which the employee may be reported to the client, or an investigation can take place. Of course, identical systems are also run by the public police today, including 'Crime Stoppers.'

Modern static access control runs the gamut from securing sensitive nuclear facilities, to embassy protection, to monitoring the rapidly growing number of gated communities where security officers replace public police. Residential security in closed communities is now a large market. Security officers not only stop unauthorized entry but also assist in emergencies and are trained in cardiopulmonary resuscitation (CPR).[187] They are ambassadors for the community and are 'impeccably dressed, exceptionally courteous and professional in attitude.' Many private police officers in the United States are also armed, proving a formidable

threat to integrative community life[188] as they police the borders between inclusion and exclusion[189] on the basis of risk knowledge.

Investigative

Type three policing, unlike the sentry-dataveillant form, is investigative
and targeted. Investigative policing is about selective, reactive policing
based on citizen information, client concerns, victim reports, or digital
dispatch. It is an individual-based, aggressive, intelligence-gathering form
of activity that includes 'stake-outs,' wire-taps, interrogations, and so
forth. Investigative policing involves research on individuals who are
under suspicion for any number of reasons, but presumably for committing an offence or being a political agitator. Unlike in sentry-dataveillant
policing, officers investigate a specific target (who may none the less be
initially unknown) rather than a general population: instead of a fine
net, a diligent hunt. Type three policing also tends to be far more
secretive and intentionally camouflaged than all other types of policing.
The trend in investigative policing is an increasing conflation with type
two sentry-dataveillant policing. As information becomes easier to trans-
mit and artificial intelligence becomes more practical, 'artificial detectives' are written into the programming of data collection systems that
investigate and collate crimes as they are entered. This is a very new
development. Type two policing becomes the routine informant for an
investigative response.

The major historical impetus for investigative policing has been largely
political. There are scores of accounts in the historical record from the
journals of the *officiers de paix* in Paris attesting to their very active
involvement in political surveillance and infiltration. *Officier de paix*
Antoine sent in daily reports of proceedings in the assize courts, noting
particularly who was present and what went on in the public gallery; he
also inspected political journals. Marlot checked all pamphlets, carica-
tures, songs, and other writings, and maintained a surveillance of reading rooms.[190] Two important circulars framed the role of the gendarmerie
in investigating subversives. First, in November 1849, General d'Hautpoul
had sent a confidential circular to his corps commanders requesting that
officers report all information that would assist in enabling him to
'combat socialism [and] halt the progress it [was] making in the countryside.' His successor, General de le Ruë, required information on three
activities: (1) events that might have an effect on the whole country such
as anxiety over grain prices or the possibility of war; (2) local events that

affect public ministries or relate to elections, assemblies of workers; and finally (3) '[t]hose which have a particular impact on a social class, amongst the superior classes the conduct of the leaders of the old parties who remain outwardly in opposition, amongst the inferior classes the conduct of the leaders of the socialists ... lack of work, insufficiency of wages, the complaints of workers, strikes, unemployment, etc.'[191] The 1820 Ordinance established the gendarmes as soldiers, and as such they were directed always to wear their uniforms when on duty. However, as before, the gendarmerie continued to employ men in civilian clothes to infiltrate dissident groups or bands of brigands.[192]

The state political model was adopted elsewhere. By the late 1800s, the *carabinieri* were 'the eyes and ears of the unified Italian state,' regularly collecting information on subversives, including anarchists, socialists, republicans, members of the International, the Catholic political parties, and separatists.[193] The Soviet militsia kept a vast reservoir of files on dissidents, including human-rights activists and religious followers. The KGB would direct the militsia to pick up and detain dissidents during visits from foreign dignitaries. For their part, the militsia infiltrated groups and maintained a complex network of informants.[194] The German Police Union's political work in the mid-nineteenth century included the surveillance of opposition parties, the ready exchange of names of organizations and persons that were politically suspect, and the confiscation of political pamphlets. They tracked the whereabouts of revolutionaries such as Karl Marx and Friedrich Engels. In June 1858, both Engels and Marx were listed as 'known communists.'[195] The swift transmission of information between and among German Police Union detachments was already regularly taking place. Known political agitators were listed in correspondence and bulletins from Berlin and Vienna to Prussia via weekly reports to the minister of the interior. The Berlin police already had a well-developed system of *agents provocateurs* and an entrenched network of informers who infiltrated dissident groups.[196]

The French system is often set against the British model, and it is undoubtedly true that the Metropolitans of London were far more restricted in infiltrating and investigating than the gendarmes. But, of course, the point again here is that they were eventually forced to make it part of their policing routine. An example of how notions of detective work differed between the German and French gendarmeries and the British police can be gleaned from their treatment of dissidents such as Karl Marx. When the Home Office wanted details of refugees from the Paris Commune, they decided that they would write to those who were most involved. A letter was sent to Karl Marx, who gave a full account of the International Workingmen's Association.[197] A Special Branch was eventually set up to monitor foreign political refugees. Critchley[198] argues that in 1878, when the Metropolitan Criminal Investigation Division was formed, most English detectives were not in the same class as the French. As Peel had wanted, their primary function was to 'prevent crime,' and their main method was to act as a visible deterrent by patrolling the streets in uniform. Of course, there are recorded instances of the police conducting undercover work contrary to their original constitution. In fact, only three years after their inception, the London police came under attack after Sgt Popay had been caught infiltrating the National Political Union as an artist. A London mob responded by stoning and stabbing three bobbies – one of whom died. The courts originally ruled the killing a justifiable homicide until that ruling was later successfully appealed. Much of the bitterness against the new police could be attributed to the fact that they were placed among the working classes to monitor all phases of working-class life – including trade union activity.[199]

Prior to the new police, there was some public police detective work being done in eighteenth-century London. The most important players were private thief-takers who themselves had shady connections to the city's underground economy and were thus camouflaged players. One of the most infamous was the self-appointed 'thieftaker-general,' Jonathan Wild, who was executed in 1725.[200] Fielding made extensive use of informers, despite his contempt for them.[201] The Bow Street Runners did have some success at investigations. Linebaugh[202] relates a case where three robbers were tracked down doggedly over two years by Fielding's men.

Soon after the London police appeared, the guardians of the Blything Union, Suffolk, formed a paid, mounted police. Three Metropolitans were hired to watch the beerhouses. They gathered information as to the 'haunts of suspected characters,' and observed the 'habits of such as were vicious' after the riots against the poor laws. Another Suffolk union near Ipswich also got three Metropolitans after anti-poor law disturbances and paid them out of union funds.[203] Very early on, rural parishes would contract with Metropolitan police to investigate crimes. After a brutal robbery and murder in the spring of 1834 in Stow-on-the-Wold, the divisional magistrates brought down a London policeman who solved the crime.[204] Private associations were formed to hire police.

The technical aspects of investigative activities need not distract us here. There is an interesting history of the use of plaster moulds of boot-prints, fingerprint identification, and eventually DNA. But in terms of the basic human activity of investigative policing, there is a veritable wealth of information about the conflation between public and private agencies that continues to the present day. While the RCMP were 'getting their man' north of the forty-ninth parallel, Allan Pinkerton was conducting investigations that led him across the United States and into Canada. In 1868, Pinkerton and his men tracked the infamous Reno Gang from Indiana to Minnesota and on to Windsor, Ontario. He arrested the train robbers and delivered them up to New Albany, before the Indiana Vigilance Committee caught up with the culprits and ex-acted vigilante justice, hanging all four Reno Gang members.[205] The Burns Detective agency has a similarly illustrious past, acting as a national detective agency long before the country could mobilize its own investigative bodies. Today, investigative policing practices are as sophis-ticated in the private realm as they are in the public realm. Former fraud investigators and chiefs of police staff top forensic accounting and investigative firms.[206]

Patrol

Patrol-based policing refers to walking about and seeing; it is arterial – acting as a visible deterrent or a mobile inspectorate to ensure the free movement of goods and people. Often, it is an end in itself. I include under arterial or patrol-based policing the transport of valuable persons and property – mobility here is the key. Patrol-based policing is ancient, probably dating from when the first human encampment resolved to have one of its group walk about the perimeter and/or within the camp to keep an eye out for trouble. To be engaged in this form of arterial or patrol-based policing means to be on call and on alert. Type four polic-ing has various media including foot, horse, train, bicycle, motor vehicle, and so forth. It is no wonder that Sir Robert Peel omitted from his plans for a new police for the metropolis both the Old City and the country-side. The policing needs of both these constituencies were largely based on static property (land) rather than mobile property (goods). The latter reflected the needs of an industrial and merchant class, and the former those of the landed gentry. Patrol-based policing is essential for the emergence of mass exchange and commodity mobility and thus is crucial for capitalism – although the opposite is not true.

The French Royal Ordinance of 17 April 1760 sought to systematize patrolling by requiring that all patrols should consist of two men, their activities to be recorded in a Journal of Service that would be inspected monthly by the local lieutenant and then the *prévôt*. On their patrols, each brigade was to liaise with its neighbours. Eventually, in 1769, these meetings became more formalized into weekly regular meetings known as *correspondances*. The Italian *carabinieri* had a similar system in place by the late 1850s. Wirion, who established the thirteen new *départements* of the gendarmerie, wrote in Year VIII after the French Revolution that patrol was essential to policing the rural areas of the former Austrian Netherlands where he was garrisoned. He implored his men to study their surroundings so that 'this positive knowledge' might be acquired from 'frequent, multiple patrols until the time is reached when there is not a single village, a single hamlet, a single house, a single wood, ravine, a single road, or even a single bush which is not recognized and known to the new gendarmes.'[207] So important was the reconnaissance aspect of the patrol to Wirion that he expected that 'by both day and night, a gendarme could leave his barracks and go to any point to which he was directed in his brigade's district with his eyes closed.'

A Treasury grant awarded to Fielding in 1763 enabled him to establish a night horse patrol of eight men to guard the roads leading into London against highwaymen, brigands, and other criminals, but in the following year the government grant was withdrawn. The horse patrol was not revived for another forty years.[208] The Bow Street horse patrol, when newly revived in 1805, conducted missions all over the country and even abroad. They cleared notorious places such as Hounslow Heath of highwaymen. They were sworn in by the magistrates of Bow Street as constables for Middlesex, Surrey, Kent, and Essex, and by an act of George IV their power was extended to within the royal palaces and ten miles thereof.[209] Their routine patrol duty encompassed the main roads up to Enfield, Epsom, Windsor, and Romford, 'giving confidence to travellers with their greeting, "Bow Street Patrol."'[210] These patrolmen were uniformed, carrying a black bat and wearing blue uniforms with scarlet waistcoats – and were known as the 'redbreasts.'[211] The foot patrol was considerably strengthened and also split into two branches. The first night patrol consisted of about 100 men. By 1818, one group, known as the 'country party,' would start their beats between four and five miles from London, patrolling inwards along the main roads leading into the capital. At the same time, the 'town party' would set out from the centre to meet them. Because of an increase in crime in the city centre, in 1821 the 'country party' were redeployed, while a strangely

named 'unmounted horse patrol' took their place in the outer suburbs.[212] The foot patrols generally started off at about dusk and remained out until one o'clock in the morning. Unlike the mounted
patrol, they did not wear a uniform but carried a truncheon, a cutlass,
and occasionally a pistol.[213] The Bow Street patrols were directed by the
government office in the following manner: 'The duty of the horse
patrol is to afford protection to persons travelling on the highroads; for
which purpose they are to patrol the roads at such a regular pace as will
bring them to the several points on the road at the time they are directed
... Every patrol is to take particular notice of all persons of suspicious
appearance whom he may see on the road and to pay attention to
whatever information he may receive of any highway or footpad robbery
having been committed or attempted, or of any suspicious persons ... he
is to make an immediate pursuit [of suspects] with such other assistance
as he may meet with, and if the party should be apprehended, to lodge
them in some place of security until he can bring them to the public
office ...'[214] By 1770, the position at Bow Street was recognized as the
senior London magistrate, and by the end of the century, the patrol
consisted of sixty-eight men divided into thirteen territorial units, and
seven police zones.[215] The Bow Street Runners were paid on a private-
profit, results-related basis – for example, for capturing a thief or recov-
ering stolen goods. This could lead to malfeasance and cooperation with
the criminals.[216]

By the late eighteenth century, French *cahiers* (hamlets drawn up at
the start of the Revolution) were protesting the lack of a police presence
and demanding the enlargement of the *maréchaussée*. The clergy at
Montargis requested more *maréchaussées* after a surge in the number of
paupers in the district. They expressly made reference to a preference
for foot brigades.[217]

Arterial policing involves tracking along with or guarding what is
mobile. Following the 1779 inspection, the inspecting general of the
Flanders company noted how burdened his men were with the pursuit
and guarding of deserters.[218] By 1807, Moncey, then head of the
gendarmerie, complained to Napoleon that his corps were stretched too
thin in having to respond to all the pretensions of some subprefects who
demanded escorts, writing that, 'If the Gendarmerie wishes to satisfy all
the requests for the useless escorts that various public functionaries
think they have the right to demand, then it will have to renounce its
duties ... to become exclusively an object of luxury and pomp.'[219] The
gendarmerie were responsible for escorting prisoners of war and super-

vising the conscription process, and for the protection of munition and tax convoys.[220] In August 1837, a gendarme stationed at Mauriac had to come to the defence of a woman who had moved in with a married man when the residents of a neighbouring commune where she now lived set out to punish her.[221] He escorted her back to Mauriac under guard.

The safe delivery of goods or people is a patrol-based activity. The Soviet militsia were in the front line of securing grain shipments to starving urban residents. They were to take whatever measures were necessary against peasants.[222] The GAI (State Automotive Inspection) is a division of the militsia overseeing licensing and safety on the roadways. Safety on the highway had been extended to safety on the seaway in England. In 1798, Patrick Colquhoun managed to cajole the formation of a private police force for a group of West India merchants. Their task was to protect goods from theft from ships in the Thames and from the wharfs and docks. The marine police were to enforce strict rules of conduct and monitor the river's proletariat by implementing dress codes, paying 'lumping rates,' managing accounting, determining wagelessness, and stopping illegal activities on London's shipping lane. They did so by applying themselves to the apparent trivialities of order maintenance: no frocks, wide trousers, jemmies, or hidden pockets were allowed on board boats; any on-the-job takings were forbidden and confiscated. In 1800 the private police of the West India merchants were taken over by the government and became the Thames River Police. By 1827 there were seven land constables and sixty-four river constables. When it was considered necessary, these men and the various other constables and patrols established in the metropolis could be summoned to assist with crowd control.

In fact, much like today, there was debate as to the best deployment of any new police. This often revolved around patrol specifics. The older watch system employed enough men to measure beats in yards – usually no more than 500 to 600 – whereas the new Metropolitan police, employing fewer men, measured their beats in miles. Any attempt to eliminate the watch system came under intense local resistance because ratepayers would get less policing for their money.[223] This is not unlike contemporary concerns about the lack of police visibility.[224] There was much concern about keeping the mounted patrol moving and not having them distracted by events that took place 'off the beaten path.' Armitage[225] reports that when it was put to the Runners by a committee that a mounted patrol might receive intelligence of a crime or burglary on a side road or off the beat, and they were asked whether, in such a case, the patrol might leave the beat, the answer was an emphatic negative. Mr Day, representing Bow Street before a special committee, added that the mounted section was intended solely for the protection of persons travelling on the road.

By Victorian times, constables were to proceed to their respective 'meets' by the nearest Turnpike Road, an early force instruction said, 'or if there be none by the nearest highway, but not diverge through lanes or fields. They will wait at the "meet" half an hour, and state in their diaries the time of arrival of the other Constables, the duration of the conference and the subject on which conferred.'[226]

Where patrol-based policing was not already in place, local ratepayers took the initiative. In November 1830, a paid collective patrol for the winter months was organized in Stoke. It was hoped that the plan would not only apprehend depredators and forestall disturbances, but also create jobs for unemployed and underemployed men in the agricultural dead season. The Stoke watch was an amateur force using local agricultural labourers set up to patrol the agricultural fields. Patrols could be publicly sanctioned or privately and collectively organized. At Tenbury, a group of locals wanted to include the parish under the Lighting and Watching Act of 1833, but were turned down by the ratepayers. They thus resolved with some gentlemen in adjoining parishes to hire some policemen. The Vicar of Tenbury remarked that the 'idle and dissolute living on plunder and poaching [had now been] checked.'[227] During the early history of the Metropolitan police in London, country parishes would occasionally band together to purchase the expertise of policemen to patrol their districts. Such was the case in Stow, where the hired police were to patrol an area six miles from the centre, keep a watchful eye on victuallers and vagrant lodging-houses, and execute summonses and warrants.[228]

By 1936, with the increased use and spread of the motor car, it was obvious that the English police needed to deploy many more officers to patrol the roads. A corps of special road patrols, paid from the national road fund, resulted in the hiring of 800 more patrolmen. They were tasked with giving verbal warnings rather than taking motorists to court. They became known as the 'courtesy cops.'[229]

Today, patrol-based policing activity is usually motorized, although the Kansas City Preventive Patrol Experiment[230] and community-based policing have reflected concerns in the general populace that a more visible police foot patrol is always needed. In any case, the private sector, as it did in the eighteenth century, is leading the way by answering consumer demand for a uniformed patrol.[231] Large multinational firms such as Securitas or Wackenhut, among others, conduct hundreds of thousands of offender transports a year in countries such as Canada, Australia, the United States, Britain, and countries throughout continental Europe. With the proliferation of twenty-four-hour automated teller machines, other subsidiaries such as Loomis, or independent firms such as Securicor and Brinks, are part of a burgeoning demand for money transport personnel. Long before this, private firms had been contracted to safeguard the transportation of goods. The Pinkerton Detective Agency was contracted by U.S. railway companies as early as 1855.[232] In many cases, private security firms conduct all arterial activity in certain communities, inviting the public police in whenever needed. So dominant has the private sector become that there is talk among some police leaders that the police may hand patrol-based policing activities over to the private sector and merely regulate them. Sussex police chief Ian Blair made a recommendation that police forces stamp security vehicles in their district with 'police compliant' decals if they come under the rubric of the local constable.

Civic-Sumptuary

The fifth and final type of policing is the civic-sumptuary category. Knemeyer[233] calls this general form of activity *polizeiwissenschaft*, referring to strategies for the general maintenance of order in Germany.[234] By civic-sumptuary policing, I am referring to regulatory and civic matters that predated the new public police. These matters included health,[235] moral and sumptuary regulation,[236] and poor relief.[237] 'Sumptuary law was one element of a process in which more and more aspects of social life were becoming objects of disciplinary or regulatory activity.'[238] While sumptuary laws may by general definition be known to encompass rules concerning the purchase of goods, Hunt adds all forms of moral regulatory regimes guiding manners, including public dress, conduct in church and school, animal control, and even the regulation of waste disposal and the water supply. It is thus no coincidence that eighteenth-century police scientist Patrick Colquhoun would express an interest in water systems, waste management, and all forms of sanitary regulation to offset disease. Type five policing thus includes many forms of regulatory activity, moral reconnaissance, arbitration in disputes, and the undertaking of tasks ancillary to crime-based policing but necessary for good administration and order maintenance. It is often assumed that civic-sumptuary policing is less and less likely to be undertaken by the public police as they relegate these duties to contracted security firms or subdepartments for by-law enforcement. However, public police (including municipal, provincial, and the RCMP) still engage in a wide range of civic-sumptuary policing, including bar security, population control on private property and roadways during festivals, train security, port security, and other regulatory functions subcontracted to them by other government authorities.

In addition to general policing duties, many new regulatory responsibilities were conferred upon English constables during the late sixteenth and early seventeenth centuries. They were the administrative agents of occupations and trades, and were servants of the justices in the enforcement of the relief of the poor and the repair of highways. During the early seventeenth century, they were made administrators of alehouse keepers and victuallers as well. The parish constable also oversaw road surveyors and would call the parishioners together yearly in Easter week for the purpose of choosing them. Constables also acquired responsibilities for implementing provisions concerning public health when an act of 1604 empowered them to order those infected with plague to keep to their own houses.[239] Constables were also tax collectors. Some were obliged to levy additional rates for particular commodities such as wax, oats, wheat, poultry, and sometimes for carts. In some cases, constables supplied actual produce such as wheat, oats, hay, straw, and butter to the royal household. Two other tasks assigned to local communities also created responsibilities for constables: to supply horses, oats, and coals to the postmaster, and to assist saltpetre men when carrying their tubs and fuel.[240] Some constables during the early seventeenth century appeared before the justices with butchers, victuallers, and alemen, requiring them to enter recognizances binding them not to dress or sell flesh during Lent.[241] Constables often had previous experience as overseers of the poor, surveyors of the highways, or churchwardens. They were usually drawn from the upper class of a village or small town.[242]

English policemen carried out tasks that were the domain of their forerunner, the parish constable: they regulated traffic, ensured that pavements were clear, watched for unsafe buildings and burning chimneys, administered aid, drove ambulances, enforced the poor law, looked for missing persons, licensed street sellers and cabs, and supervised the prevention of disease among farm animals.[243] The police of the countryside continued to concern themselves with regulating public houses, the beating or shaking of carpets in public, kite flying, the sawing of timber in the streets, or even hoop dressing and cork burning in public spaces.[244]

Police forces established charitable funds in the 1870s for the provision of shoes and clothes to children and opened up soup kitchens. Edwin Chadwick was in favour of these 'civic-sumptuary services.' He wanted police stations to be equipped with stretchers and, if close to rivers, with life-saving equipment. He also wanted police surgeons to be readily available to help anyone in populous districts, and police to undertake fire-fighting.[245] During wartime, the police handled a miscellany of duties such as finding billets for troops, controlling the movement of refugees, manning the system of advance air raid warnings, guarding secret defensive or offensive installations against public access, and collecting an astonishing assortment of arms from the public with which to equip volunteers (the Home Guard).[246]

In France, a task-specific regulatory police were plying their trade in the early eighteenth century. The *gabelous*, or salt police, were assigned to catch smugglers and collect taxes on the imports. They were heavily corrupted, however; in 1720, the minister of war, Claude Leblanc, implored his government to bring in the *maréchaussée* and then his own agents to correct this state of affairs, but he was ignored.[247] In Paris, the Cour de Monnaies were responsible for stamping out counterfeiting while the *connétablie* were assigned the task of supervising crowds outside the Comédie Française, the Comédie Italienne, and the Opéra. *Commissaires* supervised the execution of municipal regulations and took depositions in criminal cases.[248] The tasks of the *commissaires* in early-nineteenth-century Paris were many and varied. As Emsley describes, under the general heading of 'la police administrative,'[249] their duties were to encompass general good order and well-being by ensuring that the streets were clean and unobstructed, checking the registers of lodging houses and secondhand dealers, investigating passport requests and licences to carry arms, providing replacements for lost identity cards, and granting permission to establish a bakery or a meat shop. A more bizarre duty uncovered by Emsley was filed in the winter of 1800, requesting permission from Commissaire Leroux for women to go riding in men's clothes. Madeleine Gourju, a Parisian laundress, found herself in trouble for stringing a washing-line between trees on the Champs Elysées. Failure to wash the pavement in front of your home or to put down gravel or sand during icy weather could result in a small fine. *Commissaires* also checked weights and measures. Night patrols by the civilian police, as well as by guards and gendarmes, looked for cabarets open after hours and checked doors and gates to make sure that they were closed and locked.[250] By the late eighteenth century, the gendarmerie were involved in fighting forest fires as well as stamping out forestry offences such as the theft of wood from private estates.[251] Gendarmes rescued peasants during floods, fought fires, pursued rabid animals, and provided assistance during cholera epidemics.[252]

In other countries, the police also took on other diverse activities. The first Scottish police were referred to on the statute book in 1833: 'An Act to enable "Burghs in Scotland" to establish a General System of Police.' These tasks were described as watching, lighting, paving, cleansing, the water supply, drainage, and other functions. It thus 'perpetuated the broader, generic idea of policing.'[253] The *carabinieri* oversaw and reported on annual conscription, enforced quarantines, assisted the population in times of accident or natural disaster, and fought forest fires, sometimes at great personal cost.[254] The Soviet militsia, albeit mostly engaged in polemic and sentry-dataveillant policing, also undertook enforcement of sanitary regulations, ensured that food supplies reached stores, and even certified building plans for highways. It was a generalist *polizei*. Of course, in the Soviet Union there were no private police to compete for ancillary services since the Communist party had a monopoly of the means of production.[255] This resulted in a very large and ubiquitous public police force that took on many roles undertaken by the private sector in Western capitalist economies. In addition, some 13 million civilians served as auxiliary police (*druhinnikz*). In the 1950s, the militsia turned away from their political functions and focused on economic and social regulation.[256] The *miquelets* in Guipuzcoa collected provincial taxes and statistics and acted as agents of the provincial savings bank and even as a private postal service. They also engaged in various guard, traffic, and customs duties.[257] Beyond their other duties, the police of the autonomous community in Basque are also responsible for securing ports of entry, coasts, and frontiers; customs control; overseeing emigration and immigration, passports, and national identity documents; dealing with arms and explosives; and handling state protection, smuggling, and fiscal fraud against the state.[258]

Contemporary advanced capitalist societies are full of policing services that are willing to undertake a plethora of service activities only remotely related to security work. Securitas AB offers receptionist services in its Nordic region;[259] Pinkerton's, one of Securitas AB's subsidiaries, employs hazardous materials personnel at Raytheon Systems in Al Segundo, California. They also provide a fire service and a materials destruction team.[260] Group 4 Falck provides contract fire services to public authorities and private households in Denmark.[261] Wackenhut provides fire services and emergency response at Canaveral Air Station and the Kennedy Space Centre[262] as well as for the Nissan Corporation and the Rogers World Airport in Oklahoma City. Wackenhut also provides emergency medical response to public agencies on a contract basis[263] and has contracts for toll-collection booths.

Wackenhut provides ship security and inspection teams to ensure that your boat or your home are within prescribed codes. The same company even offers postal and forestry services. Of course, as we saw under polemic policing, private security firms are at the ready with a range of replacement workers during labour unrest. Secure Options provides a wide assortment of services beyond security, including interior preparation and sanitation of properties, removal of rubbish and abandoned furniture, garden tidying, and graffiti removal.[264] Burns fulfils a variety of temporary labour contracts ranging from packaging, delivery, shipping/ receiving, call-centre marketing, and other 'light labour assignments.'[265]

Conclusions

When one begins to examine the wide range of activities associated with policing, it becomes increasingly difficult to maintain old divisions between public and private. This is not to suggest that public and private designations do not, in the end, mean something – especially in judicial proceedings. But I aim to argue, as others have done before me, that this dichotomy is not particularly useful when trying to categorize the wide breadth of human labour involved in policing. I have provided the reader with a different interpretation of policing by clustering activities based on historical and contemporary practice into categories that purposefully conflate public and private policing. This is a far more productive enterprise in reaching a realistic interpretation of policing and is a better foundation both for theory building and as a general heuristic device.

In examining historical tendencies and modern manifestations of policing for the purpose of typology construction, one begins to realize how resilient and recurrent policing activities are. Today, citizens identify themselves more as consumers and make decisions on the legitimacy of taxation based on the product that is delivered. As a result, many more Canadians are purchasing private security as the cost per unit of public policing goes up and police visibility goes down.[266] We want our police to engage in far more patrol-based activity. We think this is new. But during the 1840s, rural ratepayers complained in much the same way as their London counterparts in the preceding decade about policing. In January 1842, 172 of the 240 townships in the Quarter Sessions of County Durham received petitions for the removal of the new police. In November 1842, two-thirds of the parishes in Bedfordshire petitioned for the removal of the police, whom they condemned as 'EXPENSIVE, if not INEFFICIENT.'[267] The history of English policing is littered with such examples.

In further examining the contemporary security literature in preparation for this chapter, I came across another inescapable trend: the relentless move towards an ever-increasing concentration of multinational security conglomerates. In only 2000 and 2001 to date, Group 4 Falck has announced ten takeovers – in Germany (ADS Sicherheit Group, Top Control Group), Hungary (Bantech Security Rt), Austria (SOS), Finland (SPAC), Czech Republic (BOS: Bankovi Ochranna Sluzba, a.s.), France (OGS, EuroGuard), Poland (BRE Services), and Norway (Unikey AS). And these are by no means small enterprises. EuroGuard employs 4,200 employees, ADS 1,200 employees, and BOS 1,200 employees. In 1999, Securitas AB, already employing over 210,000 people worldwide, purchased Pinkerton, increasing the employee pool by another 117,000 in the United States. Immediately after the takeover, two regional market leaders were acquired in the United States: First Security Corp. and American Protective Services Inc. This was followed by the purchase of Smith Security Inc., Doyle Protective Service Inc., and APG Security.[268] In 2000, Securitas acquired Burns, thus becoming overnight a major player in the largest security market in the world. In 2001, Securitas bought Loomis Armored car, a company with more than 220 offices across the United States, employing another 2,200 officers.

Finally, I want to return to a core conceptual argument I have made throughout this chapter. As Brogden[269] argues, 'It is critical not to confuse what the police ended up actually doing with the reasons why they were actually founded. The fact that they "may" have been effective against social disorder, crime, migrant workers, and working class people does not of itself prove that that was why they were created.' And here I find myself in complete agreement with Brogden, although I would change the emphasis. I would suggest that the real task, therefore, is to focus on the great tableau of policing as a whole – notwithstanding the formative logics of any given institution – and to analyse this mass body of human labour for its corporeal (and material) manifestation rather than for how it was imagined in the ethereal world of some planner's imagination. I optimistically offer this typology as a positive step in that direction.

Notes

1 William C. Cunningham, J.J. Strauchs, and C.W. Van Meter, *The Hallcrest II: Private Security Trends 1970–2000* (MacLean, Va: Hallcrest Systems Inc., 1990); J. Kakalik and S. Wildhorn, *Private Police in the United States* (Washington, D.C.: Government Printing Office, 1971); George S. Rigakos, 'The Significance of Economic Trends for the Future of Police and Security,' in J. Richardson, ed., *Police and Security: What the Future Holds* (Ottawa: Canadian Association of Chiefs of Police, 2000) at 176–9; Clifford D. Shearing, Margaret B. Farnell, and Philip C. Stenning, *Contract Security in Ontario* (Toronto: Centre of Criminology, University of Toronto, 1980); Karen Swol, 'Private Security and Public Policing in Canada,' in *The Juristat Reader* (Toronto: Thompson Educational Publishing, 1999) 15.

2 Les Johnston, *The Rebirth of Private Policing* (London: Routledge, 1992); Trevor Jones and Tim Newburn, *Private Security and Public Policing* (New York: Oxford/Clarendon, 1998); Nigel South, *Policing for Profit* (London: Sage, 1988).

3 See special issue of *European Journal on Criminal Policy and Research* (1999) no. 7.

4 Rigakos, *supra* note 1.

5 Swol, *supra* note 1.

6 Peter Miller and Nikolas Rose, 'Mobilizing the Consumer: Assembling the Subject of Consumption' (1997) 14:1 Theory, Culture, and Society 1; Pat O'Malley, 'Risk and Responsibility,' in A. Barry, T. Osborne, and N. Rose, eds, *Foucault and Political Reason: Liberalism, Neo-liberalism and Rationalities of Government* (London: UCL Press, 1996) at 189–207; Nikolas Rose, 'Governing "Advanced" Liberal Democracies,' in Barry, Osborne, and Rose, eds, *Foucault and Political Reason* at 37–64.

7 Thomas Hobbes, *Leviathan* (1660), ed. Richard Tuck (Cambridge and New York: Cambridge University Press, 1991). Quotation from Part II, ch. 18.

8 Philip Stenning, 'Powers and Accountability of Private Police' (1999) 7:2 European Journal on Criminal Policy and Research 325.

9 Max Weber, *Wirtschaft und Gesellschaft* (trans. as *Economy and Society*), trans. G. Roth and G. Wittich (New York: Bedminster Press, 1922/1968).

10 This Weberian notion of the state is challenged by Marxian thinkers (e.g., Ralph Miliband, *The State in Capitalist Society* [New York: Basic Books, 1969]) who would see these developments as the natural proclivity of capitalism.

11 Ian Loader and Neil Walker, 'Policing as a Public Good: Reconstituting the Connections between Policing and the State' (2001) 5:1 Theoretical Criminology 9.

12 Christopher Murphy, 'Policing Postmodern Canada' (1998) 13:2 Canadian Journal of Law and Society 1.

13 Pat O'Malley and Darren Palmer, 'Post-Keynsian Policing' (1996) 25:2 Economy and Society 137.

14 Clifford D. Shearing and Philip C. Stenning, 'Reframing Policing,' in C.D. Shearing and P.C. Stenning, eds, *Private Policing* (Newbury Park: Sage, 1987).

15 Margaret B. Farnell and Clifford D. Shearing, *Private Security: An Examination of Canadian Statistics, 1961–1971* (Toronto: University of Toronto Centre of Criminology, 1977).

16 Michael Kempa, Ryan Carrier, Jennifer Wood, and Clifford Shearing, 'Reflections on the Evolving Concept of "Private Policing"' (1999) 7:2 European Journal on Criminal Policy and Research 197.

17 Shearing and Stenning, *supra* note 14.

18 Gary T. Marx, 'The Interweaving of Public and Private Police in Undercover Work,' in C.D. Shearing and P.C. Stenning, eds, *Private Policing* (Newbury Park: Sage, 1987) 172.

19 Nancy Reichman, 'Managing Crime Risks: Toward an Insurance-Based Model of Social Control' (1986) 8 Research in Law, Deviance and Social Control, 151.

20 Kenneth D. Bailey, 'Monothetic and Polythetic Typologies and Their Relation to Conceptualization, Measurement and Scaling' (1973) 38:1 American Sociological Review 18.

21 Weber, *supra* note 9.

22 Robert F. Winch, 'Heuristic and Empirical Typologies: A Job for Factor Analysis' (1947) 12:1 American Sociological Review 68.

23 John C. McKinney, 'Typification, Typologies, and Sociological Theory' (1969) 48:1 Social Forces 1.

24 Alfred Shutz, *Collected Papers, Vol. I: The Problem of Social Reality* (The Hague: Martinus Nijhoff, 1962).

25 McKinney, *supra* note 23.

26 Ibid.

27 Bailey, *supra* note 20; A.K. Basu and R. Kenyon, III, 'Causality and Typology: Alternative Methodological Solutions in Theory and Practice' (October

1972) Pacific Sociological Review 425; Howard Becker, *Through Values to Social Interpretation* (Durham, N.C.: Duke University Press, 1950); Milton Bloombaum, 'A Contribution to the Theory of Typology Construction' (1964) 5:2 Sociological Quarterly 157; John Hendricks and C. Breckenridge Peters, 'The Ideal Type and Sociological Theory' (1971) 16:1 Acta Sociologica 31; Allen Liska, 'Strategies for Typology Construction' (1973) 7:2 Sociological Focus 21; McKinney, *supra* note 23; John C. McKinney and Alan C. Kerchhoff, 'Toward a Codification of Typological Procedure' (1962) 31:1 Sociological Inquiry 128; Winch, *supra* note 22.

28 Bailey, supra note 20.

29 Carl G. Hempel, 'Typological Methods in the Natural and Social Sciences' (1952) American Philosophical Association, Eastern Division, Vol. 1.

30 Vittorio Cappecchi, 'Typologies in Relation to Mathematical Models' (September 1966) 58 Ikon 1.

31 John C. McKinney, *Constructive Typology and Social Theory* (New York: Appleton-Century-Crofts, 1966).

32 Weber, *supra* note 9.

33 Bailey, *supra* note 20.

34 Louis L. McQuitty, 'Elementary Factor Analysis' (August 1961) 9 Psychological Reports 71.

35 Winch, *supra* note 22.

36 Bailey, *supra* note 20.

37 To confound matters, however, we must recognize that while typology construction may 'originally' have been of one form or another, subsequent researchers are free to make it whatever they desire. Udy took Weber's ideal types and converted them into types with variable characteristics: Stanley Udy, Jr, 'Bureaucratic Elements in Organizations: Some Research Findings' (August 1958) 23 American Sociological Review 415. In criminology, Gottfredson and Hirschi's *General Theory of Crime* posited a theoretical 'type' of individual most likely to engage in criminal activity – a person possessing low self-control: see Michael R. Gottfredson and Travis Hirschi, *A General Theory of Crime* (Stanford, Calif.: Stanford University Press, 1990). It was not until Gramsick and colleagues that a quantitative measure was introduced to 'identify' such risky persons and assess their criminality in a correlative, quantitative manner: see Harold G. Gramsick, Charles R. Tittle, Robert J. Bursik, Jr, and Bruce Arneklev, 'Testing the Core Empirical Implications of Gottfredson and Hirschi's General Theory of Crime' (1993) 30 Journal of Research in Crime and Delinquency 5. Notwithstanding the possibility that certain types may be redeployed using different methods, each instance of typology construction can be categorized according to the heuristic-empirical-classical triad.

38 So, in the hypothetical case of producing a historical typology of public
     policing in Russia, the use of statistical multivariate analyses is clearly
     inappropriate. To be sure, typologists of typologies are not unaware of the
     fundamental determining role played by both objects and units of analysis –
     in our example, Russian policing and historical epochs – but they have
     treated these two fundamental aspects as a series of 'dimensions.' McKinney
     introduces six dimensions in his analysis of typological construction: (1)
     ideal-extracted; (2) general-specific; (3) scientific-historical; (4) timeless-
     time-bound; (5) universal-local; and (6) generalizing-individualizing: see
     McKinney, *supra* note 31. However one decides to categorize the art of
     typology construction, what cannot be ignored is that the method employed
     for creating such classifications will be heavily conditioned by the nature of
     the phenomenon under study and the priority assigned to the unit(s)
     chosen to break down its constituent parts.

39 D.H. Bayley and C.D. Shearing, 'The Future of Policing' (1996) 30:3 Law
     and Society Review 585; Kempa et al., *supra* note 16.

40 George S. Rigakos and David H. Greener, 'Bubbles of Governance: Private
     Policing and the Law in Canada' (2000) 15:1 Canadian Journal of Law and
     Society 145.

41 C. Reith, *The Police and the Democratic Ideal* (London: Oxford University Press,
     1943).

42 Alan Silver, 'Social and Ideological Bases of British Elite Reactions to
     Domestic Crises, 1829–1832' (February 1971) 1 Politics and Society.

43 On the one hand, more conservative accounts point to the inefficiency of
     older forms of policing, including the parish constable and the watch,
     arguing that crime and disorder were rampant. The conservative accounts
     sometimes romanticize the role of 'visionary' police intellectuals such as
     Colquhoun, Chadwick, the Fieldings, and Sir Robert Peel, and overplay
     the success of the new London police. On the other hand, more radical
     accounts question whether the previous system of policing was so inefficient,
     whether crime was really so rampant, and, moreover, whether there was a
     more basic economic need to create a police body in order to pacify
     labourers. Revisionist accounts focus attention on the need to suppress
     popular revolt and fortify the position of the newly entrenched bourgeoisie.
     These police bodies were viewed as 'a plague' – as *agents provocateurs* – and
     were treated with disdain by workers and peasants: see Robert Storch, 'The
     Plague of the Blue Locusts: Police Reform and Popular Resistance in
     Northern England 1840–1857' (1975) 20 International Review of Social
     History 61. As is often the case, some intellectuals eventually positioned
     themselves 'somewhere between' these two camps: see Stanley H. Palmer,

Police and Protest in England and Ireland, 1780–1850 (Cambridge: Cambridge University Press, 1988). Intellectuals attempted to 'write a history of the police which is critical of the traditional Whig view, but is equally skeptical of the notion that the police can best be understood as an instrument of class power': see Clive Emsley, *Gendarmes and the State in Nineteenth-Century Europe* (Oxford: Oxford University Press, 1999). Reiner reviews the original two bipolar perspectives, simplifies them, and compares them against ten fundamental dimensions (or rather questions) about the emergence of the first police: see Robert Reiner, *The Politics of the Police*, 2nd ed. (Toronto: University of Toronto Press, 1992) at 11–56. He exaggerates orthodox and revisionist historiographies, conceding that none of the writers he is synthesizing 'fits the pure model in every respect' because his categorizations are 'clearly an ideal-type' (ibid., 25). Reiner, too, posits a middle position as another 'type,' seeing the merit of both interlocutory standpoints.

44 Steven Spitzer, 'The Political Economy of Policing,' in D.F. Greenberg, ed., *Crime and Capitalism: Readings in Marxist Criminology* (Palo Alto: Mayfield, 1981) 314.

45 Ronald A. Stansfield, *Issues in Policing: A Canadian Perspective* (Toronto: Thompson Educational Publishing, 1996).

46 Clifford D. Shearing and Philip C. Stenning, 'Private Security: Implications for Social Control' (1983) 30:5 Social Problems 498.

47 Bayley and Shearing, *supra* note 39.

48 O'Malley and Palmer, *supra* note 13.

49 Richard V. Ericson and Kevin D. Haggerty, *Policing the Risk Society* (Toronto: University of Toronto Press, 1997).

50 Steven Spitzer and Andrew T. Scull, 'Privatization and Capitalist Development: The Case of the Private Police' (1977) 25 Social Problems 18.

51 Murphy, *supra* note 12.

52 Rigakos, *supra* note 1. Or some time after the Second World War.

53 John L. McMullan, 'Social Surveillance and the Rise of the "Police Machine"' (1998) 2:1 Theoretical Criminology 93.

54 Clive Emsley, 'A Typology of Nineteenth Century Police' (1999) 3:1 Déviance et Société 29.

55 Thus, for Emsley, the police of metropolitan London and of Paris, commanded by government appointees and independent of local authority in both cases are examples of state civilian forces. The civilian municipal police type consisted of the borough and county police in Britain and the *gardes champêtres* in France. The third type of police, the state military form were armed like soldiers and resided in barracks; these were the Royal Irish Constabulary and the gendarmerie. Although Emsley concedes that local

practices and political structures had just as much to do with the organization of policing in Germany, Austria, Prussia, Italy, etc., he none the less
privileges the Anglo-French template as an 'ideal type' for European police
in the nineteenth century. In his view 'state civilian, municipal civilian and
state military, are sufficiently distinctive types in ways that the chains of
command and accountability functioned and that men were recruited,
equipped and deployed.' Ibid. at 36.

56 David H. Bayley, *Patterns of Policing: A Comparative International Analysis* (New
   Brunswick, N.J.: Rutgers University Press, 1985).
57 Ibid.
58 Other countries, such as Italy, have a centralized-uncoordinated-multiple
   system because the *caribinieri* and Guardia compete in all jurisdictions with
   overlapping authority. Centralized-single systems include Poland, Singapore,
   Sri Lanka, Ireland, and Israel. Decentralized-uncoordinated-single systems
   include the United States, Belgium, and Switzerland: Bayley, *supra* note 56,
   Table 3.2.
59 John D. Brewer, 'Policing Divided Societies: Theorising a Type of Policing'
   (1991) 1:2 Policing and Society 179.
60 Johnston, *supra* note 2.
61 Ibid., figure 9.1 at 195.
62 Trevor Jones and Tim Newburn, 'Urban Change and Policing: Mass Private
   Property Reconsidered' (1999) 7:2 European Journal on Criminal Policy
   and Research 225.
63 Based on Canadian employment statistics that show a 2:1 ratio in favour of
   private security over public police.
64 Peter K. Manning, *Police Work: The Social Organization of Policing*, 2nd ed.
   (Prospect Heights: Waveland Press, 1997); Peter K. Manning and John H.
   Van Maanen, eds, *Policing: A View from the Street* (Santa Monica: Goodyear,
   1978); Jerome Skolnick, *Justice without Trial* (New York: Wiley and Sons,
   1966); and, W. Westley, *Violence and the Police* (Cambridge, Mass.: MIT Press,
   1970).
65 W.K. Muir Jr, *Police: Street Corner Politicians* (Chicago: University of Chicago
   Press, 1977).
66 Anthony J. Miccuci, 'Changing of the Guard: The Transformation of Private
   Security' (1995) 18:1 Journal of Security Administration 21.
67 George S. Rigakos, 'Hyperpanoptics as Commodity: The Case of the
   Parapolice' (1999) 23:1 Canadian Journal of Sociology 381.
68 Michel Girodo, 'Undercover Probes of Police Corruption: Risk Factors in
   Proactive Internal Affairs Investigations' (1988) 16 Behavioral Sciences and
   the Law 479.

69 Carl Klockars, 'The rhetoric of community policing,' in J. Greene and S. Mastrofski, eds, *Community Policing: Rhetoric or Reality* (New York: Praeger, 1988) 239.

70 Donald Black, *The Manners and Customs of the Police* (New York: Academic Press, 1980).

71 James Q. Wilson, *Varieties of Police Behavior: The Management of Law and Order in Eight Communities* (Cambridge, Mass.: Harvard University Press, 1968).

72 Robert Baldwin and Richard Kinsey, *Police Powers and Politics* (London: Quartet Books, 1982).

73 Donatella della Porta and Herbert Reiter, eds, *Policing Protest: The Control of Mass Demonstrations in Western Democracies*' (Afterword by Gary T. Marx) (Minneapolis: University of Minnesota Press, 1998).

74 Clifford D. Shearing and Philip C. Stenning, 'Snowflakes or Good Pinches? – Private Security's Contribution to Modern Policing,' in R. Donelan, ed., *Maintenance of Order in Society* (Ottawa: Ministry of Supply and Services, 1982) 96.

75 Kempa et al., *supra* note 16.

76 Private security can be both managerial and retributive: see George Rigakos, *The New Parapolice: Risk Market and Commodified Social Control* (Toronto: University of Toronto Press, 2002). Also the public police can be both actuarial and paramilitary. See Ericson and Haggerty *Policing the Risk Society*, *supra* note 49; and Peter B. Kraska and Victor E. Kappeler, 'Militarizing American Police: The Rise and Normalization of Paramilitary Units' (1997) 44 Social Problems 1. A similar point concerning the 'velvet glove' and 'iron fist' of public policing has been made by Jean-Paul Brodeur, 'High Policing and Low Policing: Remarks about the Policing of Political Activities' (1983) 30:5 Social Problems 507; and the radical Berkeley collective: L. Cooper, E. Currie, J. Frappier, T. Platt, B. Ryan, R. Schauffler, J. Scruggs, and L. Trujillo, eds, *The Iron Fist and the Velvet Glove: An Analysis of the U.S. Police* (Berkeley: Center for Research on Criminal Justice, 1975). Besides these empirical challenges, the loss prevention-crime control dichotomy merely assigns operational terminology to pre-existing public-private divisions, a distinction that has become increasingly difficult to discern and that now means very little in terms of knowing much about what these organizations actually do.

77 Brodeur, *supra* note 76.

78 Robert J. Gerden, *Private Security: A Canadian Perspective* (Scarborough, Ont.: Prentice-Hall, 1998).

79 Ibid.

80 Jones and Newburn, *supra* note 62.

81 Ibid.

82 Tonita Murray and Erica McKim, 'Introduction: The Policy Issues in Policing and Private Security' (1983) in J. Richardson, ed., *Police and Private Security: What the Future Holds* (Ottawa: Canadian Association of Chiefs of Police, 2000) at 4.

83 Alfried Schulte-Bockholt, 'A Neo-Marxist Explanation of Organized Crime' (2001) 10 Critical Criminology 225.

84 W. Wallace, *The Logic of Science in Sociology* (Chicago: Aldine-Atherton, 1971).

85 In previous drafts I fiddled with the use of Greek derivatives roots in order to free myself from much of the conceptual baggage associated with many English terms describing policing. Unfortunately, readers found them distracting and difficult to pronounce – not a good sign for a heuristic tool.

86 Emsley, *supra* note 43 at 70.

87 Kraska and Kappeler, *supra* note 76.

88 Emsley, *supra* note 43.

89 Lorne Brown and Caroline Brown, *An Unauthorized History of the RCMP*, 2nd ed. (Toronto: Lewis and Samuel, 1978).

90 Emsley, *supra* note 43.

91 Ibid.

92 Kenneth H. Bechtel, *State Police in the United States: A Sociohistorical Analysis* (Westport: Greenwood Press, 1995).

93 Anthony Babington, *Military Intervention in Britain: From the Gordon Riots to the Gibraltar Incident* (London: Routledge, 1990); Clive Emsley, *The English Police: A Political and Social History*, 2nd ed. (New York: Harvester Wheatsheaf; St Martin's Press, 1991).

94 Ibid.

95 Mike Brogden, 'An Act to Colonise the Internal Lands of the Island: Empire and the Origins of the Professional Police' (1987) 15 International Journal of the Sociology of Law 179.

96 Clive Emsley, 'Policing the Streets of Early Nineteenth-century Paris' (1987) 1:2 French History 257.

97 Emsley, *supra* note 43 at 30.

98 Ibid.

99 Ibid.

100 Emsley, *supra* note 93.

101 Brogden, *supra* note 95.

102 Bechtel, *supra* note 92.

103 Ibid.

104 Emsley, *supra* note 43.

105 Ibid.

106 Ibid.

107 Ibid.

108 By the beginning of the nineteenth century, the authorities in the Basque province of Spain had established their own permanent police forces to deal with the rising tide of disorder and unrest. While the central government tried to create a militaristic state police service in the Basque region, repeated difficulties with recruiting Basque officers and tremendous local opposition frustrated their attempts. They were finally forced to permit provincial Basque police services to operate alongside their own: the minones, miquelets, and later the Guardias Forales; see Steven Greer, 'Decentralized Policing in Spain: The Case of the Basque Police' (1995) 5:1 Policing and Society 15 at 18. In Germany, a similar distrust of local police prevailed. 'Across the length and breadth of Germany local authorities had more confidence in gendarmes than in their own local police when it came to dealing with serious outbreaks of disorder'; see Emsley, *supra* note 43 at 21. Most German gendarmeries lay low during the political turmoil of the years leading up to 1848, but when the army moved in, like the French gendarmerie, they joined in the repression. But, of course, political repression need not be the purview of the supposed right. In the Soviet Union, the militsia, too, developed from a political, militarized body into a general police service for a complex urbanized society; see Louise I. Shelley, 'The Soviet Militsia: Agents of Political and Social Control' (1990) 1 Policing and Society 39 at 40. But in their early post-revolutionary history, the militsia were just as brutal as the army in trying to stamp out opposition to the Communists. In many parts of the Central Asian territory, where resistance by the Whites and the Basmachi was strongest, the militsia were engaged in a civil war (ibid. at 41–2). The role of the army and the Cheka in subjugating the peasantry and eliminating the kulaks has been well documented; see Robert Conquest, *Harvest of Sorrow* (New York: Praeger, 1986), but the militsia's part has not been recognized.

109 George S. Rigakos and Georgios Papanicolau, ' The Political Economy of Greek Policing: Between Neo-liberalism and the Sovereign State' (2003) Policing and Society (forthcoming).

110 Joan R. Kent, *The English Village Constable, 1580–1642: A Social and Administrative Study* (London: Clarendon Press, 1986) at 30.

111 A.R. Gillis, 'Crime and State Surveillance in Nineteenth Century France' (September 1989) 95 American Journal of Sociology 307.

112 Emsley, *supra* note 43.

113 Ibid.

114 Ibid.

115 Ibid.

116 Emsley, *supra* note 93.

117 Storch, *supra* note 43.

118 Ibid.

119 Ibid.

120 Emsley, *supra* note 93.

121 Ibid.

122 Emsley, *supra* note 43.

123 Emsley, *supra* note 93.

124 S.R. Couch, 'Selling and Reclaiming State Sovereignty: The Case of the Coal and Iron Police' (1981) Insurgent Sociologist 10 (4 and 11): 1, 85–91; Robert Weiss, 'The Emergence and Transformation of Private Detective Industrial Policing in the United States, 1850–1940' (1978) 9 Crime and Social Justice 35.

125 Cyril D. Robinson, 'The Deradicalization of the Policeman: A Historical Analysis' (April 1978) Crime and Delinquency 129.

126 Bechtel, *supra* note 92.

127 Ibid.

128 Sidney L. Harring and Lorraine McMullin, 'The Buffalo Police 1872–1900: Labour Unrest, Political Power and the Creation of the Police Institution' (Fall-Winter 1975) 5 Crime and Social Justice 5.

129 Kraska and Kappeler, *supra* note 76.

130 Couch, *supra* note 124; Weiss, *supra* note 124.

131 www.wackenhutservices.com/srs.htm. Accessed May 2001.

132 www.vancesecurity.com/services/services_templab.cfm. Accessed July 2001.

133 www.intelligarde.org. Accessed May 2001.

134 www.scott-security.com. Accessed July 2001.

135 www.1–p-i.com/L2_LUMM.html. Accessed May 2001.

136 www.specialresponse.com/strikeguide.htm. Accessed May 2001.

137 www.gettier.com/html/strike_security_.html. Accessed July 2001.

138 www.rapidformsnow.com/covert_recovery_services/. Accessed July 2001.

139 www.jemsec,com/frames_page.htm. Accessed May 2001.

140 Oscar H. Gandy, *The Panoptic Sort: A Political Economy of Personal Information* (Boulder: Westview Press, 1993).

141 Emsley, *supra* note 93.

142 George S. Rigakos and Richard W. Hadden, 'Crime, Capitalism and the Risk Society: Towards the Same Old Modernity?' (2001) 5:1 Theoretical Criminology 61.

143 Juri Mykkänen, '"To methodize and regulate them": William Petty's

Governmental Science of Statistics' (1994) 7 History of the Human Sciences 65.

144 William Petty, *The Petty Papers: Some Unpublished Writings of Sir William Petty*, 2 vols, edited from the Bowood Papers by the Marquis of Lansdowne (London: Routledge/Thoemmes Press, 1997), I, II, 11:32).

145 William Bogard, *The Simulation of Surveillance: Hypercontrol in Telematic Societies* (Cambridge: Cambridge University Press, 1996).

146 Rigakos and Hadden, *supra* note 142.

147 Mykkänen, *supra* note 143.

148 Rigakos and Hadden, *supra* note 142.

149 Ibid.

150 Kent, *supra* note 110 at 31.

151 John Styles, 'Print and Policing: Crime Advertising in Eighteenth-Century Provincial England,' in D. Hay and F. Snyder, eds, *Policing and Prosecution in Britain, 1750–1850* (Oxford: Clarendon, 1989) 56.

152 Ibid.

153 Emsley, *supra* note 43.

154 John L. McMullan, 'The New Improved Monied Police: Reform, Crime Control, and the Commodification of Policing in London' (1996) 36:1 British Journal of Criminology 85.

155 Howard G. Brown, 'From Organic Society to Security State: The War on Brigandage in France, 1797–1802' (1997) 69 Journal of Social History 661.

156 Emsley, *supra* note 43.

157 T.A. Critchley, *A History of the Police in England and Wales, 900–1966* (London: Constable Press, 1967).

158 G. Armitage, *The History of the Bow Street Runners* (London: Wishart and Co, 1932).

159 Critchley, *supra* note 157.

160 John Rawlings, 'The Idea of Policing' (1995) 5 Policing and Society 129.

161 Styles, *supra* note 151.

162 Emsley, *supra* note 93.

163 Styles, *supra* note 151.

164 Emsley, *supra* note 43.

165 Emsley, *supra* note 43 at 116.

166 Ibid. at 213.

167 Kit Carson and Hilary Idzikowska, 'The Social Production of Scottish Policing, 1795–1900,' in D. Hay and F. Snyder, eds, *Policing and Prosecution in Britain, 1750–1850* (Oxford: Clarendon Press, 1989).

168 Greer, *supra* note 108.

169 Conquest, *supra* note 108 at 43 and 50.

170 Shelley, *supra* note 108 at 49.
171 Ibid.
172 Ericson and Haggerty, *supra* note 49.
173 M.T. Klare, 'Rent-a-Cop: The Private Security Industry in the U.S.,' in L. Cooper, E. Currie, J. Frappier, T. Platt, B. Ryan, R. Schauffler, J. Scruggs, and L. Trujillo, eds, *The Iron Fist and the Velvet Glove: An Analysis of the U.S. Police* (Berkeley: Center for Research on Criminal Justice, 1975) 104.
174 Emsley, *supra* note 93.
175 Gary T. Marx and Nancy Reichman, 'Routinizing the Discovery of Secrets: Computers as Informants,' in J. Lowman, R.J. Menzies, and T.S. Palys, eds, *Transcarceration: Essays in the Sociology of Social Control* (Aldershot: Gower, 1987) 188; Reichman, *supra* note 19.
176 David Lyon, *The Electronic Eye: The Rise of Surveillance Society* (Minneapolis: University of Minnesota Press, 1994); Mark Poster, *The Mode of Information* (Chicago: University of Chicago Press, 1990).
177 Ernest Mandel, *Late Capitalism* (London: NLB, 1975).
178 C. Dandeker, *Surveillance, Power and Modernity: Bureaucracy and Discipline from 1700 to the Present Day* (Cambridge: Polity Press, 1990).
179 Richard V. Ericson, 'The Division of Expert Knowledge in Policing and Security' (1994) 45:2 British Journal of Sociology 149.
180 Rigakos, *supra* note 67.
181 George Rigakos, *The New Parapolice: Risk Markets and Commodified Social Control* (Toronto: University of Toronto Press, 2002).
182 Lyon, *supra* note 176.
183 Gary T. Marx, *Undercover: Police Surveillance in America* (Berkeley: University of California Press, 1988).
184 Lyon, *supra* note 176.
185 Stanley Cohen, *Visions of Social Control* (Cambridge: Polity Press, 1985).
186 (2000) 4 Pinkerton Solutions Magazine 23–5.
187 www.ussecassoc.com/gated.htm. Accessed May 2001.
188 Mike Davis, *City of Quartz: Excavating the Future of Los Angeles* (London: Verso, 1990).
189 Jock Young, *The Exclusive Society: Social Exclusion, Crime and Late Modernity* (Thousand Oaks: Sage, 1999).
190 Emsley, *supra* note 96.
191 Emsley, supra note 43.
192 Ibid.
193 Ibid., at 204.
194 Shelley, *supra* note 108.
195 Matthieu Deflem, 'International Policing in Nineteenth Century Europe:

The Police Union of German States, 1851–1866' (1996) 6 International Criminal Justice Review.

196 Ibid.

197 Emsley, *supra* note 96.

198 Critchley, *supra* note 157.

199 Storch, *supra* note 43.

200 John L. McMullan, 'The Political Economy of Thief-taking' (1995) 23 Crime, Law, and Social Change: An International Journal 121.

201 McMullan, *supra* note 154.

202 Peter Linebaugh, *The London Hanged: Crime and Civil Society in England* (London: Allen Lane, 1991).

203 Storch, *supra* note 43.

204 Ibid., at 232.

205 Jane Adler, "History of the Pinkerton Detective Agency' (2000) 3 Pinkerton Solutions Magazine 10.

206 Murray and McKim, *supra* note 82.

207 Emsley, supra note 43.

208 Critchley, *supra* note 157 at 34.

209 Armitage, *supra* note 158.

210 Critchley, *supra* note 157 at 43.

211 Ibid., at 44.

212 Armitage, *supra* note 158.

213 Critchley, *supra* note 157.

214 Armitage, s*upra* note 158.

215 J.J. Tobias, *Crime and Police in England 1700–1900* (London: St Martin's Press, 1979).

216 McMullan, *supra* note 154.

217 Emsley, *supra* note 43.

218 Ibid.

219 Ibid., at 69.

220 Ibid., at 70.

221 Ibid., at 114.

222 Shelley, *supra* note 108.

223 Ruth Paley, 'An Imperfect, Inadequate and Wretched System? Policing London before Peel' (1989) 10 Criminal Justice History 95.

224 Rigakos, *supra* note 1.

225 Armitage, *supra* note 158.

226 Critchley, *supra* note 157.

227 Storch, *supra* note 43.

228 Ibid.

229 Critchley, *supra* note 157.
230 George L. Kelling, Tony Pate, Duane Dieckman, and Charles E. Brown, *The Kansas City Preventive Patrol Experiment* (Washington, D.C. Police Foundation, 1974).
231 Clifford D. Shearing, 'Unrecognized Origins of the New Policing: Linkages between Private and Public Policing,' in M. Felson and R.V. Clarke, *Business and Crime Prevention* (Monsey, N.Y.: Criminal Justice Press, 1997) 219.
232 Adler, *supra* note 205.
233 Franz-Ludwig Knemeyer, 'Polizei' (1980) 9:2 Economy and Society 172.
234 By the mid-nineteenth century the German notion of policing, which encompassed a wide range of activities that included anything to do with the order and functioning of the state and the betterment of the happiness of the citizenry, had been transformed into public peace and security; see Deflem, *supra* note 195.
235 Thomas Osborne, 'Security and Vitality: Drains, Liberalism and Power in the Nineteenth Century,' in A. Barry, T. Osborne, and N. Rose, eds, *Foucault and Political Reason: Liberalism, Neo-liberalism and Rationalities of Government* (Chicago: University of Chicago Press, 1996) 99.
236 Alan Hunt, 'Governing the City: Liberalism and Early Modern Modes of Governance,' in A. Barry, T. Osborne, and N. Rose, eds, *Foucault and Political Reason: Liberalism, Neo-liberalism and Rationalities of Government* (Chicago: University of Chicago Press, 1996) 167.
237 Mark Neocleous, 'Social Police and the Mechanisms of Prevention: Patrick Colquhoun and the Condition of Poverty' (2000) 40 British Journal of Criminology 710.
238 Hunt, *supra* note 236.
239 Kent, *supra* note 110.
240 Ibid.
241 Ibid.
242 Emsley, *supra* note 93.
243 Ibid., at 3.
244 Storch, *supra* note 43.
245 Emsley, *supra* note 93 at 82.
246 Critchley, *supra* note 157.
247 Emsley, *supra* note 43.
248 Ibid.
249 Emsley, *supra* note 96.
250 Ibid.
251 Emsley, *supra* note 43.

252 Ibid.

253 Carson and Idzikowska, *supra* note 167 at 274.

254 Emsley, *supra* note 43.

255 Shelley, *supra* note 108 at 40 and 46.

256 Ibid.

257 Greer, *supra* note 108 at 18–19.

258 Ibid.

259 Securitas AB Annual Report 2000.

260 (1999) 2 Pinkerton Solutions Magazine 36–40.

261 Group 4 Falck Annual Report 2000: 23–4.

262 www.wackenhut.com/fire.htm. Accessed May 2001.

263 www.wackenhut.com/wii/services/.htm. Accessed May 2001.

264 www.secureoptions.co.uk/index-ips1.htm. Accessed May 2001.

265 (2000) 4 Pinkertons Solutions Magazine 3.

266 George S. Rigakos, 'The Significance of Economic Trends for the Future of Police and Security,' in J. Richardson, ed., *Police and Security: What the Future Holds* (Ottawa: Canadian Association of Chiefs of Police, 2000) 176–9.

267 Emsley, *supra* note 93.

268 Securitas, *supra* note 259.

269 Brogden, *supra* note 95.

6 Policing for the Public Good: A Commentary

SUSAN ENG

The growth of private policing agencies challenges the historical monopoly of the state in providing for public safety and security, raising concerns over impartiality, accountability, and incursion into public police jurisdiction and resources. However, the demand for private security services continues to grow and has expanded beyond protecting private property to include forensic services, investigations, and crime prevention. The distinctions made between the public police and private security forces now have fewer fundamental differences to support them. Yet the debate continues to focus on training standards, pay scales, and enforcement activities, while the question of the proper role of policing in society is relegated to the sidelines. The question for policy makers is to decide whether this development is a real cause for concern, and if so, what to do about it. What is needed to shape this debate is a template grounded in the fundamental principles that govern the role of policing in a liberal democracy.

The Social Contract

The role of policing in a liberal democracy is often characterized as a social contract between citizens and the state, in which each individual surrenders certain liberties to the state for the greater good of public security, and the state, in turn, guarantees that such powers will be exercised equitably and impartially. We give police powers of arrest, to use force, and to restrict our freedom in the name of social order and the public good. In exchange, the police must act within the clear parameters of their authority, and the laws that give the police their authority must not encroach on our civil liberties and human rights.

Sir Robert Peel, credited with creating the modern police institution, set out certain principles that underscore this relationship of the public police with the people they are meant to serve. The most frequently quoted of these is his direction

> To maintain at all times a relationship with the public that gives reality to the historic tradition that the police are the public and that the public are the police; the police being only members of the public who are paid to give full-time attention to duties which are incumbent on every citizen, in the interests of community welfare and existence.[1]

Among many other things, this principle encapsulates the idea that the public police are meant to be not arms of the state but agents of the citizenry; and, arguably, today's community-policing initiatives are an effort to recover that original sense of a communal responsibility for public safety and order.

On the issue of impartiality, Peel instructed his police

> To seek and to preserve public favour, not by pandering to public opinion, but by constantly demonstrating absolutely impartial service to Law, in complete independence of policy, and without regard to the justice or injustice of the substance of individual laws; by ready offering of individual service and friendship to all members of the public without regard to their wealth or social standing ...[2]

And on the issue of proportionality, Peel instructed his police

> To use physical force only when the exercise of persuasion, advice and warning is found to be insufficient to obtain public co-operation to an extent necessary to secure observance of law or to restore order; and to use only the minimum degree of force which is necessary on any particular occasion for achieving a police objective.[3]

These principles were articulated to reassure the public as much as they were to be guidelines for police conduct and attitudes. For further assurance, Peel also appointed two 'Commissioners of Police' as part of a system of checks and balances to enforce the social contract.[4] The history and development of civilian oversight agencies is beyond the scope of this paper except to serve as a reminder that they were created as a mechanism to guarantee accountability of the police function to the citizenry.

In Canada, there are different governance bodies responsible for ensuring that public needs and expectations are properly translated into policing policies and practices. There is, however, a gap between this broad mandate and actual practice. The debate revolves around the limited degree to which civilians have real access to police policy making and the societal distinctions that are magnified in the policing arena.

The Democracy Gap

A basic premise in a liberal democracy is that all are equal before the law and that the police must enforce the law in an even-handed manner. Yet it is clear that when we hear complaints about police conduct, it is not a universal voice. Rather, the pattern of who is satisfied and who complains often mirrors the societal hierarchy. Police practice reflects this distinction. The police subculture makes a distinction between the people they serve and the troublemakers – the people they do things *for* and the people they do things *to*.

The majority of the public accept this – they are prepared to let the police have whatever powers they want in order to keep the rabble from the door. A recent U.S. opinion poll found that a majority of Americans are worried enough about criminal activity on the Internet that they are willing to let law enforcement agencies intercept e-mail, despite any misgivings they might have about loss of privacy. After the World Trade Center disaster, any remaining objections would be virtually extinguished.

The definition of who are the 'public' and who are the 'rabble' has changed over time, with policing policy and laws moving towards reflecting changed social values. But there remains a readily identifiable segment of society, usually at the lower end of the socio-economic scale, that finds itself overly policed and lacking real voice in shaping policing policies. The growth of private security exacerbates this 'democracy gap,' rooted as it is in the market reality that those who pay the piper call the tune.

For those concerned about being overly policed in public or quasi-public places, much hope rests on the fact that the public police are funded with democratically controlled tax dollars and, consequently, are expected to be accountable for acting in an even-handed fashion, even towards people who make a smaller contribution to public tax coffers. With some irony, given the history of such groups with the public police, their greater concerns about the non-accountability of private security agencies may drive them to seek shelter in the bosom of the public police.

However, it may be argued that the interests of private property owners and businesses already dominate public policing priorities. These interests may now be further advanced – but their primacy was not created – through private policing services, and this has serious implications for how people are policed in public as well as privately owned spaces.

Historically, the public police were authorized to secure public spaces, and private spaces were the responsibility of their owners and the private security firms they engaged. With the growth of what Hermer and colleagues[5] call 'mass private property' such as shopping centres, privately owned spaces to which the general public is invited, the distinction of public versus private responsibility is blurred. The lines are virtually erased in Huey, Ericson, and Haggerty's[6] 'urban entertainment districts,' wherein public streets are incorporated into a designation crafted according to private, or at least mercantile, interests. Questions arise as to not only who should police such spaces but also who dictates the priorities about what people are entitled to do in such spaces. Increasingly, some public spaces are, in effect, privatized, and both the public and private police contribute to this effort.[7]

While the public police are sometimes pressed into duty to police these new communal spaces, there is some recognition that the property owners have the primary responsibility for security within their premises, and this has fuelled the growth in the private security industry. Consequently, this growth in private security should not be attributed to a failure of the public police to provide adequate protection; rather, it should be considered as reflecting a legitimate limitation on how public resources should be allocated. But what is lost is the system of democratic checks and balances in the public system.

In an environment in which primacy is accorded to commercial interests, people who do not contribute to such interests or, worse, who detract from the image created in such places to promote these interests, are unwelcome. Their behaviour in a public or quasi-public place is now judged and policed according to the overriding commercial or tourism interests. Those doing the policing owe their allegiance to their private sector employers and the property owners and not to the people being asked to move along. There is arguably no social contract between the private police and those being policed, and the democracy gap already evident in the public system may therefore be exacerbated.

Whether this is a public policy concern or is perceived as undue infringement on personal liberties, the people most likely to be aggrieved are those least likely to be able to press their case in the public domain. Indeed, it has fallen to criminologists and social scientists to raise the alarm that some fundamental democratic principles may be being undermined.

Public Good at Risk?

Policing in Western democracies is directed not at absolute order but at a measure of public safety and security that respects our core democratic values. There must be equality before the law and a guarantee of civil liberties for all citizens. The public police are required to be accountable to democratically established bodies that are mandated to examine their conduct against these broad principles. Within this public arena, some may consider the checks and balances to work imperfectly, but there are at least avenues of access and redress available to them.

Equality of access to personal safety and freedom from interference in pursuing lawful activities should be taken for granted in a community policed according to core democratic values – security in its broadest sense ought to be a 'public good,' a communal asset to which everyone contributes and to which everyone has access. What happens if policing activities become informed by commercial interests and measured according to their contribution to the security of the business enterprise?[8] Does security become commodified or co-opted by special interests? Does equality of access disappear?

If public safety and security is a 'public good,' it follows that the state should have primacy in, if not a monopoly on, the use of coercion and other policing powers, since, arguably, only the state and its agencies can be effectively subjected to a democratic system of checks and balances on the use of such powers. Indeed, the protections in the Canadian Charter of Rights and Freedoms have only been applied to governmental activities and not the private sector.[9] There is arguably greater freedom for the private police to draw upon racial profiling, to conduct intrusive surveillance and even searches, and to publish bans against people in a manner not available to the public police. Consider the public outcry if it had been the Toronto police who had drawn up a comprehensive database of the people banned from property policed by a private security firm.[10] At the very least, there would be demands for some proportionality between trespass offences and intrusive profiling.

The state has not consciously relinquished its primacy; there has been no legislative debate on privatizing policing. Rather, there has been a steady encroachment on its jurisdiction at the practical, quotidian level. Private security agencies now engage in policing activities that, on their surface, are virtually indistinguishable from what the public police do. From simply guarding property and restricting access to private property, private security agencies now enforce by-laws, monitor activities, investigate incidents, use force, and effect citizens' arrests.[11]

There is nothing to suggest that the expansion of private security services into activities that were previously carried out exclusively by the public police is in any way illegal. However, as argued by Hermer and colleagues, the emergence of mass private property or communal property requires a new legal regime to address the responsibility for maintaining order and safety on such premises, given the potentially serious impact of this phenomenon on civil liberties. Further, the appropriation and use of the techniques and symbols of the public police, while not illegal, can be a source of confusion and concern. When the use of non-lethal weapons is added to this list, questions of accountability come to the fore.

It is safe to say that the general populace are comfortable with the state's use of coercive force because the state is subject to accompanying checks and balances, including the Charter of Rights and Freedoms, to which the populace have access. The same cannot be said about privately owned and directed security services. As private security or private policing expands into the domain previously monopolized by the public police, the legitimacy of the state's primacy in providing for public safety and security is challenged.

Intuitively, this might be an open and shut case in favour of restoring that public monopoly were it not for the fact that the state itself has, in many instances, engaged private security firms to police public buildings and facilities such as airports.[12] And while concerns have been raised by the public police associations over the lack of training of private security officers and potential interference with their own activities and resources, there are a number of jurisdictions in which the public police consciously cooperate with the private firms and actively recruit from among their ranks.[13]

Either these parties, which are the most directly affected by the growth of private policing, see no risk to the public good or they have pursued the short-term goals of cost efficiency or delegation without reference to the larger debate.

The initial, intuitive reaction must therefore be tested: is private security necessarily less democratic and less equitable than public policing? Is it only the public police that can serve the public good? If not, the challenge for law reform is to determine whether and how legislative frameworks can be constructed to ensure that core democratic values are protected in an environment in which both public and private policing coexist.

Who Will Guarantee the Public Good?

It is safe to say that neither the public police nor the private firms would concede that the other does a better, or – now – even different, job of providing for public safety and security. In fact, the new typology of policing proposed by Rigakos,[14] 'cluster[s] activities based on historical and contemporary practice into categories that purposefully conflate public and private policing.' This typology takes the debate away from the premise that certain activities *necessarily* belong to the domain of public or private policing.

The new typology also allows the testing of the hypothesis that the public good may be at risk because of the growth of private policing. If no policing activity is necessarily monopolized by the public or the private police, then it is possible to consider the consequences of banning all private policing and expanding public police budgets and responsibilities or, conversely, of privatizing everything and abandoning public policing. If either of these alternatives were adopted, what would be lost or gained?

The new typology focuses on what the public and private police do but not necessarily why they do it. Citing Brogden, Rigakos reminds us that 'It is critical not to confuse what the police ended up actually doing with the reasons why they were actually founded ...'[15] If those reasons are agreed to be serving the public good by providing safety and security in accordance with democratically established principles, then the examination must concentrate on whether and to what degree all public or all private policing would ensure equality of access, impartiality, and protection of civil rights and liberties.

A general conclusion that can be drawn from Hermer and colleagues is that most of the literature shines a negative light on private policing:[16] 'the commodification of security' has led to the development of fortified spaces in which the well-to-do enjoy a high level of safety, but which tend to exclude the poor and otherwise marginalized. The concentration of non-state security in privileged non-state spaces produces a 'democratic gap' between the rich and the poor in what most would consider ought to be a general right of citizenship: some reasonable level of personal security.

This kind of analysis would suggest that the public good can only be served by the public police. However, it must be asked, How well have the public police served the public good? There is sufficient criticism of public policing to suggest that the 'democracy gap' already exists. The promise of community-based policing, when tested against actual practice and results, brought no more equity or accountability. Indeed, the 'broken windows' theory, currently popular in police management discourse, is focused on regulating signs of disorder, tends to 'intensify class-based divisions within urban neighbourhoods,'[17] and, at its worst, has been criticized as 'poor bashing.' The homeless and squeegee workers are already targeted by the public police at the insistence of business and property owners, and even laws enacted by democratically elected governments reinforce these class differentials.[18] There continue to be complaints from minority groups about overpolicing, and there are criticisms about police use of force and strip searches.

The record of the public police on accountability is also not unblemished. The most immediate example is the resistance to civilian oversight reflected in the Toronto Police Association's ongoing battle with the province's Special Investigations Unit. Some police/state surveillance already escapes democratic scrutiny. In cyberspace, there are technologies such as the FBI's 'Carnivore,' which intercepts e-mails; and 'Echelon,' a satellite-based surveillance system covering all of Europe, developed during the Cold War, is now apparently operated by intelligence agencies without any mechanism of democratic control. In the aftermath of the World Trade Center attack, Western governments are rushing through anti-terrorism legislation with limited opportunity for parliamentary debate.

While police budgets are debated publicly, it would be naive to conclude that police spending is entirely accountable. It was not that long ago that police budgets had only two lines in them, allocations and expenditures; and despite more detailed budget documents, today's debates do not stray far from that premise. And while there have been cutbacks necessitated by economic circumstances affecting all public services, few politicians have been willing to pay the political price for challenging police budgets or, conversely, to take the time required to fully understand what resources are needed to run an effective police agency. Squeezing police budgets has produced some efficiencies, but there are structural rigidities that prevent further improvements, not least of which are jobs guaranteed under common law, work structures such as the compressed work week, and traditional resistance to lateral transfers of needed civilian expertise. Finally, the pride that the public police have in their work would militate against the cost-efficiency techniques – such as waving a bar-coded wand at a sensor to measure patrol activity – employed by some private security firms. Arguably, such techniques should be resisted simply because they reduce the value of patrolling to marking territory.

Distinctions between public and private policing have blurred in more ways than just through their overlapping in apparent activities. The public police may have the mandate of serving the 'public good,' but criticisms of private policing (for differential policing, etc.) have parallels in public policing. On balance, however, people attracted to the profession of public policing are arguably more likely to be motivated by serving the public good. The police officers and fire-fighters killed in the World Trade Center attack were running into the building.

Market-driven efficiencies and the responsiveness of private security firms may be welcome antidotes to swollen public police budgets. But the public police are also obliged to serve communities not making a net financial contribution to tax coffers and to undertake activities with longer-term rather than immediate results, such as crime prevention. There is the further concern that focusing exclusively on the bottom line starts a race to the bottom, instead of raising standards: performance is measured against cost efficiency rather than effectiveness in bringing about longer-term sustainable development. It is precisely the focus on providing a 'competitively priced' service that drives the commodification of what should be a public good.

The reality is that both public and private policing will continue to coexist unless one or the other is banned as postulated. How then is it possible to capture the best of both systems for the benefit of the public good? And, while we're at it, improve the existing system of police governance and accountability?

A Not-So-New Paradigm

Hermer and colleagues' suggestion of a policing board to govern both private and public policing merits close examination, especially because it offers the opportunity to guarantee accountability and core democratic values in policing without requiring a state monopoly of policing. It also harks back to some basic precepts about the role of policing in society.

In particular, Hermer and colleagues suggest[19] '(i) that institutions for the governance of policing and the development and implementation of policing policy must recognize and provide a voice for all those in a community, whether state or non-state actors (and, of course, including the state police service), who can potentially contribute to the effective policing of the community, and (ii) that a policing budget (rather than just a budget for a state police service) should be established, for support from which all potential contributors to effective policing can compete on equal terms. We believe that such institutions of governance could be designed to reflect and promote those core democratic values to which we have referred, and, in turn, would be most likely to generate policing policies and practices that would similarly reflect and promote such values.'

In order to guarantee that core democratic values are reflected in the policing services, both public and private, a new legislative framework must be constructed, but one that would be built upon, and perhaps improve upon, many of the elements that constitute the checks and balances in the public policing system today.

Hermer and colleagues' suggestion assumes that there would be a (presumably civilian) governance body that has an overall mandate to translate community safety and security needs and expectations into policing policies, standards, and practices. This is not yet a universal model in Canadian policing, but it would be an improvement in ensuring better civilian oversight and accountability in public policing. The extension into the private policing realm could address the accountability concerns about private security activities.

Any such governance body must have a clear mandate to serve the public good and the necessary powers and authority over policing priorities to fulfil that mandate. It must be properly funded, and governors and staff must be thoroughly trained and serve on a professional, not volunteer, basis. Privately owned policing firms could be licensed and pay licence fees to help fund the governance system. Among other things, the governance body would establish and allocate policing budgets, set standards for and accredit both public and private police services, and monitor conduct and performance. A primary challenge would be to develop clear and enforceable accountability mechanisms. Many lessons can be learned from the successes and deficiencies in the existing police governance system.

Broad community representation and access are cornerstones of an effective and democratic governance structure, but the deficiencies in the existing public system must be addressed. Public input must involve more than one-way consultations; there must be some systematic feedback and incorporation of public input into the decision-making process. The 'democracy gap' is even more apparent at the decision-making level than it is in the streets or shopping centres, and it will take more than political pronouncements to bridge that gap. It will not be necessary to stray far to find the missing voices; it will only be necessary to let them be heard.

The public police have jealously guarded their independence from political interference, but some recent events have challenged this presumption.[20] Conversely, the political will and expertise to dispute police budget estimates or examine police conduct have been, at best, missing in action. On balance, a clear statutory mandate for independent civilian governors would serve the accountability agenda better than the current involvement of elected politicians, who sometimes must serve conflicting priorities.

If a governance model can be developed to ensure that both public and private policing will provide for public safety and security in a manner that protects core democratic values, then it may be argued that there would be no need to compare and contrast public and private policing. Instead, the two systems could coexist and even be encouraged to compete on the basis of skills and merit, effectiveness, and cost efficiency. Such competition might allow the attainment of the highest standards of policing services instead of the cheapest.

The challenge is to design a new paradigm in policing that accommodates changing needs and expectations while preserving the values inherent in a democracy. If standards are clearly articulated and effectively monitored, it may not be necessary to draw a firm line between policing activities that should remain within the purview of the public police and those that may be carried out by private policing agencies. If both are obliged to respect certain protections of individual civil rights and liberties, then either may be permitted to conduct surveillance, effect arrests, and use force. The flow of information between agencies would be subject to analyses applicable to both, the protection of privacy rights balanced against security needs. In essence, if the private firms can be brought within an improved system of checks and balances based on that which currently governs most of the public agencies, the concerns of accountability and protecting core democratic values may be addressed without returning to a state monopoly of policing. Meanwhile, the state retains its legitimate role in providing for the public good by establishing an effective governance model.

Conclusion

The competitive pressures introduced by the growth of private policing have forced a re-evaluation of the role of policing in a liberal democracy and the legitimacy of public power and authority. While concerns about losing accountability and core democratic values might spur calls for a return to a state monopoly in policing, a closer examination of the existing checks and balances reveals a need for improvement in the public sphere as well. And it is difficult to ignore the efficiencies and responsiveness offered by the private sector free from the historical and jurisdictional rigidities of the public system.

The opportunity arises to construct a new paradigm of policing that improves on the status quo and incorporates current demands for safety and security without casting aside the concept that public security is a 'public good.' The state may continue to fulfil its role in the social contract not necessarily as the exclusive purveyor of policing services but as the guarantor that such services are provided in a manner that protects core democratic values, impartially, independently, and accountably. Adopting the language of 'steering' and 'rowing,'[21] if the state, through its governance system, steers properly, rowing may be safely devolved to both public and private agencies.

A collective responsibility for public safety and security underlies the origins of policing in Western democracies. Societal inequities are not a modern phenomenon, but the current economic and social pressures that shape policing priorities exacerbate the 'democracy gap.' The challenge for law reform is to ensure that the public good is shared by all segments of society not just those able to pay for it.

Notes

1 Charles Reith, *A New Study of Police History* (Edinburgh: Oliver and Boyd, 1956), 288.
2 Ibid., 287.
3 Ibid.
4 Peel appointed two 'Commissioners' to oversee the London Metropolitan Police in 1829, but the modern 'Board of Commissioners,' as we know it

today, was actually an American invention that was imported into Upper Canada in 1858.

5 Joe Hermer et al., 'Policing in Canada in the Twenty-first Century: Directions for Law Reform,' in this book.

6 Laura J. Huey, Richard V. Ericson, and Kevin Haggerty, 'Policing Fantasy City,' in this book.

7 Ibid., at 195.

8 See especially ibid., and Hermer, *supra* note 5.

9 Hermer, *supra* note 5 at 31.

10 George S. Rigakos, 'Beyond Public-Private: A New Typology of Policing,' in this book, at 289.

11 Ibid. See also Christopher Murphy and Curtis Clarke, 'Policing Communities and Communities of Policing: A Comparative Study of Policing and Security in Two Canadian Communities,' in this book.

12 Rigakos, *supra* note 10. At the time of writing, private security at federal airports has been under scrutiny in Canada and the United States in the wake of the 11 September 2001 terrorist attacks. Some Canadian airport security officers have virtually admitted their lack of competence by publicly asking for more training, and the U.S. public has voiced its concerns by calling for airport security to be federalized.

13 Huey et al., *supra* note 6 and Murphy and Clarke, *supra* note 11.

14 Rigakos, *supra* note 10 at 303.

15 Rigakos, *supra* note 10 at 304.

16 Hermer, *supra* note 5 at 35.

17 Huey et al., *supra* note 6 at 148.

18 The Ontario *Safe Streets Act*, S.O. 1999, c.8, is the most comprehensive and only provincial law that attempts to police a wide range of begging behaviour, including the conduct of 'squeegee kids.'

19 Hermer, *supra* note 5 at 72–3.

20 A prime minister's role at the APEC summit, which has been the subject of a public inquiry, and an Ontario premier's involvement in the events leading to the death of Native protester Dudley George, which has yet to be reviewed by an inquiry, are two examples.

21 Murphy and Clarke, *supra* note 11 at 234, citing Osborne and Gaebler's concept of steering and rowing in which the executive sets the objective or goal for the organization (steering) and empowers those who are most capable of delivering the service (rowing). David Osborne and Ted Gaebler, *Reinventing Government: How the Entrepreneurial Spirit is Transforming the Public Sector* (New York: Penguin Books, 1993).

Notes on Contributors

Curtis Clarke is an associate professor and coordinator of the Criminal Justice Program at Athabasca University. Prior to pursuing an academic career, Dr Clarke served as a police officer in Ontario. He has carried out empirical studies on the implementation of community-based policing, police organizational/managerial change, intelligence-led policing, and the shifting boundaries between private and public policing. Dr Clarke has completed research for the Canadian Association of Chiefs of Police, the federal solicitor general, Health Canada, the Edmonton Police Service, the Metropolitan Toronto Police Service, the Alberta Association of Chiefs of Police, and the Law Commission of Canada. He also serves on the board of directors of the Canadian Association of Police Educators.

Dennis Cooley is executive director at the Law Commission of Canada, an independent federal law reform agency with a mandate to engage Canadians in the renewal of the law. He is the project manager for the commission's project 'In Search of Security,' which examines the emerging relationship between public police and private security.

Susan Eng served as the chair of the Metropolitan Toronto Police Services Board from 1991 to 1995. In this role, she tackled the sometimes sensitive issues of public accountability, police use of force, antiracism, fiscal responsibility, and the introduction of modern management methods and principles. She initiated major policy and organizational changes within the traditional police environment, overcoming many obstacles and much resistance while under intense media scrutiny. She led and directed research in major public policy issues and broadened the public discourse on the role of police in a liberal democracy. Her ability to build consensus among a diverse board of politicians and appointees made possible the implementation of many ground-breaking decisions and facilitated greater community input into the public decision-making process. Prior to her appointment to the board in May 1989, she was a partner of a major Toronto law firm, where she headed the tax department, focusing on tax planning for domestic and international clients. She is now engaged in the private practice of law, has consulted on public policy issues, including policing and security matters, and is a frequent public speaker and media commentator.

Richard Ericson is professor of criminology at the University of Toronto. He is also a fellow of All Souls College, Oxford. From 1993 to 2003 he was principal of Green College and professor of law and sociology, University of British Columbia. Prior to that he served as director of the Centre of Criminology and professor of criminology and sociology, University of Toronto. He is currently researching decision making and governance in conditions of uncertainty. His recent books include *Policing the Risk Society* (with Kevin Haggerty, 1997), *Governing Modern Societies* (edited with Nico Stehr, 2000), *Risk and Morality* (edited with Aaron Doyle, 2003), *Insurance as Governance* (with Aaron Doyle and Dean Barry, 2003), *Uncertain Business: Risk, Insurance and the Limits of Knowledge* (with Aaron Doyle, 2004), and *The New Politics of Surveillance and Visibility* (edited with Kevin Haggerty, 2005), all published by University of Toronto Press.

Kevin D. Haggerty is an assistant professor of sociology and criminology at the University of Alberta. His research interests pertain to the broad institutional, technological, and political context of criminal justice. He is currently engaged in research on the theoretical and practical implications of surveillance. His 2001 book, *Making Crime Count*, is the first institutional ethnography of the production of official statistics. He and Richard V. Ericson have combined to produce an extensive body of research on policing, risk, and governance, most prominently their 1997 book, *Policing the Risk Society*.

Joe Hermer is an assistant professor of sociology and criminology at the University of Toronto. He holds a doctorate in sociolegal studies from the University of Oxford. His recent research examines the regulation and criminalization of poverty, with a particular focus on how the subsistence activities of the homeless are policed on modern streets. Professor

Hermer is the author of *Regulating Eden: The Nature of Order in North American Parks* (University of Toronto Press, 2002) and *Policing Compassion: Begging, Law and Power in Public Space* (forthcoming from Hart Publishing), and is co-editor (with Janet Mosher) of *Disorderly People: Law and the Politics of Exclusion in Ontario* (Fernwood Press, 2002). He was recently awarded a contract with the Law Commission to examine how public social-assistance programs have been reconfigured as a crime control problem through the category of 'welfare fraud.'

Laura Huey is a doctoral candidate in the Sociology Department of the University of British Columbia. Her research interests include policing, cybercrime, exclusion, and urban communities.

Michael Kempa is a doctoral candidate within the Law Program, Australian National University. He is interested in the general theoretical problem of the interaction between institutional structure, technical innovation, and human agency as it relates to understanding how and why particular modes of governance take bite and spread at particular times and places. This theoretical work is intended to be useful towards assessing the impacts and normative desirability of innovations in governance. He engages this broad problem through the empirical window of trends and developments in policing, with a particular interest in policing reform efforts in transitional democratic contexts. This interest is reflected in his doctoral dissertation, which examines the policing reform process underway in Northern Ireland as part of that territory's broader peace process. He has begun to publish on these themes, alone and with senior colleagues, in the *British Journal of Criminology and Policing and Society*, and *The European Journal on Criminal Policy and Research*, and has contributed to several edited volumes. More normative aspects of this research program have begun to be developed in policy reports for the Law Commission of Canada and the Jamaican Ministry of National Security. Michael is now advancing this program of research at the Department of Criminology, University of Ottawa.

Michael Mopas is a doctoral candidate at the Centre of Criminology, University of Toronto. His research interests are in the areas of policing and the use of science and technology in criminal justice.

Christopher Murphy is an associate professor and current chair of the Department of Sociology and Social Anthropology at Dalhousie University, Nova Scotia. He specializes in research and scholarship on policing and security issues. Prior to coming to Dalhousie he was a senior researcher with the federal Solicitor General's Research Division responsible for police research and development. He has done various kinds of research and written articles and research reports on topics such as victims' services, video gambling, small-town policing, community-based and problem-oriented policing, police resources, Japanese policing, Aboriginal policing, neoliberal policing policy, private security and public policing, police and peacekeeping, and international police reform. His recent research focuses are on global and national trends in the governance, management, and operations of public, private, and military policing and the impact of post-9/11 security on public policing.

George S. Rigakos is assistant professor of law at Carleton University. He has published on public and private policing; policing and social theory; policing 'domestic' violence; risk (especially as it intersects with race, class, and gender); and critical criminological theory. His most recent book is *The New Parapolice: Risk Markets and Commodified Social Control* (2002) published by University of Toronto Press. Dr Rigakos is currently conducting an SSHRC-sponsored analysis of the policing of night-clubs.

Clifford Shearing is a professor in the Research School of Social Science at the Australian National University, where he co-directs Security 21: An International Centre for Security and Justice. His research and writing focus on developments in the governance of security.

Philip Stenning, formerly with the Centre of Criminology, University of Toronto, is now professor in criminology at Victoria University of Wellington, New Zealand. He earned his doctorate in law from the University of Toronto in 1983. His principal research interests include public and private policing, the prosecution process, police and criminal justice accountability, firearms abuse and gun control, and Aboriginal policing and justice. He has also studied the criminal victimization of taxi drivers in three major Canadian cities, as well as the deaths of police officers in four of Canada's major police services. In New Zealand he is currently studying the relationship between police and government, and the history of the country's prosecution system. He is a member of an international research consortium that is conducting a comparative study on the use of force by police in several countries around the world. He is the author of *Appearing for the Crown: A Legal and Historical Review of*